D0576854

Strategy and Negotiation for the International Corporation

Guidelines and Cases

Strategy and Negotiation for the International Corporation

Guidelines and Cases

John Fayerweather
Ashok Kapoor
Graduate School of Business Administration
New York University

Ballinger Publishing Company • Cambridge, Massachusetts
A Subsidiary of J.B. Lippincott Company

This book is printed on recycled paper.

Canton Drug Company and Tice Electric Company cases from *Management of International Operations* by John Fayerweather. Copyright 1960, McGraw-Hill Book Company. Used by permission of McGraw-Hill Book Company.

International Standard Book Number: 0-88410-299-8

Library of Congress Catalog Card Number: 76-10537

Printed in the United States of America

Library of Congress Cataloging in Publication Data

Fayerweather, John.
   Strategy and negotiation for the international corporation.

   1. International business enterprises—Management—Case studies. I. Kapoor, Ashok, 1940- joint author. II. Title.
HD69.17F38   658'.04'90926   76-10537
ISBN 0-88410-299-8

To Ruth and Catherine

Contents

An assessment of the company's global strategy for sewing machines on production allocation, logistics and ownership.

Negotiation of a labor contract in the strained economic, political and industrial relations environment of Britain.

TMC is threatened with a severe labor conflict growing out of internal relations strains with nationalistic and cultural overtones.

Testimony of the Chairman of Gulf Oil Corporation on contributions to a South Korean political party before a U.S. Senate Subcommittee.

Management relations and personality characteristics among U.S. and Mexican managers in solving a quality control problem.

A Mexican executive discusses his management attitudes and methods of handling relations with his superior and subordinates.

A dispute over compensation between a parent staff man and a foreign subsidiary manager involves policies and responsibilities.

Varied difficulties are encountered in pushing Indianization of management personnel replacing Englishmen in senior positions.

A broad examination of the division's system for profit and marketing planning and control in parent-subsidiary relations.

Preface

Two major components of our work in international business education have blended in the creation of this book. The first is the evolution over more than twenty years of a case-oriented course focused on the strategy problems of the international corporation (IC). The book includes all of the cases used in the current version of the course. The cases encompass the main aspects of strategy and the processes of implementing them through interaction with the environment and within the worldwide organization and administrative structure characteristic of the IC. Pedagogically the book in this respect is part of the now well established mainstream of the case method in business education. However, that approach does have some special importance in international business education because of the degree of strangeness of international problems for many students for which the reality of cases is valuable and, more fundamentally, because of the importance and complexity of the analytical and behavioral skills required for international business. The latter element places a premium on "experiential" learning for which the case method is superior. Text guidance for such learning is useful. The initial chapters in this book serve that purpose to some degree. We presume that one or more of the texts listed at the end of the chapters will be employed with the cases.

The second component is the use of simulated negotiation exercises as a teaching methodology. While role playing has been employed widely and simulated negotiations have been a part of education in other fields, this approach had not been developed in international business education in its early years. Our application of negotiation exercises started in 1968 and has since developed rapidly with application both in regular courses and in intensive negotiation projects. In the latter small groups of students devote from 20 to 30 hours per week to intensive negotiation of a sequence of major cases, including from the present set, Lube India, Bechtel, Chrysler-Mitsubishi, ESFAC, Canadian-U.S. Auto Agreement, and Ford Motor Company. The other cases in this book can be used for less intensive negotiation exercises. In most instances, the dynamic qualities of the negotiations are enhanced by having the students acquire new information so that the negotiation is placed in the immediate present. The thinking behind this approach and details of its application have been described in a previous article, "Simulated International Business Negotiations," *Journal of International Business Studies*, Spring 1972. Pedagogically its value lies essentially in the more intensive achievement of experiential learning due both to the greater involvement by the students and to the high motivation achieved through the dynamics of the process. This pedagogy has also been effectively used in training programs for corporate executives and government officials.

We would like to express our appreciation to the other authors who contributed to the writing of the cases in the various ways noted in the footnotes in the text. And most important we want to emphasize deep gratitude from ourselves and on behalf of the students and other professors who will benefit from these cases to the corporate executives and government officials whose cooperation made them possible. This form of substantive contribution of business and government to education is one of the most valuable elements of our modern culture. We have benefited greatly from its expression in the cooperative spirit of the executives and officials who helped in the preparation of these cases.

J.F.
A.K.

Chapter 1

Introduction

As the world moves towards greater economic integration and interdependence, corporate success is increasingly dependent upon achievement in a global rather than a domestic context. Applying a broad definition of a firm operating in two or more countries, the United Nations estimates there are over 7000 international corporations (ICs). Other definitions narrow the field progressively until one reaches a hard, conspicuous core of around 300 giant international corporations operating in a dozen or more countries. But regardless of what definition is used, it is clear that a competent approach to international business is a major requirement for management today.

What are the requirements of success in international management? One can enumerate an intimidating list of specific subject areas: foreign exchange management, international advertising policy, comparative labor relations methods and so on. Unquestionably a successful international corporation must have within its organization people well versed in all of these subjects.

The fundamental assumption underlying this book, however, is that for the international corporation there are two areas of overriding importance: strategy formulation and negotiation skill. The former encompasses the determination of the broad pattern of operations of the IC relating its capabilities to the environmental context. If the capabilities are effectively assessed and the opportunities and constraints of the environment intelligently perceived, the company is successful both in serving society and competing with others and, as a consequence, is profitable. If the assessment and consequent decisions are unsound, the firm suffers competitively and, being out of tune with the environment, encounters an undue amount of conflict, all at the expense of profits and perhaps ultimately survival. Thus the starting point for success in the international arena must be the conception of a sound strategy.

1

Negotiations have emerged as the most critical phase of the implementation of strategy. The world is now structured so that the interests of people are largely pursued through groups of varied composition and dimensions. The international corporation is continuously engaged in relating itself to such groups including, notably, governments, business firms and labor unions. Therefore it is essential that the IC acquire the skill to work out a pattern of operations through negotiation with these groups if it is to implement its strategy effectively.

In our book major emphasis is given to relations between ICs and host governments in strategy formulation and negotiations. This emphasis is based on four major developments over the past decade which have contributed significantly to the growing importance of the role of host governments in international business. First, for political and economic reasons, governments of many countries are playing a larger role as regulators and participants in the economic affairs of their countries resulting in greater interaction between the IC and host governments. Second, the intense competition from non-US based ICs (for example, the Japanese) both in terms of selling and direct investments is offering host countries a larger range of alternative sources of trade and investments which improves the power of the host country vis-à-vis the IC. Third, a growing range of key decision makers in the IC and host countries are developing increasing commonalty in terms of international outlook, an understanding of technology and a realistic assessment of the need of the IC and host country for each other. This commonalty is promoting a greater sense of equality resulting in growing emphasis on negotiations in reducing their differences and achieving their respective objectives. There is a growing mood among these people which does not view willingness to negotiate as a sign of weakness. Both sides recognize that the existing differences between the IC and host countries will not simply disappear but will have to be gradually and painfully resolved through negotiation. Fourth, governments are assigning growing importance to economic considerations in dealing with other governments. Consequently, the IC is faced with the necessity of interacting with governments to protect and promote its interests.

Proceeding from the assumption that strategy formulation and negotiation are primary requirements, we move to the next question. How does one acquire competence in strategy formulation and negotiation skill? For the most part, not by reading books. Both subjects are too complex, governed by too many variables and so inadequately studied today that competence in them must largely emerge from experience, accumulated knowledge and common sense. This book has been prepared from that perspective. The authors believe that the best way to improve competence in strategy formulation and negotiation skill is through guided experience. Ideally the guidance would be given continuously to people in actual on-the-job working experiences. However, a close approximation to that and one which is often more practical is guidance in simulated experiences based on real business situations.

The cases composing the main body of this book have that intent. Each poses a situation involving some degree of strategy formulation and the requirement of negotiating to implement that strategy. In a few cases the situations have fairly small dimensions encompassing strategy and negotiation within the scope of a single individual. Most of them, however, involve major situations in which critical aspects of the overall strategy of the international corporation are at stake, and substantial negotiations must be undertaken with host governments and/or other groups. By participating actively in the discussion of these situations a person learns both by doing and by the guidance received from fellow participants and instructors. In our experience the greatest learning comes from fully simulated exercises in which the participants assume active roles in the strategy formulation and negotiation processes. However, much of the same experiential learning may be achieved simply in an open case discussion process.

While participation in the cases provides the heart of the learning experience, we believe that the guidance element is capable of making valuable contributions. To a large degree the guidance must be attuned directly to the situation in each case emanating from the instructor working closely with the discussion group. To some extent, however, it is possible to provide broad guidelines to direct the overall character of the learning process. For this purpose we have provided at the start of the book two chapters outlining major aspects of strategy formulation and negotiation skill.

Chapter 2

Fundamentals of Strategy
for the International
Corporation

Fundamentally, strategy formulation for the international corporation (IC) is no different than it is for any firm. The basic
requirements are a sound assessment of the capabilities of the firm
and perceptive determination as to how those capabilities may be employed
effectively within the operating environment. There are, however, a number of
special characteristics of the global context which result in distinctive elements
of strategy formulation for the international corporation. This chapter will focus
on those distinctive elements, first considering the more significant of the
environmental factors to which the IC must adapt, then the particular capabilities of the IC, next the role of control in strategy, and finally the main strategy
options.

THE INTERNATIONAL ENVIRONMENT

The total environment to which IC strategy must relate encompasses the full
range of conditions in each country where it operates plus the additional
features of inter-nation relationships. In this brief chapter we cannot cover that
whole territory. We will not, therefore, deal with most of the questions of
determining strategy within each country which conceptually are no different
from those in domestic operations, even though significant adaptation of
approaches must be achieved to cope with their analysis in different economies
and cultures.

Our concern is confined to those international environmental features which
in practice are most critical to major IC strategy decisions and are unique to
international operations. Essentially these features emanate from the prominence of nations as the basic institutions of the world economy and polity. The

5

unique and critical environmental features for the IC are largely related, therefore, to national goals and nationalism. The goals of the nations within which the international corporation operates are best considered first, because they appear constantly as reference points against which to relate the strategic capabilities of the IC. The goals fall broadly under two headings: economic progress and political control.

Economic Progress

The daily preoccupation of nations around the world and their governments is with furtherance of economic progress. An assortment of sub-goals is recognized as central for this purpose, each having important relevance to the operations of ICs. Expansion of industrial facilities is the *sine qua non* for increased output of goods and services. It is also the primary means of providing greater employment, a pressing need in the LDCs with their great unemployment and an important consideration even in the developed countries. The balance of payments is a chronic concern in virtually all countries because the availability of foreign exchange is a critical determinant of ability to import capital goods for industrial expansion, materials for industrial output and other products to meet consumer desires which cannot be produced internally. To improve the balance of payments situation nations constantly seek to cut back on non-essential imports, increase inputs of foreign capital and expand exports. Finally, improvement of the technological capabilities of a country is perceived as essential for industrial growth. Toward that end countries seek both technology in itself and the improvement of the technological capabilities of their people.

Political Control

Political control is an objective both for its own sake and as a means for furthering economic progress. All nations today adhere at least to some degree to the concept that economic progress requires central direction by the national government. In the LDCs and even many of the developing countries this philosophy is highly developed so that the responsibility for decisions on a large portion of economic development is vested in government. National leaders perceive therefore that it is important to their ends that they have a high degree of control over economic decision making, including the nature of new investment, the allocation of funds both internally and in international transactions, and related factors. More broadly they recognize that control of national affairs is dependent upon the power of the nation in international affairs. In an economically interdependent world each nation's share of the global wealth and its role in global decision making is dependent upon its power status. Conversely, to the extent that other nations are stronger each nation finds that aspects of internal affairs are heavily influenced by interests of outsiders rather than those of its own people. Thus it is of continuing importance to its goal of controlling its own affairs to strengthen itself in the international arena.

Nationalism

Nationalism adds a strong emotional component to both the drive for economic progress and the quest for control of national affairs. The character and strength of nationalism vary substantially from country to country. However, its basic nature is universal. At its heart is the social-psychological attraction which draws people together, sharing common goals and seeking joint protection from external threats and problems. This human characteristic, which took its first strong form in the family unit, has progressed to ever higher groups, and for the past 200 years or so has firmly established the nation-state as the dominant collective group for world society. In the advanced industrial states nationalism is fundamentally very strong, the people as a whole being thoroughly committed to and accepting of the authority of the nation and looking to it as the primary governing institution. In less developed countries, nationalism to varying degrees has less depth of strength among the general population, some of whom are still essentially functioning at the level of tribalism. However, among the elites the commitment to nation building and desire to generate support of the nation among the rest of the population make for even more vociferous nationalism than is found in the advanced countries.

Fundamental to the psychology of nationalism is the desire of the people to control their own destinies through the action of their group. Thus nationalism is a powerful force resisting efforts by external groups to interfere with the political control within the nation. In addition, nationalism embodies the collective desire of the people that their society be great and strong. Thus, it provides a forceful thrust behind the efforts to seek economic progress.

ASSESSMENT OF CAPABILITIES

Within this context the first step in strategy formulation is for management to identify the basic strong points of its operations. This process is sound in general as it is the strengths of a company which give it a competitive edge and must therefore be the focus of overall emphasis in strategy. The process takes on a special importance in international operations, however, because the strengths of a company very often turn out to be the elements which are valued by host nations. They compose, therefore, a significant part of the bargaining leverage which the IC can employ at the negotiating table.

Each company, of course, has a unique set of capabilities. However, most of the areas of strength of ICs fall into a limited number of categories, each with particular strategy implications. The following outline provides a useful general scheme for analysis which each firm can adapt for its own needs. Broadly the special capabilities of firms in international business are analyzed under two headings, resource strengths and global capabilities.

Resource Strengths

The traditional rationale for the wide range of international business transactions has been the flow of resources from countries where they are plentiful or available at low cost to countries offering good demand and satisfactory price. ICs fit into this tradition, their strategies being based to a very large extent on resource capabilities. However, the resources in which their strengths are prominent take quite varied forms, and there have been significant shifts in their character in recent years. Thus the IC management needs to assess carefully both its resource capabilities and the needs for them around the world to lay an adequate base for its strategy. Four general types of resource capability exist: skills, capital, labor and raw materials.

Skills. The prominence of technical and managerial skills among the resource capabilities of international corporations is readily observed. Every IC with some patented products or processes, a good R&D program and a competent management will mark them down as key components of its resource capabilities. However, the assessment for strategy formulation cannot stop at that broad level. The management must ask a number of more refined questions about its skill capabilities to determine what sort of strategy they lead to.

In considering *technical skills* here are some key questions to be answered.

1. Are the skills quite unique or do competitors have essentially comparable capabilities? If the former is true as in a case like IBM, the company works from great strength in its strategy whereas if the latter is true, it is forced to work from a weaker position or to seek other aspects of capabilities as sources of strength.

2. Is the company constantly developing new technological innovations, or is its technology relatively stable? In the former case a company may project a strategic position in which foreign countries are continuously seeking its services, while in the latter host countries may see no value in relations with the firm beyond the minimum necessary to acquire existing technological skills.

3. How difficult is it to learn and apply the skills? If skills are relatively simple to absorb, the strategy for transmitting them will typically be much less sophisticated than that where the technology is of a complex nature requiring continuing controls, supervision and other forms of contact between the IC and application situations.

4. What is the ability of host nation personnel and companies to absorb technology? If the ability is relatively low, the strategy of the IC should be based on a much more fully integrated delivery system than is needed where the host competence is high. The difference here is well illustrated by comparing Japan, which absorbed a tremendous body of IC technology from the United States and other countries largely through licensing and minority joint venture arrangements, to relatively underdeveloped nations in which fully controlled subsidiaries staffed for extended periods by expatriates are required for optimum effectiveness.

The answers to these questions for each corporation are continuously changing, with major shifts observable over relatively short periods. Until the early 1960s United States international corporations had a wide technological lead in many product areas. However, the Europeans and now the Japanese have caught up and, in some cases, surpassed American ICs in technology in a number of fields. Thus, in a large portion of cases corporations, which may have built their early international strategies on relatively strong technological capability, must readjust to the realities that they are on a par with a number of competitors. Likewise, as the technological competence in many less developed host nations has risen rapidly, the strategic importance of IC technological capabilities has declined relatively.

Transmission of *managerial skills* is more complex in general than that of technological skills, but over the long haul it may be equally or more important to the strength of an IC's international strategy. Because they rest heavily on human behavior rather than physical-mechanical processes, managerial skills are much more difficult to transmit and acquire. For this reason strategy based on their transmission is harder to develop and manage. By the same token, however, its competitive potential and possibilities for long-term strength are considerable, especially in light of the continuing improvement of managerial systems and methods in home countries of ICs. Accepting the general proposition that ICs generally have a transmittable capability in their managerial skills, the manager must again ask more precise questions about the situation of his company.

1. What managerial skills are appropriate for the level of development of host nations? For example, sophisticated consumer behavior interviewing may work well in Europe but be overcomplicated both for managers and for economic utility in Nigeria.

2. How do the managerial skills relate to cultural contexts in host nations? Intensive superior-subordinate conferences with target setting and appraisal may, for example, be a useful export for management development in Australia but run counter to cultural patterns in Indonesia.

Capital. The role of capital in the strategies of international corporations has changed substantially over the years. In earlier times the simple process of transmitting funds from the parent company to establish factories abroad was a major component of international strategies because other sources of funds were relatively limited and establishment of fully-owned subsidiaries was the dominant strategy mode. By the mid-1970s, the provision of home country capital has fallen to a much smaller role in IC strategies, both because of the greater availability of other sources in host countries and international capital markets (e.g., Eurodollars) and because of the greater frequency of alternative strategies such as licensing and joint ventures.

At the same time other aspects of capital have become more prominent in strategy formulation as the structure of overseas investments of ICs has grown to include overseas production facilities and global marketing systems. The protection and full utilization of each form of capital calls for careful attention in strategy formulation.

Since the greater portion of foreign investment has been made in the past decade or so, the majority of foreign production sites and facilities may be presumed to be relatively satisfactory. However, for older factories and increasingly for the current generation, significant questions must be posed in the assessment of resources available to the IC in light of changing conditions both internally and externally. How do the costs of each factory compare with those of competing facilities, particularly in other countries where labor and other costs may be appreciably lower? How suitably are the facilities positioned in relation to changes in market demand?

Global marketing systems, including distribution channels, advertising structure and brand names, have always been one of the great strengths of international corporations. They have taken on a new significance as a capital resource, however, because of the strong thrust of less developed countries toward development of markets for export of manufactured goods in the past few years. There are substantial advantages to the LDCs in utilizing these well established marketing systems, compared to employing alternatives or setting up their own distribution methods.

For the most part this utilization has taken place internally within the organizations of international corporations fostered substantially by external incentives. That is, the main pattern of evolution has been for ICs increasingly to utilize plants in Southeast Asia, Mexico, Brazil and a few other countries as export supply points, and this process has been fostered by the LDCs providing export incentives and by broad international efforts, notably the provision of tariff preferences under GATT favoring import of manufactured goods from less developed countries into the advanced nations. Assessing how well the IC's international marketing structure is positioned to serve this process can therefore pay off handsomely because expansion of exports ranks as a top priority for most LDCs.

Labor. Because of their parochial viewpoint, many international corporations have experienced labor as a competitive weakness rather than as a resource until quite recently. In the early 1960s in particular, a number of United States ICs along with purely domestic corporations suffered severely from the influx of imports from Japan and other low wage-cost countries. The more competent IC managements now perceive that labor is a resource which they can use to their own advantage just as effectively as did their competitors. In the assessment of this resource, however, questions must be asked to determine how great its value is and in what ways it can be used. Is the value-weight-volume relationship of a product such that it can be shipped substantial distances making effective use of wage cost differences? Is it feasible to break down production processes so that labor-intensive aspects can be performed in low wage areas and components shipped to be assembled in marketing centers? To what extent in such a system are there problems of training, quality control and maintenance of continuity in flow of products?

Raw Materials. The typical manufacturing IC does not count among its major resources raw materials in the same sense that a mining or petroleum firm would count them. Nonetheless, many manufacturing ICs have a degree of control over raw materials which is important for their international strategies. For example, chemical and pharmaceutical companies produce intermediates (a blend of raw materials and skills) which are essential for end-product producers in many countries. To the extent that this is the case in any particular IC, the resource assessment should therefore include the relative competitive strength that raw material resources provide to the firm.

Global Capabilities

The unique capabilities of the international corporation compared to those of an essentially national corporation lie in its capacity to organize activities on a global basis. Although the transmission of resources may be accomplished by national corporations, only the international corporation is structured to integrate economic activities from a worldwide point of view. The global unification capabilities offer substantial opportunity for competitive advantage. On the other hand, there are strong forces working toward fragmentation of operations, including the economic and cultural differences among countries and the distinctive aspects of the national interests of each which are pressed by their national governments in negotiations with ICs. Thus, the second major aspect of assessment of strategic capabilities lies in examining the relative weights of these influences for unification and fragmentation of operations. The analysis focuses in large part on two broad areas of concern: product delivery system and financial management system.

Product delivery system. The product delivery system incorporates the company's product lines, research and development program, logistic system and sales promotion efforts. Great economic advantage can theoretically be achieved by a high degree of global unification of all aspects of this system through the economies of scale, avoidance of wasteful duplication of effort and location of activities in low cost areas. However, opposing influences both in the past and currently impose a substantial amount of fragmentation in the systems of virtually all companies.

(a) Product Line. The keystone in consideration of unification of this area is product line. The capabilities for unification in the other aspects are all dependent to a substantial degree on the extent of standardization of company product lines around the world. Thus the pressure of the advantages to be gained through unification in the other aspects provides strong pressures for standardization of product line.

The great majority of companies do stick within broad product categories throughout their worldwide operations except in unusual circumstances, *e.g.,* Singer took up life insurance in Brazil to help cover the overhead of its retail stores when imports of sewing machines were cut off in the 1950s. However, within their broad product categories companies typically have substantial diversity either for historical reasons (acquisitions or decentralized product decision making in earlier periods) or because of current conditions. The diversity is encouraged by variations in local tastes, standards of living, climate and assorted other factors. The incentives to move in the direction of adapting to these variations are considerable since, after all, it is market penetration and market share which are fundamentally the keys to corporate growth. The strategy assessment, therefore, must carefully weigh the potentials in this fragmentation direction against the considerable potential advantages from standardization and unification in other aspects of the product delivery system.

(b) Research and development. The advantages of a unified approach to worldwide research and development are compelling. Centralization of R&D reduces wasteful duplication of effort, makes communication among technical personnel more efficient and generally provides better coordination with global sales and production management. By comparison with R&D efforts of essentially national companies, a unified global R&D system permits amortization of R&D costs over a much broader base. Thus it is competitively feasible for the IC to mount a higher level of R&D effort than competitors operating on a more limited or fragmented basis. The practical impact of these logics is such that the great majority of international corporations do virtually all of their research in a limited number of facilities in their home countries with overseas technical work largely confined to development resulting in minor product modifications to fit local tastes, styles and the like.

This general pattern is highly unsatisfactory to host nations, however. In their quest for both economic progress and political strength they give a high priority to building up their own technical capability. The typical IC research and development organization, while it provides technological benefits to the host country, is not perceived as building up its long term technical capability. What host nations seek is for ICs to establish R&D facilities within their borders which train their people and provide on-the-spot innovative capabilities. In negotiations with ICs, pressure for this sort of technical establishment within host nations is actively pressed.

Besides this political pressure, there are additional considerations which favor some distribution of R&D facilities outside of the home nation. In particular it is a means of effectively using technical personnel of other countries and of being more responsive to market demands by closer proximity to local sales organizations. In combination these considerations have led a few companies, particularly the larger ones, to establish some global dispersion of R&D facilities, typically with units in Europe and to a lesser degree in Latin America and Japan. In some cases the full R&D effort for a particular product line may be allocated to one of the foreign units, thus preserving to a substantial degree the operational benefits of a unified system, simply shifting the geographical site of R&D work.

These varied elements suggest that the prevailing pattern of unified R&D represents the strongest capability of the international corporation but that there is sufficient logic for departure from it in some cases. Thus each corporation must make a careful assessment of the balance of factors in its own case for this aspect of the product delivery system.

(c) Logistic System. The potential capabilities from a unified global logistic system are just as promising as those from unified R&D activities. One can conceive a system in which a limited number of factories of optimum economic scale are located in sites with the lowest cost of labor and materials supplying markets all over the world. Unfortunately this is far from the reality. There are major influences both internal and external which militate against unification of logistic systems.

Among the internal factors, product characteristics are often a significant consideration. The volume and weight of products may result in transportation costs which eliminate all or a good portion of the advantages gained through large scale plants or lower-cost sites. History is another consideration, companies being reluctant to close down established facilities and make new investments, particularly if benefits from logistic efficiency are modest. Finally, proximity of production facilities to markets facilitates coordination of sales and production activities. Thus, gains in marketing effectiveness are observed by many companies to offset the limited benefits that might be provided by greater efficiency in the logistic system.

The external factors for the most part revolve around the nation-oriented drive to maximize local production regardless of global efficiency considerations. In the less developed countries, governments pressing for industrial development have established barriers to imports (tariffs and quotas) causing ICs to establish factories serving the local national market only, with costs well above those of products made in major factories serving export systems. In the developed countries, governmental actions are typically less forceful but present nonetheless. They are motivated in part by balance of payments difficulties for which one solution is restricting imports. A second factor of growing strength is the drive of organized labor in each country to hold on to existing production of ICs as well as to restrict competitive imports. This influence is reinforced by the existence in a few industries of multinational labor organizations which as yet are weak but are a growing factor.

As a consequence of these external and internal influences the extent of global unification of IC logistic systems is confined to a few patterns in which benefits are great enough to outweigh the deterrents or the latter are relatively modest. Quite commonly production is centralized on a regional basis in which the transportation and marketing communication deterrents are minor and economies of scale are substantial. This approach is particularly common where external factors have deliberately favored it, notably in the European Economic Community and to a lesser but slowly expanding degree in other regional economic groups like the Latin American Free Trade Area and the Andean Common Market. The second pattern of growing importance is the structure tieing facilities in LDCs to markets in developed countries, with emphasis on the effective transmission of labor resources noted earlier. The steady emergence of these two patterns and variations of them indicate the importance of a thorough assessment of both the potential advantages from a unified logistic organization and the varied constraints involved.

(d) Sales Promotion. The global unification capabilities of the IC in sales promotion are substantially less both in theory and practice than those in R&D and logistics. There are some efficiencies in use of common marketing methods throughout an IC including interchange of ideas and experience about similar products among units. Some gains are feasible through centralization of preparation of advertising material. Utilization of media with global or regional distribution requires a centralized approach. However, the benefits achieved in these ways are modest and a large portion of sales promotion efforts are necessarily oriented to the local level. It is essential to their effectiveness that they be finely attuned to differences in consumer attitudes and competitive conditions. So the practical possibilities of unified global approaches are limited. Nonetheless, with variations among industries, they offer sufficient advantage so that they must be included in the strategic assessment process.

Financial management system. In a unified global system there are substantial capabilities for optimizing profits by financial processes not available when foreign operations in each country are treated as separate entities. The main potentials of a unified financial management system are found in three areas:

(a) Capital management. In a unified system excess cash from varied units can be allocated by central management either for other units that need it or for investment in capital markets offering highest returns. Long-term capital may be similarly distributed among operating units as needed and new capital may be acquired from lowest cost sources. A unified system also has great flexibility in the forms of capital transfer employed, including such methods as extended terms for accounts receivable on goods shipped from the parent and high debt-equity ratios in financing subsidiaries.

(b) Geographic distribution of profits. Because of differences among countries in tax rates, freedom to remit profits, risks, and other conditions, it is often beneficial to be able to take a larger share of the profits from business transactions in one place than in another. A unified IC system has this capability

through the varied relations among the parent and subsidiaries including intra-corporate pricing of finished goods and components, licensing, management fees and the like.

(c) Foreign exchange management. In a unified system, the options open to management to deal with foreign exchange management are greater, notably the capacity to shift funds among affiliates quickly and easily. More fundamentally, a centralized decision-making system to determine foreign exchange policy is essential to a consistent and responsive approach to risk management in this field.

In aggregate these capabilities of a unified financial management system can make a quite significant contribution to IC profits. They will not, however, be developed further in this chapter and they appear only marginally in the cases for a fundamental reason derived from the role of financial management in the actual strategy patterns of ICs. Characteristically, finance plays a subordinate, implementing role in the IC strategy. The main lines of IC policies and actions are primarily determined by market-related factors—competition, technology, logistics and the like. The financial processes of the firm are geared to support the market-oriented strategy and to optimize profits as best they can within whatever constraints are fixed by that strategy. Since the primary concern in this book is with the fundamental strategy of ICs, we will therefore give no further direct attention to the overall financial management system. However, the strategy planner may well bear in mind that the potentials of unified financial management are a factor to be given some weight in overall strategic planning, including the extent of centralized control necessary to realize them.

CONTROL

Control assumes a critical role in strategic planning because of the importance attached to it by both host nations and international corporations. For the former the decision-making power held by the IC is a serious detraction from the capability of the nation to control its own affairs. It is fundamentally resisted by the basic character of nationalism and specifically it is disruptive of national efforts to control the economic development process. The fact that the decisions of the IC may be motivated by the interests of another nation and its government augment the negative feelings of host nations.

For the international corporation, on the other hand, control of its foreign operations is of fundamental importance. The IC has a fiduciary responsibility to its stockholders which requires that it exercise adequate supervision of the performance of corporate assets. Managements commonly perceive this responsibility as calling for the ability to control the main decisions affecting corporate operations. In more concrete terms key aspects of global operations call for a substantial degree of central control if they are to be effective, including transmission of skills, coordination of global product delivery systems and direction of integrated worldwide financial management.

Conflict is the inevitable outcome of these well-founded desires of both the host nations and the ICs for control. To achieve most satisfactory resolution of the conflict requires a full understanding of the objectives being sought through control and the means of achieving them. The ultimate outcome in each situation will be determined in large measure by the power of each party, but substantial accommodation of interests and effective direction of power may be achieved if the perception of the situation is clear on both sides.

Of particular importance in this stage of strategy assessment is a full comprehension of the role of ownership, an element in control which is badly misunderstood by many people, both in host nations and international corporations. Ownership is commonly perceived to be the major determinant of control. This perception stems from the obvious fact that the owners have ultimate voting power over major corporate decisions and the choice of key personnel. However, as applied to the ownership by ICs of subsidiaries in foreign countries, there is substantially more to control than that.

In the first place, regardless of the degree of ownership by the parent IC, many decisions on subsidiary operations are either potentially or actually controlled by host governments; including investments, repatriation of funds, employment of expatriates, etc. The implication of this fact for the IC is that obtaining ownership control may in fact be substantially less useful than it believes because the actual degree of control obtained is limited. The implication for the host nation is that forcing ICs to give up or share ownership with local nationals may not be as worthwhile or necessary as it perceives because the specific objectives sought may be more effectively obtained through direct controls exerted on the subsidiary decision making.

Just as the host nation may achieve control directly without national ownership participation, so the international corporation may exert substantial control even from a minority position under certain circumstances. The key to this sort of control lies in the possession by the IC of some continuing source of strength which gives it leverage in decision making in relation to local partners. The most common sources of this form of strength are a continuing flow of new technology, superior management competence or control of export marketing channels which are important to the venture.

A second critical point is that the control effects achieved by sharing ownership with local nationals depend greatly upon the character of the latter. So far as an IC is concerned an agreeable or silent partner may in many cases make little difference in the outcome of its decision making, whereas a difficult partner may complicate control in directions quite apart from any control influences intended by the host government. By the same token whether or not the host government achieves significant control gains through ownership by its host nationals in the affiliates of ICs depends upon the amenability of the local investors to government influence, a situation which will vary considerably with their politics, personalities and power.

To further complicate this picture, there are diverse views as to the economic effects of shared ownership. The basic presumption of host nations is that minimizing foreign equity reduces the long-term outflow of income from the country.

Whether or not this is a valid assumption depends upon assessment of the continuing value of the capital involved and the profitability of each particular venture. More complex are questions as to the structural effect of shared ownership. As a practical matter ICs with limited resources and the necessity to build the greatest strength for long-term operations generally treat affiliates differently according to degree of ownership in respects which are important to host nations. In particular they are much less likely to assign research and development functions to operations in which they have lower ownership shares. They are also inclined to give such units a less important role in global logistic systems. It is both more profitable and simpler to handle decision making if those plants used as export sources are fully or at least majority-controlled.

These considerations lead to a wide variety of current viewpoints toward shared ownership. In some countries there is very strong pressure on international corporations to give up majority ownership of affiliates. The Andean group countries are typical of this end of the spectrum. New investors or those seeking the free trade benefits of the Andean Common Market are expected to divest themselves of majority ownership within ten to fifteen years. At the other end of the spectrum are some countries which place no pressures on companies to give up ownership. A little short of this extreme but interesting in its philosophy is Canada. The Grey report, completed in 1973, which provides the conceptual base for present Canadian national policy on foreign investment does not take a position favoring Canadian participation in equity of foreign subsidiaries, even though the report has a strong nationalist orientation. Essentially the philosophy of the report is that the objectives of national policy can be achieved more effectively by direct controls than through the ownership. On balance it would seem that this is a sound outlook.

However, as a practical matter, the nationalistic thrust in the major portion of less developed countries, combined with the desire of many local investors to share in profits of foreign subsidiaries, provides great support for shared ownership in many countries that may be expected to continue for years to come. Thus each IC in each country situation must carefully assess how shared ownership would specifically affect its operations for that country and also determine what the objectives and outlook of the government are in order to determine what range of flexibility may be found within which it may negotiate for its own interests.

STRATEGY MODELS

The assortment of factors considered in the assessment process will lead to different conclusions for strategy in each company situation. It is impractical, therefore, to set forth detailed strategy recommendations for international corporations in general. However, it is feasible to sketch the main dimensions of a few strategy models which are logical outcomes of the assessment process outlined here and which may be observed as common patterns in international business. Many ICs pursue combinations of two or more of these strategies. There are some effects in both negotiations and operations from combining them but it is analytically desirable to consider them separately. The key elements of the models are outlined in Figure 2-1 including the corporate capabilities underlying them, the form of economic return anticipated, the requirements for effective operation, including critical points subject to negotiation with host governments, and the power or strength available to the IC in the negotiation process.

Dynamic High-Technology Model

The dynamic high-technology strategy assumes an IC capability for generating a continuing flow of product and process innovations for which demand exists in foreign countries. The profitability of the strategy rests upon arrangements rewarding the IC for transmitting the skills. The chief alternatives are satisfactory profit margins for exports of completed products or components, royalties for the use of technology and dividends from competitively profitable operation of overseas affiliates.

The most essential requirement for the satisfactory pursuit of this strategy is the maintenance of a strong R&D program which will generate the continuing flow of new technology. The importance of this requirement must be stressed because host nation goals may jeopardize it. In their desire to strengthen their own technology and independent strength, host governments often put pressure on ICs to expand R&D within their countries. The risk for the IC is that distributing R&D among a number of host countries may reduce the efficiency and effectiveness of technological work so that the heart of the strategy is weakened. Thus, concessions to host nation desires in this regard must be given grudgingly and carefully. The chief possibilities are that minor development work may be allocated to foreign affiliates or that large segments of work on a particular product line may be allocated to major R&D facilities in particular countries. If the latter type of concession is made, however, it is essential that full control over the foreign unit, including ownership, be assured because of the possible loss of proprietary rights to products which are essential to the economic base of the strategy.

The second essential requirement is that sufficient income be generated by the operating arrangements so that the global R&D program can be adequately

	IC Capabilities	Economic Return System	Operating Structure Requirements	IC Power Factors
Dynamic High-Technology Model	Continuing flow of technically significant new products	Steady flow of payments in royalties or from sales margins	Sustained high quality R&D program. Reasonable control of application of technology abroad	Strong based on desire of host nations for future technological innovations
Low or Stable Technology Model	Useful technological skill but low sophistication or slow change	Full income realized in a short period	A short-term transmission arrangement: sale or turnkey installation. Sufficient control to assure income payment	Relatively weak, dependent on value of technology and competition
Advanced Management Skill Model	High competence in marketing or other management fields	Steady flow of dividends from ongoing operations	Continuing integrated operations in fields with management skill competitively effective	Weak due to low priority for management skills
Unified-Logistic; Labor-Transmission Model	High value to weight/volume ratio. High labor intensity in production. Strong global marketing system	Regular flow of dividends from either production units or marketing system	Low cost production sites. Strong global marketing organization. Standardized products. Highly integrated control of operations. Full ownership preferred	Strong based on high priority for exports in producing countries. Weak in importing countries

Figure 2-1. Strategy Patterns for International Corporations.

financed. In the current trend of host nation negotiations, particularly in less developed countries, this requirement is increasingly difficult to achieve. LDCs in the past few years have become much more aggressive in trying to reduce the balance of payments cost of paying for imported technology. Mexico, for example, in 1973 passed a new law calling for review of all technology agreements and systematically requiring the reduction of royalties in a substantial number of cases. Thus the IC must be prepared to present a strong argument for what it regards as reasonable payment for its technological capabilities.

Some degree of control over foreign affiliates is required in this strategy but not so much as in some other strategies. A key assumption is that a substantial degree of effective managerial control can be achieved simply through the leverage of the continuing provision of technology. The minimum essential requirement is sufficient control over the application and quality of the technological work of the foreign affiliate so that the economic base of the transmission process is not weakened over the long term. That is, the IC must be able to assure that the technology is used in such a way that satisfactory products are produced. Otherwise the affiliate will not continue to generate income which will flow back to the IC. This degree of control can be achieved by relatively limited means such as a quality control arrangement with an independent licensee if the latter is a competent manufacturing organization. Beyond this minimum essential, the IC stands to gain by achieving greater degrees of control over the foreign affiliate. As a general matter, the effectiveness of the application of its technology will usually be greater if it has full control over the personnel employed in the foreign affiliates and key decisions in the operating processes. Furthermore, the greater the ownership the more readily and completely the IC may obtain full financial benefits from the technological capabilities. Thus it is highly desirable to seek majority or full ownership or, failing that, at least a strong voice in management in any shared ownership arrangement.

The strength of the IC in negotiating these points depends essentially upon the quality of its technological capabilities. A company with a significant competitive lead in a field whose technology is considered very important to host nations commands strong power in such a strategy. Leaders in specialized fields like computers and pharmaceutical products are typical examples, e.g., IBM or the Canton Drug Company (p. 271). Companies with somewhat less essential technologies or whose work is closely matched by competitors are in a weaker position. Firms producing nuclear reactors and various types of industrial machinery provide examples of this sort. A yet lower range of situations can be visualized, but it is questionable whether they really fall in the dynamic high-technology category, their capabilities placing them closer to the next strategy model.

Low or Stable Technology Model
The second strategy model assumes the IC has capability in a technological

field which has a relatively slow rate of innovation or in which the technology is of a rather unsophisticated character. The economic returns in such circumstances must be based on one-shot or quite short-term arrangements. That is, the IC's strategy calls for a system in which the technology in effect is sold in one immediate transaction or over some given period required to transfer the skills involved effectively. As compared with the first model there can be no presumption of continuing income over an extended period.

The operating requirements for this strategy call for the same sort of short-term viewpoint. The key requirements are a sufficiently secure financial arrangement to assure adequate return coupled, as may be appropriate, to sufficient control over operations to support that financial return. The specific form these arrangements may take will vary considerably according to the country circumstances.

The simplest approach is an arrangement in which the technology is sold outright. In some cases this may merely amount to selling a piece of machinery with an instruction book or perhaps the brief service of an engineer to assist in the installation and start-up process. More complex arrangements grade up to the turnkey contract for large industrial installations in which the international corporation undertakes full responsibility for construction of a plant and managing it for a period of years until local personnel are competent in its operation.

The other general approach to this strategy is the establishment of licensees, joint ventures or fully-owned subsidiaries with a guarded time horizon perspective. Host-country attitudes are generally not favorable to the long-term income costs of arrangements like this based on relatively stable or low-sophistication technology. However, the general foreign investment policies or other conditions at a given moment in a country may permit an international corporation to establish a fully-owned operation. In doing so, the IC must realistically recognize that in the future, perhaps not far down the road, adverse host national attitudes may assert themselves. Such has been the case in many situations in less developed countries resulting in pressures on ICs with weak technological positions to divest all or part of their ownership, e.g., the ESFAC case (p. 205) and terminate licensing agreements from which continuing benefits were not apparent to the host government officials. Thus the strategy of a corporation in setting up operations should presume a relatively short-term payout against the risk of termination.

Although the power of the international corporations pursuing this strategy varies with the extent of competition and the degree of sophistication of their technology, the presumptions underlying the strategy assume that they do not have a particularly strong bargaining position. The Bechtel case provides a good illustration of this weakness, the ready availability of alternative sources of fertilizer technology as well as necessary raw materials and capital leaving the consortium little power in its relations with the government of India (p. 89).

Advanced Managerial Skill Model

The third general strategy pattern is based on one or more areas of management expertise. The notable examples of this sort of strategy are found among international corporations in consumer non-durable fields whose competitive strength is based on advanced marketing skills often combined with related management competence in organization, personnel, budgeting and finance. General Foods is a good example of this model (p. 437). The economic returns in this type of strategy call for a continuing operational system which generates a steady flow of business with a high operating margin.

While in theory it might be possible to implement the advanced management strategy through management contracts or minority joint venture arrangements, in practice majority operating control seems to be a key requirement. Since advanced management skills incorporate a large degree of behavioral, non-scientific competence, it is extremely difficult to transmit them through anything but a well integrated organization system. Thus, effective strategies of this sort are typically found in those firms which have a broad network of fully controlled foreign subsidiaries in which management personnel work together over extended periods and acquire a thorough knowledge both of the management skills involved and of how to relate to other people in the organization.

ICs find themselves in a relatively weak position in pursuing this strategy if resistance is encountered in host nations. The resistance is generally greatest among less developed countries which regard advanced management skills in areas like marketing of consumer goods with substantial scepticism, e.g., the Shave-all case (p. 235). They give a low priority to this sort of skill as compared to technological skills and take a negative view therefore towards earnings involving balance of payments costs to the nation derived from their application. Among more advanced countries there is greater acceptance of the value of managerial skills, particularly in the leading countries which have ICs of their own whose earnings are based on competence of this sort. Still, even in these countries, the IC is in a relatively weak bargaining position in the pursuit of this strategy because little national benefit is perceived from the skills involved.

Unified-Logistics Labor-Transmission Model

Three elements of corporate capability are essential requirements for the fourth strategy model. First, the product involved must have a high enough ratio of value to weight and volume so that transportation over substantial distances is economically feasible. Second, the production processes must be sufficiently labor-intensive so that economic advantage greater than transportation costs is achieved by locating production in low wage areas. Third, the IC must have an effective global marketing organization. An excellent example of these elements is found in Singer's operations (p. 307) and to some degree they appear in the automobile industry (p. 133).

The economic return from the logistic strategy comes from achieving a satisfactory profit margin through the combination of the first two factors with a steady flow of business based on the third factor. The system is financially flexible, so that the profit may be taken in whatever proportions are appropriate from the production locations or the marketing system.

The implementation of this strategy calls for a well integrated and efficient global system. Furthermore, the system must have a substantial capacity for flexibility and change over time because elements essential to it are subject to considerable change. Most important are changes in wage costs which can radically alter the basis for the logistic structure. For example, in the early 1960s Japan was a sound production site for inclusion in such a strategy but with the rapid rise of wage levels there, it has become a poor competitive location compared to Southeast Asian countries. A different form of evolution is the transition of Brazil from a highly unstable political and economic status to a strong position in the mid-1970s with a booming economy providing a superior sourcing site for inclusion in a global logistic scheme.

The need for flexibility over time dictates essential elements to be included in the implementation of this strategy. It is important that there be a high degree of standardization of products so that production sites may be used interchangeably as sources for the marketing organization. Since maintenance of low costs is central to the logics of the strategy, continuing effort to improve efficiency of operations is required. Assuming the probability that rises in wage levels in some locations will reduce their competitive value while other locations emerge as more favorable sites, the strategy requires a continuing study of production locations and a sound concept as to how production mobility will be accomplished.

The control elements in implementation of this strategy are also critical. To tie together widely separated production and marketing units there must be tight internal control. Market forecasts and production plans must be worked out carefully and changes in them transmitted rapidly. Clearly quality control must be effectively maintained. There must also be thorough coordination within the system as to changes in products and particularly in the evolution of production site mobility.

Given all of these requirements, it appears that a high degree of control by the international corporation is desirable, including full ownership of all units in the system. Without this degree of ownership some questions become very difficult to deal with. In particular, the transfer of sourcing from one production site to another will raise very troublesome questions if there are equity partners in the foreign units. Likewise the extensive questions of pricing between production and marketing units are much more complicated when ownership partners are involved.

In both of these matters it may in fact be preferable as an alternative to full ownership to work with no ownership at all, handling the production phase of the strategy through manufacturing contract arrangements with independent national firms. Prices in these circumstances can be bargained over directly and cutbacks in sourcing accomplished within the terms of the contractual arrangements. However, independent manufacturers, particularly in less developed countries with low wage costs which are the natural production sites in this strategy, may be less than fully satisfactory when it comes to reliability in meeting production schedules and quality standards. Thus the achievement of full ownership control is highly desirable for this strategy, though lesser degrees of control are feasible.

The negotiating power available to an IC pursuing this strategy is great in the host countries serving as production sites and weak in those composing only marketing outlets. Among the former, with the desire to expand exports to improve their balance of payments and increase employment, the IC pursuing this strategy is looked on with great favor. In many cases, for example, the 100 percent ownership desired may be obtained on the basis of proposed export volume despite general nationalistic policy opposing foreign control of production facilities. The weakness of the IC in the marketing countries stems, of course, from the opposite psychology. The desire to reduce imports to help the balance of payments is often reinforced strongly by local manufacturers and unions protecting national production units. Where the latter are particularly strong, the IC may find that it cannot achieve entry for foreign production or the entry is limited by quotas or tariffs. A number of European countries, for example, have been quite resistant to imports from Japan and other Asian countries. However, the IC does have substantial support in the pursuit of this general strategy from the international consensus favoring greater access for exports of less developed countries into the industrial areas that has been pressed by UNCTAD and given substantive commitment through the agreements for preferential tariff treatment for imports of manufacturers from LDCs.

STRATEGY DECISION-MAKING PROCESS

The foregoing sections have set forth guidelines which represent sound goals for corporate thinking on strategy formulation. Decisions on strategy will, however, also be influenced substantially by the processes of corporate decision making. Figure 2-2 presents a basic framework for analysis of the strategy decision process. The key components are the existing pattern of corporate activities, the central actors, the influences bearing on them, the roles they perform and the specific steps in decision making.

The point of departure for strategy formulation and usually the strongest element in its outcome is the great weight of momentum and inertia in the existing operations of the firm portrayed as the central block in Figure 2-2. Each of the four elements tends to militate heavily for continuity and stability in the existing pattern. The corporations' fixed assets, notably the character of the production facilities and their geographic distribution in most circumstances

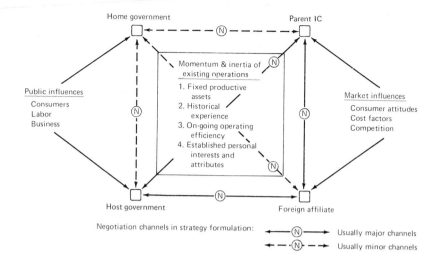

Figure 2-2. Elements of the Strategy Decision-Making Process.

represent productive employment of capital. Significant alterations in elements of strategy may reduce the return on this invested capital so its character is a deterrent to change. Likewise, managerial and production personnel focused around such facilities represent an investment and commitment which is not readily altered.

Second, the corporation contains a substantial body of historical experience which represents another form of capital. This experience is generally employed with substantial productivity as long as corporate activities continue in essentially the areas within which the experience was accumulated. Thus there is a positive economic logic for maintaining the pattern of activities within that framework. In addition, there is a negative psychological influence derived from the accumulated experience in that it often serves as a block to deter the capability of the organization to accept change along lines departing from historical patterns.

Third, the ongoing systems and structure of the organization provide a further logic for momentum. People working within the system develop patterns of expectations, communications and other elements of work behavior. The patterns have some degree of efficiency and effectiveness acquired in a learning period, and there are psychological and economic bases for resistance to change them.

Finally, the existing pattern will generally be based to some degree upon and reinforced by the characteristics of individuals within it, particularly those high in the management organization. The overall pattern of activities presumably represents to a considerable degree the viewpoint in terms of goals, values and so forth of key management people. Thus, all through the organization the existing pattern is supported by individuals with a vested interest in the maintenance of whatever economic, social, status, power and other attributes they have attained and, particularly for people at the top, the continuity of the existing strategy may involve a personal stake, in that it was the product of their thinking and administrative efforts.

Given the strength of these four elements, the whole process of strategy formulation must be perceived as similar to attempting to change the course of a massive body moving on a course with strong momentum and inertia. Major changes are possible but require great effort. More commonly, the strategy formulation consists of working out marginal and gradual alterations in direction of the ongoing body of activities over extended periods of time. And the effectiveness of elements entering into the strategy formulation process is determined in large measure by their impact on the tendency of the ongoing pattern of activities towards continuity.

Four main types of actors are indicated in Figure 2-2 as the key direct influences on strategy formulation: the parent organization of the firm and its foreign affiliates who engage in the direct processing of strategy decisions and the home and host governments which play such a major part in influencing those decisions that they may be considered direct participants in many phases of the process. But these four actors are themselves very heavily influenced by external groups. The actions of the firm are most heavily subject to impact by elements of the market, notably consumer attitudes, cost factors and competition. The governments, for their part, are substantially influenced by the publics to which they relate, notably labor, business and consumer groups as well as their conception of the interests of their national societies as a whole.

Although the firm is ultimately the determiner of its strategy, the strategy formulation process in a large portion of cases is initiated by external influences, in part because of the momentum characteristic of the firm and in part because business in its nature is an adaptive institution. That is, it essentially exists as a vehicle for performing economic service for the market, and thus its actions are substantially governed by changes it perceives in the market either from direct influences or as represented to it through the intercession of government activities. Ideally in progressive management it is desirable that the response to the market be anticipatory in the sense that management perceives trends and opportunities and initiates changes on its own timing and volition.

In fact, however, the limitations of management capability and of the range of options and assets available often result in the strategy evolving as a result of direct initiatives from external forces under substantial pressure of time. Two common examples may be cited from international business experience. First, there is the very large portion of foreign investment in less developed countries which is the result of direct government pressures resulting from import substitution and industrialization goals. The Bayer (p. 199) and Lube India (p. 53) cases are typical examples. Second, in recent years a considerable amount of investment has moved into less developed, low wage countries as the means to meet cost competition from competitors. Singer's moves into Japan (p. 127) and later into Taiwan (p. 314) fall in this category. In both of these types of situations, corporations might take the initiative in anticipating market-related opportunities; that is, companies might go to host governments seeking protection for plants which they propose themselves in LDCs, or they might go out looking for lower cost production sites to get the jump on competition. Some examples of both types of strategy approaches can be found. But in the major portion of cases ICs have moved only as a result of initiation of logics for change from external influences.

Regardless of the source of initiative for strategy decisions, the process by which the decisions are made may take quite varied patterns involving all of the main actors. The roles of each will depend upon the goals and power involved which vary tremendously according to company, country and other situational factors. Important determinants of the power of each actor are the information it has, its capacities for initiative and its structural status.

Within the corporation one would presume that headquarters had the greatest power and certainly it does have the ultimate decision-making authority. In fact, however, the foreign affiliates, particularly large, profitable ones, have a high degree of influence because they control a large portion of the information required for decision making. The General Foods (B) case illustrates varied relations in this respect (p. 437). If they are well established, the subsidiaries also have ongoing relationships with the host government which may be critical factors in interactions in the options open to the corporation, and in the way in which decision making evolves. And, of course, the power and competence of the governments involved and the way in which they employ it are of great significance in decision making, the Bechtel case providing a good illustration (p. 89).

Since each actor has considerable potential for influence in the decision-making process derived from some mix of initiative, information and authority, the linkages among the actors and the processes involved in those linkages become a vital aspect of the strategy formulation process. These aspects of the processes are what we broadly label as negotiation, the wide range of interactions within components of the firm and with major external groups. Analysis of these interactions is the subject of the next chapter.

REFERENCES

Aharoni, Yair, *The Foreign Investment Decision Process.* Boston: Division of Research, Harvard Business School, 1966.

Behrman, Jack, *National Interests and the Multinational Enterprise.* Englewood Cliffs, N.J.: Prentice-Hall, 1970.

Duerr, Michael G., *R&D in the Multinational Company*. The Conference Board, 1970.

Fayerweather, John, *International Business Management: A Conceptual Framework*. New York: McGraw-Hill, 1969.

Fayerweather, John, (ed.) *International Business Policy and Administration: A Compendium of Concepts, Experience and Research*. Hastings-on-Hudson, N.Y.: The International Executive, 1976.

Franko, Lawrence G., *European Business Strategies in the United States*. Business International, 1971.

Knickerbocker, Frederick T., *Oligopolistic Reaction and Multinational Enterprise*. Boston: Division of Research, Harvard Business School, 1973.

Robbins, Sidney M. and Robert B. Stobaugh, *Money in the Multinational Enterprise*. New York: Basic Books, 1973.

Robinson, Richard, *International Business Management*. New York: Holt, Rinehart and Winston, 1973.

Robock, Stefan and Kenneth Simmonds, *International Business and Multinational Enterprise*. Homewood, Ill.: Richard D. Irwin, 1973.

Stopford, John M. and Louis T. Wells, *Managing the Multinational Enterprise*. New York: Basic Books, 1972.

Chapter 3

Introduction to International Business Negotiations

The international company (IC) is used to a particular business philosophy, operating procedures and patterns of interaction with the broader political, economic, social and cultural environments as they are reflected in the home country. However, in establishing operations in a foreign country, the IC has to adapt to the particular context of the host country. To a lesser extent, the host country also has to adapt to the business approach of the IC. In brief, both the IC and the host country seek an acceptable degree of mutual adaptation. Negotiation is an important means by which each party seeks adaptation by the other.

This chapter describes the nature of negotiation, discusses the nature of IC and host country contributions and the implications for negotiation, and highlights considerations in approaching negotiation. Appendix A lists the major mistakes committed in negotiations, especially by American ICs.

The primary focus of this chapter is on negotiations of the IC with governments, especially of developing countries, because such negotiations are particularly demanding. However, the general principles and observations presented are relevant for all types of negotiations including those with business and labor.

NATURE OF NEGOTIATIONS

In general, negotiation occurs within a context composed of five concentric circles (see Figure 3-1). First, negotiation is characterized by four Cs which represent common interests (something to negotiate for), conflicting interests (something to negotiate about), compromise (give and take on points) and criteria or objectives (determining the bases for its achievement).

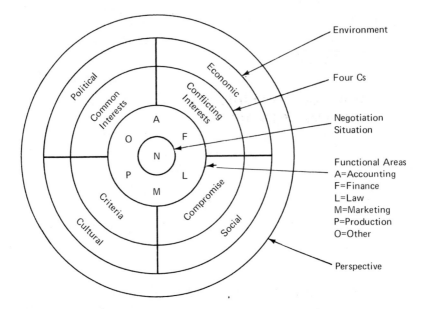

Figure 3-1. The Context of Negotiation.

For example, the IC wishes to undertake a project in a country and the host country wishes for it to do so; they have common interests. However, the IC might seek a level of ownership which the host government does not prefer to offer; the two parties have a conflict. In the negotiations, the IC agrees to accept minority ownership if the host country will offer assurances of management control; the host country might concur with this requirement if the IC offers guarantees of exports of a specified volume or amount; the parties to a negotiation compromise on specific points to gain a total package which is more advantageous to them. The criteria used by the host government might be to show political interests in the country that the IC is not being offered ultimate control authority even though it has effective operational control and that the project will have a positive balance of payments effect on the country. The IC might stress achieving a shorter payback period through operating control which encourages it to accept less attractive long-term control through lack of majority ownership. Considering this sort of compromise evolution we may broadly define negotiation as the use of common sense under pressure to achieve objectives of an organization in interacting with other organizations. However, reaching explicit agreement on all points is not necessarily the only objective of negotiation; in fact, agreement may be reached on only some of the explicit proposals being negotiated. Even then agreements vary widely in their degree of specificity and in the extent of disagreement which is left unsettled. The outcome of negotiations is more than merely an explicit agreement.

Second, the political, economic, social and cultural systems constitute the environment of a country and directly influence the approach to negotiation adopted in that country. For example, in contrast to an American executive, a Japanese executive in keeping with the consensus approach to decision making will not commit his company without detailed review and discussion within his group. The importance of group harmony, the role of the chief executive to maintain harmony, the role of middle management in initiating decisions and the importance of informal interaction both within the organization and with external groups—these characteristics of Japanese companies are significantly different from US companies.

The unique characteristic of international versus domestic business negotiations is that international negotiations are influenced by a wide variety of environments which determine the selection of appropriate tactics and strategies of negotiations to be adopted. Specific groups in different environments have their own concept of what is "right," "reasonable" or "appropriate" in negotiations; each group also has its own expectations of the likely response of an opposing group to an issue, event or mood determined by its "self reference criterion"—that is, the unconscious reference to one's own cultural values. Effective negotiation requires an understanding of the social, cultural, political, and economic systems as well as an expertise in technical, financial, accounting, and legal analysis.

Third, the negotiator must develop a broad perspective that includes the larger context within which he negotiates. This perspective is developed through answering such questions as "Besides the factors directly related to the ongoing negotiation, what other developments influence the approach to negotiation of the opposite group(s) and of various levels of the organization I represent?" For example, in negotiating with a government, the IC should recognize questions such as "What other similar and related projects has the government negotiated in the past? What has been the reaction of political and economic interest groups within the host country to the terms of investment granted to foreign investors in these projects? What pressures are being placed by external groups on the host government for a particular pattern of development of the industry? In essence, perspective requires that the negotiators understand the characteristics of the broader framework within which they negotiate and be able to interpret the framework for its implications for the specific negotiations they are engaged in.

Fourth, over time, the four Cs change. The information, know-how and alternatives available to the IC and the host country also change, resulting in a fresh interpretation of the four Cs, the environment and perspective.

Fifth, especially in countries where host governments have to approve the terms and conditions of entry of the IC, negotiations are rarely bilateral (only between two private companies) but multilateral, as reflected in Figure 3-2. The host government is fully informed of the negotiations between the private parties either throughout the negotiations or at later stages when government

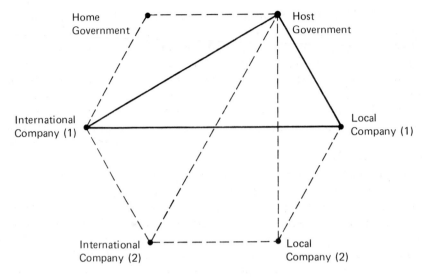

Figure 3-2. Multilateral Negotiations.

approvals have to be secured. In a trilateral or multilateral context, each party to the negotiation possesses a wider range of approaches and strategies to negotiation than is true in a bilateral context.

Sixth, multinational competition leads to multinational negotiations as outlined in Figure 3-3. For example, the negotiation situation marked A on Figure 3-3 might deal with an investment in a fertilizer plant in a country. ICs from several countries may be interested in the project. In negotiating with the host government, the American IC for example must not only know the broader context of negotiations being used by the host government but also the context of negotiations of each of the other interested parties from different countries. The approach of the Japanese to the negotiations is likely to be different from that of the Americans and the Europeans which in turn will be different from that of the communist countries. The essential point is that effective negotiations require that the negotiator for any one group be able to understand and interpret the context of negotiations of groups from other countries.

Seventh, negotiation requires the integrative expression of many different skills illustrated in Figure 3-4; functional skills in areas such as finance, marketing, production, accounting, political science; awareness of environmental factors (social, cultural, economic, political); understanding of the nature and orientation of group dynamics; awareness by the individual of his own capabilities and behavior.

CONTRIBUTIONS AND NEGOTIATION IMPLICATIONS

The IC and the host country seek each other, for each party offers contributions of a political and economic nature to assist the other in achieving its

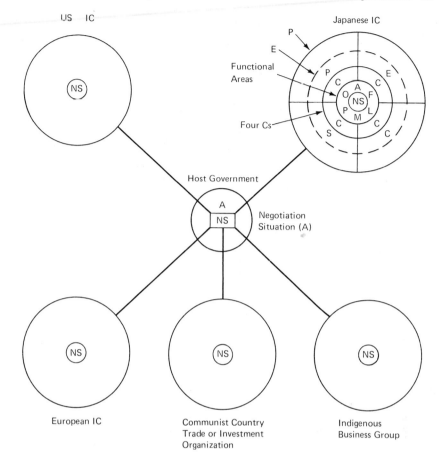

Figure 3-3. Multinational Negotiations.

objectives. Figure 3-5 is an illustrative list of the types of contributions made by the IC and the host country.

In a specific investment proposal, the IC offers a contribution package composed of different components. It may only offer advanced technology through a pure licensing agreement, or it might undertake a wholly owned operation closely integrated with IC's international operations providing capital and management skills. The host country, on its side, seeks certain types of contributions from the IC. It usually would not prefer a wholly foreign owned operation for domestic political and economic considerations even though it would reduce the initial foreign exchange drain on the country. But, the host country may offer preferential tax treatment, import privileges, allocation of land on concessional terms and management control to the IC as a contributions package to induce the IC to offer a package acceptable to the host country. In brief, the IC and the host country negotiate to achieve what each deems to be the optimum contributions package it can secure from the other. Thus, at any

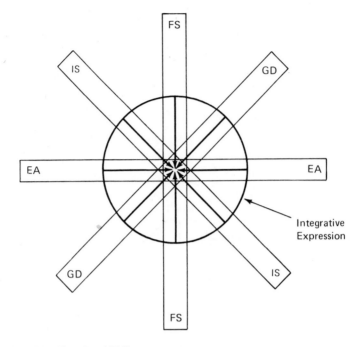

FS = Functional Skills
IS = Individual Self-Awareness
GD= Group Dynamics
EA = Environmental Awareness

Figure 3-4. Integrative Expression of Skills.

given moment each party is assigning a value to the individual and collective contributions of the other.

However, over time, the values assigned by each party to the other's contributions changes. For example, the IC may have originally introduced the manufacturing of transistors into country A at time period X. The host government welcomed this technology introduction because it assigned a high value to it. To encourage the IC, the host country may offer special incentives such as tax relief (for a specified period of time, say seven years), faster governmental approvals and others. At time period X plus seven years, the host government may believe that there has been significant local absorption of technology pertaining to transistor manufacturing. Thus, at time period X plus seven years, the original technology contribution of the IC has a lower value in the eyes of the host government than it did at time period X. At this stage, the host government encourage the IC to undertake local manufacturing of inte-grated circuits reflecting a higher level of technology than transistor by offering additional incentives in the form of tax relief and other benefits.

IC   Host Country

1. Technology

A. Access to range of existing technology and know-how and subsequent developments

A. Access to range of existing local technology and know-how and subsequent developments

2. Finance

A. Providing external capital
B. Activating local capital sources

A. Assistance in organizing and/or approval of foreign exchange transactions
B. Providing local finance
C. Providing favorable tax package.

3. Marketing

A. Skills for development of local markets
B. Exports to other units of the IC
C. Exports to buyers outside of the IC

A. Access to local markets
B. Assistance for exports by the IC

4. Organization Capacities

A. To activate, package and effectively deliver contributions
B. To provide managerial expertise

A. Offer assistance in packaging and delivery

5. Political Relations

A. Through effective delivery of contributions, assist overall attitude toward IC and assist host country decision making elites in maintaining positive investment climate
B. Assist economic/political relationship between home and host countries and between host and third countries

A. Offer contributions consistent with political/economic preferences of decision making elites
B. Develop and interpret policies consistent with broader bilateral and international relations

Figure 3-5. Types of Contributions.

The IC, on its side, has to review the value of its contribution package to the host country and vice versa. By undertaking local manufacturing of integrated circuits in country A, the IC may be faced with having to modify its global production, logistics and marketing programs for integrated circuits. The special incentives offered by country A might not be sufficiently attractive to the IC to undertake modifications of its global operations. Within this context, the IC might decide to postpone manufacturing integrated circuits in country A. However, it would then be faced with a contributions package in time period X plus seven which is assigned a lower value by the host government than when it was originally introduced.

The IC can increase the value of its contributions package by offering something other than higher level technology sought by the host government. It has several options available to it within the framework of broader corporate policy. The IC can agree to export a larger amount of transistors it manufactures in country A, thereby assisting the host country in earning foreign exchange.

The host country, especially if it is in a difficult foreign exchange position, may assign a particularly high value to such a contribution by the IC. Consequently, at time period X plus seven years, the overall value of the ICs contributions package with the export feature is far more acceptable than it would be without the export feature and without local manufacturing.

The central theme of the foregoing discussion is that both the IC and the host country can change the composition of their respective contributions package in a manner which assists in achieving each other's objectives at a particular moment in time. The implication of this theme for negotiations by the IC and the host government is critical: the contributions package of each party must change over time in a direction sought by the recipient to retain value in the eyes of the recipient.

Additionally, both the IC and the host country seek a contribution package from the other which best reflects their requirements at a particular moment in time. It is unlikely that the contributions package sought by the host country will contain everything offered by the IC and vice versa. However, serious difficulties emerge between the IC and the host country when the package offered by either one is significantly different from what is sought by the other.

During time periods A and B both the IC and the host country offered contributions packages which were within their respective ranges of acceptable differences. However, at time period C, if the IC refuses to manufacture transistors in country A and also refuses to export (Y_1) then its contributions package is outside of the range of acceptable differences as far as the host government is concerned (X_1). However, the contributions package consisting of the original technology introduced in time period X but including exports in time period X plus seven years (Y_2) falls within the range of acceptable differences for the host government (X_2). The implication for negotiation is not merely the direction of change in the contributions package of the IC and the host country but also the timing of the change.

If the IC and the host government remain outside of each other's respective ranges of acceptable differences for too long, their relationship is strained leading to mutual antagonism, distrust and discord. Of course, such a relationship is a strong hindrance to developing a contributions package acceptable to either side.

It should be noted that at times one party may offer a contributions package which is simply not acceptable to the other. Thus, the host government might not permit management control to be with the IC. Yet, management control may be a requirement of the IC. Or the IC may seek collaboration with a local private party while the host government requires collaboration in a particular industry to be with a public sector enterprise. In brief, each party regards certain issues as non-negotiable.

Economic-Political Contributions

As highlighted in Figure 3-5, the economic nature of the contributions package consists of technology both existing and subsequent developments, provision of external and local capital, access to markets (within and outside of the IC) and access to local markets, and provision of organization capacities in packaging projects and in their management. The political side of the contributions package often consists of assisting in achieving the political/economic objectives of decision making elites of the host government without hurting the chances of the IC in achieving its own objectives and in offering linkages between two or more countries. The objective here is to highlight the general nature of negotiations on the economic and political contributions packages between the IC and host country and the changes in relative emphasis over time.

The IC typically uses economic arguments to influence the host government, such as the effect on the foreign investment climate and the economic benefit to the host country (including the effect on the domestic investment climate). A favorable investment climate is likely to increase the inflow of technology, capital and other contributions by the IC and sought by the host government to facilitate achievement of its economical political objectives. The foreign investment climate of a country is influenced by many factors such as taxes, customs, foreign investment procedures, delays in decision making, violation of contract terms and general attitude toward private enterprise. The IC often tries to persuade the host country that it will benefit by maintaining a favorable investment climate. This is easier to accomplish when the host country feels that foreign investment is very desirable. For example, the potential effects on the foreign investment climate is a strong argument with the Egyptian government in 1976 but carries less weight with the Indian government.

Another determinant is the relative attractiveness of a country for foreign investors. Iran, Brazil and Japan are some of the countries attractive to most foreign investors which increases the host government's choice and reduces the need for heeding the requirements of any single source of investment. Again, Thailand might attach particular weight to the preferences of United States companies since the Thais wish to reduce the predominant role of Japanese investors.

Additionally, the IC stresses potential economic benefits or losses related to foreign investment to influence the host government. Foreign investments have a multiplier effect on the host country's economy, resulting in benefits which are often greater than those of the original investment, by offering constructive competition, improving working conditions, contributing to the development of local resources and of local managerial and entrepreneurial skills. For example, an IC in Britain when pressured by the host government to reduce the scope of its activities informed the government that seven wholly indigenously owned companies were almost entirely dependent upon the IC for their business. Therefore, any damage to the IC would directly effect the local companies.

The economic benefit/loss argument has varying degrees of impact in negotiation between the IC and the host government. In the developing countries, the argument does not usually change the existing attitudes of the host country on fundamental points such as policies toward economic development and the role of the public and private sectors, including the role of the IC. Policies of host governments in these areas are based on considerations which extend considerably beyond mere economic factors. However, specific policies of the host government on operational elements (import policies, foreign technicians, etc.) might be influenced especially if it is attempting to attract foreign investments.

Economic/Political Weighting

Because of the political implications of their decision, an important consideration for host government negotiators becomes how to achieve the necessary economic benefits without exposing themselves to political attack notably on issue of control (including charges by the indigenous business community). Of course, it is often impossible to do so. However, to the extent possible, officials will attempt to achieve at least the appearances of national control even though the real situation might be quite different. At times the appearance is as important as the reality. For example, in 1975 an Asian government would not grant an IC majority ownership but was anxious for the IC to accept 49 percent ownership along with an ironclad management contract providing the IC with exclusive management control. With this arrangement, the host government would not be exposed to attacks by interest groups of permitting foreign equity control; at the same time, the IC would have total authority in the management of the company.

The range of acceptable differences for the IC and the host country are composed of economic and political contributions. Over time it is likely that an IC's project will be exposed to greater political considerations than at the initial stages of entry into a country for three reasons. First, local companies may begin to experience intense competition from the IC in a direct sense or for labor, raw material and capital and begin to object through politicians and government agencies. The economic challenge of the IC to the local business community often arouses a desire for protection through political means. Second, an IC often occupies a significant position in a particular industry in the host country.

This creates anxiety on the part of the host government, not because the IC is economically inefficient but because a foreign company is exercising significant control over an industry. Political considerations become particularly important if the industry involved is considered vital by the host government. Third, an IC often gains a high profile in a host country because of aggressive marketing, expansion into new or related industries or involvement in a controversy. The high profile encourages the host government to review the IC's contributions package with particular emphasis on the political implications of the package. The high profile typically emerges after an IC has been operating in a country for some time.

If the political components of the IC's contributions package turn negative in the eyes of the host government, it becomes important for the IC to review its overall contributions package to determine whether it could be modified to retain a positive value in the eyes of the host government. For example, a leading beverage company has operations in several countries. In a developing country, the host government insisted on reducing the equity interest of the IC from 100 percent to a minority position. The IC was known to be highly efficient with a good product (which had become a household name) and an excellent marketing network. The host government informed the IC, off the record, that local economic interests were exerting pressure on the government to curb the presence of the IC in the country. The officials added that in general the government was impressed with the IC's contributions to date but under the new set of political circumstances in the country, especially the influence of the business community with key political elites, it was important that the IC emerge with a revised contributions package to reduce or neutralize the political pressures on the officials.

The IC carefully concluded that it would not be sufficient to add purely economic contributions to its package. Rather, its fresh contributions should have important political benefits for the decision making groups in the host government especially those favoring the IC. After informal discussions with appropriate host government officials and with selected political leaders, the IC added three contributions to its existing package.

First, it volunteered the use of its excellent marketing network for distribution of birth control material. This remains a critically important area for the host government decision making elites. The IC did not incur a significant cost but made an immensely important political contribution to its package in the eyes of the host government.

Second, it offered to introduce a low cost, high protein food drink into the country to be developed through collaboration of leading nutritional experts in the country. Such a product had a definite nutritional value and was eagerly sought by the host government. Therefore, this move contributed positively to the overall package offered by the IC.

Third, the IC offered to sell up to 15 percent of its shares in the host country to the workers. The government viewed this move favorably as it wished to encourage other ICs to provide for worker share in ownership.

The net result of these fresh contributions was that the host government considered the revised package of the IC to be within the range of acceptable differences. The IC's equity was reduced to 74 percent over a period of five years and the scope of its operations was not curtailed. The contribution package offered by the host government was within the range of acceptable differences for the IC.

CONSIDERATIONS IN APPROACHING NEGOTIATION

The objective in this section is to offer an illustration of some of the considerations in approaching negotiation and must be seen within the larger context of negotiation outlined in Figures 3-1 through 3-5.

Precedent Orientation of Decision Maker

Both the IC and host government officials evaluate terms of investment with reference to terms provided in the past. Officials favor this approach as it provides for relatively safe decisions, especially where officials do not possess experience in dealing with ICs and is preferred in situations where there is an unclear allocating of authority and responsibility.

The IC also favors a precedent-oriented approach to decision making largely because such decisions are safer for the individual executive. Furthermore, in the last ten years, especially in developing countries, host governments have sought reduction of the areas and extent of participation of the IC. In this context, the IC uses precedents to assist in maintaining a situation which is more favorable for it than what is sought by the host government.

The IC is particularly concerned about global precedents. If it accepts certain terms of investment in a particular country, the IC thereby establishes precedents which are used by governments in other countries to negotiate with the IC. For example, when Esso was selling its fertilizer plant in the Philippines in 1970, the terms of divestment by Esso in Aruba emerged as a precedent which could be used by the host government. (See ESFAC, p. 205).

Both the IC and host governments should recognize the critical role of precedents in negotiations. Proposals should be structured and negotiated in a manner which reduces an obvious conflict with precedents.

Stressing Short-Term Effects

Both the IC and governments assign individuals to a particular function for a specific period of time normally ranging between two and four years. Thereafter, in keeping with normal rotation policy to provide wider experience, the individual is shifted to another area of the organization where his functions and responsibilities are of a different order than in the previous assignment. Thus, both the IC executive and the government official are assigned to a particular area for a relatively short period of time.

Both government officials and IC executives stress achieving short-term effects because their performance is measured over the short term. A minister wishes to show results (increase in exports, greater employment, etc.) during his term in office which seldom extends beyond two or three years. Similarly, an executive wishes to show concrete results (higher profits, greater share of the market, etc.) during his stay typically for three years in a particular country.

Often the conflicts which arise between the IC and the host government negotiators deal more with questions of how to ensure that the short-term effects of both sides can be achieved. Conversely, the IC and the host government experience relatively limited conflict over the longer term effects of the project such as improved foreign investment climate, increased foreign exchange earnings or enhanced domestic skills. However, the long-term effects are important to each party and conflicts over such effects are likely to appear after a project has been in operation in a country for a few years.

Responsibility, Authority and Credibility

An executive's credibility in the eyes of host government officials is determined by what the officials perceive his power to be—whether he is a decision maker or merely serves as a mouthpiece for higher levels of the organization. For example, after several months of negotiation with the American manager of an IC in France, the host government officials concluded that the manager possessed limited decision making authority because all policy decisions were being made at headquarters in the United States. Therefore, they did not take the views of the expatriate seriously and insisted that senior management from the United States visit France for face to face negotiations with the host government.

At times, especially when a new project is being considered for the first time in a country, the level of investment is large or when serious bottlenecks arise, the senior levels of management from the regional and headquarters level become involved in direct negotiations with the host government. However, when this occurs, it is important that the credibility and standing of the country-level manager not be damaged in the eyes of the host government. Unfortunately, too often headquarters personnel especially force their way into a country level negotiation with seriously adverse consequences on the on-going negotiations and the company's presence in a country.

The timing, extent and areas of involvement of regional and especially headquarter personnel in negotiations at the country level should be carefully organized.

As with any organization, the IC and governments contain several levels. Requirements of protocol, nature of the issues and personal relationships and interests influence which levels of the IC interact with the host government as reflected in Figure 3-6.

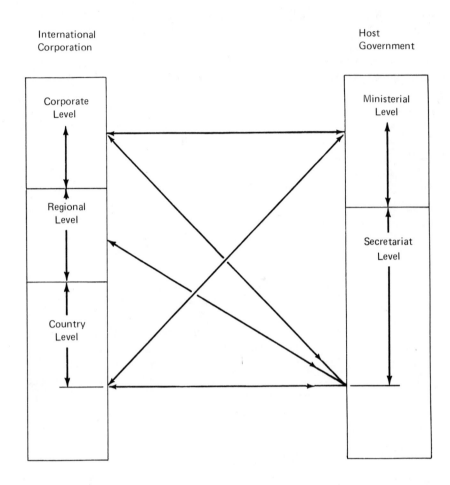

Figure 3-6.   Internal and External Levels of Interaction.

The country-level manager of an IC may negotiate with an official of the host government at the secretariat level for expansion of operations, special incentives or other issues. However, while he is negotiating with the external group (the host government) he is also making representation of his views and recommendations to the regional level of the corporation. Similarly, the secretariat official of the host government is making representations to its senior levels and other related ministries. Therefore, both the IC executive and the host country official are negotiating with an external party and also within their respective organizations at the same time.

The IC initiates discussion with host government officials either at the secretariat or the ministerial levels. It is most important to think through the appropriate approach in view of the relative role of each level.

The secretariat level is in most cases powerful as it is solely responsible for analysis and in developing a common viewpoint within the concerned ministries on a foreign investment proposal. It is proud and jealous of its role and frowns upon companies which attempt to bypass it. However, rejection of a proposal at the secretariat level still allows the IC to proceed directly to the minister. The reverse is seldom the case as long as the minister rejecting the proposal is in office.

Initial contact with a minister is used under special circumstances such as a close relationship between a minister and an IC executive, a major bottleneck which is critical to an ongoing operation or a new agency of the host government which simply has not developed a significant secretariat level.

At times, the decision making center for a particular project within the host government is not clearly known to the IC. Because of shifting organizational responsibilities and interministry rivalries, two or more ministries might wish to adopt the key role in negotiating a particular project. In such a situation, the IC might have to interact with the ministerial level of one ministry and the secretariat level of another.

In general, the IC must understand the relative power structure of the secretariat and ministerial level in a government and it should avoid actions which violate existing practices.

Informal Explorations

Informal explorations are the most important means of gaining the views of government officials and searching for areas of commonalty without either side seeking or offering a commitment. This approach offers both sides time to think through a proposal, engage in internal deliberations, reduce exposure to pressures from various groups, avoid public disagreements which cause loss of face by one or more parties and insure that relatively safe decisions are made.

Informal explorations for a project are expressed through several visits to government officials at the middle and senior levels. The discussions which occur are not reduced to writing except for internal memoranda. Cordiality and an effort to learn the view of government officials who might oppose the formal application are stressed. Gradually over time some sort of an official position begins to emerge which then offers the IC an idea of what is likely to be considered favorably by the government if the IC was to make a formal application.

The informal process is time-consuming and requires considerable patience and an understanding of the local context. The IC must have an intimate knowledge of individual decision makers, of host government processes and of the unique characteristics of a proposal.

The nationality of the company's representative also affects the interaction process especially when officials are more comfortable with fellow nationals than with foreigners, particularly where sensitive issues are discussed. The IC must therefore have nationals who can be entrusted with this most delicate function but who can also keep in mind the company's objectives. At times, the host country national is placed in a most difficult situation of loyalty conflict—should he act in the best interests of the company or of the country?

Personal Relations

Good personal relations with the appropriate host government officials are at least as important as an excellent feasibility or cost-benefit study. While technical skills are particularly important during the implementation and operations of a project, human skills are critical at all stages.

However, sound personal relations develop only through considerable expenditure of time and effort especially by the more senior country levels of management interacting with host government counterparts. Unfortunately, more often than not, executives do not devote sufficient energy to this function.

Information

Information refers to facts relating to a particular industry, project or developments of a relatively objective nature. The IC has a comparative advantage in this area vis-à-vis the host country especially when a particular industry is being introduced into the host country for the first time. However, over time, the host country gains experience and learns about the various sources of information thereby positioning itself in a relatively favorable position vis-à-vis the IC. For example, the IC is required to submit periodic reports to the host government on the scope of its operations thereby adding to the sum total of the governments information about an industry and the IC's operations. Additionally, in some cases, the host government has undertaken projects on its own in competition with existing projects of ICs in the country, thereby gaining information allowing for comparison with the information provided by the IC. Information plays a critical role in negotiations. The IC and host governments develop and seek information both on macro (industry) and micro (specific project) aspects. The IC is faced with an important policy question: would negotiations be more effective and agreements more lasting if the IC provided more information on its activities and objectives to the host government? Should host governments specify the types of information they seek from ICs for more effective assessment and negotiation with ICs?

Publicity

The ICs activities are the subject of growing interest, concern and controversy in most parts of the world and are therefore accompanied by publicity. Negotiations are often influenced by effective use of publicity to secure a specific response from an opponent, to encourage public discussion especially where a project has political implications, to justify a particular decision in the eyes of the public and to reduce alternative courses of action by adopting a particular stance.

The public media in many countries are controlled by the government or leading indigenous business organizations. Additionally, in most cases the intelligentsia (editors, correspondents and the like) retain a critical attitude toward the IC. Therefore, if the IC is embroiled in a public controversy in a foreign country, it is likely to be dealing with public media which are neither investigative nor favorable toward the IC.

Both the IC and the host government should think through the following types of questions: should the IC respond publicly to comments in the public media or should it adopt a "no comment" approach? should there be a single spokesman for the IC in responding to questions of the public media? how should public pronouncements of headquarters be coordinated with the needs of the country level?

SUMMARY

Any negotiation situation must be viewed within the larger context composed of a vast range of complex political and economic considerations, a changing cast of characters and a shifting interpretation of common and conflicting interests between the parties to a negotiation. The contributions package offered to each other by the IC and the host country is subject to change in order to better reflect what each is seeking from the other to achieve its respective objectives. The composition of the package and carefully timed changes in it play a critical role in negotiations between the IC and the host government. Additionally, a negotiation must be carefully approached for a wrong approach has a detrimental effect on the outcome.

The central theme, however, is that skills of negotiation are required in all aspects of interaction between and within governments, business firms, unions and inter-governmental organizations. The development of negotiation skills requires training and study. In the evolving context of international business, negotiation skills must be viewed as an essential part of the expertise of the IC executive and government official. Additionally, negotiating is simply too important an activity to be approached in an ad hoc manner. It requires careful planning in an immediate and a long-term sense.

Appendix 3A:
Major Mistakes in
Negotiations

Developing a list of "do's" and "don'ts" in negotiation is always fraught with dangers of simplification and oversight. However, the following list illustrates types of mistakes committed by the IC, especially in negotiations with host governments in developing countries and should be seen with reference to the context of negotiation outlined in Figures 2-1 through 2-5. The mistakes are organized into four broad and interrelated categories of empathy, role of governments, decision making characteristics and organizing for negotiation.

A. Empathy
1. *Failure to place yourself in the other person's shoes:*
It is not sufficient to merely know the position and approach of your opponent in a negotiation; even more important is to understand the reasons which prompt him to adopt the particular stance.

2. *Insufficient understanding of different ways of thinking:*
Reaching the same conclusions is important, but in negotiations it is even more important to know the thought processes by which individuals from different cultures reach the same conclusions.

3. *Insufficient attention to saving face of the opponent:*
"Winning" in a negotiation situation should not result in a loss of face for the opponent, especially in countries where personal honor is a sensitive issue.

4. *Insufficient knowledge of host country:*
Often the negotiator does not have sufficient knowledge of the history, culture and political characteristics of a country in which he is negotiating.

B. Role of Government

5. *Insufficient recognition of the nature and characteristics of the role of government in centrally planned economies:*

The desire for rapid development, distrust of private enterprise, lack of indigenous entrepreneurial talent—these and other considerations have prompted host governments to play a major role in planning for the economic development of their countries.

6. *Insufficient recognition of the relatively low status assigned to businessmen:*

Not only are government officials in planned economies powerful, but they often look down upon businessmen who are viewed as being concerned only with questions of profits and not the broader national aspirations of the society.

7. *Insufficient recognition of the role of host government in negotiations:*

Negotiations in developing countries are generally tripartite in nature, involving the foreign company, the local company and the host government.

8. *Insufficient recognition of the perception of host countries of the role of the IC's home government in negotiations:*

Regardless of what the reality of the situation is, the host government believes that the foreign company uses the muscle of its home government in negotiations with the host government.

C. Decision-Making Characteristics

9. *Insufficient recognition of the economic and political criteria in decision making:*

Host government officials place particular stress on political considerations in evaluating investment proposals in keeping with the general orientation of the type of organization to which they belong.

10. *Insufficient recognition of the difference between approval at one level and implementation of such approval at other levels of government:*

Gaining approval of the central government for an investment does not mean that other levels of the government will automatically implement the approval.

11. *Insufficient understanding of the role of personal relations and personalities in decision making by the host government:*

Host government officials possess considerable discretion in interpretation of policies and regulations relating to foreign investments.

12. *Insufficient allocation of time for negotiations:*

It simply takes longer in certain countries to present a proposal, to gain a reaction and to offer a response because of distance, mutual suspicion, different ways of thinking and the internal decision-making structure of the government and the IC.

D. Organizing

13. *Insufficient attention to planning for changing negotiation strength:*

The negotiation strength of the IC and the host country changes over the duration of a project.

14. *Interference by headquarters:*

Headquarters personnel sometimes interfere directly in negotiations, causing serious damage to the credibility of the country-level managers and the field negotiations.

15. *Insufficient planning for internal communication and decisions:*

Several parts of an organization have an interest in an on-going negotiation, and their views and preferences have to be recognized in negotiating for a particular package of terms of investment.

16. *Insufficient recognition of the role of the negotiator in accommodating the conflicting interests of his group with those of the opposing groups:*

The negotiator plays a crucial role as interpreter, intermediary and counselor both to this own group and to the opposing group on what can be achieved in a particular negotiation.

17. *Insufficient recognition of the loci of decision-making authority:*

Decisions are seldom made by any one branch of government but are shared across agencies and ministries because of the particular characteristics of government organizations.

18. *Insufficient recognition of the strength of competitors:*

The tendency to underestimate the competitive strength and negotiation skills of non-American companies is a source of weakness in the American company's planning for negotiation.

19. *Insufficient attention to training executives in the art of negotiation:*

Executives are seldom trained or encouraged to develop negotiating skills.

SELECTED REFERENCES

Bartos, Otomar J. *Process and Outcome of Negotiations.* New York: Columbia University Press, 1974.

Behrman, Jack N. *U.S. International Business and Governments.* New York: McGraw Hill, 1971.

Behrman, Jack N., Jean Boddewyn, and Ashok Kapoor. *International Business-Government Communications: U.S. Actors, Structures, Issues.* Lexington, Mass.: D.C. Heath and Company, 1975.

Drickman, Daniel. *Human Factors in International Negotiations.* Beverly Hills, California: Sage Publications, 1973.

Fayerweather, John (ed.). *International Business-Government Affairs.* Cambridge, Mass.: Ballinger, 1973.

Fayerweather, John. *The Mercantile Bank Affair.* New York: New York University Press, 1974.

Fisher, Roger. *International Conflict for Beginners.* New York: Harper and Row, 1969.

Ikle, Fred C. *How Nations Negotiate.* New York: Harper and Row, 1964.

Kapoor, Ashok. *International Business Negotiation: A Study in India.* New

York: New York University Press, 1970; paperback Princeton: The Darwin Press, 1973.

Kapoor, Ashok. *Planning for International Business Negotiation.* Cambridge, Mass.: Ballinger, 1975.

Mikesell, Raymond F. *Foreign Investment in the Petroleum and Mineral Industries.* Baltimore: The Johns Hopkins University Press, 1971.

Schelling, Thomas C. *The Strategy of Conflict.* Cambridge, Mass.: Harvard University Press, 1960.

Smith, David N., and Louis T. Wells, Jr. *Negotiating Third World Mineral Agreements: Promises as Prologue.* Cambridge, Mass.: Ballinger, 1976.

Zartman, I. William. *The Politics of Trade Negotiations between Africa and the EEC: The Weak Confront the Strong.* Princeton, N.J.: Princeton University Press, 1971.

Zartman, I. William (ed.). *The 50% Solution.* New York: Doubleday, 1976.

Cases

Part A

Lube India Ltd.

NEGOTIATION FOR AN INTERNATIONAL MIXED VENTURE

Esso Standard Eastern (ESE) has had a presence in India since the 1880s. It established refining and marketing operations in India in 1954 that grew to substantial size, making ESE one of the largest single foreign investors in India. The relationship between the Government of India (GOI) and ESE has changed for the worse over time to such an extent that the two parties have a pathological reaction to each other.

The GOI and ESE initiated negotiations in October 1959 for a lubricating oil manufacturing plant. After protracted and detailed negotiations, extending over five years, the two parties signed a lube refining agreement in September 1965. In April 1966, Lube India Ltd. was incorporated as a mixed venture equally owned by the GOI and ESE. In February 1970, the lube refinery was formally inaugurated by the Vice President of India. The primary focus in this study is on the negotiations for a mixed venture with particular emphasis on the terms of sharing management responsibility between the GOI and ESRC (Esso Standard Refining Company).

BACKGROUND

The objective in this section is to present a brief outline of major developments in the petroleum industry in India from the mid 1950s to the mid 1960s for their effect on the negotiations relating to the lubricant project.

This case is based on a larger study by A. Kapoor in A. Kapoor, *Planning for International Business Negotiations.* Cambridge, Mass.: Ballinger 1975.

The major development in the 1950s was the signing of agreements between the GOI and three major international oil companies for establishing refineries in India: Standard Vacuum* with nine million barrels per year (1954), Burmah-Shell with fifteen million barrels per year (1954) and Caltex with five million barrels per year (1957). The essential terms of these agreements were: (1) the private companies had the right to import crude oil from their own sources; (2) they owned 100 percent of the refineries; and (3) the companies could not be nationalized by the GOI for a specific period of time. These agreements were hailed when they were first concluded. Foreign direct investment in petroleum facilities in India increased from $47 million in 1948 to $218 million in 1955, or from 8 to 24 percent of total foreign direct investment in the country.

However, starting in 1955 with the second Five Year Plan period (1955-1960), several interrelated developments contributed to the growing conflicts between the private international oil companies and the GOI. Imports of crude oil were having a negative impact on the deteriorating foreign exchange position. Between 1955 and 1960, imports increased from $1.4 billion to $2.3 billion, while India's gold and foreign exchange reserves dropped from $1.9 billion to $0.7 billion. The Soviet Union offered to supply crude oil and refined petroleum products to India on a barter basis which would save the country $33 million in foreign exchange expenditures. However, the foreign oil companies refused to handle Soviet products through their refining and marketing networks in India, thereby causing a severe strain in their relations with the GOI.

The GOI's reaction resulted in several types of activities to reduce the country's dependence on the major international oil companies operating in India. More specifically, it consisted of the following five moves: (1) investigating the pricing policies of the oil companies to determine whether they were making unreasonable profits; (2) moving rapidly to develop an integrated, state owned petroleum exploration, refining and marketing network that could process Soviet crude; (3) refusing to allow development of additional refining capacity by the international companies; (4) encouraging the development of independent oil companies such as Philips Petroleum Company, American International Oil Company, and state owned enterprises such as ENI of Italy and National Iranian Oil Company of Iran to enter into crude oil supply and refining agreements with the GOI; and (5) growing pressure especially on the major oil companies for admitting local ownership. Of course, all these moves resulted in growing pressures and conflicts between the GOI and the established majors in India.

Other developments also occurred. In April 1965, India Oil Company (owned by the GOI) planned to import about 2.3 million tons of refined products from the Soviet Union accounting for almost 20 percent of the total market demand. But the established majors in India refused to market the Russian products through their facilities and the GOI's network was not sufficiently established at

---

*Standard Vacuum Co., a joint venture of Standard Oil (N.J.) and Socony-Vacuum Co.

the time. This led to shortages of products in the country as well as a confrontation between the GOI and the established majors. The GOI took steps under the Defense of India Act in June 1965 to position itself to compel the oil companies to distribute the refined products.

In sympathy with the GOI's cause, the nationwide union of oil workers called for a strike against the oil companies in order to force them to distribute Soviet products. However, the strike was called off at the behest of the GOI. Thus the relationship between the oil companies and the GOI was highly strained throughout the period of negotiation between Esso and the GOI on the lubricant project.

LUBE INDIA NEGOTIATIONS:
A CHRONOLOGY

Most of India's lube oil requirements were satisfied by imported lubricants or by lubes blended in India from imported lube base oils. The need to import these products added to the increasingly severe drain on the country's foreign exchange resources especially after the first Five Year Plan, which prompted the GOI to consider development of local facilities to meet this growing demand (Exhibit 1). Various estimates available to the GOI indicated that between $6 million and $8 million in foreign exchange could be saved each year for each 100,000 tons of indigenous lube oil production. A sample calculation of potential foreign exchange savings is shown in Exhibit 2. India's foreign exchange shortage remains a critical determinant of its development policies and programs.

Exhibit 1. Industry Lube Oil Supply/Demand Forecast (thousands of metric tons)[a]

| | 1966 | 1968[b] | | 1970 | |
		Min.	Max.	Min.	Max.
Demand—all grades	470	515	—	590	600	—	750
Indian production					
Barauni	45	45		45	
Koyali	50	100		100	
South India	—	75		75	
Calcutta	—	—		50	
Total production	95	220		270	
Import requirements	375	295	370	330	480

[a]Developed by Esso India (May 3, 1963).

[b]Actual consumption in 1968 reached 486,860 tons with the forecast for 1975 projected at 881,000 tons (Esso India News, March 1970).

Negotiations—Exploratory

In 1959 the Government of India (GOI) invited tenders for the construction of a 100,000 ton per year, high viscosity index (VI)* lubricating oil base stock manufacturing plant. The tenders were requested with the understanding that the lube plant was to be entirely owned by the government. At least ten companies submitted proposals in answer to the GOI tender. In March 1960, Stanvac, with the concurrence of the Boards of Jersey Standard and Socony-Vacuum, advised the GOI of its desire to design, construct, manage and operate a lube oil manufacturing plant for high VI lubes with a 100,000 ton per year capacity, integrated with and adjacent to its existing Bombay refinery. Feed preparation facilities would be located in and owned by Standard Vacuum Refining Company (SVRC). The lube plant would be owned 50 percent by SVRC and 50 percent by the GOI and operated by SVRC under management contract.

There were several reasons for Esso's interest in the lubricant project: (1) the demand was high, suggesting an attractive profit potential; (2) the integration with the refinery would offer additional economies and profits; (3) the lubricant project would be a logical extension of Esso's activities in the country; (4) it might offer a forum for exploring policies and action, which might subsequently be considered for the larger petroleum refining and marketing operations in India; and (5) company executives were optimistic about business prospects in the country.

The Government paid little attention to Stanvac's proposal until early 1961, nearly twelve months later. Preliminary discussions were begun. The first major

Exhibit 2.   Estimated Foreign Exchange Savings (per 100,000 tons production)

Exchange Saving	
Decreased lube product imports	$8,712,000
Additional Expenditures	
Repatriation of overseas loans	540,000
Interest on overseas loans	180,000
Non-rupee operating costs	870,000
Dollar dividends	131,000
Crude oil imports	1,702,000
	3,423,000
Net Foreign Exchange Savings	$5,289,000

Based on overseas loan requirement of $5,400,000, ten-year term at 6 percent interest to finance new facility in India. Developed by Esso Standard Refining Co. of India, July 1962.

*A measure of the grade or quality of a lubricating oil with high VI for automotives and medium and low VI oils for industrial applications.

conflict arose over ownership of the vacuum pipe still to be used for preparation of the lube plant feedstock. Stanvac had proposed that the vacuum pipe still be owned by SVRC and erected at its refinery. But the GOI insisted that this facility be owned and operated by the lube plant and Stanvac reluctantly agreed so to modify its proposal.

There were other areas of disagreement as well. The GOI modified its initial position of 100 percent ownership and agreed to share ownership with a foreign company for two key reasons: this would result in the foreign partner's providing most of the foreign exchange cost of the plant; and the GOI did not possess the necessary technology or personnel to undertake the project on its own.

The Government also made it clear that it would not grant Stanvac a management contract. Furthermore, it stipulated that the managing director of the proposed joint company would require specific approval of the board of directors with regard to certain management decisions. The GOI also indicated its desire to have the management structure of the lube oil project conform to the "pattern" of recently concluded agreements with other international companies. Stanvac was willing to concede this point, provided limits of authority of the managing director were made as broad as possible. At the suggestion of Jersey Standard five key provisions of Stanvac's acceptance of the GOI's management "pattern" were:

1. Stanvac and the GOI shall at all times have equal effective representation and voting rights on the board of directors.
2. The managing director will be a Stanvac nominee.
3. The managing director will be authorized to continue to conduct business in a normal course whenever the board may be deadlocked, and that such authority shall continue until the deadlock is resolved by arbitration.
4. Succession of a Stanvac nominee as managing director will be insured if the incumbent should become incapacitated during any deadlock period.
5. Additionally, the agreement should clearly delegate to the managing director the general authority to supervise and direct construction and operation of the lube refinery.

These provisions became the cornerstone of any mixed management concept acceptable to Esso. Although these provisions were destined to be discussed and debated for the next four years, Esso remained firm in its position that these provisions were essential to sound management of the new company.

By November 1961 Stanvac was able to advise New York that the principal unresolved issues were price, return on investment and management. In late 1961 and early 1962, the proposed lube oil project received considerable attention by Stanvac, in both Bombay and New York. Other matters under discussion at the same time included lube oil pricing, crude oil supply, sharing of plant output, potential construction contractors, and competitive lube oil projects being considered by the Government of India.

During this period and subsequently, Esso and the GOI engaged in a wide range of informal explorations. Esso was well established in India and knew the Indian business context, particularly as it related to interacting with the Government. The typical pattern of negotiation was first to seek the views of carefully selected officials in the operative ministries (and other individuals familiar with the operative ministries) on a given issue. This informal exploration would suggest what might be acceptable to the GOI, the various forces at work within the Government, and the manner in which the issue might be presented for more detailed and formal consideration. This activity took time and effort, but Esso already possessed the necessary organization and personnel to engage in such informal explorations. The references to the actual meetings must, therefore, be seen within this framework of exploration and negotiation.

Negotiations—Detailed

On January 18, 1962 the Secretary of Mines and Fuels and the general manager of Stanvac's activities in India met to discuss the lube plant proposal. It was an exploratory meeting in which a number of issues were discussed. However, no commitments were sought or made by either party. Negotiating teams were named to represent each party with the first session scheduled for the following day. Stanvac's attitude at this point was a mixture of optimism and caution. It informed headquarters that while the first response of the GOI appeared to be favorable, it did not necessarily mean smooth sailing ahead or an early agreement.

The first negotiating session, held on January 19, 1962, reviewed all aspects of Stanvac's proposal. The Under Secretary of Mines and Fuels and the Joint Secretaries of Economic Affairs and of Oil comprised the GOI negotiating team, while Stanvac was represented by its assistant general manager for refining, an American assistant, and an Indian national long employed in its Bombay operation. (The equivalence of organizational levels represented at the negotiations was maintained by both sides.) At this meeting there was no attempt to negotiate on differences between Stanvac and GOI positions but merely to point out where these differences existed.

Three days later a follow-up session was held in which substantive issues were discussed. The most important feature of this meeting was discussion on management control including the first full explanation of GOI's "concept" of management. This concept or pattern of management had evolved from earlier negotiations which resulted in the formation of Oil India Ltd., an exploration and petroleum producing company established as a 50-50 mixed venture by the Burmah Oil Company and the GOI. The GOI had adopted the management structure in the Oil India charter as the pattern for all manufacturing ventures between the Government and private sector companies. This pattern established the position of financial director (a government nominee) as a substantial check on the managing director, who would be a nominee of the private sector company. (See Appendix B for general pattern.)

The development and use of this pattern was based on a number of considerations on the part of the GOI: (1) it would offer greater monitoring and direct control of activities of foreign companies, especially in strategically important and sensitive areas; (2) it would assist in the development of a management cadre within government ranks with the experience to move into the managing director's position; (3) it would safeguard the government from those who criticized the unchecked presence of foreigners in key sectors of the economy; (4) the GOI wished to gain acceptance of the new precedent it was attempting to establish by a major international oil company, which would make it simpler to seek acceptance from others. Also, the shared management approach in a small venture such as the lube project could be extended at a later date to large ventures, including the refinery and marketing operations of Esso in India.

Esso, on its side, was seriously concerned with the implication of shared management with the Government not only because of operational efficiency in India but also because of the potential for creating an undesirable precedent for the company's worldwide operations.

Stanvac presented its basis for pricing feedstock to the plant and lube base stocks from the plant. Minor issues discussed included foreign exchange loans, Indian tax position and product blending and packaging requirements proposed by the GOI. Pricing and taxes were later to become breakpoints for Esso.

On February 2, 1962, a third meeting of the negotiating committee was held. Some of the issues such as management control were discussed; however, many of the key topics remained under government review. A ten-day recess was provided to give the GOI time to study the proposed pricing basis as well as its requirements for blending and packaging, and to give Stanvac time to review the management provisions in the charter recently negotiated between the GOI and Burmah Oil. At this point there was some feeling among Stanvac personnel that an agreement with the GOI was imminent. Stanvac emphasized to Jersey Standard that prompt resolution of the management question was essential if the company wanted to conclude an agreement with the GOI.

Following considerable restudy of the various proposals and some minor formal contact between the parties, the next meeting of the negotiating committee was held on March 30, 1962. The major topic of the discussion was management control of the lube oil company, and on this topic the parties appeared to be narrowing their differences. Stanvac felt that unless there were further changes in the official attitude of the GOI, the memorandum on management control would be acceptable to the GOI.

On April 1, 1962, Mobil's joint ownership with Jersey Standard of the Standard-Vacuum Oil Company was terminated. Refining and marketing activities continued under the sole ownership of Jersey Standard, with the new regional company named Esso Standard Eastern (ESE) and the name of the refining company in India changed to Esso Standard Refining Company of India, Ltd. (ESRC). Esso was able to continue negotiations without interruption since the original Stanvac negotiating team continued on its behalf.

The major unresolved issue at this point, in ESRC's opinion, was the basis to be used for pricing lube oil base stocks from the plant. This had already proved to be a major obstacle in reaching an agreement with the GOI. However, there was considerable feeling within Esso that a modified pricing proposal which it had submitted to the GOI in May 1962 would settle this issue to the satisfaction of both parties. ESE informed Jersey Standard that in its view an agreement with the GOI could be concluded if the GOI accepted the company's pricing proposal.

This optimism soon subsided following the June 6 meeting of the negotiating committee. During this meeting, the GOI indicated its desire to add a clause to the management provisions that would allow the GOI to elect the managing director after a three- to five-year operation. Esso would, in turn, be able to elect the financial director. The GOI's attitude was that equal ownership should also present each partner with the right to fill a particular function.

The GOI also indicated that it desired that any setting of prices should be left to the lube plant board—no price formula should be established beforehand. Esso's position was that its partnership with the GOI and the wide powers of the Government on price controls would result in a pricing structure that would not be attractive for the company. The GOI, on the other hand, was of the opinion that the pricing decision should not be prejudged, but rather should be in the hands of the board of directors, as would be the preferred practice in a private enterprise economy. Esso maintained that the economy was not sufficiently private or exposed to free market forces to permit this approach.

The GOI's stand on management sharing and pricing were not acceptable to ESRC and ESE. On August 22, 1962, the Executive Committee of ESE adopted a revised pricing basis which, in general, satisfied the GOI's desires. No change was made in its management proposal for the lube oil company. By late October 1962 the negotiating committee was able to complete a draft agreement that satisfied both teams. In early November this draft was initialed by ESE and submitted to the GOI for review and approval. However, government action was delayed six months until May 28, 1963, when the Indian Cabinet initialed and thereby granted conditional approval of the Indian Government to the preliminary agreement. At this point ESRC was anticipating an early conclusion of the formal agreement. Its technical affiliate, which would be responsible for plant construction, was projecting design completion by end of 1962, with plant startup scheduled for early 1966.

However, these projections proved to be highly optimistic. Each draft of the final agreement created new issues for contention or expanded existing minor issues. As time passed there was also some change of position on issues previously considered resolved. The preliminary agreement initialed by the parties stated that a final decision regarding capacity, product yields and costs would be taken by the GOI after receipt of the detailed project report to be prepared by ESE. In other words, the agreement initialed was of a "heads type" nature, which permitted both ESE and the GOI room for change depending on the results of the study.

In July 1962, the GOI informed Esso that it would not sign the contract for the lube plant if the size was less than 145,000 tons per year unless Esso's project study clearly demonstrated that the larger size was not practical. Since Esso's studies at that time indicated that its Bombay refinery could provide enough feedstock without refinery expansion for up to 145,000 tons per year of lube base stock, and since ESE was concerned about the lube manufacturing plans of its competitors, especially Shell, Esso decided to accept the GOI's demands and push for signing at the earliest possible date.

On August 20, 1963, a draft of the lube plant agreement was reviewed by the Jersey Board, which concluded that there were a number of amendments which should be made to the financial and foreign exchange sections of the draft. Jersey's main concern was that some sections of the agreement could be interpreted to mean that Esso would bear a disproportionate share of the financial burden even though it was the stated position of both parties that such a burden would be shared equally. The GOI agreed to modify the wording to more clearly reflect the understanding of the parties.

However, a major issue arose as the parties attempted to write the companion agreements that would formalize Esso's design, engineering and technical services input to the construction and operation of the lube plant. Following a meeting on November 11, 1963, ESE reported to Jersey Standard that the GOI's attitude was highly critical on what it felt to be an expensive and possibly one-sided agreement. The GOI's specific objections to the Technical Services Agreement (TSA) and Design Engineering Agreement (DEA) concerned (1) the fees to be paid by the lube company to Esso for its technology and efforts in completing the plant, (2) Esso's position that patents developed by lube plant employees be assigned to Esso, (3) Esso's reluctance to accept responsibility in the form of a performance and operational guarantee on the plant design, and (4) Esso's desire to arrange a long term Technical Information Service Agreement (TISA) with the lube company. These items had not previously been discussed in detail, and they were to prove difficult to resolve. (See Appendix C for final terms of the agreement.)

On December 9, 1963, the GOI raised a new major issue by advising ESE that they now felt that the plant should be designed to produce base stock for both high and medium viscosity index lube oils. This presented a major problem, since the design changes necessary to produce medium VI lubes would require additional capital and might reduce the net worth of the project. Of even greater significance to Esso was that this requirement would reduce the plant capacity for high VI lubes and thus frustrate Esso's attempt to become the sole indigenous source for high VI base stocks. Realization of this advantage had been one of the incentives for Esso's continuation of the project up to this point. The project was conceived at a particular time when market needs and government policies reflected certain characteristics. However, as negotiations continued, the concept of the project in the GOI's mind changed, which required subsequent changes by the ESE. Moreover, as the parties started to focus on the project, specific terms emerged that were either not recognized or only vaguely recognized during the initial stages of negotiation.

Although the disagreement over design and technical service agreements and the proposed change in project scope presented major obstacles, ESRC was convinced that it was in Esso's best interest to protect its market in India by concluding an agreement before its competitors were able to establish other lube projects. In the second week of December, ESRC offered Jersey Standard an assessment of the GOI's attitude towards the project. It strongly recommended that the company should proceed quickly with the revised project. The management in India was convinced that the key GOI officials responsible for this project were anxious to reach an agreement as soon as possible, and preferably with Esso instead of the other applicants. ESE informed Jersey Standard that Shell had presented a formal proposal for a competing project. This development required a quick decision by Esso, otherwise the negotiations would be interminable and the GOI would attempt to play off one applicant against the other.

The management in India was strongly in favor of the revised project required by the GOI on the grounds that in the long term it would be more advantageous, realistic and viable for Esso. Without a lube plant, Esso would be at the mercy of other suppliers; with one it would have a guaranteed source of base stocks. Esso management in India warned headquarters that the worst thing that could happen to the company in India would be if its decision not to modify its original proposal was interpreted by the GOI as a step by Esso to break off negotiations. Inherent in this warning was the potentially adverse reaction of the GOI on several important issues still outstanding between Esso and the GOI on crude oil imports, refining and marketing in India.

A central feature of ESRC's strategy was to reach agreement on the general terms as soon as possible, with the specific details of the project guided by the detailed study to be undertaken by Esso. The main reason for adopting this approach was to secure a commitment for the project from the GOI. If Esso insisted on detailed negotiations upon completion of the study, it would be exposed to danger in two ways: other bidders for the plant would then attempt an agreement in principle with the GOI; and the negotiations resulting from the detailed study would be longer and more frustrating.

Within 24 hours of receiving the communication from India, ESE headquarters in New York cabled its affirmation of the position of the management in India. It advised, however, that the management in India explore all aspects of the agreement with the government to avoid any misunderstanding. In addition, it specified that the GOI be informed that both ESE and Jersey Standard were doing everything possible to structure a proposal that would accommodate the wishes of the GOI.

For the next twelve months Esso and the government continued to negotiate in an attempt to reach an agreement. Their differences concerning plant product and the design, engineering and technical services agreements were eventually resolved. However, new issues arose as quickly as existing ones could be settled.

The main issues at this point were all of an economic nature, and concerned the following: (1) excise duties to be levied on the products of the lube plant, (2) exposure of the ESRC refinery to additional taxes on the feedstock it supplied to the plant, (3) income tax exemption for interest on foreign exchange loans for the plant, (4) tax liability on design and engineering fees and technical information fees and (5) magnitude of the design and engineering agreement (DEA) fee to be paid to Esso.

Of the above issues Esso was most concerned with the matter of excise tax. In Esso's view, the GOI had originally accepted a ceiling for excise duties applicable to the lube plant that would be equivalent to the import duties on base oils. It was now clear that the government had changed its position considerably. At this point Esso believed that the GOI's position not only jeopardized profits of the lube plant but also those of its existing refinery which would be supplying feedstock to the new plant.

On April 22, 1965, the GOI informed Esso that it would accept the reduced DEA fee of $1.6 million. However, a week later the GOI presented a list of fourteen modifications to Esso for consideration. This list included a clause that would change the equity ratio to 51:49 percent in favor of the GOI after ten years of operations. Another clause provided that all board deadlocks would be referred to the President of India for decision during the initial ten years.

The GOI's strategy at this point was to test the determination of Esso not to renegotiate the terms already agreed upon. From a negotiation standpoint, the worst outcome for the GOI would be to withdraw the new demands. At best, the GOI might find some potential gains in the terms and language of the agreement. In either case the GOI would have raised an issue that would come to Esso's attention even if it was not included in the agreement. Thus, as contract terms were to be renegotiated, the GOI could always point out that it had sought a particular term in the original negotiations.

The presentation of the fourteen new demands generated rapid activity within ESRC to determine from reliable sources if the government was serious about them or only engaging in a negotiation ploy. Informal and discreet explorations were conducted with people within and outside the departments concerned with the negotiation. Esso India's conclusion was that the GOI was engaged in a negotiation ploy. It also realized that consideration of any of these terms would reopen all other terms for renegotiation, which in turn would create innumerable delays in reaching the agreement. The management in India was also aware of the potential damage to its credibility with corporate levels in New York if its stand and approach did not lead to the desired objectives. For these and other reasons, Esso India recommended to corporate headquarters not to accept the fourteen modifications proposed by the GOI.

On May 4, information regarding the developments in India, along with Esso India's recommendations, were referred to Jersey Standard's executive committee for review. Some executives doubted that the GOI seriously meant to proceed with the project especially in light of the long and drawn-out negotiations. One view expressed was that the company should have withdrawn from the project long before. If it needed a reason, the fourteen demands of the GOI could be used to terminate negotiations followed by a withdrawal of the project.

However, a stronger view that prevailed was that the company should agree with the recommendations of the management in India. Withdrawal of the proposal at this phase of negotiations would create considerable ill will with the GOI. In particular, key officials who also had authority over Esso's crude oil importing, refining and marketing operations would be placed in a difficult and embarrassing situation. Of course this could adversely influence their outlook toward the larger operations of Esso in the country.

However, the executive committee cabled Esso India on May 4, 1965 that it concurred with Esso India's recommendation that it inform the GOI that the company would not accept the fourteen modifications. Esso India's stand was strongly supported by corporate management, a point that was conveyed to the GOI, thereby raising the credibility of the country-level management with the GOI. However, both parties desired to reach an agreement. The negotiations had continued for so long that failure of either side would expose it to criticism. The GOI in particular was conscious of this point. Also, by May 1965 it realized that the much publicized negotiations it held with the consortium of United States companies for one million annual tons of fertilizer capacity would end in failure. This further endorsed the need for a successful outcome to the negotiations. Both Esso and the GOI tried to arrive at terms of an agreement, but Esso refused to expose itself to the possibility of renegotiating the entire project if it accepted any of the fourteen demands of the GOI.

The GOI and Esso engaged in informal explorations with each other, each attempting to determine what would be accepted by the other party. This process further convinced Esso that the large majority of the fourteen demands of the GOI would be rescinded. On May 24, 1965 the GOI and Esso met formally. The GOI insisted on two key points: change of equity to 51:49 percent in favor of the GOI, and that the GOI be the arbitrator of deadlocks. Esso refused to accept these terms, informed New York of its stand, and was supported by headquarters. Both the country and corporate levels viewed these terms as break points for them.

On June 9, 1965, the GOI informed Esso that it was prepared to set aside its request for consideration of the fourteen points.

On September 15, 1965, the Lube Refinery Agreement was signed by the President of India and Esso Standard Eastern, Inc., thus concluding negotiations that had spanned nearly five years (see Appendix A). On April 4, 1966 a new company, Lube India Limited, was incorporated and in February 1970 the lube refinery was formally inaugurated.

Nearly five years of negotiation had finally resulted in an agreement. The key issues are summarized in Exhibit 3, which states Esso's position, the GOI's position, and the final outcome.

Appendix A presents the Lube Refinery agreement and Appendix B offers a detailed listing of allocation of functions between the managing director and the financial director.

Exhibit 3. Summary of Key Issues

Issue	Esso Position	GOI Position	Final Outcome
1. Ownership	Esso-GOI equal shareholders.	Initially sought 100 percent ownership. Then accepted equal basis. Later pushed for GOI majority position in 10 years.	Esso-GOI equal shareholders.
2. Management control	Esso appoints managing Director. M.D. has broad powers to operate plant. M.D. continued to operate during deadlock.	GOI appoints financial director as check on M.D. M.D. works through board. No M.D. authority for deadlock. GOI to resolve disputes. GOI has right to appoint M.D. after five years.	Managing director appointed by Esso, financial director by GOI. M.D. continues to operate during deadlock.
3. Product pricing	Parity with price for lubes imported from USA with transportation costs from Persian Gulf.	No parity formula. Board to decide product pricing. GOI right to control industry prices.	Initial pricing formula based on parity. Thereafter board can adjust price subject to GOI price controls.
4. Tax liability.	No greater tax liability than that on imported products. Written guarantee from GOI.	Initially willing to provide some written guarantee. Later opposed to guarantee. GOI as sovereign has right to tax.	General statement on parity with imports and other domestic products. GOI as sovereign has right to tax.

✳️ *Appendix A*

Lube Refinery Agreement

This Agreement is made on the Fifteenth day of September One Thousand nine hundred and sixtyfive between THE PRESIDENT OF INDIA (hereinafter called "Government," which expression shall unless excluded by or repugnant to the context be deemed to include his successors) of the First Part and ESSO STANDARD EASTERN, INC., a Corporation organized and existing under the laws of the State of Delaware, U.S.A. and having its registered office at 100 West 10th Street, City of Wilmington, County of New Castle, State of Delaware, and having its Principal office at 15 West 51st Street, New York 19, N.Y. (U.S.A.) (hereinafter called "ESE" which expression shall unless excluded by or repugnant to the context be deemed to include its successors and assigns) of the Second Part.

(WHEREAS the Government and ESE, formerly known as "Standard-Vacuum Oil Company," have been negotiating for the establishment of a Lubricating Oil Manufacturing Plant in India (hereinafter called "The Lube Refinery"), AND WHEREAS several letters have been exchanged and a number of Conferences have been held between representatives of the parties, AND WHEREAS the terms and conditions agreed between the parties for the establishment of the said plant have been embodied in this Agreement which supersedes the said letters and the decisions arrived at in the said Conferences.

NOW IT IS HEREBY AGREED BY AND BETWEEN the parties hereto as follows:

[1.In this Agreement the following expressions shall have the following meaning that is to say:]
(i) "Esso Standard Refining Company of India Ltd." ("here-

67

inafter called ESRC)—shall include its successors and assigns.

(ii) "The Indian Income Tax Act of 1961" includes any reenactment or modification thereof from time to time.

(iii) "Tonne"—means a Metric Tonne of 2204 lbs.

Name and Capital Structure

2. A company, hereinafter called "The Lube Company" shall be incorporated and registered in India, limited by shares under the Companies' Act of 1956 with the object of establishing the Lube Refinery. The Government will own 50% of the shares of the Lube Company and ESE will own the other 50%. The authorized capital of the Company shall be Rs. 3.5 crores divided into 35000 equity shares of rupees 1000 each. The initial subscribed capital shall be Rs. 2.86 crores and will be paid in equally by the Shareholders as required by the Company. Any further issue of Capital shall be issued to the Government and ESE in the same proportion and on an equal basis. The Memorandum and Articles of Association of the Company shall be approved by the Government and ESE.

Management of the Company

3. The Management of the Lube Company shall be vested in a Board of Directors, consisting of eight members. The Government and ESE agree to elect from time to time four Directors nominated by the Government and four Directors nominated by ESE so that at all times there will be an equal number of Directors nominated or selected by each party. All provisions for filling any vacancy on the Board of Directors or for the appointment of alternate Directors will be designed to preserve this equal representation.

The quorum for the meeting of the Board of Directors shall be one-third of its total strength (any fraction contained in that one-third being rounded off as one). No question arising at any meeting can be decided without an affirmative vote from at least one Director nominated by the Government and one Director nominated by ESE.

The Board of Directors shall elect one of its Members as Chairman. ESE will cooperate in causing a Director nominated by Government to be elected Chairman. In the absence of the said Chairman, ESE further agrees to cooperate to elect a Government nominee to act as Chairman during such absence. The Chairman will *not* have a casting vote.

4. The quorum for all General Meetings whether Annual or Extraordinary shall be Members present in person not being less than five in number, subject to their holding more than 50% of the shares. The voting power of both the parties shall

always remain equally divided. No Resolution may be passed, unless approved by the shareholders holding more than 50% of the subscribed share capital of the Lube Company.

Management

5. The Board of Directors shall elect one of its members as Managing Director. The Government agrees that it will cooperate in causing a Director nominated by ESE to be elected Managing Director. In the absence of the said Managing Director, Government further agrees to cooperate to elect an ESE nominee to act as Managing Director during such absence.

6. The Board of Directors shall elect one of its Members as Financial Director. ESE will cooperate in causing a Director nominated by Government to be elected Financial Director. In the absence of the said Financial Director, ESE further agrees to cooperate to elect a Government nominee to act as Financial Director during such absence.

Duties and Responsibilities of Managing Director and Financial Director

7. The powers, functions, responsibilities and duties of the Managing Director and Financial Director shall be as set forth in Schedule "A" attached hereto which shall form part of this Agreement. The Managing Director and Financial Director shall be responsible and accountable to the Board of Directors for the execution of their duties. Neither the Managing Director nor the Financial Director shall be eligible for the office of Chairman of the Board of Directors.

The foregoing provisions insofar as they relate to the appointment of the Managing Director and the Financial Director shall be subject to review by the Government and ESE at the end of five years from date of the respective appointment of the first Managing Director and first Financial Director.

Indian Personnel

8. To the extent that qualified individuals are available the Lube Company shall give preference to the employment of Indian Nationals, ESE shall provide or arrange local training facilities to the extent it can do so, and where local training facilities are inadequate ESE will train Indians abroad. Local training and training abroad both shall be carried out at the expense of and solely for and on behalf of the Lube Company.

In order to obtain the high quality of personnel required to operate the Lube Refinery in the most efficient manner possible, it is agreed that the Lube Refinery will be free to compensate its employees at a rate comparable to that paid by major industries in the area.

ESE & ESRC Personnel

9. To construct, start up and efficiently and effectively operate the Lube Refinery for about three years after startup, or such longer period as the Board of Directors may decide, it may be necessary and desirable to utilize the services of experienced

personnel of ESE such as Operating Superintendents, Shift Superintendents, Mechanical Superintendent, Startup Operators, Administrative Superintendent, Chief Engineer, Project Engineer. As and when such key personnel are required, they will be procured from ESE, ESRC and/or from and of ESE's associated and affiliated companies and ESE shall nominate and make available to the Lube Company qualified personnel on the following conditions:

(a) The Lube Company agrees to pay ESE the total emoluments and benefits of such personnel which they enjoy under the policies of ESE and, in case they are procured from ESRC and/or any of its affiliated and associated companies, according to the policies of ESRC or any such companies for the time being in force.

(b) ESE shall have the right to recall such personnel after giving three months prior notice to the Lube Company.

As and when such qualified personnel are required for the continued operation of the Lube Refinery and they are not available within India for permanent employment by the Lube Company they will in the first place be procured from ESE, ESRC and/or from any of ESE's associated and affiliated companies, and ESE shall nominate and make available to the Lube Company the personnel on the terms stated above.

Taxation 10. (a) The Government will use its good offices with the Maharashtra Government for according to the Company the same treatment in regard to exemption from sales tax on their intercompany transfers and/or sales between the Company and ESRC and/or ESE and/or other oil companies for so long as any of the oil companies enjoy exemption from sales tax on their inter-company sales or transfers of their products.

(b) Government will use its good offices to ensure that ESRC and Lube Company are not placed at a disadvantage —

(i) in the imposition or in the method of levy of customs duty on their products as compared to any like products imported from abroad; or

(ii) in the imposition or in the method of levy of Excise duty on products manufactured or processed by them as compared to any like products manufactured or processed in the country.

Distribution
of Profits

11. After making adequate provisions for Income Tax and re-serves as further stipulated in this Agreement the net profits of the Lube Company available for distribution as shown in its audited accounts will be distributed annually by way of dividend to its shareholders unless otherwise agreed by the Board of Directors.

Reserves

12. All reserves to be established by the Lube Company other than such as may be required by law, and except sums required to be retained in the Development Rebate Reserve shall be agreed upon by the Board of Directors from time to time.

Location of
Plant

13. The proposed Lube Refinery shall be located adjacent to ESRC at Mahul, Bombay 71.

Scope of
the Project

14. The Lube Refinery shall process reduced crude and will have such other associated facilities to manufacture initially about 145,000 tonnes per annum, or such other increased quanti-ties as may be agreed upon, of base oils from which can be blended high and medium viscosity index automotive and intermediate industrial oils depending on the design and total cost of the project. The design, capacity of the plant, its product yields and the cost of the project will be as mutually agreed between Government and ESE after receipt of a detailed project study which ESE has undertaken to prepare.

Project Study

15. ESE will forward to the Government a techno-economic study covering prospects and economic survey of the project, general processes, total estimated cost and general product pattern within one month from the date of this Agreement and shall also forward within six months from such date a detailed Project Study, including economic survey to indicate the prospects of the project, the design data, the associated and other facilities required, tender specifications, total estimated cost based on current price of equipment, materials and profitability of project and the expected return on the capital to be invested.

It is agreed that confidential information which may be furnished to the Lube Company by ESE or any of its subsidiaries or affiliates shall be kept entirely confidential, and the Government and ESE agree to cause the Lube Company to take all reasonable precautions to prevent the disclosure of such information except as required under the laws of the country.

Cost of

16. Subject to the detailed study as mentioned in para 15, and

the Plant
and
Finances

any variations of total cost as may be agreed upon by Government and ESE the estimated fixed capital cost of the project is Rs. 7.16 crores. The funds required to finance the construction, erection and start-up operations of the lube refinery shall be raised as under:

a. Subscribed and Paid-up Capital of the Lube Company shall be Rs. 2.86 crores divided into 28,600 shares of Rs. 1000 each to be subscribed by Government and ESE equally.

b. Loan Capital—Rs. 4.30 crores to be raised as long-term loans on terms acceptable to both the Government and ESE.

c. Working capital of approximately Rs. .076 crores to be secured from short-term rupee borrowing facilities in India which facilities will be utilised to the extent consistent with the net cash requirements of the Company.

The above estimate is based on an initial annual production capacity of 145,000 tonnes of base oils as mentioned in Clause 14 and on the details available at present. A more precise and accurate estimate in respect of cost and finance will be available when the detailed Project Study will be completed. In case this estimate is increased or decreased after mutual agreement, such changed cost shall be financed so far as practicable on the same basis and proportions as mentioned in sub-clauses a, b and c of Clause 16. Any loans to the Lube Company in accordance with b and c above, whether in rupees or foreign currency will be arranged without shareholder guarantees if possible. If shareholder guarantees are required by the creditors then unless otherwise agreed the loans shall be guaranteed severally by the Government and ESE each with respect to 50% of the liability under each loan requiring such a guarantee. Each party will itself arrange the foreign exchange to meet one half of the total guaranteed foreign liability in case the need for fulfilling such guarantee arises.

Foreign
Exchange

17. Out of the estimated fixed investment cost of Rs. 7.16 crores for the establishment of the Lube Refinery, about Rs. 4.30 crores will be required in foreign exchange. ESE will contribute their equity amounting to Rs. 1.43 crores, in foreign exchange and the balance of the foreign exchange requirement, estimated at about Rs. 2.87 crores, is to be raised in the form of foreign exchange loans. ESE will, at the earliest

practicable time after the incorporation of the Lube Company, use its good offices to bring about such foreign exchange loans on the best available commercial terms prevailing at that time. The terms of any such loan are to be mutually agreeable to the shareholders. The objective shall be to obtain loans for the Company at attractive interest rates and on a basis permitting drawdowns during the construction period as required. If required by foreign creditors, Government will guarantee that the Lube Company will be permitted to convert rupees to the required foreign currency for payment of interest and repayment of principal, as due. The extent of the foreign exchange loan requirements will be reassessed and may be slightly increased or decreased as necessary after contracts for construction and equipment are awarded. ESE will notify to Government as soon as the details are known the amount of changes, if any, in the foreign exchange loan required.

Supply of Reduced Crude

18. ESE shall have the right and the obligation to supply the Lube Company with the requisite quantities of reduced crude oil. ESE undertakes to supply such reduced crude oil from ESRC unless ESRC is prevented from supplying because of reasons of force majeure. Supplies of reduced crude shall be delivered by ESRC on behalf of ESE on consignment to the Lube Company for processing into lubricating base oils. If ESRC is unable for reasons of force majeure to provide the reduced crude oil ESE will as promptly as possible arrange for supplies from other sources.

The Lube Company shall retain only the lube base oils which include all operating losses, fuel required for the Lube Refinery's operation and if further required by the Lube Company such extract from the Treating Unit as is suitable for sale as carbon black feedstock. The remaining portion of the total hydrocarbons delivered to the Lube Refinery (i.e., the quantities of reduced crude delivered to the Lube Refinery less the quantities of lube base oils, fuel for operation of the Lube Refinery, extract retained as carbon black feedstock and manufacturing loss), will be returned to ESRC. The Lube Company shall not acquire ownership of any of the stocks not retained by it and such stocks shall remain the property of ESRC at all times.

To enable ESRC to maintain its production of fuel products Government agrees with ESE that ESRC shall be permitted to import from its normal sources and process additional crude equivalent to the quantity of lube base oils, fuel, carbon black feedstock and operational losses to be sold to the Lube Company by ESRC.

Price of
Reduced
Crude

19. The price of the lube distillates, reduced crude and/or any other residue retained, used or lost in operations by the Lube Company under Clause 18 above shall be equal to the Landed Cost of crude to ESRC, plus a handling charge of Rs. 1.5 per tonne of net feedstock billed to the Lube Refinery, plus excise duties if any levied on such net feedstock, plus an amortization of the additional facilities which ESRC will be required to install. Calculation of the amortization of the additional facilities is as described in Clause 20. The billing shall be on weight basis.

Calculation
of Amortiza-
tion Charges

20. The Lube Company will pay to ESE or at its request to ESRC Rs. 20 lakhs to be spent in installing certain additional facilities at the Combination Unit and Propane Separating Unit, including the pipeline from ESRC to the Lube Refinery fence, by straight-line amortization extending over a period of fifteen years, plus interest at the rate of 6 per centum. Such interest shall be paid yearly and calculated on the mean of the outstanding value at the beginning and the end of each year. This amortization amounts to approximately Rs. 1.0 per tonne of net feedstock as billed to the Lube Refinery.

Sale of
Lube Base
Oils

21. Government and ESE shall each have the right to 50% of each of the lube base oils and other products manufactured by the Lube Company. If one of the parties does not uplift its full share of each of the lube base oils and other products, the Lube Company will give the other party the first option to purchase the uplifted share of the first party.

Packing
and
Blending

22. Packing and Blending facilities shall not be provided by the Lube Refinery. If, in future, at any stage such facilities are required by the Lube Refinery each proposal shall be examined on its own merits by the Board of Lube Company. In case the Government desires that ESE arrange to blend/pack Government share of base oils produced by the Lube Refinery from its blending plants at Bombay and Calcutta it shall be separately and independently negotiated by the Government with ESE and shall be arranged on the terms and conditions mutually agreed between the parties.

Raw
Materials

23. The Lube Company shall maximize the use of indigenous materials and supplies, subject to their being available in sufficient quantities, of required quality and competitive in prices and delivery terms to those available from imported

sources. Any imported materials and supplies, as are required to be imported shall meet the specifications as set out in the project report and subject to the Import Control Policies of the Government of India from time to time.

ESRC
& ESE

24. ESE will supply and/or shall procure from ESRC and from any of its associated and affiliated companies, certain utilities, mechanical repairs and other services to the Lube Refinery on contract basis as mutually agreed. ESE or one of its subsidiary or affiliated companies will enter into separate agreements with the Lube Company to provide technical services to the Lube Company at a cost mutually satisfactory to both parties. Such technical services shall include assistance in respect to the Lube Refinery in resolving technical problems, attaining efficient operations and producing suitable products, including new techniques applicable to this plant.

Acquisi-
tion

25. Government shall use its good offices to assist the Lube Company to acquire land on a fair and reasonable basis, adjacent to ESRC at Mahul, Bombay.

Transfer
of Shares

26. ESE shall be entitled to transfer any or all of its equity shareholding to Standard Oil Company, N.J. or to a subsidiary of Standard Oil Company, N.J. which may succeed to a major portion of ESE's assets. Except as aforesaid, neither party shall transfer any or all of its shareholdings without prior consent of the other party unless it has first offered such shares to the other party. If the party does not wish to accept the offer, the shares may be sold to a third party purchaser provided that the sale is not made on terms more favorable to the purchaser or at a price lower than the price at which the shares were offered to the other party without first reoffering them to the other party on the same basis; and provided further the purchaser shall be bound by the provisions of this and all other applicable agreements.

Notices

27. All Notices required or permitted to be given under this Agreement shall be deemed to be given if in writing and sent to the other party on the following address by post under a certificate of posting or by Registered Post. Any change in address of either party shall be intimated to the other party immediately:

(1) Government - Secretary
                            Ministry of Petroleum and Chemicals
                            (Department of Petroleum)
                            Government of India
                            New Delhi

(2) ESE

Arbitra-
tion

28. Any dispute on difference between the Government on the one hand and ESE on the other, of any kind whatsoever at any time or times arising out of or in connection with or incidental to this Agreement (including any dispute or difference regarding the interpretation of this Agreement or any clause thereof) shall be referred to the arbitration of two arbitrators, one to be appointed by the Government and one by ESE (which arbitrators shall appoint an Umpire before taking upon themselves the burden of the reference under this Agreement) and such reference shall be deemed to be a submission to arbitration within the meaning of the Indian Arbitration Act 1940 or any statutory modification thereof. In the event of the arbitrators failing to agree upon the Umpire such Umpire to be appointed by the Chief Justice of India.

Assign-
ment

29. Except as provided in Clause 26, the rights, interests and obligations arising out of this Agreement shall not be assignable by either party in whole or in part without the previous approval in writing of the other party.

Force
Majeure

30. Neither party shall be liable for any delay or failure for the performance of any obligation under this Agreement due to force majeure which term shall mean and include Acts of God, Wars, Revolutions or other disorders, acts of enemies, embargoes, import and export restrictions, strikes, lockouts, fires, floods, order or decrees of any Government or Governmental authorities, perils of the sea, accidents of navigation, breakdown or injury to ships or by any other cause, whether or not of the same class or kind as those set forth, not within the control of the parties.

Either party affected by Force Majeure shall give notice in writing to the other party immediately.

Marginal
Headings

31. The marginal headings appearing herein are for purpose of reference only and shall have no effect on the meaning or substance of any clauses of this Agreement.

32. This Agreement will be subject to the laws in force in India for the time being.

33. The name of the Lube Company shall be Lube India, Ltd., and in case this name is not available, any suitable name agreed to by the parties.

Sign for and on behalf of   For ESSO STANDARD EASTERN, INC.
THE PRESIDENT OF INDIA

※ *Appendix B*

Schedule A

1. The Board of Directors will be authorized by the Articles of Association to delegate certain of its powers to the Managing Director, and pursuant to this authority and subject to its supervision and control and such directions as it may give from time to time shall delegate to the Managing Director the power to supervise and direct the construction and operation of the plant and facilities of the Company, to hire and discharge employees to obligate the Company for necessary or appropriate facilities, supplies and services, and to make appropriate arrangements for the disposition of the goods produced by the Company.

2. The Managing Director will keep the Financial Director fully advised as to all business affairs of the Company and will consult with him in all matters of financial policy and those matters requiring concurrence as described under the following specific powers.

3. The Financial Director will be responsible for advising the Managing Director and the Board of Directors on all matters where financial policies and considerations are involved.

4. The Financial Director may call for papers and reports from any of the Heads of Departments or officials of the Company relating to the exercise of his (the F.D.'s) duties and responsibilities.

5. Where there is any difference of opinion between the Managing Director and the Financial Director on any matter of financial policy or on any matter specifically requiring the Financial Director's concurrence, the matter will be referred to the Board of Directors.

6. Recognizing the value of continuous operation of the Lube Plant to both

parties to the Agreement, the parties agree to cause their nominee directors to pass, at the first meeting of the Board, a resolution providing the Managing Director with the necessary powers to complete the construction of the refinery or to continue to conduct the business and operate the Lube Plant in a safe and efficient manner during any period of deadlock which might occur in the Board of Directors. These powers shall include authority to carry on the routine operations of the refinery including acquisition of raw materials, making necessary repairs and replacements, maintenance of staff and payment of wages, and disposition of products, but will not include powers to change the scope of the plant or to alter the nature of the business or to take any steps that will prejudice either party in the resolution of the deadlock. During any such period, the Managing Director will keep the Board of Directors fully informed of his actions.

Delegation of Specific Powers

7. Subject to the general provisions above the following powers as given to the Annexure are delegated to the Managing Director and the Financial Director. All instances not covered by these delegated powers would be a matter for decision by the Board.

8. While the Managing Director and the Financial Director would be held responsible for the exercise of these delegated powers, they may in consultation further delete the exercise of specified authority within the ambit of these delegated powers to the Managerial staff. All cases of such sub-delegation should be approved by the Board.

Schedule of Powers of Managing Director & Financial Director

Schedule of Powers of Managing Director & Financial Director
(R.B.—Report to be made to the Board of Directors)

Nature of Powers	Managing Director	Financial Director
A. *Establishment*		
1. Creation of posts on approved scales of pay	Full powers except for posts carrying a starting salary of Rs 1,600 and above (R.B.)	Concurrence for posts carrying a starting salary of Rs 1000 and above.
2. Appointments and fixation of initial pay	Full powers except for posts carrying a starting salary of Rs 1,600 and above (R.B.)	Concurrence when higher initial pay is proposed.
3. Grant of:		
(a) Leave in accordance with rules	Full powers	—
(b) Special Disability Leave	Full powers	—
4. Declaring an officer as controlling officer for purpose of personnel control	Full powers (R.B.)	Concurrence
5. All matters relating to grant of travelling allowance according to rules	Full powers	—
6. Travel by air	Full powers	—
7. Transfer of officer and staff	Full powers	Concurrence where officers of Finance & Accounts Dept.
8. To permit handing over charge away from headquarters	Full powers	—
9. Temporary and officiating appointment of a Company servant to more than one post and fixation of pay and allowances.	Full powers (R.B.)	Concurrence

No.	Item	Powers	Remarks
10.	To make officiating arrangements.	Full powers subject to a maximum period of 6 months where Senior Executive posts are concerned (R.B.)	—
11.	To restrict the pay of an officiating employee.	Full powers (R.B.)	Concurrence
12.	Fixation of pay on promotion	Full powers	Concurrence when there is a departure from the normal rule.
13.	Grant of increments	Full powers	—
14.	Extension of joining time	Full powers	—
15.	Advance of Pay and T.A.	—do—	—
16.	Advance of purchase of conveyance	—do—	—
17.	Sanction of Permanent Advance Imprest.	—do—	Concurrence
18.	Grant to or acceptance by Company employee of: (a) honoraria or fees (b) rewards	Full powers up to Rs 1,000	—
19.	Retention of Company servant after 55, up to 60 years of age one year at a time subject to Certificate of Fitness.	Full powers except for posts in Senior Executive Grade (R.B.)	Concurrence
20.	To prescribe the form of surety Bonds to be executed by staff handling cash and stores, etc.	Full powers	Concurrence
21.	To fix installments for recovery of over payment of pay & allowances	—do—	—do—
22.	Investigation of arrear claims	—do—	—do—
23.	Acceptance of resignation	Full powers except for posts starting salary of Rs 1,600 and above (R.B.)	—

Schedule of Powers of Managing Director & Financial Director (cont.)

Nature of Powers	Managing Director	Financial Director
24. Termination of services	Full powers except for posts on starting salary of Rs 1,600 and above (R.B.)	—
25. Ex-gratia payments in case of injury sustained while on duty	Up to Rs 1,000 in each case	Concurrence
Note: Powers enumerated at items 3, 8, 14, 18, 21, 22, and 25 above shall not be exercised by the Managing Director in his own case.		
B. Works		
26. Approval to works detailed estimates of which have been cautioned by the Board	Full powers	—
27. Excess over such approval	Full powers up to 5% over original figure subject to total not exceeding Rs 20 lakhs (R.B.)	Concurrence for expenditures in excess of 5% of original figure and Rs 2 lakhs in value
28. Approval to works which have been approved in principle by the Board and for which detailed estimates are also now presented.	Up to Rs 5 lakhs (R.B.)	Concurrence
29. Excess over approval in item 28 above	Up to 10% over original figure	Concurrence
30. (a) Acceptance of tenders for approved works when more than one valid tender is received and the lowest tender is to be accepted.	Full powers up to Rs 20 lakhs (R.B.)	
(b) When only a single tender is received (to be treated as negotiated tender)	Full powers up to Rs 10 lakhs (R.B.)	Concurrence

31. Invitation to an acceptance of limited tenders for reasons to be recorded in writing.	Up to Rs 10 lakhs (R.B.)	Concurrence
Note: R, 30 & 31 all tenders would be limited to invitation to a selected list of contracting firms. This list would require concurrence of Financial Director. The list of contracting firms will be reviewed periodically and approved by the Board. (*At least 3 firms from the approved list would be given the opportunity to tender for each minor works costing in excess of Rs 10,000.*)		
32. Acceptance of contracts without calling for tenders in emergency cases for reasons to be recorded in writing.	Full powers up to Rs 2 lakhs (R.B.)	Concurrence
33. Acceptance of contracts where the lowest tender is not being accepted for reasons to be recorded in writing.	Full powers up to Rs 2 lakhs (R.B.)	Concurrence
34. To sanction commencement of work on an urgency certificate after administrative approval but before technical sanction to the estimate.	Up to Rs 5 lakhs (R.B.)	Concurrence
35. Maintenance and repairs to roads and buildings, plant, machinery and vehicles.	Full powers	Concurrence for any item exceeding Rs 2 lakhs.
36. To fix rents for quarters, shops, land and business premises.	Full powers	Concurrence
37. (a) to fix rates for the hire of machinery	Full powers	Concurrence
(b) to fix rates for the hire of tools, equipment & furniture	Full powers	Concurrence
38. To sanction extra/supplementary items and/or minor deviations in contracts for works.	Up to a 10% excess over original value subject to above delegations and to total not exceeding Rs 20 takhs. (R.B.)	Concurrence

Schedule of Powers of Managing Director & Financial Director (cont.)

Nature of Powers	Managing Director	Financial Director
39. To award contracts for loading, unloading, handling, transport, etc.	Full powers for contracts not exceeding 24 months. (R.B.)	Concurrence if over Rs 50,000.

The original contract for the construction of the lube plant and any subsequent contract relating to an expansion or modernization of the plant would be let either on turn-key basis, or on the basis of specific job projects as may be decided by the Board of Directors. If the contract is given on a turn-key basis the company would be chosen from a selected list of international construction companies who would be given due opportunity to submit bids. The Managing Director will evaluate the bids and recommend to the Board of Directors a contractor taking into consideration such factors as cost, adequacy of engineering, completeness of design and general approach to project. The construction company would be expected to use local facilities, materials and talents to the maximum possible extent consistent with the time schedule, quality and cost of the project.

C. *Purchase:* (For schemes & works already approved by the Board)

All tenders would be limited to invitations to a selected list of suppliers. The list of suppliers would require concurrence of Financial Director. (*At least 3 firms from the list would be given opportunity to tender for each order totalling over Rs 1,000.*)

Nature of Powers	Managing Director	Financial Director
40. (a) Acceptance of tenders when open tenders are invited, more than one valid tender is received & where lowest tender is accepted.	Up to Rs 20 lakhs (R.B.)	Concurrence above Rs 2 lakhs
(b) Purchase acceptance of tenders without calling for tenders at controlled rates or specified (*ceiling*) rates prescribed by the Board.	Up to Rs 20 lakhs (R.B.)	–do–
41. Acceptance when only a single tender is received after calling for open tenders.	Up to Rs 10 lakhs (R.B.)	Concurrence
42. Acceptance of limited tenders	Up to Rs 10 lakhs	–do–
43. Acceptance by negotiation after invitation to tender for reasons to be recorded in writing.	Up to Rs 10 lakhs (R.B.)	–do–

44. Acceptance of any tender other than the lowest tender, reasons to be recorded in writing.	Up to Rs 2 lakhs (R.B.)	—do—
45. Supplementary agreements on purchases	Up to excess of 10% on original value subject to powers delegated above and the total not exceeding Rs 20 lakhs (R.B.)	Concurrence
46. Purchase without calling for tender in a case of emergency for reasons to be recorded in writing.	Up to Rs 2 lakhs (R.B.)	
47. To waive liquidated damages in cases of late deliveries:		
(a) Where no loss is incurred.	Full powers	Concurrence
(b) Where an actual loss is incurred.	Up to Rs 20,000 (R.B.)	Concurrence
D. Contingencies & Miscellaneous		
48. To sanction contingent expenditure	Full powers	
49. To sanction expenditure on ceremonial occasions	Up to Rs 10,000 in each case subject to a maximum of Rs 20,000 a year (R.B.)	Concurrence
50. To sanction purchase of stationery and stores including office equipment (other than for works).	Full powers	—
51. To sanction residential telephones	Full powers	—
52. To sanction advertisement charges	Full powers	Concurrence for items over Rs 5,000
53. To sanction legal charges	Full powers	Concurrence for over Rs 5,000
54. To sanction Reserve limit for stores and spares	Up to Rs 20 lakhs (R.B.)	Concurrence
55. Execution of instruments, deeds, leases, contracts, etc.	Full powers except where common seal of the Company required under the Companies Act.	—

Schedule of Powers of Managing Director & Financial Director (cont.)

Nature of Powers	Managing Director	Financial Director
56. To sanction write-off of losses: (a) Not due to theft, fraud or negligence	Up to Rs 20,000 in each case (R.B.)	Concurrence
(b) Due to theft or negligence	Up to Rs 5,000 in each case (R.B.)	Concurrence
(c) Of amounts due to the Company such as rent, hospital dues becoming irrecoverable.	Up to Rs 10,000 in each case (R.B.)	Concurrence
57. To sanction claims for demurrage wharfage.	Full powers	Concurrence over Rs 5,000
58. To sanction expenditure for transport of materials by other than the cheapest mode in emergencies (reasons to be recorded in writing)	Full powers (R.B.)	
59. To incur expenditure on immediate safety of employees, plant, machinery, etc. within works premises and township.	Full powers (R.B.)	
60. To sanction re-appropriations between the detailed heads of expenditure in the sanctioned budget.	Full powers (R.B.)	Concurrence
61. To institute, defend, compound or abandon legal proceedings, or refer claims to arbitration and execute powers of attorney, and sign plaints, written statement and all other.	Full powers except for instituting, compounding or abandoning legal proceedings and referring claims for arbitration.	
61. Documents and papers in connection with cases in Law Courts, etc. on behalf of the Company.		

E. *Sales*

62.	Full powers for all sales of oil and gas in accordance with the prices and principles approved by the Board.	Full powers	Concurrence
63.	Sales of stores to contractors at book rate plus 10% or market rate whichever is higher.	Full powers	Concurrence for any item exceeding Rs 2 lakhs.
64.	(a) To declare stores as surplus/ unserviceable, to fix their selling price and to prescribe the mode of their disposal.	Up to Rs 5 lakhs per annum	Concurrence
	(b) Writing down the value of surplus obsolete stores on the books.	Up to Rs 5 lakhs per annum	Concurrence

Bechtel Corporation

UNSUCCESSFUL NEGOTIATION FOR A MASSIVE FERTILIZER PROGRAM IN INDIA

In November 1963, the Bechtel Corporation explored with the Government of India (GOI) the possibility of a program designed to establish a massive fertilizer manufacturing capacity in India. The idea was extensively studied by a consortium of large United States oil, chemical and engineering companies, and a feasibility report was submitted to the Government of India in January 1965. The consortium and the GOI negotiated various terms of a proposal for a massive fertilizer program (mfp) until May 1965, when the consortium formally withdrew its proposal because of irreconcilable differences with the GOI. This case is a study of the negotiations for the massive fertilizer program.

BACKGROUND

A very large percentage of India's population is dependent on agriculture. India's agricultural output has been handicapped by such considerations as uneconomic size of land holdings, antiquated farming techniques, very limited use of fertilizers, inadequate transportation and storage facilities, *ad hoc* nature of official policies toward development of agriculture, and the political sensitivity of issues concerning agriculture.

In the early 1960s certain quarters in the United States government (USG)

For a detailed study see A. Kapoor *International Business Negotiations: A Study in India.* New York: New York University Press, 1970; Princeton, N.J.: The Darwin Press, 1973.

were beginning to be concerned with the limited attention being paid by the Government of India (GOI) to long-term development of agriculture. The Ford Foundation in 1959 analyzed many of the problems facing India in improving agriculture performance. Feeling that adequate growth of agriculture was a major requirement for Indian development, the United States Government initiated a dialogue with the appropriate circles in India to encourage an effective long-range program of agriculture development.

An adequate supply of fertilizers was an essential feature of raising agriculture output. Indigenous manufacturing capacity in fertilizers—existing and proposed—is indicated in Appendix A. The consumption targets by the end of the First Five-Year Plan were 176,000 tons of nitrogenous (N), 68,000 tons of P_2O_5. The actual consumption during this period reached 122,000 tons of N and 14,000 tons of P_2O_5. The consumption targets for the Second Plan were as follows: 370,000 tons of N; 120,000 tons of P_2O_5; 30,000 tons of K_2O. The actual consumption was 210,000 tons of N; 70,000 tons of P_2O_5; 26,000 tons of K_2O. The Third Plan targets were as follows: 1,000,000 tons of N; 400,000 tons of P_2O_5; and 200,000 tons of K_2O. A mid-term appraisal of the Plan revised the targets to 800,000 tons of N; 250,000 tons of P_2O_5; and 150,000 tons of K_2O. Exhibit 1 provides additional details about the comparative availability of fertilizers as against the targets for some years of the Third Plan.

There were many reasons for the limited development of fertilizer production. The private sector—domestic and foreign—was not eager to invest in

Exhibit 1.   Comparative Availability of Fertilizers as Against Targets

(Figures in Million Tons)

Year	Target	Indigenous Production	Import	Total Availability	Despatches from Pool Factories
		Nitrogen (Central Fertilizer Pool Supplies)			
1961-62	0.400	0.167	0.138	0.285	0.281
1962-63	0.525	0.184	0.285	0.429	0.350
1963-64	0.650	0.222	0.223	0.465	0.456
		P_2O_5			
1961-62	0.100	0.064	–	–	0.060
1962-63	0.150	0.079	0.010	0.089	0.083
1963-64	0.225	0.104	0.011	0.115	0.116

	K_2O		
	Target	*Import*	*Despatches*
1961-62	0.082	0.028	0.028
1962-63	0.100	0.047	0.036
1963-64	0.130	0.062	0.057

fertilizer manufacturing facilities because of more profitable opportunities in other industries. Also, the state played a major role in the industry. The "fertilizer pool" arrangement placed distribution of almost all fertilizers in the hands of the GOI. Again, the GOI determined the price at which it would purchase fertilizers from the private sector units. The GOI also determined the price charged to the consumer.

Major technological developments had taken place in fertilizers. Large projects up to 200,000 tons annual capacity were being advocated. Neither the public nor the private sector in India possessed the necessary technology to undertake such projects without foreign assistance.

Certain ministries of the GOI were becoming concerned about the limited fertilizer resources of the country in the light of its ever-increasing food needs. They were gradually recognizing the very important role of fertilizers in any program of increased food production. While some political and administrative groups of the GOI felt that the public sector possessed the necessary know-how (or would be able to acquire it within a short space of time), some others recognized that development of indigenous technology was quite some time away, while the problem of adequate food supplies was immediate.

Officials of the US Agency for International Development (AID) in India were credited with the view that greater consumption of fertilizers was the only quick way to step up food production. AID estimated that four million tons of fertilizers would be needed to meet the Fourth Plan food requirements target of 120 million tons. Appendix B provides estimates of fertilizer consumption during the Fourth Plan.

Thirty percent or more of the investment for a modern fertilizer plant would consist of foreign exchange. India, however, was critically short of foreign exchange. Government-to-government aid was not expected to increase materially. Also, the GOI could not turn to the Soviet Bloc for assistance because it did not possess the necessary technology in fertilizers.

Petroleum refining capacity in the country had increased, leading to a surplus of naphtha. Exports were not feasible because of the worldwide glut in the product. The GOI wished to determine the best way to utilize the excess naphtha. Fertilizer manufacturing was one useful method.

A few influential members of the GOI were concerned about the country's unfavorable image overseas as a place for foreign private investment. The USG was encouraging the GOI to provide foreign private enterprise with the opportunity to assist India in its development efforts. The GOI had sought USG assistance for the Bokaro steel project. In September 1963, the assistance had been denied because the project was to be located in the public sector. The Russians had then offered to assist the GOI in the Bokaro project. Some quarters of the GOI felt that General Lucius Clay's testimony to Congress on the Foreign Aid Bill in which the Bokaro project was proposed had had an adverse effect on India's image in the eyes of the United States Government.

The US Ambassador to India at the time was Dr. Galbraith, who described the report of the Clay Commission as the "observations of a distinguished group of private citizens whose suggestions on public and private sector investment naturally reflect their personal views."

In private, Galbraith was strongly critical of Clay.

(General Clay) has decided that there must be no assistance to Bokaro as long as it is in the public sector. In other words, for blatant ideological reasons, he is going back to the policies of the Eisenhower Administration. These were a grievous failure. Nothing substantial was done to advance private investment; and they talked about it enough to cause everyone to suppose our concern was to sustain capitalism rather than help Indians. I have shifted to a purely pragmatic policy of doing whatever works.

The Business Council for International Understanding (BCIU), with the cooperation of the United States Department of State organized a delegation of leading United States business executives to hold off-the-record discussions with GOI officials in New Delhi. The delegation visited India in April 1964, and both the foreign companies and the GOI felt that the discussions were "frank and constructive" and that "much misunderstanding had been removed." Oil, chemical and other industries were represented in the delegation. The Bechtel Corporation was also a member. In the course of discussions with the top levels of Indian officialdom, the US companies secured the distinct impression that the GOI would encourage foreign private investment in fertilizer and also in other industries in accordance with overall Plan targets. Certain quarters of the USG along with some US corporations were interested in continuing and furthering the favorable dialogue established with the GOI during the April visit. Some individuals in the GOI reciprocated that feeling.

By 1963 and to an ever-increasing degree thereafter, some fundamental policy issues were being debated within the GOI. Is it desirable to have large concentrations of economic power? Since the private sector had not fulfilled its role in developing the fertilizer industry, should it be allowed to participate in the fertilizer industry? Perhaps the public sector should be solely or largely responsible for the development of this industry since it is of vital interest to the country? Should the public sector collaborate with the private sector; and if so, what should be the policies for such collaborations? What should be the policies when foreign private companies collaborate with the GOI? In what ways should they be different from foreign private collaborations with the domestic private sector? Does the existing system of marketing provide for adequate movement of the quantities of fertilizers which the country is likely to need? Does the existing pricing structure provide the necessary incentive for foreign and domestic private investment? Such fundamental questions were being debated within the GOI. Opinions of the officials varied according to their political and economic ideologies. Agricultural policy (of which fertilizers are a major component) affects all levels of Indian society. The consequences—political, economic, social—had to be carefully weighed by members of the GOI in arriving at policies.

The Ministries of Finance, Petroleum and Chemicals (P&C), and Food and Agriculture (F&A) were the ones mainly concerned with foreign exchange, fertilizers, and food production. The Ministry of Finance (often regarded as the most powerful Ministry) played a major role in the disbursement of foreign exchange. It was hard pressed from various quarters to meet their respective needs for foreign exchange. The Ministry of P&C was responsible among other areas for increasing indigenous manufacturing capacity of fertilizers. The Ministry of F&A was responsible among other areas for distributing fertilizers and developing a general program for better fertilizer use. Each ministry had its particular set of priorities; and while they all sought the development of the country, their respective requirements did conflict at times.

CHRONOLOGY OF NEGOTIATIONS

The Bechtel Corporation was engaged in business in India. It was in partnership with the GOI on a 50:50 ownership basis in a company known as Engineers India Ltd. and was familiar with the developments in food and fertilizer policies taking place within the GOI. The company had developed a favorable image in India, and GOI officials thought highly of the company and its intentions. The Bechtel representative, R.M. Dorman, had explored the general subject of food and fertilizer needs in India with various knowledgeable groups including AID and the Ford Foundation. The prevailing feeling was that food production must be increased and that this could be achieved only through much greater use of fertilizers. The BCIU-sponsored meetings with top GOI officials further clarified the importance attached to this field by the GOI.

April-June 1964

Dorman explored the interest of his corporation in undertaking a major program for fertilizer manufacturing in India. S.D. Bechtel, Chairman of Bechtel Corporation, expressed keen interest in the concept. He felt that India should establish a series of fertilizer plants using standardized design and technology in order to achieve fertilizer production within as short a period of time as possible. He noted that India was faced with an emergency situation regarding foodgrain production. During the Second World War, Bechtel Corporation had built ships on a standardized design basis, and the same approach could be adopted for fertilizer plants. S.D. Bechtel also felt strongly about the humanitarian considerations and was willing to expend considerable time and effort to develop the concept of a massive fertilizer manufacturing program for India. He also realized the vast scope for profitable business undertakings in India. With this support from his Chairman, Dorman proceeded to explore in somewhat greater detail the attitudes of USG and GOI officials in India. Bechtel Corporation had informed the US Ambassador to India (Chester Bowles) of its initial ideas for massive fertilizer program (mfp) and Bowles was enthusiastic about it. He felt that an mfp in India undertaken by US companies would create a positive image of the US in India especially after the negative consequences on Indo-US relations as a result of Bokaro.

Dorman also had detailed discussions with J. Lannigan, Commercial Counselor of the US Embassy in Delhi. Lannigan had promised himself that during his assignment in India he would attempt to attract $1 billion of additional US investments into India. The Bechtel proposal for an mfp would contribute significantly in the realization of Lannigan's objective. Lannigan served as a source of information for Dorman in terms of thinking within the embassy, status of proposals by other US companies and for explorations with selected GOI officials.

At this stage, explorations with the Indian Government were largely conducted by senior officials of the US Embassy. Ambassador Bowles met with Kabir, Minister of Petroleum and Chemicals, to gain his reactions to the idea of an mfp. Kabir was not against the idea but raised several questions regarding financing, marketing, plant location and investment terms likely to be sought by US companies. He also noted that such a project would require major policy decisions from the GOI which would evolve only over a considerable period of time.

US Embassy officials felt that the Ministry of Finance (MF) would be more receptive to the massive fertilizer program than Petroleum and Chemicals (P&C) because Finance possessed more dynamic individuals and also because it was a more powerful ministry. Therefore, embassy officials interacted with the senior secretariat level of Finance. The officials strongly encouraged the embassy to ask Bechtel to develop a proposal which could be reviewed by the GOI and encouraged Bechtel to interact directly with Finance as they did not consider the senior levels of P&C to be "sufficiently imaginative" and decisive.

The US Embassy relayed this information to Dorman and urged him to proceed with due speed and promised all possible assistance. Dorman recognized the conflict which existed between the Finance and P&C ministries. Given the sensitive nature of the fertilizer industry, the wide range of unresolved policy issues which would be raised by the mfp proposal and the involvement of the US Embassy, Dorman was fully aware of having to proceed delicately in dealing with the two ministries. Dorman also realized that if the mfp idea was to generate and retain a desirable momentum, specific information would have to be provided to the GOI within a matter of months. Otherwise, both the GOI and his own principals would lose interest in it.

July-August 1964
On July 31, 1964, AID officials in India informally indicated to the GOI that

massive American assistance would be forthcoming for India's fertilizer needs during the Fourth Plan. However, AID felt that fertilizer targets should be pitched much higher than current Planning Commission estimates. It proposed that nitrogenous fertilizer targets should be pegged at 3 million tons against the 2.2 million tons envisaged by the Commission. AID also expressed reservations about the big role assigned to the public sector in the Fourth Plan. AID made it clear that the United States could not offer assistance in coal-based fertilizer technology since it had not been developed in the United States. Some GOI officials viewed these "recommendations" as a means of encouraging India to accept the mfp being developed by Bechtel.

In early August, Kabir left on a four-week tour of European countries to explore possibilities of foreign participation in India's fertilizer industry. On his return to India in late August, Kabir stated that India's Third Plan target for fertilizer production—80,000 tons by 1966—would be only half fulfilled. Also, the most valuable foreign assistance offered so far had been from the Bechtel mfp for one million tons of fertilizer by 1971.

By this time, the GOI had a few proposals from foreign companies for fertilizer manufacturing, but none of these proposals had progressed very far. Additionally, after the general concept of the mfp became public knowledge, all foreign companies decided to withhold significant development of their proposals until the outcome of the mfp was known. If the mfp materialized, it was unlikely that their individual plant proposals would be of significant interest to the GOI. Conversely, if the mfp did not materialize, the GOI would be particularly keen to proceed with a final determination of the existing proposals.

Indian farmers were beginning to show an interest in fertilizers. Also, certain quarters of the GOI were convinced about the price elasticity of demand, i.e., the lower the price, the greater is the amount of fertilizer used by the farmer. Therefore, the GOI was anxious to reduce the price of fertilizer to farmers. With larger production units located near coastal areas and refineries, the GOI felt that the cost of production could be reduced. The aim would be to bring down the prices of fertilizers to the level of current import prices and then reduce them even further.

Dorman met O.V. Alagesan, Deputy Minister of P&C, and formally conveyed the desire of a United States consortium led by Bechtel Corporation to participate in the development of the Indian fertilizer industry. He also discussed the question with Nakul Sen, Secretary to the Ministry of P&C, and with various other senior officials in the same and other ministries. The GOI learned that the consortium would consist of the Bechtel Corporation (an engineering company), a petroleum company, two chemical engineering companies, and companies specializing in hydrocarbons and coking coke processes. It was anticipated that as the project developed, West German, Italian and Japanese companies would also participate in the program in one capacity or another.

By this stage, the major decision had already been made by the GOI to proceed with the first stage of the mfp idea, namely, the development of a feasibility study. Dorman, however, was meeting with various GOI officials in order to keep them informed of what was happening and also to give them a certain degree of importance as their inputs would have a bearing on the eventual decision of the GOI.

The feasibility study was to be undertaken by Bechtel Corporation with appropriate involvement of officials of the GOI. The GOI agreed to this approach because then the results of the study would be more acceptable to the foreign companies than under an arrangement where the study was done by the GOI alone. The GOI agreed to pay up to $400,000 in Indian currency. It could have approached AID for counterpart funds to pay for the GOI's part of the cost of the study, but the government elected not to do so because of the larger strategy of the Ministry of Finance in promoting the mfp.

There were several components of Finance's larger strategy. First, it wanted to demonstrate to Bechtel and the consortium that the GOI was serious about the mfp and the rupee contribution offered additional evidence of its seriousness. Second, Finance wanted to convey to the USG that India was not discouraging US companies from participating in the development of the Indian fertilizer industry, and the prompt action on the mfp idea was a demonstration of its intent in this respect. Third, by taking the initiative in approving the feasibility study, Finance clearly established its leadership role within the GOI as far as the mfp was concerned. Fourth, the high publicity and the results of the feasibility study would offer additional means of convincing certain elements of the GOI that immediate attention must be paid to the development of the agriculture sector on a realistic and consistent basis. In brief, Finance was hoping to achieve several objectives through approval of the feasibility study.

S.D. Bechtel had taken personal control of the development of the project. While Dorman was conducting initial explorations in India and after he relayed a positive reaction from the US Embassy and the Ministry of Finance, S.D. Bechtel took steps to inform selected US companies of the overall mfp concept and seek their involvement. He contacted executives at the most senior levels of management, individuals whom S.D. Bechtel knew personally through many years of joint business and personal relationship. Some of the companies contacted who expressed interest were Texaco, Gulf, Hercules, Esso, Mobil, Shell and General Lucius Clay of Lehman Brothers. However, in September 1964 the consortium consisted of one committed member, Bechtel Corporation, while the other companies had merely offered an initial expression of interest.

US companies were interested in the mfp for two reasons. First, several chief executives were personal friends of S.D. Bechtel and did not wish to decline his invitation to participate, especially at a stage when they were not being asked to offer a commitment. Second, the companies reasoned that by being associated with the mfp they could gain access to information which would be useful to them in developing their own projects at a later stage if the mfp project did not materialize.

However, the companies expressing an interest also imposed two conditions which had to be honored by Bechtel. First, their names would not be disclosed to the Indian Government. The companies feared that such disclosure might harm their existing operations or ongoing negotiations in India or it might result in the Indian Government assuming that the companies were in fact committed to the project whereas in reality the companies were only offering an expression of interest. Second, the companies stressed that the decision to participate in the feasibility study did not imply in any way that they were committed to the project. They would make a final decision depending upon the outcome of the study and their independent assessment of the investment climate in India.

Several of the companies participating in the feasibility study (Esso, Shell) were highly experienced with the Indian business scene and maintained extensive operations in the country. Bechtel, in contrast, possessed comparatively limited experience in the country. Therefore, the experienced oil companies would not depend only upon the interpretations of Bechtel but would place far more weight on the views of their own management in reaching a decision.

September 1964

S.D. Bechtel and General Clay were proceeding to Tokyo for meetings. The US Embassy and Dorman had urged that they visit India for face-to-face meetings with key GOI officials. However, Clay was hesitant to become associated with the project because of a negative reaction from GOI officials as a result of his stand on the Bokaro project. S.D. Bechtel convinced him to accompany him to India. However, it was understood between Bechtel and Clay that Clay's presence would not mean that Lehman Brothers was involved and that Clay would make a final decision on his role in the mfp depending upon the outcome of their discussions in India. However, the private understanding was not revealed, and Clay was to discover upon reaching India that in the mind of the Indians he was involved with the project. Thereafter, it became extremely difficult for him to withdraw from the mfp.

General Lucius Clay and S.D. Bechtel arrived in Delhi on September 13, 1964 as representatives of the United States consortium. They held a series of talks with Union Ministers and officials including the Ministers of P&C (Kabir), Food and Agriculture (Subramanyam), External Affairs (Swaran Singh) and Finance (Krishnamachari). Clay and Bechtel expressed confidence that the entire project could be worked out to the mutual benefit of the GOI and the United States consortium.

Clay and Bechtel were in India for about five days. The discussions with the GOI covered two areas: first, the feasibility study would ascertain the over-all fertilizer requirements of the country along with a breakdown of regional needs. This would provide the basis for determining the size and ideal location of each plant; second, the study would evaluate the current fertilizer pricing, marketing and distribution patterns in the countryside with the objective of suggesting improvements. The feasibility report would recommend courses of action and ways to implement them. If the GOI accepted the recommendations, the first of the proposed five plants would be in production within 30 months. Clay and Bechtel made it clear that the consortium would not offer its final terms until completion of the feasibility study. The GOI on its side stated that it would await the recommendations of the feasibility study before making a statement of its terms for foreign investment.

In a press conference on September 17, 1964 Clay stated that he and Bechtel were returning to the United States that night to discuss the various aspects of the proposed collaborations with other United States investors on whose behalf he and Bechtel had come to India. Clay and Bechtel had discussed certain issues of foreign investment with the GOI—issues which in their opinion would be of particular and immediate importance. Thus, Clay is reported to have stated that the project would be a 50:50 collaboration with the GOI and that the consortium would seek an abolition of the existing pool price system in favor of a competitive selling arrangement. The consortium would seek a reasonable rate of return. Through modern machines and technology and economies of scale, Clay felt that prices would be reduced. The question of supply rights for crude oil, naphtha and other raw materials associated with fertilizer manufacture was not discussed.

The GOI got the impression from Clay's participation that the United States financial community would be involved with the project. The question of foreign exchange financing was discussed to a limited extent.

The GOI suggested five sites for study: Madras, Cochin, Haldia, Barauni and Durgapur. The consortium, however, could suggest alternative sites if it did not consider any of these sites favorable. There was not a firm agreement between the GOI and the consortium representatives that the GOI would be bound to offer these sites or that the consortium was bound to accept them. During this visit, Clay and Bechtel were highly pleased with the enthusiastic response they received from the GOI officials. Issues of investment, which they considered to be important, were discussed. They were neither seeking nor offering a statement of terms of investment. Both the consortium representatives and GOI officials felt that it would be premature at this stage to get into the details; this would be done only after the feasibility study was received by the GOI.

The public statements by Clay and Bechtel had an adverse effect on the development of the mfp. A senior AID official commented:

> Clay's stand was that if he and Bechtel could raise the money for the mfp, the least the GOI could do was to approve it. He showed a complete lack of understanding of how things are done in India. He committed a major mistake in telling the GOI what it should do for India's best interest—an approach which arouses deep resentment in a country with a long colonial history and where the scars of colonialism are still obvious.

Again, some GOI officials felt that at the press conference Bechtel and Clay said things best left unsaid at the time. Questions of ownership, distribution, cost and price, etc. were disclosed in their replies to Indian reporters. The comments were tantamount to saying that the US companies were anxious, willing and able to proceed with the mfp if the GOI would permit them to do so. That is, they seemed to place the burden of proof on GOI. Yet, India could not take the next step until it had the results of the feasibility study or a firmer basis for further discussion. Some Indian officials felt that Bechtel and Clay, in creating their strong impression, were unfair to the GOI and the key officials associated with the mfp.

October-December 1964

By the end of the visit by Clay and Bechtel, there was a great deal of enthusiasm in various circles of the GOI about the massive fertilizer program proposed by Bechtel Corporation. Thus, addressing the informal meeting of the State Ministers of Agriculture, Subramanyam, Minister for Food and Agriculture, stated that the program of the American consortium would be finalized by March 1965. The first unit would go into production about 18 months after the finalization of the agreement; and after that, one unit would be completed every few months. In view of the impending increase in supply of fertilizers, the Minister urged the farmers to be prepared.

The visit by Bechtel and Clay was highly publicized. The mood reflected in the press and by statements of some GOI officials was that India's fertilizer and foodgrain problems would be solved by the mfp. However, this mood of high expectation was being viewed with considerable alarm within certain quarters of the US embassy, particularly AID, the Indian government and the Indian business community, and each group had its own particular reasons for concern. AID was disturbed because in its view Bechtel was permitting the Indians to develop the viewpoint that the project would in fact solve India's fertilizer and food production problems. However, this was an utterly false expectation. Additionally, within such an expectation framework, the Indian Government was ignoring the fundamental changes in agriculture policy required for lasting and meaningful change in India's foodgrain production.

Within certain quarters of the Indian Government, there was concern on three points. First, if the Bechtel proposal materialized, it would mean that a significant part of an essential industry would be controlled by foreign companies. This was totally unacceptable within the context of the country's policies of local control of essential industries. Second, with the high publicity attached to the project, if it did not materialize for any reason, the party blamed would be India and not Bechtel or other companies, and this would further reduce India's image with the international business community. Third, the US government, through the US Embassy, was directly involved in the development and promotion of the project, and Indian Government officials were resentful of this role of the US Government.

The leading Indian business establishments were concerned that a major industry in the country would be exclusively in the hands of major foreign companies which would prevent them from participating in the growth of the industry. Bechtel Corporation had not discussed the possible involvement of the leading Indian business organizations in the venture. In order to safeguard their respective interests, such Indian houses started independent interaction with select government officials to emphasize the drawbacks of dependence on foreign companies in a vital sector of the nation's economy.

The GOI was continuing to study its agriculture policies. It appointed a seven-member committee to recommend an effective system of distribution of chemical fertilizers. The committee was also asked to consider the question of pricing, role of cooperatives in marketing fertilizers and the role of extension services in promoting the use of fertilizers. In October 1964 AID in New Delhi made several recommendations for changes in GOI policies on fertilizers. It placed particular emphasis on complete freedom of pricing and distribution mfp favored.

Appendix B lists the demand estimates for fertilizers developed by different groups. Each group emerged with a different figure based on the assumptions and the methodology it used. However, there were other areas of differences on demand estimates between these groups and also among the various companies considering investments in fertilizer manufacture. Estimates of market demand varied, i.e., the amount of fertilizers which could be consumed within a given time period in the Indian market. Also, estimates of effective demand varied, i.e., the amount of fertilizers which could reasonably be expected to be consumed by the farmer in the light of economic, transportation and other considerations.

Clay and Bechtel returned to the United States in late September 1964, and proceeded to develop the consortium. Selected companies were formally asked to participate. It was clearly understood that participation by any company in the consortium did not mean that it would have to continue as a member for the duration of the consortium or that it would be required to make an investment in the event that the consortium reached an agreement. The various companies, as part of the consortium, would evaluate the general idea of an mfp and the terms under which they would recommend an investment by the consortium.

In October 1964 the consortium considering the mfp consisted of Bechtel Corporation in the position of overall leadership and Esso, Shell, Texaco, Mobil, Asiatic, Allied Chemical, Food Machinery Corporation and Lucius Clay of Lehman Brothers. The high publicity and the favorable response from the GOI during Bechtel and Clay's visit to India encouraged the companies to remain associated with the mfp idea. In general, the participating companies felt that the mfp idea was something too big not to be associated with. While several of the participants remained highly skeptical of the prospects of the mfp in India, they wanted to be associated just in case the mfp was accepted and approved by the GOI.

Consortium members offered selected personnel from their respective companies to assist in completing the feasibility study. The Stanford Research Institute undertook studies on certain aspects of the fertilizer situation in India. Committees composed of representatives from the participating companies were established to consider various issues which would be fundamental to the development of any concrete proposal for the GOI. Some of the committees were steering, finance and legal. By October a working consortium had been established and it proceeded with considering the various questions which would effect their decision to undertake an investment.

The consortium was faced with a wide range of issues to be resolved. Understandably, the different participants had their respective objectives and terms of investment they would seek. And Bechtel Corporation in particular realized that the feasibility study was due to the Indian government by January 1965, followed by a specific proposal by March 1965. The momentum had to be maintained in order to retain the interest of the GOI and of the members of the consortium.

In brief, the major issues of discussion within the consortium were as follows:

— The project: number of plants, their location, equity investment, foreign exchange requirements and nature of the end product.
— Corporate entities: separate manufacturing and marketing companies, extent of ownership split with the GOI and within the consortium and the debt-equity ratio for the project.
— Marketing: responsibility of the GOI or the consortium.
— Profitability: what price for the end product, guarantee of purchase of production by GOI and guarantees of specified return on investment.
— Supply rights: all raw material (crude and others), engineering, design and construction and allocation of such rights between the GOI and the consortium.
— AID guarantees: long-term and short-term debt investors and for equity investors.

The participating companies experienced serious differences on almost all issues, and Bechtel Corporation was finding it increasingly difficult to offer leadership to the consortium, negotiate for a compromise between the conflicting requirements of various members and still achieve the deadlines for submission to the Indian government. In general, the more experienced members with extensive experience in India were convinced that Bechtel's time estimates for submitting the study and gaining GOI approvals were totally unrealistic. The unprecedented nature of the project would require considerable review and debate within the GOI before any decisions would be forthcoming. Some companies felt that the consortium should initially undertake only two plants with an option for three more at a later date depending upon the outcome of the first two plants. Others felt that the consortium's responsibility should be limited to manufacturing, and the GOI should be exclusively responsible for the marketing of the fertilizer. Additionally, the GOI should be asked to offer guaranteed purchase of total production of mfp plants or of a certain percentage of production at a predetermined price. However, some members felt that this was an unreasonable requirement, and General Clay was strongly against such a demand as it would be tantamount to asking the GOI for a guaranteed profit. The oil companies were interested primarily in securing supply rights for crude oil while the chemical companies had no interest in crude oil rights but sought supply rights for potash and other non-oil raw materials. Again, some of the members were against accepting less than 100 percent equity in the mfp and at most would settle for 51 percent. But they were not enthusiastic about accepting a minority equity interest for the consortium on the grounds that it would establish an undesirable precedent for their operations in other parts of the world. There were also personal differences between the representatives of the various participants often reflecting differences between their respective organizations. A few members were disturbed by the slow speed with which decisions were being formulated within the various committees of the consortium.

By November a major oil company with extensive experience and operations in India withdrew from the consortium on the grounds that it did not wish to accept minority equity interest. However, its true reason was that it did not feel that the consortium would be able to develop an mfp acceptable to the GOI. In late December another major oil company withdrew from the consortium on the grounds that the decision makers were not coming to grips with the fundamental questions of financing the mfp. Another oil company was seriously reviewing its association. The vast majority of the remaining members of the consortium were reassessing their association especially in light of the withdrawal of the two companies with extensive Indian experience. However, the GOI was ignorant of these withdrawals.

In November 1964 the consortium wanted part of the foreign exchange financing for the project to come from governmental assistance to India. The GOI, on the other hand, argued that the objective of encouraging private foreign investment was to secure foreign exchange from sources other than governmental assistance. The consortium also sought majority ownership, management control and an improvement in distribution channels leading to a 10 percent to 15 percent reduction in the price of fertilizer to the farmer.

In late November 1964 the Deputy Minister for Petroleum and Chemicals, in response to a question in the *Lok Sabha* (Lower House of Parliament) stated:

> It is too early to say anything. Nobody wishes to run into difficulties. In fact, regular negotiations will start only after the report has been submitted and specific proposals have been made about finances which also will form part of the report.

He added that the sites under consideration included Madras but added that the location of the plants would be decided only after the feasibility report was received. The Deputy Minister insisted that "as far as he could see, there is no difficulty" in consortium developments.

January-March 1965

The feasibility report was submitted to the GOI in January 1965. Minister Kabir disclosed on January 22, 1965 that the feasibility report had recommended two plants in North India and one each in Southern, Western and Eastern regions. The report added that the first of the five plants of 200,000 tons capacity would go into production 28 months after final approval by the government. The foreign exchange requirements for these plants would be met by the consortium outside of the assistance received under the AID consortium. It had not been decided whether the projects would be in the public or the private sectors. No decision had been taken about the location of the plants. But the GOI would have the final say in the matter of plant location. Appendix C offers additional details of the feasibility report.

The feasibility report submitted by Bechtel Corporation aroused considerable publicity and controversy in India. The report represented the specific thinking of the consortium on the mfp which to date had been a general concept. The negative reactions within the GOI were along three lines. First, the GOI maintained that the report did not contain anything which it did not already know and therefore was unhappy about having paid a significant sum of money for a report which was largely a repetition of known facts. Bechtel Corporation maintained that the summary observations contained in the report were backed up by considerable analysis, and Bechtel had decided to submit a summary in order to encourage all parties to consider the broader policy issues as against getting enmeshed in details of methodology. Second, the GOI challenged the cost estimates for the five plants. Bechtel maintained that the estimates were subject to review and further discussion. Third, the GOI had hoped for a concrete proposal by this time if the overall time targets for the mfp were to be achieved. Instead, Bechtel had merely presented a general summary. Bechtel maintained that the specific proposal would emerge from the summary.

Bechtel's approach to negotiation at this stage was first to gain a heads type agreement with the GOI on broad policy issues (ownership split, raw material supply, foreign exchange financing) before entering into detailed negotiations. In Bechtel's opinion, if it agreed with the GOI's approach of discussing the details of each of the terms of investment the negotiations would be interminable. Additionally, Bechtel hoped that if a heads type agreement with the GOI could be achieved quickly, it would be of considerable help in retaining the association of the existing members of the consortium and perhaps might even help in gaining additional members.

The discussions with the consortium figured prominently in debate in the

Lok Sabha on March 2, 1965. The Finance Minister, T.T. Krishnamachari, assured the House that the "interests of the country and the interests of finance" would be taken care of in the negotiations. He described the Bechtel proposal as being very sketchy and added that "we will bargain and bargain very hard . . . If I do anything else, I serve the purpose of turning down many of these offers." Appendix D illustrates the nature of the discussions in Parliament.

More specific areas of differences between Bechtel and the GOI began to emerge in March. On March 11, the consortium objected to the GOI's decision to collaborate with the National Iranian Oil Company (owned by the Iranian Government) and the American International Oil Company (a wholly owned subsidiary of Standard Oil Company of Indiana) for the fertilizer-cum-refinery complex at Madras. The consortium representatives argued that Madras was the most desirable site. Also, the GOI had violated its earlier understanding with Bechtel Corporation that the Madras site would be reserved for the consortium. The GOI argued that there was no such agreement and the NIOC/AIOC collaboration with the GOI for the Madras site had been considered for quite some time. Bechtel stated that the loss of the Madras site meant that the entire basis of negotiations for mfp would need to be changed.

Bechtel Corporation in fact had been aware of the GOI's discussions with NIOC and AIOC for the Madras site. Lannigan of the US Embassy had assisted Dorman in attempting to encourage AIOC to participate with Bechtel in the mfp instead of promoting a separate project of its own. Lannigan had gone to the extent of stating that the US Embassy would not help AIOC in gaining USG guarantees and financing if AIOC decided not to associate with the mfp but would offer all possible assistance if it joined the consortium. However, AIOC decided against associating with the mfp because it was not confident of the prospects of the project. Additionally, it felt that Bechtel had slighted Standard Oil Company of Indiana by not asking it to participate in the consortium when it was originally launched.

An event which occurred during S.D. Bechtel and General Clay's visit to India might have contributed to Bechtel Corporation's interpretation of the award of the Madras site by the GOI to AIOC/NIOC. During the visit, Clay and Bechtel met with the Minister of Finance. During this meeting in the course of discussing several aspects of the mfp, Bechtel noted that Madras was an important site for the mfp and that he did not want the GOI to award it to other companies unless the consortium had first bid for it. The Minister merely nodded his head and asked Bechtel to raise the next point. Bechtel interpreted this to mean that the Minister had agreed. The Minister and the GOI maintained that such an interpretation was totally incorrect. If Madras was in fact so important to Bechtel, it should have been made a specific point of detailed discussion and expressed in writing.

The adverse reactions to the feasibility report and the decision on the Madras site had a seriously adverse effect on the remaining members of the consortium.

The existing doubts about the viability of the mfp became much stronger. The approach of Bechtel on the question of the Madras site in negotiations with the GOI had another objective as well. By making it a "break-point," Bechtel hoped to plant the first seed for withdrawal from the mfp if discussions within the consortium and with the GOI failed to become positive.

By late March it was stated that Bechtel was unable to raise the huge sums of money required except with the cooperation of international oil companies, and the oil companies could not be made to take interest in the fertilizer program without giving them a share in oil refining in India. Bechtel stated that its associates among the oil companies should be invited to become partners in the Haldia refinery on the terms on which other foreign companies had been invited to join the Cochin and Madras refineries. This demand had taken the GOI by surprise. It replied that fertilizers and refining were two different things and could not be tied together. See Appendix E for an editorial in the Indian press.

On March 30 the consortium demanded that it should be assured of recovery of its investment within five years of the commissioning of the five units and that it should be permitted to import crude oil, rock phosphate, sulphur and other raw materials required for manufacture of fertilizers by the proposed naphtha-based plants.

April 1965

In early April some of the principal issues, the stand of the consortium and GOI, and the possible solutions to the issues were generally of the following types. Bechtel Corporation was beginning to conclude that realization of the mfp as originally conceived would be extremely difficult.

1. Supply rights
   a. WIC:* Insisted upon supply rights, including those to crude oil, commensurate with equity participation.
   b. GOI: Would not grant rights to WIC to import crude oil/naphtha while indigenous supplies were available.
   c. The possible solutions: (1) Award of Haldia refinery to a consortium member; (2) Award of Haldia refinery to KNPC co-jointly with consortium member (e.g., Gulf), which would provide crude oil requirements of KNPC for Haldia refinery; (3) Long-term contract for finished petroleum products between WIC and GOI; (4) Inclusion in consortium of an oil company which currently had crude oil supply rights (e.g., AIOC), and which could then share such rights with other consortium members.
2. Supply Rights (cont.)
   a. WIC: Insisted upon supply rights to raw materials for mfp other than crude oil or naphtha.

---

*To avoid adverse publicity for Bechtel Corporation, it formed the Western Industrial Corporation (WIC) to develop and negotiate the mfp.

b. GOI: Mfp must utilize indigenous substitutes whenever possible.

c. The possible solutions: (1) Mfp would use indigenous substitutes if they met competitive conditions of price, quality, quantity, etc. (2) Product pattern of mfp plants could be modified to use only or largely indigenous substitutes; (3) Barter of indigenous raw materials for imported raw materials; (4) Securing credits from foreign nations for imports of raw materials.

3. Equity Participation

a. WIC: Insisted upon equal (50-50) equity participation with the GOI.

b. GOI: In public-sector projects, GOI insisted upon majority ownership.

c. The possible solutions: (1) WIC could collaborate with the Indian private sector and hold majority ownership; (2) The manufacturing company (with equal ownership split) and the marketing company (with GOI holding majority ownership) could be combined, giving GOI majority ownership on the whole; (3) GOI and WIC could have 49 percent each of the manufacturing company with 2 percent held in a non-voting trust; (4) Both GOI and WIC or WIC alone could agree to surrender a stipulated equity at an agreed time in the future; (5) WIC could take a tight managerial control of mfp, obviating the need for equal equity participation.

4. Offtake Guarantees

a. WIC: Insisted upon GOI guarantees to purchase products that the marketing company could not sell.

b. GOI: Potential market for fertilizers suggested good commercial risk and guaranteed offtake established a dangerous precedent for GOI.

c. The possible solutions: (1) The mfp should export some part of fertilizers manufactured; (2) GOI could purchase at "distress prices" (i.e., prices lower than existing market prices) the product that the marketing company could not sell; (3) GOI could purchase a portion of the mfp output at market prices (not "distress prices"); (4) WIC could secure financing from sources which did not require any offtake guarantees; (5) The mfp plants could sell their output for a specified period of time to the fertilizer pool; (6) For a two-plant program, the mfp could assume the same commercial risks now expected of other private-sector plants.

5. Financing

a. WIC: Insisted upon financing outside of AID India Consortium though the final decision would depend on terms of investment approved by GOI, availability of ERG from AID, and attitude of private financing sources in United States.

b. GOI: A substantial part of the foreign exchange financing would have to be outside of Aid India funds.

c. The possible solutions: (1) The mfp should be financed by a combination of private and public (Aid India) funds; (2) The mfp could seek collaboration of Indian private sector for some part of rupee, and if possible, foreign exchange financing.

6. Some Basic Issues (for WIC's consideration)
   a. Establishment of fewer plants, for example, two or three, but of a higher production capacity, say 300,000 instead of 200,000 tons per year of nitrogen equivalent;
   b. Extent and areas of managerial control for WIC;
   c. Supporting evidence for rate of return on investment required by the consortium for discussions with GOI;
   d. Designation of sites for mfp plants;
   e. Review of cost estimates for construction, engineering, operations, etc.;
7. Approach to Negotiations
   a. WIC: Insisted upon agreement in principle with the GOI on the key areas of the mfp before a detailed discussion of the specifics of engineering, construction, costs, marketing, etc., could ensue.
   b. GOI: Insisted upon negotiating details first and then deciding on whether it could agree on the broader principles of investment.

The mood within the GOI and the Indian press was cautious if not negative about the mfp. Indian papers stated that USG officials had identified themselves so much with the Bechtel proposal as to hold out a threat for change in United States' attitude toward aid to India. *The Indian Express* of April 2nd stated:

It is known that the U.S. government attaches great importance to this deal. Apart from the U.S. Ambassador in India, Mr. Chester Bowles, Mr. Averill Harriman, the U.S. President's roving envoy, who visited India recently, is also believed to have urged expeditious finalization of this deal.

By mid-April 1965 Bechtel Corporation argued that western enterprise could be attracted only if a reasonable profit commensurate with risks and efforts could be provided. Bechtel pointed out that this could be achieved within the existing level of fertilizer prices in India. On April 19, 1965, Minister Kabir stated in Calcutta that the GOI would wait until May 15 for Bechtel to finalize its offer. Otherwise, other projects would be considered.

May-June 1965
The period between May and June 1965 was a hectic one. Bechtel Corporation knew that the original concept of the mfp was not feasible. It was wondering whether a substantially scaled-down version would have better prospects. There were other considerations influencing Bechtel's approach. Given the high expectations and publicity aroused by the mfp, what would be the consequences of a failure of the project for Bechtel Corporation and other

members remaining with the consortium? Given the involvement of the US Embassy, what would be the effect on Indo-US relations? Should the US Embassy be asked to assist in terminating the negotiations for the mfp? What would be the best approach for terminating the mfp with least consequences for all parties concerned? While Bechtel Corporation executives in India proceeded to negotiate with the GOI for a scaled down project, they were also planning for termination of negotiations.

The GOI, on its side, was concerned about several points. If the mfp did not materialize, it would be blamed on the GOI and thereby have a seriously adverse effect on the foreign investment climate in India. Other companies which had expressed interest in fertilizer projects might decide to withdraw or negotiate for terms which would be difficult for the GOI to accept. Additionally, certain members of the GOI were concerned that they would be blamed for not having learned about the characteristics and make-up of the consortium at a much earlier date so that the GOI would not have lost valuable time in negotiating with a consortium which simply could not deliver. Therefore, by May the GOI became particularly anxious to salvage something out of the original proposal by Bechtel. It offered several alternatives to Bechtel, including one for establishing only two plants.

By this stage, Bechtel Corporation at the headquarters level had concluded that the right time and mood for the mfp had passed. Involvement with a single plant would not be of interest to the company. Also, several of the oil companies which had been members of the consortium were encouraging corporate management of Bechtel to terminate any further negotiations for fertilizer plants with the GOI. A major reason for this suggestion was that some of the oil companies were planning to reactivate their own projects in India and felt that the GOI would be more attentive to their needs once the mfp idea was dead and buried. When Bechtel Corporation did not accede to this request promptly, the oil companies started to review new contracts they were negotiating with Bechtel Corporation for engineering, design and construction of facilities in various parts of the world. As a result, Bechtel Corporation finally informed the GOI that for the time being the mfp was being withdrawn.

Appendix A

Indigenous Fertilizer Manufacturing Capacity—Existing and Proposed

A. *Existing and Planned Capacity*

  1. *Public Sector*

    (a) *Present Capacity in the Public Sector*

Plant	N	P_2O_5	K_2O
Sindri (FCI)	.120	—	—
Rourkela (H. Steel)	.120	—	—
Alwaye (FACT)*	.070	.032	—
Nangal	.080	—	—
Total	.390	.032	—

*Capacity by Spring 1965, Present Capacities; N, 030, P_2O_5, .014

    (b) *Public Sector Plants Under Construction*
      (Million tons)

Plant		Date of Completion	N	Capacity P_2O_5	K_2O
Trombay	(FCI)	1965	.09	.045	—
Namrup	(FCI)	1966	.05		—
Gujarat	(GSF)	1968	.125	.057	—
Neyvelli	(NF)	1967	.07		—
Gorakhpur	(FCI)	1968	.08		—
			.415	.102	—

(c) *Total Capacity of the Public Sector by 1968*
   (Million tons)

	N	P_2O_5	K_2O
Present Capacity	.390	.032	—
Capacity under Construction	.415	.102	—
	.805	.134	—

2. *Private Sector*

   Present and Projected Private Sector Capacity
   (Million tons)

	N	P_2O_5	K_2O
Total July 1963	.040	.130	.042
Projected for completion by 1968:			
Coromandel	.085	.075	—
Kothagudam	.080	—	—
Misc.	.020	.090	—
Total by 1968	.225	.295	.042

3. *Total Capacity and Anticipated Deficits*

   (a) *Total Capacity by 1968*
      (Million tons)

	N	P_2O_5	K_2O
Private	.225	.295	.042
Public	.805	.134	—
	1.030	.429	.042

   (b) *Deficits (Requirements Minus Projected Capacity)*
      (Million tons)

	N	P_2O_5	K_2O
1970/71	1.948	1.060	.628
1975/76	3.814	1.993	1.048

Appendix B

Estimates of Fertilizer Consumption in the First Plan

(Figures in million tons)

Year	Working Group's Targets			U.S. AID's Targets			Stanford Research Institute's Targets*		
	N	P_2O_5	K_2O	N	P_2O_5	K_2O	N	P_2O_5	K_2O
1966-67	0.85	0.37	0.19	0.89	0.31	0.16	–	–	–
1967-68	1.00	0.50	0.23	1.17	0.45	0.23	–	–	–
1968-69	1.30	0.65	0.27	1.53	0.64	0.33	–	–	–
1969-70	1.60	0.80	0.31	2.00	0.93	0.48	–	–	–
1970-71	2.00	1.00	0.35	2.65	1.34	0.68	2.08	1.29	0.67

*Targets for 1970-71 alone were set out in this study.

Summary Report

The report submitted by Bechtel Corporation to the GOI was entitled *Fertilizer for India: Summary Report of a Study Conducted for the Government of India.* A considerable body of background information was not included with the report. The major characteristics of the report were:

1. Exhibit 1 highlights the projected production capacity in India including the mfp plants. Almost 90 percent of the 1970-1971 target of two million tons per year could be realized by 1969 if feasibility of the mfp is established and it is authorized without delay by the GOI.

2. Out of the five plants, each with a capacity of 200,000 tons per year of nitrogen, three will be in coastal locations in Zones 2, 3 and 4 and two will be inland plants in Zone 1. (See Exhibit 2.)

3. The estimates of capital costs for the five plants (see Exhibit 3) was $425 million with 46 percent in rupees and the balance in other currencies.

Exhibit 1.   Projected Production Capacity Including Massive Program Plants

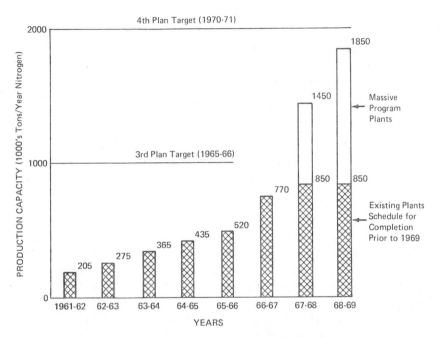

Source: Bechtel Corporation, *Fertilizer for India: Summary Report of a Study Conducted for the Government of India* (San Fransisco: Bechtel Corporation, January, 1965), p. 20.

Exhibit 2. Fertilizer Production by Zones Including Massive Program Plants

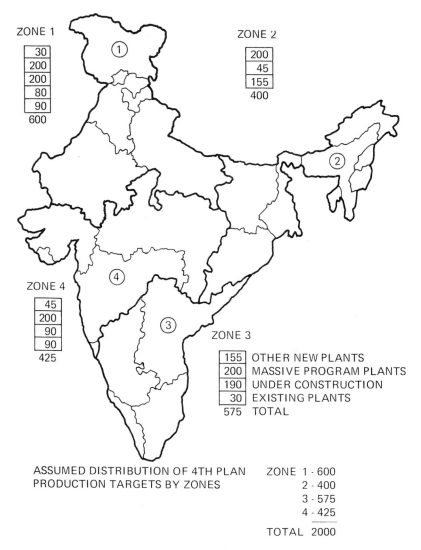

ZONE 1

| 30 |
| 200 |
| 200 |
| 80 |
| 90 |
600

ZONE 2

| 200 |
| 45 |
| 155 |
400

ZONE 4

| 45 |
| 200 |
| 90 |
| 90 |
425

ZONE 3

155	OTHER NEW PLANTS
200	MASSIVE PROGRAM PLANTS
190	UNDER CONSTRUCTION
30	EXISTING PLANTS
575	TOTAL

ASSUMED DISTRIBUTION OF 4TH PLAN
PRODUCTION TARGETS BY ZONES

ZONE 1 - 600
2 - 400
3 - 575
4 - 425

TOTAL 2000

Figures are 1000's Tons Per Year of Equivalent Nitrogen

Source: Bechtel Corporation, *Fertilizer for India: Summary Report of a Study Conducted for the Government of India* (San Fransisco: Bechtel Corporation, January, 1965), p. 21.

Exhibit 3.   Estimates of Capital Costs for Five Plants

	Rs.	U.S. $
1. Processing units including ammonia plant, urea plant, acid plants and granulator facility	97,82,00,0000	205,500,000
2. Non-processing facilities including raw material receiving, handling and storage facilities, power generation, water supply and recovery, steam supply, site development, fencing and general facilities, administration building, shop, maintenance warehouse, laboratory, cafeteria and the like	59,33,00,000	124,650,000
3. Housing facilities for plant staff	9,51,00,000	19,970,000
4. Special facilities as required at specific plant sites, mainly wharves and ship unloading systems	4,21,00,000	8,840,000
5. Cost of land	1,35,00,000	2,840,000
Sub-total: Fixed capital	172,22,00,000	361,800,000
6. Preproduction costs including startup and training costs and initial charges of catalyst, etc., and owner's cost during construction	9,36,00,000	19,670,000
7. Working capital including allowance for spare parts, 30 days storage of raw materials, interest during construction, insurance during construction, etc.	20,72,00,000	43,530,000
TOTAL ESTIMATED CAPITAL REQUIREMENT	202,30,00,000	425,000,000

Analysis of the above costs indicates present conditions and availability of supply in India would permit a currency distribution as follows:

	Rs.	Other Currencies
1. For facility construction costs	48%	52%
2. For initial materials and services for operation (working capital)	35%	65%
3. In total, the ratios are	46%	54%

Source: Bechtel Corporation, *Fertilizer for India: Summary Report of a Study Conducted for the Government of India* (San Francisco: Bechtel Corporation, January 1965), pp. 29-30.

Appendix D

Parliamentary Digest,
April 1, 1965
(Questions asked in
Rajya Sabha)

Shri A.D. Mani: Will the Minister of Petroleum and Chemicals ... state (a) whether the American consortium, which had offered aid for setting up fertilizer plants in India, has raised certain objections to government's policies in the feasibility report recently submitted by it; and (b) if so, what are those objections?

Shri O.V. Alagesan: No sir. In their report, however, the American consortium made a number of suggestions which in their opinion will help in the achievement of the massive fertilizer programme.

Shri A.D. Mani: According to my information the consortium is believed to have objected to the government's decision to collaborate with the National Iranian Company for the setting up of a fertilizer plant in Madras which, it is claimed, is the keypoint in the scheme of five plants offered by it. Can he deny the statement?

Shri O.V. Alagesan: I would like to tell the Members that the negotiations with the Iranian party and the American party with regard to the Madras refinery were started much earlier. The Bechtel people came much later into the picture. Certainly they would have taken it that Madras might be available to them but as it has been decided earlier that we shall collaborate with the Iranian party and the American International Oil Company, there is no question of Madras going to them.

Shri A.D. Mani: On a point of order. I asked him a straight question. Can he deny the statement since they have raised this objection (and) because this House is entitled to discuss the implementation of the policy if their claim is accepted: There is another question. This consortium has submitted a feasibility report on its estimates and the cost of the project will be Rs. 202.30 crores. They also wanted 50 percent equity participation and they have mentioned that without this 50 percent equity participation of American capital they will not be able to raise funds in America. Can he deny this statement?

Shri O.V. Alagesan: All these are under negotiation with the parties. We are discussing these things, and it will be very difficult to discuss the details of the terms at this stage.

Shri Arjun Arora: May I know if this firm has, as its head, the ill-famed General Clay who was responsible for wrecking the government's plan for getting American aid for Bokaro and, if so, why has the government of India negotiated with this firm which has, as its head, a General who has achieved only one victory, and that victory is against American collaboration in our steel industry?

Shri O.V. Alagesan: I do not think General Clay has anything to do with this particular firm. This is called Bechtel and Company and behind them there is a consortium of American firms which is composed of oil companies and several other firms. Perhaps General Clay comes in as a financier. We do not have any more information than that.

Shri P.K. Kumaran: May I know our policy regarding foreign participation in such collaboration agreements? Are the GOI thinking of giving 50 percent equity participation or are we thinking of giving them only minority participation as before?

Shri O.V. Alagesan: The question of equity participation and other connected matters are the subject of present discussion. As far as the general question of foreign participation in equity capital in India goes, that has been made clear more than once by the Prime Minister and the Finance Minister.

Appendix E

"On whose terms?"

Financial Express
March 3, 1965

For any American official or officials to suggest or even give the impression to the GOI that US aid might be limited to any particular project is, to say the least, most disturbing. And yet, if New Delhi reports are correct, this is exactly what seems to have happened in the case of (the) much advertised Bechtel proposals for a massive fertilizer programme in the country. The Minister of State for Petroleum, Mr. O.V. Alagesan, gave no direct replies to the queries of members in the Rajya Sabha on Friday last which could dispel the misgiving that the Bechtel Corporation had demanded almost impossible conditions for collaborating in setting up fertilizer plants. Apparently the high politics involved did not permit him to make a feasible statement. The question of 50:50 equity participation in this Rs. 200 crores project (now remedied down by Americans to 1.75 crores) between Bechtel and GOI has been there right from the beginning, and it is no secret that there are various differences of opinion between the two parties on the sharing of ownership. Faced with facts and figures that its original estimates were on the high side, that its feasibility report offered no solution to the present high prices of fertilizer the Indian farmer has to pay, and that its proposal for control over management for a reasonably long period was prompted more by its anxiety to retain control than to streamline the industry, Bechtel Corporation would now seem to be seeking to withdraw from the cooperation it had extended to New Delhi by putting new conditions which it must have known are impossible of acceptance. Without resolving the issues laid earlier, that corporation demands not only that it should be assured recovery of its investment within five years of the commissioning of the five units, but also that it should be permitted to import crude oil, rock phosphate, sulphur and other raw materials required for manufacture of fertilizer by the proposed naphtha-based plants.

Surely the corporation is aware that there is excess naphtha produced in this country and that more of it will be available as new refineries expand. The obvious implication is that the American consortium wants its oil partners to be entrusted with the setting up of the Haldia refinery since the issue in the case of Madras refinery is now settled. The disappointment of Americans on the rejection by New Delhi of the attractive offers of the US companies for collaboration in the Madras refinery is understandable. It is too much to expect Western Oil Company to process Soviet oil and sell petroleum products from this country in the context of oil politics and economics. To attempt, however, to gain by backdoor methods in Haldia what has been lost in Madras is neither good business nor good politics. *What is shocking is that US officials should identify themselves so much with the Bechtel proposal or to even hold out a threat of change in American attitude towards aid in this country.* Though now forgotten, Bokaro still remains a sour point in the relations between the two countries. And Bechtel promises to dig deeper in this wound unless US industrialists and officials realise quickly that New Delhi would welcome foreign private or official capital only on its own terms.

Massey-Ferguson

NEGOTIATION OF COOPERATION ARRANGEMENT FOR PRODUCTION OF CONSTRUCTION EQUIPMENT IN ROMANIA

Late in 1972 Massey-Ferguson (M-F) was well advanced in negotiations with the Romanian Foreign Trade Enterprise, Mecanoexport, for a cooperation arrangement to produce wheel loaders. However, a few key points remained to be resolved and it was not clear how strong the intentions were of the Romanian officials to carry the arrangement through to effective implementation.

COMPANY BACKGROUND

Massey-Ferguson was a Canadian-based multinational farm equipment and machinery manufacturer with factories, sales offices, export distributors and associate companies throughout North and South America, Europe, Africa, Asia and Australia. In 1972 the company's consolidated sales reached a record level of US $1,190 million.

M-F operated on the basis of two key principles of organization: (1) decentralized marketing and manufacturing operations and (2) general supervision by corporate headquarters of policies and strategies, including product strategies, treasury management, facilities location, flow of trade, planning and control

This case was adapted from C.H. MacMillan and David P. Charles, *Joint Ventures in Eastern Europe: A Three-Country Comparison.* Montreal: Canadian Economic Policy Committee of the C.D. Howe Research Institute. Copyright © C.D. Howe Institute. Reproduced by permission.

processes, organization structure and senior executive personnel administration. Applying these principles in the evolving international environment, the company established in 1972 a new worldwide management structure intended to place it in a better position to compete with increasing effectiveness on a worldwide scale. In essence, it was a mixed geographic-product line structure in which regional groupings made strategic product proposals representing the needs of their particular market areas, while the product divisions maintained worldwide control of their respective product lines.

Thus the negotiations with Mecanoexport in the fall of 1972 were handled by M-F's London office. The special operations division of this office was responsible for concluding all such cooperation agreements for Eastern Europe, Africa, Asia and Australia. This division negotiated licensing arrangements for the local manufacturing of M-F products and handled the development of new trading approaches. However, even though the negotiations were conducted by London executives and would be supervised out of that office, operational arrangements and goods flows would involve a plant in Aprilia, Italy and a plant in the United States. Both these plants produced the wheel loaders that the Romanians were interested in manufacturing.

ARRANGEMENTS IN EASTERN EUROPE

M-F did not have any other cooperation agreements in Eastern Europe in 1972. It did have a licensing agreement with a Yugoslav enterprise for the manufacture of tractors, but this had been allowed to lapse. It was currently negotiating a very large cooperation agreement with a Polish enterprise for the production of tractors. The tentative arrangements involved a major licensing agreement to increase production at the Ursus tractor plant outside Warsaw to 80,000 units a year, from the present level of 45,000 machines, by introducing a new range of tractors. Initially, M-F would be responsible for supplying both the necessary technical knowledge and the component parts until the Polish enterprise was capable of assuming complete manufacturing responsibility. The total contract was estimated at approximately $250 million.

Prior to the current negotiations, M-F had had only straightforward trading transactions with the Romanians. In 1970 the Romanians approached M-F regarding the manufacture of wheel loaders, and discussions opened in terms of a prospective joint venture, shifting later to the contractual mix of licensing, technical assistance and marketing arrangements which were under negotiation in 1972. Although the Romanians were still anxious to discuss a joint venture arrangement, M-F felt that such a sophisticated arrangement should evolve out of some form of previous cooperation, through which both parties could establish a sound working rapport, realize each other's productive capabilities, and develop a common desire to work towards a mutually advantageous end.

M-F was interested in the Romanian arrangement because it viewed the

Comecon area as a large untapped market for wheel loaders, which it regarded as superior to any equivalent piece of machinery that the Eastern European countries were currently producing. A cooperation arrangement with Mecanoexport would provide M-F with a direct means of entering the Romanian and Comecon markets. It might also improve M-F prospects in the Chinese market, given the special relationship which existed between Bucharest and Peking. Other reasons for M-F's interest in such a project were the attraction of a stable, low-cost alternate source of quality machines and components. The bilateral clearing agreements between Romania and a number of developing countries could also facilitate more ready access to these soft-currency countries than was currently possible for M-F machinery.

On the Romanian side, there were a number of reasons for desiring such a relationship with a Western enterprise. First, there was the prospect of having continuous access to Western know-how. Second, there was the need to obtain the necessary technical assistance, documentation, training and continuous exchange of information on the wheel loaders. Third, the Romanians desired a quality product which would be readily marketable in both the East and the West. Fourth, Mecanoexport wanted to obtain a certain amount of marketing know-how, to develop contacts, and to acquire easier access to Western markets.

After extended discussions an operating arrangement along the following lines had emerged as essentially satisfactory to both parties. In return for Romanian provision of the necessary manufacturing facilities, including plant and certain pieces of equipment as well as the necessary labor force, M-F tentatively agreed to furnish the Romanian enterprise with the following:

a. Manufacturing rights to certain wheel loader models.
b. Technical assistance for setting up local manufacturing and production operations.
c. Production organization skills as required.
d. Marketing rights and privileges:
   i) non-exclusive marketing rights for the Comecon bloc and China. M-F was anxious not to upset trade transactions that it was currently conducting with other Eastern European countries;
   ii) exclusive sales rights to the Romanian market for the products produced under license, although M-F would retain the right to sell other products to Romania;
   iii) the right to sell finished machines produced under license to M-F, which in turn would market the equipment through its worldwide sales network; and
   iv) the option to sell directly to the rest of the world upon approval of M-F, such approval being readily granted in cases of soft-currency countries having special bilateral payments arrangements with Romania.
e. After-sales servicing facilities. This was particularly important in the case of

machinery sales because a prospective buyer was interested not only in purchasing the equipment but also in comprehensive after-sales servicing, maintenance, and the availability of spare parts. Thus it was necessary for M-F to ensure that the Romanians were thoroughly trained to provide these services. This was of particular importance to the Western firm because all of the Romanian machines produced under license would bear the M-F trademark.

M-F agreed to supply the necessary percentage of components so that the Romanians would be able to produce a finished product domestically. It was anticipated that the Romanian content in the finished machines would be gradually increased as Romanians acquired more experience in the production process. Mecanoexport would pay for the required M-F components, technical assistance, licensing fees and other services in convertible currency. In a similar fashion, M-F would also pay hard currency for any complete machines and/or components that it purchased from the Romanians. To the extent possible, the Romanian hard-currency outflow in this arrangement would be balanced with the hard-currency inflow from M-F purchases.

M-F would arrange the necessary credits for Mecanoexport, which would vary in accordance with the size of the project. Although there was no definite price tag on the project as yet, it would be in the area of several million dollars and would be determined in the long run by the Romanian enterprise's production volume.

M-F would provide training for Romanian technicians in its Western factories and would send engineers to Romania to assist in setting up initial production operations. M-F also envisaged having a small technical and quality control staff in Romania on a full-time basis.

PROBLEMS ENCOUNTERED IN NEGOTIATING
THE AGREEMENT AND ITS PRESENT STATUS

One aspect of the arrangement that was still unresolved centered upon differing approaches to market forecasting and management planning. In essence it was a conflict between the Western business need to adapt constantly to rapidly changing market conditions and the constraints placed upon Eastern enterprises by the rigid nature of Eastern planning practices. M-F was in a highly competitive world market and could not establish rigid long-term plans and commitments to Eastern European countries, since this might work to the detriment of the company. On the other hand, in such arrangements the Comecon countries often desired a seven- to fifteen-year fixed purchase agreement from the Western firm. Mecanoexport initially wanted a long-term fixed purchase agreement from M-F for the wheel loaders. This was not acceptable to M-F as the company would not commit itself to such a rigid and highly vulnerable position, given the competitive nature of its business and widely fluctuating world market conditions. A compromise was being considered under which M-F would accept a three-year agreement to take a certain amount of the Romanian production for marketing in the West, with the condition that the quality and quantity of the Mecanoexport deliveries were in accordance with Western market demands. Within this three-year period, the Romanian content in the finished product would be gradually increased in line with domestic production capabilities for the basic machine and with the ability of Romanian sub-suppliers to provide such accessory equipment as batteries, tires and engines. M-F would accept any product component for the Romanian-produced machines as long as it met M-F specifications and quality control standards.

A second area in which agreement had not yet been reached concerned the marketing arrangements. The critical issue here was marketing rights in Greece, the Near East and Africa. The Romanians wished to export to these markets; however, M-F already had direct sales arrangements there which it did not wish to disrupt.

A third question concerned the range of wheel loader models which would be produced in Romania. This decision required considerable analysis of market needs, particularly on the part of the Romanian machinery industry officials, as it would relate to other aspects of their industrial development program.

In the background of the negotiations also were the roles of various Romanian government organizations and officials. Mecanoexport with which Massey-Ferguson was negotiating was a structurally integrated enterprise functioning under the direction of the ministry of industry responsible for producing construction equipment. However, the Ministry of Foreign Trade also had a major interest in the arrangement because of its responsibility for exports and imports and the balance of trade in general. It was therefore essential that this Ministry also concur fully in the nature of the agreement. Although M-F had no direct knowledge of the viewpoints of specific officials at high levels on this proposed arrangement, it was aware that there was some degree of lack of support at the ministerial level. It was understood that certain ministry officials were not satisfied with some aspects of the contract. It had also been the company's experience that progress of the agreement had been delayed by various changes in personnel at the ministerial level. A significant factor in the role of individuals in the negotiation was the extent of personal responsibility of key officials in contractual agreements. According to Romanian practice if, in certain important respects, an agreement did not work out satisfactorily, the individual responsible for negotiating it bore a direct personal responsibility.

Singer Company (A)

CONSIDERATION OF INVESTMENT IN FACE
OF OPPOSITION BY JAPANESE INDUSTRY

In late 1954 the Singer Manufacturing Company was confronted with strongly adverse comment from Japanese groups concerning its proposed investment in the Pine Sewing Machine Company of Japan. The Japanese Finance Ministry, to whom the Singer-Pine contract had to be submitted for approval, neither approved nor rejected the proposal but allowed reports to filter out that the government hoped it would voluntarily be withdrawn.

After World War II the sewing machine industry appeared a logical specialty in which the Japanese could compete on the world market. In 1947 the Ministry of International Trade and Industry took steps, in cooperation with the Japanese Sewing Machine Industry Association, to improve design and to standardize production. Simplification and interchangeability of parts contributed to the rapid growth of the industry in the next few years. However, it also resulted in the entry into the industry of hundreds of small, weakly financed producers, some of them no more than home workshops which supplied great numbers of the cheaper machines which reached the export market.

Japanese export of sewing machines and sewing machine heads for assembly into machines averaged 10,000 units monthly by 1949. It averaged over 70,000 units monthly by 1952 and fluctuated between about 60,000 and 100,000 units monthly thereafter. Sewing machines and sewing machine parts constituted

Written from newspaper reports compiled by Willard Hanna, American Universities Field Staff. Copyright by the President and Fellows of Harvard College. Reproduced by permission.

Japan's second largest machinery export (textile manufacturing machinery came first) and earned Japan about $30,000,000 annually. Approximately 60 percent of the Japanese sewing machine output—which provided a livelihood for some 300,000 families—went into the export trade. The best customer was the United States, which in 1953 bought 46 percent by number and 35 percent by value of Japan's exports. Japan exported in quantity also to South America, India, the Near East, Australia, Africa and Europe.

In 1954 the Japanese sewing machine industry found itself in a state of crisis. It was faced with apparent saturation of the home market and declining prices on the world market. It had resorted to cutthroat competition in both the domestic and the international markets. The government, meanwhile, in an effort to meet its over-all economic problem of an adverse trade balance, had adopted a tight money policy. Sewing machine manufacturers, being accustomed to operating primarily on short-term capital and now being unable readily to get bank credit, resorted more and more commonly to sacrifice sales. The larger companies attempted to diversify production by turning to such items as washing machines and motor bicycles; they attempted also to develop a nationwide home market for a name brand product and to withdraw more and more from the export market. Small manufacturers, however, lacking the better financial resources of the larger companies and lacking the brand appeal to the nationwide home market, tended to resort to price and quality paring for quick export sales, or to promotional stunts for home sales. Small manufacturers frequently contracted with foreign purchasers at officially set rates, then gave generous rebates. They developed such devices as the "Quiz Sale." In one "Quiz Sale" persons offering correct answers to easy questions received checks valid for $27 in payment on a machine priced at about $64.

Competition was severe in the US market against European and domestic firms. Higher priced Japanese models were comparable to European machines in quality, but they constituted only a relatively small part of the total Japanese exports. Reductions in price and quality of the cheaper machines tended to bring the whole Japanese export industry under suspicion for shoddy merchandise and selling practices. The report became widespread in Japan that American manufacturers were demanding an increase in the 10 percent tariff rate on imported sewing machines and enforcement of antidumping regulations. United States imports from Japan dropped from 520,000 units in 1952 to 450,000 units in 1953.

Japanese manufacturers, large and small alike, lacked their own distribution channels abroad and had not engaged in overseas promotional campaigns which might have helped sustain prices and quality. Whereas in 1950 Japanese manufacturers had maintained a standard price of $26 each for grade A sewing machine heads, they received only $20 per head in 1951. Small manufacturers had been known to accept as little as $10 per head. One manufacturer accepted $11.50 per head on an order of 50,000 for delivery to Brazil. Exports were generally in the hands of export agents rather than the manufacturers themselves, and export of unmarked machines or machine parts for imprint of the seller's own brand name had been a common practice. The situation became so alarming that on September 16, 1954 the government banned all further export to North America, pending achievement of some satisfactory means of regulation. Three months later the ban remained in effect, no satisfactory system having as yet been worked out.

As prices fell further, leading members of the Japanese industry and government authorities had become gravely alarmed by the situation, including the dangerous loss not only of markets but of prestige. Leading manufacturers, therefore, organized an export cartel early in 1954 for regulation of price and quantity of exports. According to the cartel agreement, minimum export prices were linked to quantity of sales ranging from $18 per head for from one to 99 machines f.o.b. Japan to $16 per head for more than 2,000 machines. Each maker was permitted to export according to this price scale only 70 percent of his export total for the previous year. Above this limit he received a bonus quota if he exported at prices higher than the export prices quoted in the agreement. Members of the cartel, in cooperation with the government, attempted in addition to establish strict quality inspection prior to export to make sure that shoddy machines were not shipped. It proved impossible, however, to enforce the provisions of the cartel agreement. Price-cutting, rebates and export of inferior quality machines continued.

A possible but controversial solution to the industry's problems lay in trade with Communist China. Prior to the war China had been a major market for Japanese machines. In the early 1950s Japan had received repeated feelers from Communist China regarding export to China of Japanese sewing machines. Many people felt that the China market could absorb all of Japan's excess production.

THE SINGER MANUFACTURING COMPANY
IN JAPAN

In July 1954, Singer announced it proposed to buy into the Pine Sewing Machine Company, a subsidiary of Japan Steel Company. Pine made application to the Finance Ministry for approval of a tentative contract with Singer, which included the following provisions: Pine would double its capitalization from Y10 million to Y20 million and Singer would purchase all of the new stock issue, thus acquiring a 50 percent interest in the firm. Singer would provide $70,000 for factory expansion and $250,000 in machine tools; this total of $320,000 would be repaid by Pine at the end of ten years, but during this period the obligation might be converted in part or in its entirety into capital stock. Singer would also provide Pine with certain technical assistance. Pine would pay Singer a royalty of $4.50 depending upon the type of machine for each unit produced, and the machines would be sold under the Singer trademark. The original production goal was set for 5,000 units monthly, increasing to 7,000 in five years. Pine workers would be required to sign an oath of secrecy on the know-how offered by Singer.

The proposal immediately stirred up severe opposition in the Japanese sewing machine industry and in other Japanese circles as well. Labor unions opposed the Singer plan and there were a few mass worker protests including some rioting. The Japanese Sewing Machine Industry Association submitted a petition to government agencies protesting the plan for the following reasons:

1. The tie-up would "oppress" the domestic sewing machine industry.
2. The project promised no technological benefits.
3. It promised no contribution in foreign exchange earnings.
4. It foreshadowed a serious social problem as it would affect the livelihood of numerous Japanese employed in the sewing machine industry.

It was argued that Pine's tie-up with such powerful foreign capital interests would make survival of Japanese manufacturers, particularly small manufacturers, extremely precarious; that Japanese manufacturers were already fully as advanced technologically as foreign manufacturers; that rather than bringing dollars into Japan's economy, the necessity for royalty and other payments would drain dollars out; that the whole industry was suffering from manufacturing and employment problems which Singer's entry would aggravate, not ameliorate.

The industry was aware of Singer's strong competitive position. In other Asian markets Singer machines provided the Japanese with their toughest competition. Singer intended to sell machines in Japan at low prices and on an easy installment plan. Some Japanese manufacturers had announced plans for installment selling but none had as yet been put into effect.

Reactions of Japanese government authorities, as reported by the press, were that an investment such as that proposed by Singer was primarily for production of Japanese consumer goods which would lead to further inflation of the Japanese economy and that foreign investment would be looked upon with favor when it improved Japan's foreign exchange position. Japanese government authorities were further quoted as disapproving the "oath of secrecy" regarding Singer know-how, the exclusive marketing privileges conferred upon Singer, and the alleged effort of Pine Sewing Machine Company to solve its own financial difficulties by tying in with a foreign firm to the obvious detriment of its Japanese competitors. Japanese government authorities were reported as having been troubled by the prospect that Singer, if its tie-in with Pine were disapproved, would come to an agreement with some other Asian manufacturer, and thus confront Japan with a formidable Asian rival. This last possibility was not considered too likely since only in Japan, and nowhere else in Asia, was there a sewing machine industry sufficiently developed for tie-in with Singer to be possible.

In response to the criticism Pine argued that the Japanese industry was maintaining itself only by accepting "calamity prices" on its exports, that introduction of Singer techniques would reduce costs and thus make profit possible once again. It argued further that the Singer trademark carried such prestige that exports would automatically increase, not only to the United States but to the rest of the world. It was anticipated that most of Pine's increased output would be sold in export.

If the Japanese government did not approve the Pine proposal, Singer could either withdraw or go ahead without validation of the two agreements involved in the arrangement. The investment agreement covered the capital investment (equity and debt) with provisions for dividends, interest and repayment. The licensing agreement covered the royalties to be paid to Singer. Both agreements had to be validated by the government if foreign exchange were to be obtained for payments to Singer.

The Chrysler-Mitsubishi Automobile Joint Venture

In 1971 the government of Japan gave its approval to the joint venture formed by Chrysler Corporation and Mitsubishi Heavy Industries to develop various aspects of the global automobile business of the two firms. Although the agreement had contemplated eventual 65 percent ownership by Mitsubishi and 35 percent by Chrysler, the latter had taken up only a 15 percent interest by 1976 and other elements of the collaboration were subject to continuing evolution according to changing interests of the parent firms.

BACKGROUND

The Chrysler-Mitsubishi agreement emerged as a major element in the progress of Japan toward a more open posture in international economic relations. Other nations were challenging the reasons for restrictions on imports and foreign direct investment: the unstable balance of payments situation, the scarcity of natural resources, the need for reorganization of Japanese companies to prepare them for more effective international competition and the weak position of a vast range of small and medium size industries. An important element underlying the reluctance of the Japanese was a basic fear of disruption of the carefully managed Japanese society—particularly the harmony between business and government—through the unrestricted presence of foreign companies which might neither understand nor wish to work harmoniously within the Japanese system.

Prepared by Prof. John Fayerweather, New York University, on the basis of an earlier case by Prof. Ashok Kapoor and Masaru Sakuma in A. Kapoor, *Planning for International Business Negotiations.* Ballinger, 1975, supplemented by information from the companies.

Japan was anxious to receive greater recognition in the global economic system. In July 1967 the government of Japan announced a program with the aim of decontrolling investments in most industries by March 1972. The Foreign Investment Council, responsible for implementing the program, recognized several advantages and disadvantages. The advantages included: (1) introduction of superior foreign *technology* to raise Japan's technology level; (2) promotion of economic efficiency through *competition*; and (3) rationalization and modernization of Japanese industrial operations through modern managerial techniques. The disadvantages included: (1) *domination* of firms or industries by foreigners with technological and/or financial strength; (2) retardation of Japan's *R&D* growth by foreign countries using centralized R&D of their home country; (3) stimulation of *industrial strife* among many small Japanese companies forced by excessive competition; and (4) disruption of long-term structural policies and short-term economic adjustment policies if foreign capital refused to *cooperate with the GOJ*.

The July 1967 announcement was viewed as the first step in the liberalization program, but there were significant differences of interpretation of the term "liberalization" between the Japanese and the foreigners. To the foreigner, liberalization meant a rapid opening of the Japanese economy consistent with the policies and practices of other major industrial countries. To the Japanese it meant a very gradual pace of opening the Japanese economy to foreign investment with the extent, terms and areas of investment determined by the GOJ. They planned to liberalize only those industries in which the Japanese possessed a competitive edge over foreign capital. The automobile industry was regarded as one of the key industries whose liberalization in the early phase of the program would be detrimental to Japan's economic and national interests.

The US auto industry was very critical of this exclusion of automobiles from Japan's new capital program. Japan's exports to the US were not discriminated against by the US Government. The GOJ engaged in many non-tariff barriers to the import and sale of US cars in Japan. The US auto industry made strong representations to the US Government to demand changes from the GOJ and the US Government placed pressure on the GOJ for liberalization of the auto industry.

In response to these pressures, the GOJ announced in October 1969 that foreign investments in the Japanese automobile industry would be liberalized. The policy announcement consisted of the following points: (1) direct investments by foreigners in the manufacture of automobiles and parts and sales of cars would be liberalized as of October 1971; (2) only newly established joint ventures (those which did not utilize existing manufacturing facilities in Japan) would be approved; and (3) foreign ownership would be limited to 50 percent.

Japan's auto industry was understandably concerned about this program. They felt that a rapid pace of liberalization would prevent them from achieving effective reorganization and strength. One particular fear they had was that smaller automobile companies in Japan would seek to grow through collaboration with foreign companies. The essential argument of the industry and of the Ministry of International Trade and Industry (MITI) was that the Japanese industry, despite ranking second to the US in terms of total production, was not strong enough to compete with the American big three—GM, Ford and Chrysler.

Japanese companies were considerably smaller than US companies. The sales of the top company, Toyota, were one-quarter of those of Chrysler in 1968. Nissan was similar to Toyota but the remaining ten firms were much smaller. Another aspect of concern to the Japanese auto industry was their weak position in terms of research and development activity. Despite size and R&D status, Japanese companies were well placed to produce passenger cars at competitive prices because of efficient (though small) production facilities coupled with relatively inexpensive labor costs.

The Japanese automobile industry recognized the inevitability of liberalization. Therefore, when the GOJ announced its plan to decontrol foreign capital investments in the auto industry, the industry did not publicly show surprise or panic. In private, however, the industry was concerned because it believed that the GOJ's announced plan of liberalization would eventually lead to 100 percent foreign ownership, free investments in kind, and a limitless acquisition of stocks in existing automobile manufacturers—investment terms which the American companies had been persistently demanding through formal and informal channels. The takeover of existing auto companies would be rather easy in Japan, for the stock was publicly traded. This Japanese fear was reinforced by a number of takeovers previously achieved by American companies in Europe: French Simca, British Rootes and Spanish Barreiros by Chrysler Corporation and minority holdings by Ford in Britain and Germany.

MITI being responsible for the development of key industries in Japan was more Japan-oriented than was the Ministry of Finance which could adopt a more international outlook. The Japan Automobile Manufacturers Association (JAMA) issued a special statement at a meeting in Hakone in July 1968 declaring the unity of national auto capital and stating its opposition to an early liberalization policy in the industry.

MITI then devised a plan for liberalization of the auto industry. The essential component of MITI's plan was to seek mergers between Japanese companies which would enhance their financial, technical and production strengths. MITI had planned to liberalize foreign capital investments in Japan's auto industry only after the reorganization was completed, that is, when no Japanese automobile manufacturer remained which might want to approach foreign capital for assistance. In effect, this meant the formation of two giant groups, one centered around Toyota and the other around Nissan.

The Mitsubishi group of companies was a powerful one and had a long tradition of working closely with the GOJ. The immense size of the group was highlighted by a few facts. It was composed of 47 companies whose total sales in

1969 were $19.5 billion (vs. $7.4 billion for Chrysler), whose aggregate assets were $15 billion (vs. $4.4 billion for Chrysler), and whose group employed 349,000 (vs. 231,000 for Chrysler). Mitsubishi had a long history of involvement in the automobile industry starting with the manufacture of the Mitsubishi Model A in 1917, the first passenger car produced in Japan. However, the requirements of the military authorities, coupled with the lack of a significant domestic market, removed Mitsubishi from the passenger car area. But the experience and know-how acquired in producing various items for the armed services—e.g., engines, trucks—were to prove beneficial for the company's reentry into automobiles.

Makita, the president of Mitsubishi Heavy Industries at the time of negotiations with Chrysler, was largely responsible for development of Mitsubishi's auto division. He was experienced in establishing joint ventures and licensing agreements with companies such as Westinghouse and Caterpillar and stressed the benefits of US technological, management and marketing know-how. The automobile industry was important to Mitsubishi. In 1969 the sales of Mitsubishi's Automobile Division accounted for almost 34 percent of the total sales of the company. The remaining areas of sales included machinery (33%), shipbuilding (29%), prime movers (10%) and aircraft (4%). Mitsubishi made a heavy commitment to the automobile industry for two reasons. First, the automobile market had grown rapidly in the previous decade as a result of the development of a loan finance system. Second, Mitsubishi wanted to diversify the product mix to include more products for the mass market at home and abroad. Mitsubishi, however, recognized its weakness in international marketing. Hence, it was convinced of the need for a joint venture with an established foreign company. It was strongly against the MITI policy of reorganizing the automobile industry into two giant groups. Unlike smaller firms, Mitsubishi could not be subordinate to either Toyota or Nissan because it meant admitting defeat for the automobile division. Kono, Chairman of Mitsubishi Heavy Industries, stated, "For Mitsubishi to survive in the auto industry, there is no way but tying up with foreign capital."

Mitsubishi realized that there would be strong objections to a joint venture with a foreign company. The decision to seek a foreign firm raised two implications for Mitsubishi: (1) the most senior levels of the Liberal Democratic Party would have to be approached, as they would be more receptive to the positive aspects of a joint venture and (2) the foreign company would need to strongly encourage its government to make increasingly firm and specific demands on the GOJ for concrete evidence of capital liberalization. This joint venture would be a test case for the GOJ's intent to liberalize trade.

On the American side the main factors in the situation were the US Government, the automobile industry and Chrysler Corporation. All three were quite interested in benefiting from Japan's trade liberalization. Chrysler's interests were distinct from General Motors (GM) and Ford in key respects. The sub-compact car had been introduced by GM and Ford, but in 1968 Chrysler lacked this important product category. Unlike Chrysler, Ford and GM had a long history of pre-World War II operations in Japan. In 1925, Ford established a 100 percent-owned company for assembly operations which was followed by GM's assembly operations in Osaka in 1927. In 1929 Ford and GM assembled 29,383 units compared to 437 assembled by Japanese automobile companies. Before the war Ford had sought to establish a joint venture with Toyota and then with Mitsubishi. The Japanese military command, however, rejected the proposals. GM, on its side, had sought association with Nissan which had been rejected by the government. Both companies had made efforts to gain entry into the Japanese market through a joint venture after the war but had not been successful.

Prior to the joint venture discussions, Chrysler was in an extremely good position from almost every point of view. Its revenues and earnings were at a record high. In 1969, however, earnings fell almost 70 percent, and were at their lowest levels since 1962. For the entire year of 1969, Chrysler netted just $99 million on revenues of $7.1 billion, down from $7.4 billion in 1969. During the final quarter of that year the company had a $4,400,000 deficit, the first time it had been in the red since the third quarter of 1961.

Chrysler's international operations were smaller than those of Ford and GM. Outside the US and Canada, Chrysler accounted for 21 percent of the car sales by American companies, compared with 40 percent for GM and 39 percent for Ford. Considering the great potential of the growing foreign market for motor vehicles, Chrysler realized that its international operations would have to be greatly expanded. Chairman Lynn Townsend had persuaded the company to buy a 25 percent share of Simca in France in 1958. Subsequently it increased its Simca holding to a majority and also bought an interest in Rootes Motor Ltd. of Great Britain. As of 1969, Chrysler had plants in eighteen foreign countries.

Chrysler's total investment abroad amounted to $500,800,000 at the end of 1969, the bulk of it in three European companies: Simca—77 percent, Rootes—74 percent, and Barreiros Diesel S.A. of Spain—86 percent. In 1969 Chrysler's net from overseas operations came to $19 million, a return of 3.8 percent on investment, and a margin of only 1.2 percent on revenues of $1.6 billion.

Chrysler was attracted to Mitsubishi for four key reasons: (1) Japan was the only market that had not been previously invaded by GM and Ford; (2) Mitsubishi was one of the leading heavy industry companies in all fields. Thus it would be beneficial for Chrysler to tie up with Mitsubishi in case it wanted to enter into any other heavy industry field beside that of the auto industry; (3) Chrysler would be able to compensate for some of its weaknesses, for example, in truck production, one of Mitsubishi's strong areas; and (4) Chrysler wanted to obtain a share of the small car market by importing Mitsubishi cars to the United States.

Mitsubishi was strongly inclined toward choosing Chrysler as its joint venture partner for several reasons: (1) Chrysler had an excellent reputation for both management and technological skills; (2) Chrysler could compensate for Mitsubishi's weakness in worldwide passenger car production (while complementing Chrysler's weakness in the truck production area); (3) Chrysler appeared to be more flexible in terms of ownership. It would accept a 20 to 30 percent basis while Ford sought a 50:50 split and GM insisted upon 100 percent ownership of subsidiaries; (4) Chrysler could not take over the joint venture as it had done in France and Spain because none of the joint venture shares would be available on the market; and (5) most important, Chrysler could provide an international marketing network.

THE NEGOTIATIONS

Two stages of negotiation were involved: the agreement between Mitsubishi and Chrysler and the approval of the proposed joint venture by the GOJ. Mitsubishi conducted the negotiations in the second stage for the two firms.

Mitsubishi-Chrysler Agreement

The first advances by Chrysler came during June 1968 when A. Newton Cole, Vice President of Chrysler International, arrived in Japan with some of his staff. They expended much effort to meet the top leaders of the Japanese business world and made the purpose of their mission (to form a joint venture) quite well known. The proposal at this stage was to establish a joint venture with a Japanese firm with Chrysler holding 20 to 30 percent of the equity of the new company. The balance of the proposal was understandably general at this stage.

During Cole's initial visit, he met with the leaders of Isuzu, Toyo Kogyo, Nissan and Mitsubishi. The first three were adverse to Cole's proposals, but Mitsubishi and Chrysler struck an accord from the beginning. They also recognized that in order to save time, they should reach a "heads type" agreement quickly between the most senior levels of management and then have lower levels negotiate the specific features. During the next nine months a series of communications, meetings, visits and policy and technical discussions convinced the parties that they could work well in a joint venture. By March 1969 everything concerning the joint venture, except the exact percentage share of equity each was to hold, was agreed upon and documented in a memo ready for the signatures of the top men of both companies. In early May 1969, Makita flew to Detroit to complete this phase.

From the very first discussion between Cole and Makita, because of the delicacy of the situation, it was decided by both sides that no information was to be disclosed. The GOJ was at this time backing the MITI's reorganization of the automobile industry, and it might not have allowed Mitsubishi to negotiate at all until the reorganization policy was effected. The other Japanese automobile companies, particularly Toyota and Nissan, would be very much against the joint venture. Mitsubishi and Chrysler combined would be formidable competition. Circles opposed to the tie-up could make negotiations infinitely more complex by leaking news to the press, making disparaging remarks which might force Mitsubishi to justify its actions by disclosing· all details of the negotiation or simply undermining Mitsubishi's position by accepting terms less beneficial to the Japanese company than Mitsubishi could or would accept. Chrysler was as anxious as Mitsubishi to keep negotiations secret because it also could be easily undercut by either Ford or GM.

Makita's visit to Detroit in May 1969 continued within this shroud of secrecy. In the negotiations the most crucial point was the capital investment share of the new company. Mitsubishi wanted 70 percent ownership and wanted Chrysler to have 30 percent. Chrysler, on the other hand, insisted that it was to have 40 percent with Mitsubishi holding 60 percent, for two reasons: first, under Japanese law, the minority shareholder has the right to prevent major changes in the objectives and scope of the enterprise if it owns more than 33 percent; second, Chrysler wanted to see how strongly Mitsubishi would react to a 40 percent ownership request which was higher than the 20 to 30 percent sought by Chrysler during Cole's exploratory visit to Japan in July 1968.

Finally, on the afternoon of May 12, just before Townsend was to go to the White House to attend a dinner at the invitation of President Nixon, both parties reached a satisfactory agreement that Mitsubishi would have 65 percent ownership and Chrysler 35 percent. Of course, it was understood that the final figure of foreign ownership would depend upon the GOJ and the MITI. The 35 percent offered Chrysler protection against major changes in the enterprise. Also, it permitted Mitsubishi to argue with the GOJ that Chrysler was significantly below the 50 percent ownership level allowed by the capital liberalization policy.

An agreement on May 12 between the two companies was important. Both companies were keenly aware of the opposition likely in Japan once the joint venture plans were announced. The favorable activation of the GOJ would be best achieved through representations by the US Government which might present the proposed Mitsubishi-Chrysler venture as a test case of the true intent of the GOJ in the capital liberalization program. Townsend's dinner invitation to the White House would offer a unique opportunity to present the essential features of the proposed venture and secure US Government support at the highest levels of the government.

The specific terms of the initial agreement, in addition to the equity division, were along the following lines:

1. International operation. Both companies agreed to develop their international operations by cooperating in overseas markets and through mutual usage of existing marketing networks.
2. Exporting to the US market. Chrysler would import the Mitsubishi Galant which would be sold through the Dodge network.

3. Exporting to overseas markets. The Mitsubishi Galant would be exported to overseas markets, except for the US and Canada, through the existing sales networks of both companies.

Various technical problems involved in automobile production, such as production control, assembly control, etc. and financial, legal and other areas of joint venture operations were discussed.

Negotiations with GOJ

It was decided that Mitsubishi should conduct all negotiations for approval of the joint venture with the government of Japan and make public statements in Japan. The negotiations were set in motion when the first public disclosure was made by Makita at a press conference at Tokyo International Airport on May 18, 1969. He set forth the key elements of equity division and operating arrangements. Chrysler opened offices at the Mitsubishi headquarters in Tokyo in May 1969. The initial staff included specialists in marketing, finance and engineering.

The central theme of Mitsubishi's strategy to gain approval of the GOJ was present in subsequent public statements. The proposed joint venture with Chrysler was consistent with and in fact would promote the objectives of the automobile capital liberalization program announced by MITI. Of course, Makita was silent concerning the key objective of MITI which was not to involve foreign companies at this stage of development of the automobile industry. However, MITI could not state this objective publicly because of strong criticisms which would follow, particularly from the US Government.

The more significant level of negotiations for securing GOJ approval was the private level where the major objections of MITI would be discussed. In the Japanese system this informal process of exploration with government officials is far more important than the formal application which, in fact, often serves as the concluding, rather than initiating stage of negotiation. A major element in MHI's strategy was to seek support at the highest levels of the GOJ. The top Mitsubishi executives had good connections with senior members of the Liberal Democratic Party and the Cabinet. Because of the attitudes of the *Zaibatsu*, men at this level would be more receptive to the joint venture than MITI.

Makita's May 18 public announcement had a great impact upon both Japanese government and business circles. The crucial point was that it infringed upon the government policy which prohibited joint ventures with an existing Japanese auto company. MITI was particularly agitated. It was open defiance, and it could destroy MITI's plan by providing the auto industry with a precedent for bringing in foreign capital. The first official reaction was that of H. Yoshimitsu, Director of the Heavy Industry Bureau of MITI. This Bureau was in charge of executing the governmental plan to develop the auto industry and was in a position to examine and decide upon all applications for foreign investments.

At a press conference Yoshimitsu stated that the government would make its decision on the Mitsubishi-Chrysler joint venture in time for the forthcoming ministerial talks because there were various questions confronting the industrial reorganizations of the auto industry. He denied that there was any possibility for an immediate approval of the joint venture plan.

In contrast to the negative position taken by Yoshimitsu, several members of MITI seemed to be in favor of the Mitsubishi-Chrysler tie-up. An influential MITI source outside the Heavy Industry Bureau, for example, said that in the announced joint venture plans, the Japanese side would have a larger share of the capital, and that Japan should take advantage of the joint venture because it gave the auto industry the means of liberalizing foreign investment in a way which would be favorable to Japan.

The formal position of the government was given by Kumagai, Deputy Minister of MITI. He mentioned that the project would have great influence on those Japanese industries facing liberalization. MITI would therefore have to give very serious thought to granting permission. On May 21, Ohira, Minister of MITI, made a formal statement about the Mitsubishi-Chrysler project at a press conference. He said the government would not change its fundamental policy of developing the auto industry into two factions, but that the liberalization date would be moved ahead. The GOJ said it was interested also in learning the opinions of Isuzu (with whom Mitsubishi had been pursuing a joint venture discussion prior to Chrysler's interest).

The orientation of Ohira's statement was political. His more sophisticated attitude toward the possible implications and benefits of the project was affected by the overall point of view placing prime emphasis on the international implications involved. He said that MITI would consider the Mitsubishi-Chrysler project not as a Mitsubishi problem alone, but rather as the problem of Japan's auto industry in an international context. The reaction of the various Cabinet ministers was even more open-minded. Prime Minister Sato had stated in the Cabinet meeting of May 20 that as far as the liberalization of foreign capital was concerned, each Bureau concerned should be flexible in its considerations. These and other comments showed that there was no single viewpoint within MITI on the Mitsubishi-Chrysler joint venture, with negative reactions stronger at the lower level.

Japan's big business community, the *Zaibatsu*, was in favor of the Mitsubishi-Chrysler tie-up, because it foresaw obstacles to future international business if Japan continued to close her market to foreign capital, and it feared increasing protectionist sentiment in the United States. The proposal had quite an impact on the leaders of Japan's auto industry. This move reduced the power of the Japan Automobile Manufacturers' Association as some of its members started to doubt the ability of the association to control the course of events in the industry.

The proposed joint venture talks between Mitsubishi and Isuzu mentioned above had progressed to a mutual use of dealer networks and a mutual purchase of assembly parts. Mitsubishi had not given Isuzu any prior notice about the Chrysler agreement. Hence, the day after the public disclosure, Isuzu canceled the proposed Mitsubishi-Isuzu tie-up.

The US Government welcomed the Mitsubishi-Chrysler joint venture project because it thought it might pave the way for a speedier liberalization of the foreign investment policies in the Japanese auto industry. However, a note of criticism and growing pressure on the GOJ was present in the comments of some US government officials. They noted that the relatively small percentage of stock Chrysler was to hold in the joint venture could hardly satisfy US businessmen and that they would urge the US Government to press Japan for a freer inflow of capital.

GOVERNMENT APPROVAL AND THE
FINAL AGREEMENT

On June 11, about three weeks after Makita's announcement of the proposed joint venture, MITI's attitude toward the liberalization schedule changed to a more favorable one. Ohira announced that the government liberalization schedule for the auto industry would be considered for revision in the fall. Then, on August 14, the Auto Industry Committee of the Liberal Democratic Party held a meeting to which it invited Sato, executive vice-president of Mitsubishi Heavy Industries, in order to question him regarding the Mitsubishi-Chrysler project. The committee members exchanged views with each other as to what policy they should take towards the proposed joint venture.

The forthcoming summit meeting between Prime Minister Sato and President Nixon influenced the speed and manner in which the joint venture would be considered by the GOJ. The GOJ realized that an important area of discussion between the two leaders would deal with economic relations of the two countries. The US Government would press Japan for a more rapid and a wider range of capital liberalization. It was more than likely that the Mitsubishi-Chrysler joint venture would be raised as one of the specific examples. Broader and more explosive issues were on the scene. The US-Japan Treaty of Mutual Cooperation and security was to be renewed in 1970. The renewal in 1960 had resulted in riots and downfall of the government at the time. The time of the summit established some sort of a deadline by which the GOJ would need to emerge with a statement on its intentions behind capital liberalization in a general sense and in the specific context of the Mitsubishi-Chrysler joint venture.

The foregoing considerations also had implications for the speed with which Mitsubishi and Chrysler should present a formal proposal. For one thing, some members of MITI continued to have a negative reaction to the proposed joint venture. Under these circumstances, Mitsubishi did not feel that it should push the government any harder than it already had. The Heavy Industry Bureau, which was responsible for the auto industry, had been preoccupied with the merger creating the Nippon Steel Corporation. Mitsubishi decided that the filing of the application to the government should be put off until after the Prime Minister's return from his visit to the US in November. Mitsubishi expected that there might be considerable change in government policy after Sato's return.

While Chrysler had access to the highest levels of the US Government, it could only hope and encourage the government officials to impress upon the GOJ the need for favorable and speedy action on the joint venture. But, in the changing context of international relations, it was possible that the US Government might not single out the venture for favorable treatment. Therefore, one specific thing which Chrysler had to promote was favorable support of the US Government. Eventually, the US Government played a decisive role in pushing the Japanese Government to a decision. On October 10, Trezise, Assistant US Secretary of State, visited Ohira to discuss the Japanese liberalization program at the MITI offices. Tresize had been briefed by Chrysler executives in Tokyo prior to his meeting with Ohira. Tresize said that the US had a keen interest in the liberalization of certain items and dates. He added that as far as the liberalization schedule of the Japanese auto industry was concerned, it was difficult for the US to understand the reasons behind the Japanese Government's policy. In addition, he requested that the Japanese Government consider the collaboration between Japanese and US car makers in a more positive light. He also asked for Ohira's special consideration in reviewing the Mitsubishi-Chrysler case. To the request of the US Government, Ohira replied that (1) the liberalization date would be announced within a few weeks, and that (2) the application for the Mitsubishi-Chrysler joint venture project would be examined right away, even if the application were filed before the liberalization date.

On October 14 the GOJ announced that the liberalization of the auto industry would be effective in October 1971, half a year earlier than the previous date set for liberalization. As expected by Mitsubishi, Prime Minister Sato was placed under severe pressure by US companies during his visit to the US. The Emergency Committee for American Trade (ECAT) was one of the business groups which made a number of demands on Sato regarding the liberalization of the auto industry. The terms of these demands were basically that (1) the liberalization schedule for the auto industry should be set ahead, from October 1971 to October 1970, and that (2) the restriction of 50 percent maximum foreign ownership in a joint venture should be abandoned. With this sort of pressure put on the Prime Minister, Mitsubishi felt that he would be encouraged to accelerate the liberalization date.

At the board of directors' meeting of MHI on October 28, the joint venture was approved. At this stage the project provided for establishment of (1) an export and import company to (a) export the Mitsubishi Galant, now called the Colt, to the US and sell it through the Chrysler network, and (b) import parts for the Chrysler Valiant for assembly in Mitsubishi factories. Chrysler cars would be sold through the Mitsubishi network in Japan; (2) an auto production company.

The scope of the joint venture was being negotiated at this time by Makita and the most senior levels of Chrysler in Detroit. One key consideration for both companies was to include dimensions in the project which would be particularly appealing to the MITI in order to gain approval and to compensate in some way for violating certain aspects of the MITI's policy on capital liberalization in the automobile industry. As a result of high level discussions in Detroit, Makita announced that all types of Mitsubishi's auto products, including cars, trucks and buses, would be manufactured in Chrysler's overseas factories and would be sold through Chrysler's overseas sales network. As the first step in this cooperative effort, 5,000 Mitsubishi Colt cars and light trucks would be manufactured annually in Chrysler's factory in South Africa.

This announcement pleased MITI as it would lead to exports of a range of Japanese automobiles. Also, the sharing of Chrysler's international production facilities would result in offering Mitsubishi access to markets which could not be reached through exports. Additionally, it would provide Mitsubishi experience in international production which would prove useful as Japanese companies undertook foreign direct investments.

Mitsubishi decided that it would not file the application in the current year but would postpone the filing until a new Cabinet was elected in December 1969. It was expected that after the election at the end of the year some Cabinet members would be shuffled, and at that time the Mitsubishi-Chrysler project would be considered in a more favorable light. Mitsubishi had reason to believe that Miyazawa would become the new Minister of the MITI. He possessed a greater international orientation than was true of Ohira and would not be bound by the policies for reorganization of the automobile industry developed under his predecessor. The decision to postpone the formal application was based on informal discussions by Mitsubishi with the leading members of the LDP, the *zaikai* and other political contacts who were in a position to know the developments within the inner circles of the GOJ.

On February 15, 1970 Mitsubishi and Chrysler reached final agreement on the terms of the joint venture. The companies revised their original idea of establishing two joint venture companies and decided instead only to form the auto production company. The export and import company was not established because the companies decided to export the Colt through the present Chrysler organizational network. The outline of the final agreement was as follows:

1. Mitsubishi would separate its automobile division and establish Mitsubishi Motor Company (MMC).

2. The joint venture's capital would be increased to $125,000,000 upon approval of the Japanese government, the additional sum representing the amount added by Chrysler, which was its allotted capital share.

3. The joint venture would have 20 members on the board of directors,

thirteen representing Mitsubishi and seven representing Chrysler. Those directors sent by Chrysler would not have the right to represent the company; for example, they could not sign binding contracts.

4. The joint venture company would carry on sales activities for the Mitsubishi Colt through Chrysler's worldwide network, and would do assembly work for Chrysler's compact car, the Valiant, in Japan.

5. The joint venture would do research and development work on new cars.

6. Financial and management control would be with Mitsubishi.

While all this was being decided, a new Cabinet had been formed with Miyazawa replacing Ohira as the Minister of the MITI. On March 18, 1970 Townsend, Chairman of Chrysler, visited Japan to meet with Prime Minister Sato and Miyazawa. On the same day he held a press conference jointly with Makita, and he expressed his desire that the Mitsubishi-Chrysler project would be considered and approved before October 1971. He added that the filing date would be left to Mitsubishi's judgment. When asked about his meeting with Prime Minister Sato and Miyazawa, Townsend said that both men seemed favorably inclined toward the proposed tie-up.

On March 30 Miyazawa told the Finance Committee in the Diet that as far as the Mitsubishi-Chrysler project was concerned, the government would accept the application and take all action necessary for its approval, provided that the project would be effected according to government policy, and that it did not harm the national interest in any way. He added that this would be done even if the application were filed before the liberalization date of October 1971.

On June 1, 1970 the Mitsubishi Motor Corporation was formed by the separation of the automobile division from the other manufacturing sectors of Mitsubishi Heavy Industries. On February 22, 1971 Makita and Sato, President of Mitsubishi Automobile Corporation, stated in a press conference that Chrysler's investment in the joint venture company would be a 15 percent capital ratio at the formation of the company. Chrysler's investment would be increased to 25 percent in 1973, and would finally reach 35 percent in 1974. Chrysler's members of the board of directors in the joint venture company would increase gradually in compliance with the amount of investment, to three in 1971, five in 1972, and seven in 1973.

Miyazawa stated that MITI would try its best to approve the tie-up project as soon as possible after April 1, 1971, the liberalization date set for the auto industry, which was six months earlier than that originally planned. The reason that Mitsubishi and Chrysler decided to change their capital ratios at this point was that (1) because of the financial difficulties Chrysler decided to make a smaller investment at the time, and (2) the smaller ownership ratio for the foreign company would make it easier to get MITI's approval. By this point the joint venture was being viewed as a desirable precedent from MITI's standpoint for negotiations with other foreign automobile companies seeking to establish joint ventures in Japan. MITI recognized that other companies would seek investments in Japan. The Japanese would have to accept them. The major question was of the terms and conditions which would be acceptable to the Japanese and yet satisfy, at least in the beginning, the foreign companies. The Mitsubishi-Chrysler joint venture possessed characteristics which would be favorable precedents in the new international context faced by the Japanese. The joint venture placed managerial or financial control clearly in the hands of the Japanese company.

Ford was negotiating with Toyo Kogyo for a 25 to 75 percent ownership split, while GM was seeking a 35 to 65 percent arrangement with Isuzu. The shares of Isuzu and Toyo Kogyo were both sold in the open market. The fear of foreign control was a critical feature of these negotiations. In fact, Henry Ford II visited Japan in March 1971 to assure Prime Minister Sato and Miyazawa that the final agreement with Toyo-Kogyo would clearly stipulate that Ford would not attempt to take over the joint venture or Toyo Kogyo.

On April 1, 1971 the automobile industry was liberalized, resulting in removing some of the formal protections from international competition it had enjoyed in the past. However, informal and administrative forms of protection would remain for some time to come. In contrast to the purely Japanese orientation visualized by MITI under Ohira, by April 1971 the GOJ's thinking was that the Japanese automobile industry would be organized into two categories—pure Japanese (Toyota, Nissan, Honda), and joint ventures (Mitsubishi-Chrysler, Ford-Toyo-Kogyo, GM-Isuzu).

Shortly thereafter the joint venture between General Motors and Isuzu was finalized with GM purchasing 34.2 percent of the equity in Isuzu. The main product line was light pickup trucks, but with GM's help, Isuzu planned to enter the small car field soon. The proposed Ford-Toyo-Kogyo venture was never finalized because the Toyo-Kogyo rotary engine Mazda proved an overnight success and convinced the Japanese manufacturer that it needed no foreign partner. The Japanese, however, expected Ford to continue seeking a local partner with Honda the most likely candidate. This would give Ford access to Honda's CVCC (compound vortex controlled combustion) engine and it would give Honda an overseas outlet for its four-wheeled vehicles.

On May 1, 1973 the auto industry became fully liberalized as the GOJ put into effect a trade liberalization program that permitted 100 percent foreign direct investment in both new and existing companies, with some significant exceptions.

EVOLUTION OF THE JOINT VENTURE

Shortly after the final Chrysler-Mitsubishi agreement was approved in 1971, the companies agreed that Chrysler's participation would continue at 15 percent rather than rising to the 35 percent initially contemplated. Two factors supported this decision from Chrysler's point of view. First, changes in the exchange rate had substantially altered the price relationships which had previously been strongly favorable to exports from Japan to the United States. Thus the importance of MMC as a production base for Chrysler had decreased, temporarily at any rate. Second, the company was not looking for new investment locations because of strains in its financial position. This factor increased in importance in subsequent years. By 1975, in fact, Chrysler was seriously considering divestment of units which could not contribute to its profits. Possible disposal of its complete UK operation had been averted only by major support by the British Government agreed to in late 1975.

Despite its disinclination to invest further in MMC, Chrysler on the whole felt that the arrangement had been worthwhile thus far. The company had received no dividends on its investment as MMC was operating very close to the breakeven level. This condition was due to the relatively depressed state of the Japanese auto market domestically and the low market share achieved by MMC. When the Chrysler-Mitsubishi joint venture began in 1970, it had a production capacity of 400,000 vehicles/year and had jumped into third place behind Toyota and Nissan. However, its share of the Japanese auto market had steadily declined in subsequent years, totaling only 8.5 percent of the market for 1972. Subsequent market share data appear in Exhibit 1.

The value of the arrangement for Chrysler, however, lay in the availability of MMC as a source of small cars and trucks for a variety of markets around the world. For its part, MMC valued the arrangement with Chrysler because its marketing system took about 50 percent of its car production, about 25 percent of the total MMC output.

Exhibit 1. 1973 Production and 1974 Plans of Japanese Auto Companies (1000 units)

	Production		*Domestic Sales*		*Exports*	
	1974	*1973*	*1974*	*1973*	*1974*	*1973*
Toyota Motor	2300	2308	1500	1565	800	721
Nissan Motor	2000	2039	1200	1283	800	711
Toyo Kogyo	800	739	400	398	400	344
Mitsubishi	560	563	460	445	100	91
Honda Motor	450	355	300	298	150	74
Daihatsu Kogyo	310	307	300	293	10	9
Suzuki Motor	260	244	250	235	10	4
Fuji Heavy Ind.	230	208	150	163	80	43
Isuzu Motors	220	218	140	149	80	60
Hino Motors	76	77	60	69	16	8
Nissan Diesel	25	24	20	23	5	2
Imports	–	–	30	32	–	–
Total	7231	7082	4810	4954	2451	2068

The MMC automobile line consisted of five basic models as follows: The Debonair was a luxury car sold in relatively limited volume to upper class customers. The Colt fell roughly in the size range of US subcompact cars and was produced in two-door, four-door and station wagon models. The Lancer was a somewhat smaller variation of the Colt, sold also in two-door, four-door and station wagon form. The Celeste, a new model introduced in 1975, was roughly similar in size to the Lancer but made only in a two-door hatchback model. The Minica was a smaller model of a type not sold in North American markets. In addition MMC produced a range of small and large trucks and some buses and special vehicles. The company had four large factory complexes employing some 22,000 people. It also had a substantial center for research, development and testing. Its models were held basically constant through the early 70s but improvements within them were being made regularly. Most significant in the automobile line was the introduction in 1975 of the silent shaft engine. Four cylinder engines are inherently prone to vibration and noise. MMC developed a new system of drive shaft alignment and position which resulted in significant reduction in vibration and noise. This "silent shaft" engine was demonstrated to a group of US automotive editors and other experts in mid-1975 and received very favorable reactions. It was to be offered as a two-liter option to the standard 1.6 liter engine in MMC cars sold in the US for $231 extra.

Chrysler drew on MMC substantially as a source for subcompact cars for which it did not have production within the United States. It had recently introduced the Chrysler 1307/1308 in Europe. It was not immediately contemplated that it would be imported into the United States. The market response had been excellent, so that full production capacity from the French Simca 1307/1308 was being absorbed in the European market. It was also to be made in the UK plant under the new program for that operation. The 1307/1308 had a front-end drive car and thus not directly comparable to those available from Japan. In 1975 Chrysler announced its intention to produce a four-cylinder car in the US, but it would not be avaliable until 1978. It would be similar in some respects to the 1307/1308. The US model would be slightly smaller than the Celeste and differ also in being front-wheel drive, so it was anticipated that there could be an adequate market for both. An arrangement was completed in 1976 to purchase engines and axle-transmissions for it from Volkswagen to save on costs and get into production sooner.

International sales of MMC products were handled by either Chrysler or MMC according to a division of areas agreed to by the companies. Chrysler handled all sales in North America, most other countries in which it had factories and certain other areas. MMC handled Southeast Asia. Initially Europe had been reserved for Chrysler but recently portions of it had been opened up to MMC including Benelux and the United Kingdom into which MMC imported in a joint venture arrangement with another Japanese firm. All of the MMC exports were of completely builtup (BU) vehicles except that portions of the shipments to

Australia, South Africa, the Philippines and New Zealand were of knockdown (KD) units for assembly. In some cases the KD units were incomplete to provide more locally procured content. The distribution of MMC exports by models is shown in Exhibit 2.

The major market for MMC products was the United States which absorbed about half of all export sales. These vehicles were all brought in BU. The US tariff structure provided no advantage for imports of parts as compared to complete vehicles. The transportation advantages of shipping KD vehicles were not sufficient to justify the cost of assembly in the United States, especially as wages were still lower in Japan than in the United States. Initially imports were limited to the MMC Colt which was sold through the Dodge distribution organization in the United States and through both Dodge and Plymouth dealers in Canada. The Plymouth portion in Canada was sold under the name Cricket with variations in the grill to distinguish it from the Dodge Colt. The Canadian Plymouth organization had previously sold a British Chrysler model also called the Cricket. The acceptance of this model was disappointing but the organization liked the name so the Colt variation was brought in to substitute for the British line. MMC was very anxious to broaden its distribution base in the United States, and after some period of negotiation the MMC Celeste was introduced early in 1976 for sale through the Plymouth distribution system using the name Arrow, thus roughly doubling MMC product outlets in the United States.

The next largest country for MMC exports was Australia. Japanese auto sales in Australia had been highly successful in the early 1970s. For some time Australia had had local content regulations which required that all firms assemble cars with considerable local procurement within the country. Regulations required 60 percent local content but the main US vehicles (Chrysler Valiant, GM Holden and Ford) had about 95 percent. However, the demand for Japanese models had been so great that it exceeded the production capacity within Australia and import of some BU cars had been allowed. Subsequently when demand weakened in 1974-75 this relaxation was partially withdrawn and companies were allowed to bring in BU vehicles only to the extent that BUs would not exceed 20 percent of industry volume.

Chrysler imported two MMC automobiles into Australia, the Colt, which was locally called the Galant, and the Lancer. Together they composed about 40 percent of Chrysler's Australian sales. The Galant was the first model introduced and it was produced within the 60 percent Australian content regulations, engines, transmissions and sheet metal parts being the only imported content. The Lancer was brought in as a fully-BU vehicle at a later date in the period when the local content requirements were relaxed. With the subsequent limitation of this relaxation Chrysler was forced to restrict its imports of Lancers substantially as it had no facilities for local assembly or component procurement.

The various developments in the Australian situation led to a proposed

Exhibit 2.   Production and Sales of Mitsubishi Motor Corporation

Model by Calendar Year	Total Production	Total Exports	Sales through Chrysler System					Sales through MMC		
			United States	Canada	Australia	South Africa	Other	S.E. Asia	Europe	Other
Colt										
1972	191,281	66,430	33,213	8,698	5,664	1,485	8,418	7,249	—	1,703
1973	181,664	66,277	25,146	6,570	10,708	2,358	10,382	8,254	—	2,859
1974	168,907	119,368	64,820	10,912	17,819	3,265	13,116	6,529	1,164	1,743
Lancer										
1972	376	—	—	—	—	—	—	—	—	—
1973	82,925	4,486	—	—	—	—	769	3,663	—	54
1974	69,698	20,843	—	—	4,211	—	7,601	7,519	1,136	376
Trucks/Buses										
1972	252,675	14,301	—	—	62	1,470	1,277	10,458	139	895
1973	295,243	20,768	—	—	64	—	1,246	18,050	244	1,164
1974	256,913	37,655	—	—	406	4	2,030	31,960	487	2,768

change in part of Chrysler's production operation. Because of a shift toward purchase of smaller cars, the company's foundry and machining plant was underutilized. At the same time, Toyota and Nissan were forced by the government restrictions to use more local components. Chrysler proposed that a consortium be formed of Nissan, Toyota, Chrysler and the Australian government to take over the plant and sell its output to the firms according to their needs. In late 1975 negotiations for this arrangement were being pursued.

Chrysler started to import the Colt into South Africa under a special restricted quota arrangement as a low content vehicle (about 25 percent). In 1976 the company had under-way plans to increase local content above the regular 66 percent level to qualify as full manufacture and be free of import restrictions.

When the arrangement was reached with Mitsubishi, Chrysler sold all but 5 percent of its equity in its Philippine assembly plant to a local Philippine firm, MMC and a Japanese trading company. By mutual understanding among the investors, Chrysler also continued to provide the manager of the plant. This operation assembled imported Colts and some MMC trucks and manufactured transmissions. It also assembled some Chrysler trucks imported from the United States. The KD exports to New Zealand were purchased by an independent assembly plant in which neither MMC nor Chrysler had an investment.

The Chrysler-Mitsubishi agreement also had contemplated export of Chrysler products to Japan. This process had, however, developed only to a very small degree with volume amounting to about 1,500 units per year. These were relatively large cars whose demand was substantially based on prestige. Their owners gained status not only from their size but from their distinctive American character in being left-hand drive rather than right-hand drive as was normal to Japanese-made cars. The Chrysler cars were handled through a company representative in Japan and sold by an independent dealer system, although some of these dealers were also part of the MMC dealer organization.

Organization

Organizationally the relations between Chrysler and MMC were handled through directors, two liaison offices and some exchanges of personnel along with regular negotiations between the operating managements of the two companies. Chrysler had four directors on the MMC board. Three were resident in Japan working regularly with the operating organization in finance, product planning and sales and marketing respectively. The fourth member of the MMC board was a high level member of the Chrysler international organization resident in Adelaide, Australia where Chrysler had its Pacific area headquarters.

Chrysler maintained a liaison office in Japan. For the most part this office was concerned with the implementation of operating arrangements between the two companies such as the handling of shipments. MMC had a small office in the United States staffed by three executives. They handled a multitude of functions including the facilitation of communication between the Japanese and Americans. They were available to help in overcoming special problems which might arise. For example, in 1975 when the Celeste was to be introduced in the United States, a problem arose in getting Plymouth name plates. An MMC executive expedited their procurement and air shipment to Japan. His main concern, however, was in the area of marketing. As a regular practice he kept informed of marketing and advertising programs in the United States for MMC products and routed this information back to Japan both for possible use in other countries and for reactions which the Japanese management might wish to communicate to the US organization. He also devoted considerable time to visiting dealerships to ascertain reactions to MMC products, marketing problems and improvements which might be contemplated.

While these organizational elements facilitated communication between MMC and Chrysler, the main arrangements between the two firms were handled in direct negotiation between senior executives of each company.

Operating Arrangements

The aspects of operations in which negotiations between the Chrysler and MMC organizations were pursued included production planning, pricing, marketing and product development.

Production and procurement planning was complicated because of the difficulty of predicting sales in the cyclical automobile market and the transportation time between Japan and the United States which was up to two months longer than from US plants. Chrysler placed orders for production with MMC for output up to six months ahead. However, because of changes in sales, it frequently found it necessary to negotiate for increases or decreases in the planned schedule.

Chrysler purchased products from MMC landed at a North American port with shipping arrangements handled by MMC. The prices for the sales were negotiated once or twice a year. Since there were distinct variations in products because of the nature of markets, anti-pollution requirements and other factors, separate prices were negotiated for each product for each country of shipment. The negotiations were essentially conducted on an arm's length basis even though Chrysler had a 15 percent interest in the selling company. The Chrysler members of the MMC board were expected to function as MMC employees in this matter, not taking Chrysler's part or revealing to Chrysler any of the pricing negotiation strategy of the firm. The pricing was based primarily upon cost and competitive conditions. Because of their much greater volume, Toyota and Datsun were the price leaders in the field. With its smaller volume MMC was competitively at a disadvantage, but Chrysler had to press for prices which would permit it to compete effectively with the leading Japanese firms. Variations in the quantity ordered by Chrysler also resulted in some variations in prices.

Chrysler had full authority for all marketing decisions for MMC products. However, the company was open to proposals and ideas from MMC in marketing matters, recognizing the joint interests of the two firms in marketing effectiveness and the possible benefits of ideas from MMC in this area. Thus all merchandising, advertising and other sales programs were communicated to MMC and discussions of them held regularly by Chrysler executives with MMC personnel. The chief change in marketing resulting from discussions was the addition of the Celeste line for distribution through Plymouth organizations. Other changes in marketing had evolved over time with some inputs of MMC. At the outset Chrysler had not emphasized the Japanese origin of the Colt. Subsequently, however, as Japanese cars became well accepted in the US market, they found it advantageous to emphasize the Japanese origin in their promotion programs. While the made-in-Japan image had value in the marketplace, the sourcing point had some marketing disadvantages in Chrysler's experience. For one thing, roughly nine months were required for individually ordered cars to reach purchasers. The effect of this factor was limited by the fact that Japanese models had relatively few options so more people bought models from dealers' stock than was true of American-made cars. However, for a few buyers it was a disadvantage. Another concern was the greater number of shipping stages resulting in more damage to cars than those from domestic plants. Continuing attention was being given to attempts to minimize these problems.

As relationships between Chrysler and MMC evolved, joint product planning had received progressively more attention. The managements perceived that coordination of their product plans would be of substantial value to future success. Thus by 1975 very close integration with intimate negotiations about products for 1978 and later years was under way. Related to and somewhat supporting this process was a considerable amount of exchange at the technical level in product design and production.

CONDITIONS IN THE JAPANESE AUTO INDUSTRY

In the background of the Chrysler-Mitsubishi joint venture were general conditions in the Japanese auto industry. Japan experienced a minor recession in 1970-71, and its major suppliers (Australia, Indonesia, the Philippines) felt the impact with a drop in their exports to Japan. The same chain reaction was experienced in 1974-75 as the Japanese economy struggled with inflation, high labor settlements, steel and electric power price increases and continued material shortages. Labor costs, which for years gave Japanese manufacturers a strong competitive advantage over American producers, had been rising at an annual rate of 15 percent. The two US dollar devaluations since the formation of the Chrysler-Mitsubishi joint venture also had their effect. The oil crisis compounded Japan's economic problems because Japan was 99.7 percent dependent upon overseas supplies of crude oil which in turn produced 75 percent of Japan's energy demands.

Japan's automobile exports had grown rapidly in the late 1960s (Exhibit 3). However, by 1975 the rate of growth had diminished substantially, indicating that the potential for further expansion was limited. 1974 had been a relatively good year for exports because the yen was cheap and with business recession at home, there was an export drive and a rapid increase in demand in the Near and Middle East and some other countries. However, in 1975, with the global recession, sharp price competition and import controls in a number of countries, prospects were weak for further export expansion. The industry therefore was concerned with the prospect that the competitive status for the Japanese auto industry had reached a critical turning point with rough going expected for subsequent years.

The Japanese industry had benefited from special circumstances in its early export surge because its small cars complemented the large car output of the major firms. By the beginning of the 1970s, however, the big three had started to turn out smaller models, and sharp competition for this segment of the market developed between US, Japanese and European auto makers, encouraged by the desire to economize brought on by the energy crisis.

Exhibit 3. Exports of Major Automobile Producing Nations (In 1,000 units and percentages)

Calendar Year	Japan	U.S.	W. Germany	G. Britain	France	Italy
1965	194(10.4)	168(1.5)	1,527(51.3)	794(36.5)	638(38.9)	327(27.8)
1970	1,087(20.5)	486(5.9)	2,104(54.8)	862(41.1)	1,525(55.5)	671(36.2)
1971	1,779(30.6)	487(4.6)	2,293(57.6)	915(41.7)	1,592(52.9)	681(37.5)
1972	1,965(31.2)	624(5.5)	2,188(57.3)	767(32.9)	1,769(53.2)	700(37.7)
1973	2,067(29.2)	771(6.1)	2,348(59.4)	762	1,931(53.7)	705(36.0)
1974	2,618	868	1,881	728	1,949	734

Note: Export ratios against production given in parentheses.

Japanese Export Shares by Destinations (Percentages)

	1969	1970	1971	1972	1973	1974
N. America	39.3	45.6	53.2	51.1	44.2	43.4
Europe	10.2	11.6	12.1	18.7	19.6	14.8
Near-Middle East (Incl. Africa)	13.6	12.7	11.5	9.3	10.8	11.2
Southeast Asia	18.9	13.8	9.3	8.4	10.6	11.2
Oceania	10.0	9.0	7.4	6.3	8.8	11.2
Latin America	8.0	7.3	6.5	6.1	5.9	8.2
Total Exports (1,000 units)	858	1,087	1,779	1,965	2,068	2,618

The US market was of prime concern to the Japanese industry. Exports to the US rose rapidly and by 1971 accounted for 53 percent of Japan's exports. Subsequently the percentage declined, and there was even some absolute drop in export volume by 1973. Thus even before the oil crisis there was a marked turn in the state of Japanese automobile business in North America because of (1) the repeated revaluations of the yen in 1972-73, (2) the trade directive in the first half of 1973 requiring self-constraint in exports to the US, and (3) the shortage of automobiles for exports resulting from the overheated domestic demand in the first part of 1973. Exports recovered in 1974, but it was observed that this was substantially due to replenishing of inventories and did not reflect a substantial improvement in the basic market situation. Thus total Japanese sales in the United States which reached a peak of 760,000 units in 1973 dropped back to 600,000 in 1974. Market share data are given in Exhibit 4.

Despite the emphasis on economy in cars, the market for subcompact autos in the United States was weaker than that for compacts. The switch from larger models was largely towards compacts whose sales rose even in the recession year of 1974. At the same time it appeared that the decline in income of buyers resulted in a tendency to hold back on purchases of subcompacts in the main category of demand for that class of car, notably as second and third car purchases by middle income families. Despite efforts by the big three to maintain their competitive position in the subcompact market by foregoing price hikes in the face of two price increases in 1974 by the Japanese, the US firms suffered most from the weakness of the subcompact demand. It appeared that the US companies, which were new in this field, had not as yet developed products which could match the imports in overall performance despite having some price advantage in competition with them. The big three were, however, continuing their efforts to develop new models of even lighter weight and lower gas consumption with the expectation of introductions in the 1976-77 period which would put them in a stronger competitive relation to the Japanese models. Suffering already from a price disadvantage, the latter therefore could expect severe competition in the near future. The present price differences were indicated by the fact that the prices of the Nissan Blue Bird (engine capacity 2000 CC) and the GM Vega (2300 CC) were roughly equal in 1972 but as a result of revaluations and price increases for the Blue Bird in 1974, it cost $800 more than the Vega. Some difference was due to the US subcompacts offering as options features which were standard equipment in the Japanese cars but even allowing for this difference, the Japanese products were roughly $300 to $400 higher in price.

Higher costs in Japan were due in part to the increase in oil prices which had a greater effect there than in other countries. In 1974, for example, it was estimated that oil price increases had caused manufacturing cost rises of 9.9 percent in the US, 8 percent in West Germany and 11 percent in Japan. Further differentials were found in the higher rate of increase of cost of materials in Japan where such materials already accounted for a higher percentage of the cost

Exhibit 4.   Import Shares in the U.S.

Year	Ratio of Total Imported Cars	Import Ratio of Japanese Cars	Shares of	
			Japanese Cars	VW
1960	7.6%	0.0%	0.4%	32.1%
1965	6.1	0.3	4.5	67.4
1967	9.3	0.8	9.0	57.2
1969	11.2	2.0	17.7	53.1
1970	14.9	3.6	24.1	46.6
1971	15.1	5.7	37.6	34.7
1972	14.5	6.3	43.1	34.4
1973	15.3	6.6	42.6	27.1
1974	15.8	6.8	42.7	24.0

	U.S. Sales		Percent Change
	1975	1974	
Toyota	283,909	238,135	+19.2%
Volkswagen	267,718	334,515	−20.0
Datsun	263,192	189,026	+39.2
Honda	102,389	43,119	+137.5
Fiat	100,511	72,029	+39.5
Mazda	65,351	61,190	+6.8
Colt	60,356	42,925	+40.6
Volvo	59,408	52,167	+13.9
Capri	54,586	75,260	−27.5
Mercedes	42,093	35,294	+19.3
Subaru	41,587	22,980	+81.0
Opel	39,730	59,279	−33.0
BMW	19,419	15,007	+29.4
British Leyland*	70,839	54,161	+30.8

*Jaguar, MG, Austin, Triumph, Rover

of manufacture. In 1974 wages of auto workers were roughly one-half those in the United States, but the cost of labor was rising more rapidly, wages having gone up 20 to 30 percent a year in Japan compared to about 10 percent in the United States and Europe. The effect of these changes was moderated by the fact that personnel expenses were less than one-third of that in the case of the United States as a percent of total production (6.6 percent in 1971 as opposed to 27 percent in the case of the United States on a value-added basis). All factors considered, it was estimated that by 1976 there would be practically no gap in production costs between Japan and the United States. The Mitsubishi Research

Institute estimated production cost indexes for Japan and the United States at 145 and 141 respectively (base year 1970), with West Germany estimated at about 133.

The major advantage of the Japanese cars in 1975 was fuel economy. In the US Environmental Protection Agency ratings Japanese models held four of the top ten positions among 250 models tested. At this time Japanese cars also had an image of high product reliability, good quality, uniformity and few malfunctions. It was felt that the Japanese firms benefited from a high level of production and quality control and an outstanding labor force as compared to the type of labor currently available in European and US auto plants. They had also establshed a strong service network in their major markets.

Outside the North American and European markets, the Japanese faced a mixed picture. The best prospects lay in the oil-producing countries where the market for passenger cars and trucks was expected to expand rapidly. With manufacturers in other countries having little extra capacity to supply trucks, the Japanese were fast becoming a base for supply of those vehicles. In other countries, however, varied restrictions and problems were encountered. In the Andean area, auto policy had recently been reappraised with the result, for example, that in Peru, Toyota had replaced Nissan. In Southeast Asia it was expected that export sales would decline because of emphasis on building local assembly production. Since the Japanese auto makers had been slow to invest directly overseas, expansion of KD exports would hurt them. The location of Japanese overseas facilities are indicated in Exhibit 5 along with those of other major international firms. With the prospects for the industry as a whole uncertain there were reports that basic structural changes might be made in the smaller companies (see Exhibit 6).

Exhibit 5.   Production Activities of World's Automakers in Developing Countries

	GM (U.S.)	Ford (U.S.)	Chrysler (U.S.)	BLMC (Britain)	VW (W. Germany)	Mercedes-Benz (W. Germany)	Renault (France)	Fiat (Italy)	Toyota (Japan)	Nisson (Japan)
Australia	□	□	□	□	O		□	□	□	□
New Zealand	O	O	O	O	O			O	O	O
Brazil	●	□	●		□	□			●	
Argentina	●	●	●	O		□	□	□		
Mexico	●	●	□		□		□			●
Chile	□	□	□	□			□	□		●
Peru		●	●	□	□	□	□	□	●	●
Venezuela	●	●	●		□	□	□	□	□	□
Colombia	O	O	▲	O	O					
India				□		□		□		□
Indonesia	O		O		O	O			▲	O
Philippines	□	●	●	□	□	□	□	□	□	□
Thailand		O				O		O	▲	O
Taiwan		□								□
ROK	O	O								
Malaysia	O	▲			O	O	O	O	O	O
Singapore		O			O	O	O			▲
S. Africa	●	●	●	□	□		□	□	□	□
Rhodesia		O	O							
United Arab		▲								

□ Production   O assembly only   ● production with capital participation
▲ assembly with capital participation

Exhibit 6. Japan: The Merger Scramble to Save Car Makers

At a time when Japanese auto makers are looking forward to their best year in history, they are also bracing for a round of corporate mergers. The paradox arises because nearly 60% of the market—an estimated 7.3 million vehicles this year—is shared by two giants, Toyota Motor Co. and Nissan Motor Co., leaving the nine other manufacturers to scramble for the rest.

Reorganization of the industry is now under intensive study by the Ministry for International Trade & Industry (MITI), which would like Toyota and Nissan to take over some of their weaker competitors to save jobs in an economy already sapped by recession. Neither MITI nor car company officials will say exactly what is going on, but it seems clear that some mergers—or "business relationships," as the Japanese call them—will be implemented by yearend. There is no betting at the moment which solution will eventually be chosen.

A prime prospect. The top candidate for merger is Toyo Kogyo Co., maker of the Mazda, which last year lost $5.7 million on sales of $1.6 billion and is saddled with more than $1 billion in debt. Toyo Kogyo has an inventory of 80,000 unsold cars in Japan, and an industry spokesman calls the company "our biggest problem."

MITI officials have held a series of secret meetings with Toyota and Nissan officials to persuade them to take over the Mazda maker, offering them a substantial government subsidy as inducement. "They tell us it is our social responsibility to aid another Japanese company," says one source. "If we require [the subsidy], they will include it in next year's budget. It would be disguised in some way; they are very clever people."

If that fails to work, industry sources believe a second possibility is a link between Toyo Kogyo and Isuzu Motors Ltd., another troubled manufacturer, which lost $29 million in the fiscal year ended last October. Under that plan, Isuzu, a major truck maker that has suffered because of the lag in construction, would concentrate on truck-building while Toyo Kogyo turned out passenger vehicles.

Any Toyo Kogyo-Isuzu tie, however, is complicated by the fact that General Motors Corp. owns 34% of Isuzu and recently instigated a management reshuffle. Some observers think it is significant that executives of C. Itoh & Co., the big trading concern that brought GM and Isuzu together, recently joined the boards of both Toyo Kogyo and Isuzu. But other sources say flatly that MITI does not favor that linkup because "it cannot control GM." Robert Lockwood, vice-president of General Motors Overseas Operations, who has also just become an Isuzu vice-president, says his company would not even consider a marriage with Toyo Kogyo.

A three-way deal? One further possible solution to Toyo Kogyo's woes is thought to be a three-way tie with Isuzu and Mitsubishi Motors Corp., which is 15% owned by Chrysler Corp. Although Mitsubishi is said by its executives to be profitable, relations with Chrysler are "very delicate" over the issue of how Mitsubishi-built autos should be sold in the U.S. Mitsubishi Corp., the big trading company that represents the car maker's parent, sees no advantage in the present arrangement under which Chrysler markets Mitsubishi's Dodge Colt and Plymouth Arrow through its own dealer network.

Finally, there are merger rumors involving Suzuki Motor Co., which is best known in the U.S. as a motorcycle maker but which also produces small cars in Japan and Jeep-like vehicles for export. Suzuki's auto sales fell from 185,000 units in 1974 to 168,000 last year, and profits slumped an estimated 45% to $3.7 million. Talk of a Suzuki-Toyota tie gained credence recently when the smaller company asked Toyota to help it meet new exhaust emission standards.

Collaboration on technical, marketing, and other levels is likely to become more prevalent in Japan, as it has in Europe, as small companies struggle to compete with the industry giants. "They are going to be driven to it in order to keep costs down," says GM's Lockwood. "It makes economic sense. It's sort of sharing the load without losing identity."

Business Week, March 4, 1976.

The Mercentile Bank

A DISPUTE WITH THE CANADIAN GOVERNMENT
OVER FOREIGN OWNERSHIP

In early 1967 The First National Bank of New York (Citibank) was engaged in strained negotiations with the Canadian Government over its ownership of the Mercantile Bank of Canada.

ACQUISITION OF MERCANTILE

The Mercantile Bank was set up in 1953 by the Rotterdamsche Bank of Holland. There was moderate resistance to the granting of its charter from the eight major banks whose country-wide branches dominated Canadian finance. But it was supported by the government and business community because of the contribution the Dutch could make to foreign trade, especially with their Far East connections. Everyone assumed Mercantile would be an inconspicuous factor in Canadian banking, and so it was until 1963.

Apparently Mercantile was not a particularly successful venture. Its condition, along with changes in the parent bank situation, led to the decision of the Dutch owners to sell out. Late in 1962, they let it be known in banking circles that Mercantile was available for sale. Several Canadian and foreign banks, including First National City Bank of New York (Citibank), came forward with offers. By mid-June 1963, Citibank was close to agreement with the Dutch for Mercantile's purchase.

On June 20, 1963 Robert MacFadden, Citibank's vice president in charge of

---

This case summarizes information derived from a research study reported at length in *The Mercantile Bank Affair*, John Fayerweather, New York University Press, 1974.

Canadian affairs, visited Louis Rasminsky, Governor of the Bank of Canada, to inform him of Citibank's intentions. While the prospective sale of Mercantile was being openly discussed, the identification of the actual bidders had been kept secret. The negotiators had determined that Canadian government approval was not required for the sale of a bank by one foreign owner to another. However, in later testimony Citibank executives said they had felt that it was wise for Mr. MacFadden to visit Mr. Rasminsky, partly to confirm this legal point and to get a direct reading of official Canadian reaction and partly as sound diplomacy to assure that the Canadians would hear about the purchase directly and promptly from Citibank.

Mr. Rasminsky dictated the following notes on the conversation with Mr. MacFadden. (These notes and subsequent quotations are from the hearings before the House of Commons Committee on Finance, Trade and Economic Affairs, before which Citibank appeared on January 24, 1967 and Mr. Rasminsky on January 30, 1967.)

"MacFadden indicated that if the Minister of Finance or I expressed very strong views about their coming in, the bank would certainly reconsider their decision. I said that the administration of the Bank Act was a matter for the Government and not the central bank and I strongly urged them to see the Minister of Finance and hear his views before concluding their negotiations with Mercantile. He said he had intended to speak to the Minister of Finance at the same time as he spoke to me but as he was involved in the Budget Debate it was clearly impossible to see him. I urged him not to push the matter to a conclusion with the Mercantile before seeing the Minister of Finance, and he undertook that they would not do so."

In his testimony, Mr. Rasminsky made the following comments on the conversation:

"I would like to make it clear that I was not then urging Mr. MacFadden not to come in here; the urging consisted of urging him to see the Minister of Finance before he came in here. I felt that their coming in here would create quite a stir, and I was anxious that they should realize that at the beginning and not be confronted with an unpleasant situation later. . . ."

"Mr. Munro: Mr. Rasminsky, were you aware at any time during this period in 1963 or 1962 of American interests indicating a desire to buy out or to buy a substantial portion of the shares of any of our chartered banks?"

"Mr. Rasminsky: Not in any concrete way, Mr. Munro. I cannot be specific about this because it was never sufficiently documented to really get down to cases on it, but I did hear market rumors from time to time that one or another American bank was interested in acquiring interests in the banking field in Canada."

Mr. MacFadden wrote the following memorandum on the meeting:

"1. We were completely right in going directly to him first to discuss our plans. He was most appreciative and had heard no intimation of our plans so at this date there had been no leak. I did not feel that he was too surprised at our proposal.

"2. He strongly recommended our going the route of the Mercantile as easier for us but did not back away from a charter application on our own. He suggested the timing could be complicated by the revision of the Bank Act.

"3. In either case he would be called to testify before the Treasury Board and would want to think through carefully two points on which he would have to give answers:

(a) Would this open up an influx of applications from American banks, and

(b) What would be the effect on close working arrangements with chartered banks when discussion would be reported promptly to our Head Office and could he and the Bank of Canada live with it?

"4. He approved the sequence of steps we proposed to take and I assured him we would come back to him when the deal is firm and before signing and at the same time to clear with the Minister of Finance."

. . . .

On June 26, 1973 representatives of Citibank and Rotterdamsche Bank signed a memorandum of agreement subject to approval by the central banking authorities of their governments and formal ratification by their boards of directors. After a brief time lapse due in part to the intervention of a weekend, Mr. MacFadden advised Mr. Rasminsky by telephone on July 2 that a firm deal had been made with the Dutch. He asked Mr. Rasminsky to arrange a visit with Mr. Gordon. Speaking from memory in his testimony, Mr. MacFadden said that he asked that the appointment be made as soon as possible but that Mr. Rasminsky did not call until July 16, setting up a date for a visit on July 18 with Mr. Gordon. Mr. Rasminsky in his testimony, speaking from notes he had made of his conversations, said that Mr. MacFadden specifically asked for an appointment on July 18 and that he telephoned to Mr. MacFadden on July 3 to confirm this date. He also stated that he was on vacation on July 16 and could not have made the telephone call that day. In his testimony he indicated that he understood Mr. MacFadden to mean that the "deal" amounted to a "firm option" to purchase Mercantile but not a final contract. Thus he assumed that Citibank was still in a position to withdraw, and he again encouraged Mr. MacFadden to ascertain Gordon's views before completing the purchase. He read a section of the Gordon report (see Appendix A) on foreign banks to impress Mr. MacFadden with the feelings which might be aroused by this action.

On July 18, James S. Rockefeller, Chairman of Citibank, and Mr. MacFadden met with Walter Gordon, Robert Bryce, Deputy Minister of Finance, and Clayton F. Elderkin, Inspector General of Banks. Henry Moquette, President of Mercantile Bank, had accompanied the Americans but Mr. Gordon asked that he not join the meeting. The Canadian version of this meeting was given in a memorandum written by Mr. Elderkin which was endorsed by Mr. Bryce:

"Mr. Rockefeller said that National City had made an arrangement with the shareholders of Mercantile to acquire the shares of the latter bank, but that no firm commitment had been made. He said his people considered that Canada was one of the more important countries in the financial world, that they would like to participate in its growth and that he had asked for this interview to obtain the viewpoint of the Government with respect to the proposed purchase.

"The minister said that he was glad to have the opportunity of expressing the views of the Government regarding the transaction as he considered it of great importance. He stated that while he had a very high regard for the National City, he was going to be quite candid in explaining some of the objections of the proposed purchase.

"He said that owing to rather unique circumstances it was possible for National City to acquire a banking subsidiary in Canada through what amounted in effect to a loophole in the law which required the bank charters be approved by Parliament. There is nothing in present Canadian legislation to prevent the transfer of Mercantile shares to another non-resident group.

"This could enable a non-resident bank to establish a subsidiary here which could be expanded into a large foreign-owned banking institution, unless subsequent action is taken. If National City enters the Canadian banking field by this method, it is very probable that other American banking corporations would want to do so as well, but in that case charters would have to be obtained.

"It is highly unlikely that a charter would be granted by this Parliament for a bank that was to be non-resident controlled. Not only would the Government not be in favor of such action, but both of the minor parties have expressed opposition to an extension of foreign control in financial institutions.

"The minister emphasized that the situation now is different from that in 1953 when the Mercantile received its charter. Since that time, the Royal Commission on Economic Prospects has recommended that control of Canadian chartered banks (and insurance companies, Mr. MacFadden noted) should be in the hands of Canadians and it suggested that appropriate action be taken to prevent control passing to non-residents.

"The minister also referred to the matter of relations between Bank of Canada and the chartered banks which had been discussed with the governor of the bank. Problems might arise in carrying out monetary policy if a foreign-controlled bank was prevented from cooperating because of laws or regulations in the country of the parent. Mr. Rockefeller said that this presented no problem as any branch or subsidiary of theirs would be entirely governed by the laws of the country in which it was licensed or chartered.

"He said that National City had always maintained good relations with the Bank of England but the minister said circumstances here were quite different. He was told that there had been one instance when American anti-trust legislation appeared to interfere with the central bank's attempt to control credit here. Moreover, at times there have been difficulties over United States treasury attempts to extend foreign asset control regulations into Canada through the banks.

"The Royal Commission on Banking and Finance is expected to report before the end of the year. The minister said it is quite possible that the Commission will have some recommendations regarding foreign participation in Canadian banks. The Bank Act will be up for revision in 1964 and the Government then will have to decide what it will do in respect of this particular matter.

"In response to a question, Mr. Rockefeller was told by Mr. Elderkin that it was the practice to revise the Bank Act every ten years and that the Act was each bank's only charter; it would be possible to stop a bank carrying on business when the revised Act comes into force if its charter were not continued thereby. The minister remarked that while he himself might not have volunteered this information, no doubt Messrs. Rockefeller and MacFadden were quite aware of it. Mr. Rockefeller recalled that the licenses of Canadian banks to do business in New York State come up for renewal annually.

"At one stage, Mr. Rockefeller said that National City would prefer to operate in Canada through a branch rather than by means of a charter and asked if this could be permitted as it was in many other countries and, with some restricted powers, in certain American states. He was told that it has always been considered the best policy in Canada to have commercial banks chartered and subject to uniform legislation.

"The minister said that it would normally be unfair to apply retroactively any legislative restrictions on control of banks by non-residents, but since the National City people were now aware of the Government's views about the possibility of their acquiring the shares of the Mercantile, the Government would not consider that they would be entitled to exemption from any legislation in respect of foreign ownership that might be enacted in the future.

"In conclusion, the minister said that if the National City proceeded with its plan, it might tend to encourage restrictive legislation and advised Messrs. Rockefeller and MacFadden not to proceed with their proposed action. Mr. Rockefeller then said, 'In other words, if we do so, it will be at our own peril.' The minister said that he would not have volunteered this expression but that he thought Mr. Rockefeller had sized up the situation correctly.

"The interview was conducted on a very amicable basis, but left no doubt as to the views of the Government on this subject."

In the hearings Mr. Elderkin clarified the nature of Gordon's warning:

"Mr. Gregoire: Is it not a fact that at the same meeting a very precise concrete warning was given by the then Minister of Finance to the effect that section 75 or something to that effect would be included in the new Bank act?

"Mr. Elderkin: No, the warning was only that there might be legislation restricting foreign-owned banks."

The following memoranda were written by the Citibank executives:

Mr. MacFadden's Memorandum

"Mr. Gordon knew of our plans to acquire the Mercantile Bank and had discussed it with Mr. Rasminsky, Governor, Bank of Canada. He raised the same questions as had been previously raised by Rasminsky in my conversation with him on June 20:

(a) This action of ours would open the flood gates for charter applications by other American banks, and
(b) The confidential nature of the relations of the Governor with the Canadian banks would be disrupted by the presence of a subsidiary of a large American bank who would perforce report on all discussion to its Head Office. Concern was also expressed over the possible interference of some of our U.S. laws, such as the Clayton Anti-Trust Act.

"Mr. Gordon admitted that there was nothing the Government could do to prevent our proceeding with our plans, because of a loophole in the present Bank Act whereby no provision had been made to prevent foreign ownership of a chartered bank. He stated that if we were to apply for a charter today we would be turned down under the temper of the present Parliament. He pointed out that the report of the Royal Commission on Banking was due to come down in the fall and would be followed by hearings in connection with the revision of the Bank Act due in June, 1964. With a minority Government having to deal with vociferous minority parties, he could not predict what restrictions on foreign ownership of Canadian banks would be included in the new Act. We pointed out that it had always been the practice of Anglo-Saxon countries not to enact retroactive legislation. We were reminded that all bank charters expire with the old Bank Act and he made it clear that possibly the Mercantile charter would not be renewed. He said the Government does not welcome our contemplated move, and he can obviously be counted on to use any influence he has to get us out, if we go ahead. He referred several times to the Gordon Commission report of 1957 (of which I was the Chairman) in which he recommended specific legislation to prevent foreign control of Canadian banks.

"Mr. Rockefeller indicated that we were committed to our plans but had not yet filed for approval with the Federal Reserve. In answer to our question about the foreign-owned former Barclay's Bank and the present Mercantile, he said that they were small and inconsequential and consequently they could live with them. Mr. Rockefeller reminded Mr. Gordon of the activities of Canadian banks in the U.S. He brushed that off as inconsequential, even including the operations of the Agencies in New York.

"We had previously called on U.S. Ambassador Butterworth to inform him of our plans and he was most enthusiastic about our going into Canada."

Mr. Rockefeller's Memorandum

"A call was made with Mr. MacFadden on Finance Minister Gordon. There were present his associates, Bryce and Elderkin. The meeting was very friendly but the result unfavorable. It lasted 45 minutes. The Minister had been asked to see a representative of the U.S. Treasury who had been sent up to explain President Kennedy's tax bill at the same time as our appointment and the Treasury man was deferred until we had finished. Gordon also extended apologies for not being able to take us to lunch. Preliminary arrangements had provided for Moquette of the Mercantile Bank to accompany us, but when we arrived he was told that Gordon wanted to see us privately.

"Gordon had been advised of the matter by Rasminsky. He said he would like to talk from a memorandum and had a memorandum in hand during the conversation. The Mercantile Bank was permitted to come in in 1953 under a different set of circumstances. Its entry into the market provoked considerable discussion at that time. Gordon went on [to say] that he had been chairman of a banking commission to review the laws several years ago and that that commission did not look favorably on the presence of a foreign bank in the market. He stated that if we enter the market through purchase of the Mercantile Bank it would be considered as taking advantage of an unforeseen loophole. It would be further considered inopportune at this time because another banking commission is being established this fall to review the banking laws again with changes in the laws contemplated in 1964 or 1965.

"The argument was that Canada was a small developing country in which banking played a more important part than in mature countries. They now enjoy a very flexible working arrangement with the Governor of the Central Bank and the chartered banks. They pretty much ignore the Mercantile Bank under Dutch control on account of the scope of its activities. While highly complimentary to FNCB and its personnel they feel [that] under our management the Mercantile Bank would become a more important factor. He expressed fears of an American manager and an American subsidiary being more responsive to our interests and those of the U.S. than those of Canada. He made vague allusions to the U.S. tax and antitrust laws. He reiterated his published views as to being concerned with the extent of U.S. ownership of Canadian industry. He stated that U.S. manufacturing subsidiaries were more interested in Canadian business than manufacturing for export from Canada and did not assist in combating Canada's balance of payments problem.

"Another major argument was that if we were permitted to come in there would undoubtedly be a flood of applications from other U.S. banks and other foreign banks. The inference was that Rasminsky and he were at a loss as to how to cope with this problem and preferred to avoid it by keeping us out. In reply to a question he stated that without any doubt if we attempted to obtain a new charter in Parliament it would be refused.

"He dismissed our presence in the London market and [our] friendly relationship with the Bank of England as inapplicable as London is an international market with many foreign banks. He dismissed the existence of Canadian agencies, branches, and subsidiaries in the U.S. saying that they were an inconsequential factor in our market, whereas we would be an important factor in the Canadian market. In reply to another question he said that he would feel just the same way if matters were arranged so that we had a branch rather than a subsidiary in Canada.

"It was called to our attention that the renewal of the charters of all the Canadian banks will be due for revision next year and that the one of the Mercantile Bank would not necessarily be renewed. He said that he would have no compunctions about opposing a renewal for us, having advised us so far in advance. He knows that licenses of foreign banks operating in New York are renewable annually. He said the Government looked on the transaction with disfavor and he advised against completing it. Fortunately at the very beginning we opened the conversation by saying that we had made a deal with the Dutch and were coming to advise him of it. This was the one thing that seemed to disturb him and to shake his overall attitude of telling us what we should do. We made no commitment as to our course of action. We said that we of course would consider his views and appreciated them but might feel that our contractual obligation with the Dutch was such that we were committed. We further said that we also had an obligation to our shareholders to take advantage of an opportunity that was open to them. His disapproval was very clear. He did not forbid us to proceed and made no direct threats of reprisal. On being asked that if we decided to proceed that it was at our own peril he said that he would not use those words but it was a correct appraisal of the situation."

A significant point in these discussions was the status of the deal between Citibank and the Dutch. Some comments by the Citibank executives elaborate on their views on this point.

"Mr. Harfield (Citibank's lawyer): . . . Now, you come to the other question whether you can repudiate your own deal. And I suppose that, . . . the board of directors could have declined to act on this, and that would probably have been an excuse. It would have been a repudiation of what their officers had done. But they might have had a legal technical out on that. Clearly if the Federal Reserve Board had failed to give its approval . . . that would have been an act beyond the control of the parties, which would have made the agreement unenforceable, and no longer binding."

"Mr. Rockefeller: . . . May I elaborate on your other point just a second. We live in a practical world. If the Citibank in New York and the Rotterdamsche Bank in Holland are making a deal, produce the paper signed by authorized officers, and either one of us had wheeled out of it on a technicality, our name would have been worthless in banking circles in a week. That is just practical. As to legal, you can do—I do not care what the legal is. But it would go around Europe that the Citibank had welshed on the deal."

On July 26, Mr. MacFadden telephoned to Mr. Rasminsky. From his notes the latter reported that Mr. MacFadden said Mr. Gordon had registered disapproval but "after serious consideration they [the bank] had decided to go ahead." On July 29 Mr. MacFadden accompanied by Mr. Moquette, President of Mercantile, visited Mr. Gordon. In his testimony Mr. MacFadden said "the purpose for the meeting was to advise the minister that we appreciated the time that he had given us and that we appreciated his views but that we felt we had to honor our commitment to our Dutch friends."

On September 30, 1963 Citibank took control of Mercantile. At the time the bank had branches in Toronto and Vancouver in addition to its main office in Montreal. By 1967 branches had been opened in Calgary, Halifax, Quebec City and Winnipeg. In this period the bank also improved its financial performance, recording its first operating profit under Citibank in 1966, although this was offset by substantial bad-loan write-offs. The bank also undertook some innovations, including staying open later hours, introducing a new type of savings deposit and providing credit for livestock, a practice other Canadian banks had not undertaken.

THE BANK ACT PROPOSALS

On May 6, 1965 a proposed new Bank Act was presented to the House of Commons by Finance Minister Walter Gordon. The act included severe restrictions on foreign ownership of Canadian banks and operations of banks controlled by foreigners. Clause 53 provided that no individual could own more than 10 percent of any bank and that foreign ownership in a bank could not exceed 25 percent. This provision, however, was not to apply to the ownership pattern of any bank that had been in effect prior to September 22, 1964. That was the date on which the government had first announced officially its intentions to restrict foreign ownership of banks, it being Canadian practice not to make laws retroactive before the date on which their terms are initially proposed. Thus Mercantile was exempt from the restrictions of Clause 53. However, a related section did restrict Mercantile by requiring that any new shares had to be sold to Canadians until the foreign ownership was down to 25 percent and individual ownership (i.e., Citibank) to 10 percent.

The major debate centered around section 75(2)(g) which applied only to Mercantile, the sole foreign-owned bank. It read as follows:

> "Except as authorized by and under this Act, the bank shall not, directly at any time after the 31st day of December 1965, have outstanding total liabilities (including paid-up capital, rest account, and undivided profits) exceeding twenty times its authorized capital stock if more than twenty-five per cent of its issued shares are held by any one resident or non-resident shareholder and his associates as described in section 56."

During a debate in the House of Commons on June 14 Mr. Gordon defended the restrictions against Mercantile in the proposed Bank Act. In this speech he gave publicly for the first time his version of the 1963 interview with the

Citibank officials. He declared that Citibank had been forewarned of possible restrictions before they had purchased control of Mercantile and had gone ahead despite these warnings. On July 17 Mercantile issued a press release responding to Mr. Gordon's statements. The bank asserted that Citibank bought control in an entirely legal manner and the deal was complete before the conference with Mr. Gordon. They expected that it would be accepted in Canada since only the transfer of ownership from one foreign bank to another was involved. They had advised the Canadian officials of their action "with the full expectation that it would be welcomed since it made available to Canadian exporters the overseas facilities of First National City Bank in 41 countries." The proposed legislation was opposed as discriminatory and retroactive.

Gordon's proposed Bank Act was never voted on because of a national election that fall. After he resigned (see Appendix A) Mitchell Sharp became Minister of Finance, and on July 7, 1966 Mr. Sharp introduced a new bank act with essentially the same provisions affecting Mercantile except that the effective date was changed to December 31, 1967. At this point Mercantile had already issued all the stock which was authorized, and its liabilities were slightly in excess of 20 times the authorized stock. The proposal meant in effect, therefore, that it would either have to reduce the ownership of Citibank to 25 percent or undertake no further growth.

On April 7, 1966 the US Government dispatched a diplomatic note to the Canadian Government objecting strongly to the treatment which had been proposed for Mercantile. While this note was never officially released, a copy of its alleged text, given in Appendix B, was printed in a book. This text seems consistent with the tenor of the note described by prominent figures at the time.

In early May 1966, Gordon's book, *A Choice for Canada* was published. In the book he reasserted that Mercantile was being fairly treated because he had warned the Citibank officials before they were committed to purchase of the bank. On May 10 the bank issued a press release restating its position as set forth in its 1965 press release and concluding, "We believe it improper to engage in debate with the former finance minister over who said what at a meeting over three years ago. Suffice it to say we voluntarily made the full details of the transaction known to Mr. Gordon at the time and our understanding of what transpired at the meeting with him is not in accord with his."

Two days later Mr. Gordon rose in the House of Commons to protest against the bank's statement on a point of personal privilege. He quoted the press release and then reinforced his own position by disclosing publicly for the first time the memorandum written Mr. Elderkin. He then charged that "Mr. MacFadden, president of the Mercantile Bank, has now seen fit to question the accuracy of the statement which I made to the House on June 14, 1965. In doing so he has cast a reflection upon my integrity, both as a member of this House and as a former member of the government." Later in the day, a member of the House of Commons also raised the Mercantile issue by asking Mr. Sharp if he had been subjected to pressure to eliminate the provisions affecting the bank in the new act. Mr. Sharp responded that he received representations on this and many other subjects regularly. He asserted, however, "There is an imputation in this question that I yield to pressure from anyone. I yield to pressure from no one, and neither does this government." On May 17 the Speaker of the House ruled against Mr. Gordon, saying "To my mind the fact that someone outside the house places a different interpretation than does the hon. member in his then capacity as Minister of Finance does not constitute an infringement of the rights and privileges of the hon. gentleman as a member of the house."

In public discussions of the Mercantile affair there was prominent mention of the possibility of US Government retaliation against Canadian interests if restrictions against Mercantile were enacted. The obvious targets for retaliation were the agencies of the Canadian banks in New York which had assets of about $2.5 billion mostly invested in call loans in Wall Street. Fear of retaliatory action appeared in newspaper articles shortly after Gordon's first proposals and continued throughout the affair. It was reinforced by certain actions in the United States. The latter included a July 1966 study by Dr. Zwick for a congressional committee recommending federal control of foreign banking and an implementing bill proposed by Senator Javits. It appears that the timing of these actions was purely coincidental, with no direct relation to the Mercantile affair. However, much of the Canadian press felt there was a direct relation, and the fears were encouraged by a few subsequent actions, notably another version of legislation introduced by Congressman Fino of New York who explicitly exhorted President Johnson to support the bill to permit retaliation against Canada. Likewise the Federal Deposit Insurance Corporation, in approving a merger in California involving a Canadian bank, took occasion to make a critical observation about the treatment proposed for Mercantile. The press reported late in 1966 that a second diplomatic note from the United States Government had explicitly contained threats of retaliation. (See Appendix C.)

In November 1966 hearings on the Bank Act commenced in the House of Commons Committee on Finance, Trade and Economic Affairs. The first witness heard on the sections affecting the Mercantile Bank was G. Arnold Hart, President, Bank of Montreal. He presented a vigorous case supporting Mercantile's position that the provisions were retroactive and discriminatory. Earle McLaughlin, Chairman of the Royal Bank, did not undertake the same vigorous support. But he indicated that he felt the status of the bank should not be changed. No other bankers testified specifically on this point. However, from press reports and other information, it was known that opinions in the banking community ranged from vigorous support of Mercantile through neutrality to mild opposition. The eight large chartered banks which dominated Canadian banking felt little concern about Mercantile as a competitive threat. Some, like Mr. Hart, objected on principle to the type of legislation proposed and among them there was some degree of concern about the possible retaliation against their operations in the United States.

On December 24 an interview appeared in the Toronto *Star* in which Prime Minister Lester Pearson made his first statement on the Mercantile affair:

"QUESTION—The specific issue between the two countries now is the Bank Act changes vis-à-vis the Mercantile Bank. Does the government intend to stand firm on this?

"ANSWER—Certainly we see no reason for changing the position that we have taken, especially in the light of our own knowledge of the discussions between Mr. Gordon, when he was minister of finance, and the officers of the bank concerned, and of our strong feeling that a country should maintain control over its banking and insurance companies. While we should welcome foreign capital, we should also insist that Canadian subsidiaries of foreign corporations, and, of course, I am thinking primarily of American, must behave in every respect as Canadian, and that their business policies must be consistent with Canadian policies and Canadian interests.

"That is one reason why we would be very reluctant—and reluctant is too mild a word—why we would not find it possible to agree that foreign banking concerns should be allowed to develop in Canada in a way where their policies could be determined by their head offices in a foreign country; or where the expansion of a foreign bank because of contacts, say, between the home office in New York and industries in the United States with subsidiaries in Canada might be given preferential treatment over Canadian banks. That's the problem.

"QUESTION—Where a country loses control of its monetary instruments, then there is no economic sovereignty left.

"ANSWER—I think that is true. But having said that, I think of the matter in larger terms than those concerning only United States banks. I think of it also in terms of central and international bankers now controlling our economic and financial destiny to such a large extent, irrespective of the political agencies of a country. It's very easy to say that we are not going to allow outside control of our financial development, but sometimes we have to go to New York—by we I mean Canadian corporations, Canadian governments—even when we want money. We haven't enough Canadian capital for our own development. Some bankers in New York who have no branches in Canada, no banking interests in Canada at all, will say we don't like your policies so we won't give you the money. That is their right, but by this very action, our financial position can be weakened. So when we talk about one American bank being a potential threat to Canadian control over our financial system, by its growth in Canada, we must recognize that this can happen without any American bank being in Canada at all. So this is a far bigger problem than the Mercantile Bank."

The House of Commons committee received the testimony of Mercantile on January 24, 1967. The bank was represented by James Rockefeller, Robert MacFadden, Stewart Clifford, General Manager, two Canadians who were Directors of the bank, Andre Bachand and Kenneth B. Palmer, and Henry Harfield of a New York law firm. The discussion ran through three sittings, morning, afternoon and evening, consuming a total of six and a half hours. The bank presented a brief (Appendix D) prior to the session, and short introductory comments were made along this line by the bank representatives at the outset. Most of the time was spent answering questions by the MP's.

The greater part of the discussion was devoted to the retroactivity issue. In essence the bank group contended that there was a failure of communication in the 1963 meetings which was unfortunate but did not affect their position that they had acted quite legally.

There was considerable debate over whether Citibank was so committed after June 26 that it could not withdraw from the deal with the Dutch. Several committee members contended that the clause in the agreement making it "subject to the approval of our Boards of Directors and of all the Governmental authorities concerned" gave Citibank an opportunity to withdraw after hearing Rasminsky's cautioning comments on June 28 or Gordon's stiff warnings. They felt that the deal could have been turned down by the Board of Directors on July 16 or that Mr. Gordon's position should have been interpreted as failure to obtain approval of a concerned government authority. The Mercantile representatives asserted that the "authorities" had been clearly understood to mean only those with legal authority over the deal, namely the Dutch and US Governments. Unless one of them had turned the deal down, they contended that the agreement was legally enforceable as of the date of initial signing, the approvals of the boards being a formality.

Perhaps a quarter of the testimony, in short slugs of time throughout the day, was devoted to discrimination. Most of this discussion centered on US treatment of foreign banks, committee members pressing the point that the United States discriminated in a variety of ways. The Mercantile officials were reluctant on this point at first, stressing in particular the special advantages which foreign bank agencies in New York had in such matters as not being confined by Federal Reserve Board controls of reserve ratios. But under pressure from the committee members, who drew heavily on Dr. Zwick's report as a reference, the officials conceded that there were many states where foreign banks could not operate and others where some form of discrimination did exist.

There were a few attempts by committee members to redefine the issues, perceiving in various ways the inappropriateness of the retroactivity-discrimination-punitive characterizations. Mr. Wahn made two attempts. In a brief comment early in the day he suggested that one might say the provision was "undesirable" but not retroactive. Later in the day he had formulated his ideas more fully. He rejected all three terms and defined the provision quite simply as "an attempt to carry out a legislative purpose which may or may not be right." The purpose was to bring all banks under essentially Canadian ownership. He argued that the provisions could have been even stricter, for example, by specifically requiring divestiture and that the Act really made a sincere effort to positively recognize the special situation of Mercantile, by giving it leeway to adjust.

Mr. LaFlamme and Mr. Davis took another tack, emphasizing that the provisions pertained only to future events, specifically the limits to growth, and could not therefore be termed retroactive as that would pertain to the past. Mr. Davis also tried to divert the discussion from the legal argument about whether Gordon's warning constituted an official position. He related the warnings rather to Citibank's evaluation of future risks in making the investment. His idea was not fully developed but seemed to be that the problem now confronting Mercantile was in the nature of a business risk and expectation of a variety of such risks had to be accepted in making investments. These suggestions for restructuring the issues fell on deaf ears as far as the Mercantile group was concerned.

The possibility of Citibank selling 75 percent of its stock in Mercantile was raised three times during the hearings. There was also some discussion of a related philosophical idea, exhortation by committee members to the bank officials to act like a Canadian bank and not seek special concessions. The exchanges on divestiture were quite brief, the Mercantile people taking a negative position on two counts: (1) that Mercantile was so unpromising an investment now, because of the Bank Act provisions, that "we do not have anything that we could sell to any one at any price," and (2) it would be unprofitable for Citibank. Mr. Rockefeller said "[We will sell] only if forced to do so, because after all there is no percentage in doing all the work and giving somebody else 90 percent of the benefit of it." A final suggestion was made that ten years might be allowed for divestiture but Mr. Rockefeller said this did not change his position.

There were just a few short periods devoted to the alleged detrimental effects of Citibank ownership of Mercantile. A quite long exchange, largely handled by Mr. Harfield, refuted the risks of extraterritorial control by the US Government through anti-trust laws or other means. Mr. Clifford could be quite specific in assuring the committee that Mercantile had consistently conformed to the Canadian Government guidelines and regulations bearing on monetary and fiscal policy and that he had been entirely cooperative in not passing on to his parent organization confidential information given by government officials. There were a couple of exchanges on the idea that if Mercantile were given a free rein, a number of other foreign banks would seek permission to enter Canada on the same basis. These did not lead far, however, as the Mercantile officials disclaimed ability to speculate on the question.

Interspersed among the main body of comments on retroactivity and discrimination were questions by members of the committee about the knowledge of Canadian nationalism and Mr. Gordon among the Citibank officials. Seven times during the day this subject came up in one way or another. Each time, the Mercantile officials indicated that they had not expected an unfavorable reaction to their purchase of Mercantile and that Mr. Gordon's position came as a great surprise. When Mr. Rockefeller was asked if he was not aware of the nationalistic provisions proposed in Mr. Gordon's budget in the spring of 1963, he claimed, "I was completely ignorant." Mr. MacFadden said, "I was aware of Mr. Gordon's economic views" but that confronted by Gordon's position, "I was completely taken aback and quite dismayed . . . " The committee members generally indicated disbelief in these expressions of ignorance. An element of skepticism also seemed to be present in the exchange with Mr. Basford started by his observation that Citibank went ahead with buying Mercantile ". . . believing that the State Department would rescue them if need be." Rockefeller: "I can assure you that we are not relying on the State Department." Basford: "When did you start to rely on the State Department?" Rockefeller: "We did not rely on the State Department. The State Department injected themselves into this. We did not call on the State Department." Encouragement to skepticism on this viewpoint was given by a comment by Mr. Palmer earlier to the effect that there was nothing improper about US Government aid, that a Canadian firm in a similar situation would reasonably expect its government to intercede for it with a foreign government.

The Rockefeller and MacFadden memoranda on the July 18, 1963 meeting were released at the time of the testimony. They had brought insufficient copies of MacFadden's memorandum on the June 20 meeting with Mr. Rasminsky so it was given to the chairman of the committee the following day. Both among committee members and the press to whom the memorandum was released, MacFadden's statement that he would "clear with the Minister of Finance" before signing the deal was interpreted to indicate that he had made a commitment which he had not fulfilled. In a telephone explanation to newsmen printed in two papers, Mr. MacFadden observed that "we often use words we don't intend," indicating that he had not meant to imply that he would see Gordon before a firm deal was made. He asserted that the words used and the intent technically referred only to the final signing of the contract which was accomplished in September 1963, so the bank had in fact fulfilled his stated intention.

On January 26 Mr. Sharp expressed his views on the Mercantile issue in a television interview. He spoke mainly on two points—US pressures and divestiture. He was quite firm on the first point, stating that the government would not be "bullied" into modifying the Bank Act by threats of retaliation from the United States. He expanded considerably on the divestiture idea, clearly indicating that this was the route the government hoped Mercantile would follow. He expressed the view that the bank's stock was "a very saleable proposition" and reported that a number of people had shown an interest in buying it. He observed that once the 25 percent provision was met, there should be no limit to the growth of Mercantile and that he felt it was desirable for it to become a strong competitor in Canadian banking. He appeared to be inviting Mercantile to negotiate a compromise on the effective date by suggesting that a reasonable time should be allowed Citibank to sell its shares. During the interview Mr. Sharp rejected the discrimination and retroactive charges. He departed somewhat from the previous government position in observing that "all legislation is to some extent retroactive."

Mr. Rasminsky testified on the Mercantile Bank situation on January 30. Most of the time was devoted to the 1963 meetings. His comments on them have already been presented earlier in the case. A small portion of the time was devoted to the various effects of Citibank control of Mercantile on Canadian banking. Mr. Rasminsky defended the general concept of retaining national control over domestic credit policy, pointing out that all countries including the United States followed this general principle. He observed that, "A small foreign bank certainly would not jeopardize monetary control or monetary policy." His comments along these lines were rather brief and generalized, no specific analysis being offered as to the form or degree of undesirable action that might stem from foreign control of Mercantile.

He was more explicit on the possible decrease in effectiveness of moral suasion. He cited instances in the past (e.g., the exchange crisis in 1962) when cooperation by the banks was sought to adopt certain lines of action. "Such requests can succeed only if there is universal compliance, because, if a single bank refuses to comply, its competitors are not going to stand by and let it get business that they, the complying banks, are turning away." He also "was concerned at the possibility that the foreign funds control legislation of the United States might be given extraterritorial application in Canada" through the Mercantile Bank.

On the question of communications, Mr. Rasminsky took pains to define the nature of the concern he had expressed to Mr. MacFadden. In 1963 he had recently started a practice of meeting three times a year with the chief executives of the nine chartered banks. He felt that regular intimate communication would improve relations and lead to better decision making through exchange of knowledge and thinking. He also found that a close working relationship made it easier to get the banks to go along informally with policies without formal government action. He noted that for the most part he preferred to use direct government action to implement monetary policy but that from time to time the moral suasion approach was more practical. His concern was that the presence of an executive from a foreign-controlled bank would impair the effectiveness of this intimate relation. "This is really not a question of confidential information, because at these meetings I do not really give any confidential information . . . the contacts with the general managers and with the presidents of the banks did provide a useful opportunity for an informal exchange of views and information. . . . The question in my mind was what effect the presence of what might be regarded as a large American bank at these gatherings might have."

He more or less dismissed this as a current consideration, however, by saying, ". . . as things have turned out, Mr. Stewart Clifford has attended the meetings . . . and I have not the slightest criticism to make of the way he has conducted himself in what for him must have been a very difficult situation."

Questioned by a committee member about why such objections would be raised about a US-controlled bank when they had not been made when it was Dutch-owned, Mr. Rasminsky responded in terms of both present and future conditions. He felt "that it was one thing . . . when the owner was rather distant—a small Dutch bank—and another thing to have in Canada a bank the owner of which was a nearby, large, very enterprising and aggressive American institution." An important factor in his thinking was the fact that there were many US subsidiaries in Canada while the Dutch had very few. He noted at this point that Mercantile actually did only a small portion of its business with US subsidiaries. But later in his testimony he returned to the same line of thought, ". . . there probably would be an inclination to direct the Canadian [subsidiary's] business to the subsidiary of the American bank." He expanded considerably on this hypothesis indicating that he felt it was sound.

The other distinction was "that Citibank coming in would be regarded as the harbinger of things to come . . . people would assume that competitors of the Citibank in the United States would also certainly want to establish in Canada once Citibank had done so." He agreed that the new Bank Act would effectively prevent this, but his feeling in 1963 was that it would be hard for the government to have to keep rejecting US banks' applications for charters once Citibank had made the initial entry. "I thought it would be likely that if the Citibank acquired the Mercantile, this would increase the desire of the Citibank's competitors in the United States to come into Canada and that it would increase the pressure from others to apply for charters here. Yes, I think it would be a problem to keep rejecting applications of American banking institutions for charters here."

In response to an earlier question he had expressed some views on allowing foreign bank agencies in Canada similar to the agencies of Canadian banks in New York. "It would seem . . . a rather odd situation that Canadian banks can operate in a great many countries of the world, but there is no means at all by which foreign banks can operate in Canada." He felt that the foreign agencies would probably have some beneficial competitive effect, even though they would draw some business away from Canadian banks. He did anticipate some loss of monetary control if they were admitted. He declined to state "a categorical view on the subject" but his position seemed relatively favorable.

At one point in the testimony a committee member asked about what would happen if Citibank sold 75 percent of its stock, ". . . can Citibank still control the policy of Mercantile Bank and of course grow, under the Act as revised; are we still up against many of the same problems you mentioned earlier this evening?" Mr. Rasminsky replied, "There are so many problems to worry about that worrying about the situation that will prevail when the stockholdings of the Citibank are reduced to 25 per cent, seems a somewhat remote problem."

On February 1 Prime Minister Pearson made a nationally televised speech, most of which was devoted to general policy toward foreign investment and relations with the United States. He affirmed that, "We are going to continue to need foreign capital for Canadian development and the know-how that often goes with it—we must avoid discriminatory or unfair treatment which would create the kind of atmosphere that discourages necessary foreign investment." But he insisted that foreign enterprises be "subject to Canadian law only and responsive to Canadian policy" and he hoped that Canadians would own as much of industry as possible and retain control of their economy. He recognized that interdependence was the nature of the modern world but the Canadians wished to retain "our own national identity . . . preserving those national values which have a special meaning for us."

Mr. Pearson saw problems in US-Canadian relations arising from limited viewpoints on both sides. Canada had to avoid "oversensitive nationalism, defensive rather than aggressive, based on the fear that as the weaker partner we are too dangerously vulnerable to the effects of the decisions of the friendly giant that lives beside us." Americans, on the other hand, were not sensitive to the Canadian desire to remain independent and there was an "inability on their part to understand our refusal to accept the doctrine that what is good for the US must not necessarily be good for Canada too."

As to the particulars of the Mercantile affair, Mr. Pearson affirmed the government decision that the Bank Act proposals were sound in the interest of retaining effective control of Canadian development and achieving greater competition in banking. "These changes are not unfair to any foreign or domestic interests; and they will be followed through. They have been misrepresented by some voices across the border, but as a result of recent evidence given before a Parliamentary committee, they are now better understood, I believe, in both countries."

MODIFICATION OF PROVISIONS

In late January, Bryce Mackasey, a liberal member of Parliament, acting on his own initiative but with the knowledge of members of the Cabinet, had gone to New York to discuss the situation with the Citibank executives. He impressed upon them that the primary objective of the government was to have Citibank ownership of Mercantile reduced to 25 percent. In response to Mr. Mackasey, Mr. Rockefeller observed that he did not rule out the sale of some Mercantile shares to the public at some future time. In the days that followed there was some direct discussion between Mercantile representatives and Mr. Sharp. On February 14 Mr. Clifford sent the following telegram to Mr. Sharp:

> As there appear to have been some conflicting reports about the position of our Bank regarding the current revision of the Bank Act, we would like

to make the record clear. Being a legally constituted Canadian chartered bank since 1953, we of course have been and are now subject to and governed by Canadian law. Any increase in our authorized capital is subject to the control of appropriate Canadian authorities. At the present time it would be inappropriate to offer shares in the Bank to the investing public as some years are needed to build profitability. We would appreciate a period of time to accomplish this work. If the proposed special ratio of liabilities to authorized capital becomes law, this time is needed. We will give consideration to making shares available to Canadian residents when it is appropriate to do so.

The same day Mr. Sharp met with the Commons Committee. The telegram had conveyed to them a feeling that Citibank was now prepared to sell 75 percent control in the bank. The discussion was mainly directed towards action which would facilitate this end. Specifically it was felt that the bank should be given time in order to establish itself on a sound and profitable basis. To accomplish this an amendment to extend the effective date to the end of 1972 was proposed and approved by the committee with Mr. Sharp's concurrence. Citibank responded to the announcement of this action with a brief press statement: "If this clause is to become law, then certainly deferral of its effective date is desirable."

The change of date was not, however, acceptable to Walter Gordon who had returned to the Cabinet as Minister without Portfolio in January. He made a major issue of the question in a cabinet meeting and furthermore contended that the percentage of control permitted should be reduced to 10 percent. The dispute among the cabinet members continued for about two weeks, finally ending in a compromise under which the five-year extension was retained but made subject to review by the cabinet from year to year. The phraseology was as follows: "December 31, 1967 or after such later date not being a day later than the 31st day of December of 1972 as may be prescribed from time to time by the Governor in Council [Cabinet] ." The result was to make it possible for the cabinet at any time it was dissatisfied with Mercantile's performance to shorten the time period. Mr. Mackasey objected strongly to this change, referring to it as "dirty pool," evidently implying the terms were contrary to the basis on which he had talked to Citibank. After the Act was passed on March 21 the bank issued a strongly worded press release:

We are disappointed that the Canadian lawmakers have apparently framed legislation looking towards the expropriation of the lawful and legitimate investment made by United States investors in the shares of the Mercantile Bank of Canada, which were acquired from other foreign holders at whose instance Canada granted the bank's charter. The method chosen to transfer this U.S. investment to Canadian hands through a forced sale is tantamount to nationalization with no provision for prompt, adequate or effective compensation—a right which has long been recognized in international law.

Advised of this statement in Ottawa, Mr. Sharp promptly replied:

> Mercantile Bank does not have to sell any shares to Canadians if it does not want to expand. It can remain a small bank if it chooses to retain all its shares. No nationalization whatever is involved. I do hope that the Mercantile Bank will follow its stated intention of selling shares to Canadians. It will receive sympathetic consideration when it applies for an extension of time under the new Bank Act in order to prepare itself to sell shares.

PRESS OPINIONS

The Mercantile affair received a large amount of attention in the Canadian press. The diversity of Canadian press opinions can be seen in Exhibits 1 and 2 which summarize an analysis of 180 editorials which are believed to be virtually all of those in Canadian papers on the affair. As Exhibit 1 shows, at the outset Mercantile was generally supported, the basic norms of fair treatment being dominant at that stage. Subsequently the weight of support steadily shifted away from Mercantile. The change was partly due to a broadening of interest with a greater number of papers, especially in smaller cities, supporting the Canadian Government position and partly due to shifts in positions. There were eight papers which changed their positions during the affair, two shifting at least partially in favor of Mercantile and six away from it.

Exhibit 2 shows the frequency of mention of various subjects in the editorials. The dominant concern with control of national affairs stands out as most frequently mentioned (104 times) but the fairness aspect is close behind it (94 mentions). US government pressure ranked fourth overall (63 mentions), but this somewhat understates its importance because it did not appear until the later stages. In the period January 24-31, 1967 with the largest number of editorials US government pressure ranked third.

The considerations in the eight papers which shifted their positions are instructive as to critical factors in Canadian thinking. In seven cases the papers expressed concern over fairness considerations. Three turned against Mercantile because of judgments based on specific evidence, notably the release of the MacFadden memorandum. In three cases aggravation of worries about loss of control of national affairs evidently outweighed earlier judgments based on fairness considerations (two cases) and need for foreign capital (one case). In two cases, fairness considerations resulted in pro-Mercantile changes but not really at the expense of concern about monetary control. In summary, the basic value standard of fairness stands out but it is shown in these cases on balance to be subordinate variously to deep concern over control of national affairs or to counteracting moral-value judgments in which nationalistic bias worked to the disadvantage of the foreigner.

Exhibit 1. Editorials on Mercantile Bank Affair

Period	Major City Papers*				Minor City Papers*				All Papers			
	Pro Govt.	Pro Merc.	No Pos.	Tot.	Pro Govt.	Pro Merc.	No Pos.	Tot.	Pro Govt.	Pro Merc.	No Pos.	Tot.
Up to May 1966	0	9	0	9	0	0	0	0	0	9	0	9
May to Nov. 1966	3	6	4	13	2	3	0	5	5	9	4	18
Dec. 1966 to Jan. 23 1967	9	16	2	27	7	2	1	10	16	18	3	37
Jan. 24-31, 1967	13	16	2	31	18	5	8	31	31	21	10	62
Feb. 1967 on	21	11	8	40	11	1	2	14	32	12	10	54
Total	46	58	16	120	38	11	11	60	84	69	27	180

*Major cities are defined as those with 1967 metropolitan populations of over 200,000. Minor cities include the balance.

Exhibit 2.   Frequency of Mention of Subjects in Editorials by Time Period

Subject	June 1965 to May 1966	May to Nov 1966	Dec 1966 to Jan 23,1967	Jan 24- 31,1967	Feb 6- Apr 1967	Total
Loss of control of national affairs	2	13	21	41	27	104
Fairness of treatment of Mercantile	6	10	22	38	18	94
Possible retaliation by U.S. against Canadian bank agencies	6	12	26	17	12	73
Direct U.S. Government pressure	–	3	16	31	13	63
Competitive threat to Canadian banks	2	4	5	10	6	27
Danger of scaring off U.S. capital	–	–	4	10	8	22
Citibank did not show proper respect for Canadian officials and national opinion	–	–	–	13	6	19
Allowing Mercantile full freedom may open door to flood of other U.S. banks	–	2	2	7	6	17
Doubts about credibility of Citibank	–	–	–	5	2	7

✳ *Appendix A*

NOTES ON THE CANADIAN CONTEXT
OF THE MERCANTILE CASE

Encouraged by high tariffs and an open and very favorable investment climate, foreign capital poured into Canada after World War II,
both in the traditional natural resource industries and to develop
manufacturing plants. Foreign companies, notably those from the United States,
anxious to protect their markets, built hundreds of factories, creating what has
come to be known as the "branch plant economy."

Initially, this massive influx of foreign investment was welcomed without
reservation. By the mid-1950s, however, the Canadians began to realize that with
industrial progress were coming other consequences of a disturbing nature. The
problems were brought into focus with the publication in 1957 of the report of
a royal commission to study the Canadian economy which is commonly known
as the Gordon report after its chairman Walter Gordon.* By and large it was
favorable to foreign capital, observing, "The actual or potential adverse effects . . . are not frequent and that economic benefits far outweigh economic
disadvantages." However, it did recommend action to increase the degree of
Canadian control of the foreign subsidiaries by a greater inclusion of Canadians
in management and boards of directors, increase in Canadian equity in subsidiaries, and the publication of financial reports.

Also in 1957 there occurred an incident which, while small in magnitude, has
received much publicity. The Chinese Communists came to Canada seeking a
quantity of vehicles. Some initial negotiations led to a proposed shipment by

*Royal Commission on Canada's Economic Prospects, *Final Report*, Ottawa: Queen's
Printer, 1958.

183

Ford. However, when word of this proposal reached the Ford headquarters in Detroit, it was vetoed. It would have been a criminal offense under the US Trading With the Enemy Act for parent company Ford executives to permit a subsidiary to sell such goods to Communist China. When this action became known through the press in Canada, it caused a strong adverse reaction. Ford of Canada was a Canadian company and the Canadians felt the US Government had no business telling a Canadian company with whom it should and should not trade.

Politics

The Liberal Party, which had been in power since 1935, was firmly entrenched in the immediate post-World War II years. In 1957 the Conservatives, led by John Diefenbaker, unseated the Liberals by a small margin, and a year later in another election they received an overwhelming majority. The Diefenbaker government proved ineffective in dealing with an assortment of national problems. In an election in 1962 it lost substantial ground to the Liberals and in 1963 the Liberals won 129 seats in Parliament to 95 for the Conservatives. This was four short of a majority of all seats so the Liberals, to stay in power, required the support of some members of either the National Democratic Party (NDP) with 17 seats or the Social Credit Party with 24 seats. The Liberals were generally considered more pro-American than the Conservatives. However, on the foreign investment question their victory marked another major turning point in Canadian policy. Walter Gordon who was a close friend of Lester Pearson, the new Prime Minister, and a leading party strategist became Minister of Finance.

Since the publication of the Gordon Report, he had made the foreign investment situation his prime subject of interest. In 1961 he published a book, *Troubled Canada*, which took a substantially more adverse view of foreign investment than was contained in the 1957 report.

Actions on Foreign Investment

With the power of a cabinet position and the support of the Prime Minister, Mr. Gordon moved promptly to implement his determination to halt and, hopefully, to reverse the extent of control of the Canadian economy by US capital. His first budget proposals included a 30 percent tax on the take-over of shares of Canadian companies by non-resident corporations and individuals. The budget was presented to Parliament on June 14, 1963. While some features were controversial, the take-over tax created the most extreme reaction. Businessmen, particularly those close to the securities markets, immediately sensed that it would have an extremely adverse effect on the image of Canada in foreign business circles, resulting in a reduction of new investment with severe effects both for security prices and the economy in general. Confronted by this opposition and fearful of bearing the onus of creating a stock market panic, Mr. Gordon withdrew his take-over proposal on June 19.

After the budget debacle it appeared for a while that Walter Gordon might resign from the Cabinet. However, his closeness to Lester Pearson was such that the Prime Minister remained loyal to him and he continued in office until the end of 1965. As chief party strategist, Mr. Gordon recommended that a new election be held in 1965. Working without a clear majority, the Liberals were in a weak position. Mr. Gordon persuaded the party leadership that a new election would result in a clear majority. However, the Liberals gained only two seats in the election held in November 1965, so that they still had to function as a minority government. Mr. Gordon, taking responsibility for this result, resigned from the Cabinet, being replaced as Minister of Finance by Mitchell Sharp. Mr. Sharp shared Gordon's concern about control of the Canadian economy by American business, but he believed in more moderate means to reduce it.

While he had been forced to withdraw his tax proposals, Walter Gordon sought in other ways to stem the tide of American investment during his tenure as Finance Minister. His actions in the Mercantile affair were one facet of this effort. The other prominent undertakings were aimed at US investment in insurance, trust and loan companies, and in press media. The former created little stir because it proposed no change in ownership or operations of firms already controlled by foreign capital. The law passed in 1964 simply provided that in companies set up in the future no more than 25 percent of the shares could be held by non-residents, and no more than 10 percent by any one resident or non-resident.

The proposals for the press media led to a major Canadian-US conflict, however. Walter Gordon included in his 1965 budget a provision that "the deduction of income tax by a taxpayer of expenditures incurred from advertising directed at the Canadian market in a foreign periodical wherever printed be disallowed." For the *Reader's Digest* and *Time*, enactment of this provision would have been a severe competitive blow. With the Canadian corporate tax rate standing at 50 percent, it would in effect have doubled the cost of placing advertising in their Canadian editions as compared to placing ads in Canadian-owned publications. The publications, with the support of the US government, protested vigorously against the proposals. As a result, they were specifically exempted when the tax provision was passed.

There were no official accounts of the conduct of the US government in this case. The press conveyed an image of extreme pressure by the US State Department, acting at the behest of the US publications. Walter Gordon in a subsequent book charged that the United States threatened to withdraw support of the proposed automotive trade agreement which was vital to Canada for the development of its automotive manufacturing and easing of its balance of payments problems.* A book by Peter Newman describes in intimate terms various forms of strong pressure exerted on the Canadian Government because of the press tax measures.**

*A Choice for Canada, Toronto: McClelland & Stewart, Ltd., 1966.
**The Distemper of Our Times, Toronto: McClelland & Stewart, Ltd., 1968, pp. 224-226.

While Walter Gordon pursued his aims with vigor but limited success, others in the Pearson cabinet were taking a milder tack towards foreign investment. The general approach they advocated was moderate pressure to encourage foreign firms to work for Canadian national interests. The chief specific action was the issuing in 1966 by Robert Winters, Minister of Trade and Commerce, of the 12 "guiding principles of good corporate behavior for subsidiaries in Canada of foreign companies" which encouraged use of Canadian management, sale of equity to Canadians, etc.

GENERAL REFERENCES

John Fayerweather, *Foreign Investment in Canada*. White Plains: International Arts & Sciences Press and Toronto: Oxford University Press, 1973.

David Godfrey and Mel Watkins, eds., *Gordon to Watkins to You*. Toronto: New Press, 1970.

Isaiah A. Litvak (ed.), *The Nation Keepers*. Toronto: McGraw-Hill, 1967.

John Lindeman and Donald Armstrong, *Policies and Practices of United States Subsidiaries in Canada*. Washington: National Planning Association, 1969.

A.E. Safarian, *Foreign Ownership of Canadian Industry*. Toronto: McGraw-Hill, 1966.

Task Force on the Structure of Canadian Industry, *Foreign Ownership and the Structure of Canadian Industry*. Ottawa: Queen's Printer, 1968.

 *Appendix B*

DIPLOMATIC NOTE HANDED TO A REPRESENTATIVE OF THE EXTERNAL AFFAIRS DEPARTMENT ON APRIL 7, 1966, BY THE AMERICAN EMBASSY IN OTTAWA

The Embassy of the United States of America refers to the recent meeting in Washington of the Joint Committee on Trade and Economic Affairs, and in particular to the statement of the Minister of Finance that the Government of Canada expects to introduce new banking legislation during the current session of Parliament.*

The Embassy has been instructed to remind the Government of Canada of the concern with which the United States Government viewed certain aspects of the banking legislation introduced in Parliament last year but not enacted (Bill C-102 of May 6, 1965), and to express the hope that the banking legislation to be introduced this year will not contain provisions discriminating against American-owned banks.

The United States Government wishes to remind the Government of Canada that Canadian banks are not subject to discrimination in their United States operations. Indeed, in some respects they enjoy a privileged position relative to United States banks in that their banking operations are not restricted to one state. As a result of favorable United States treatment, major Canadian banks play a significant role in United States banking activities, particularly in New York City's financial market.

The United States Government recognizes the right of the Government of

---

*Reprinted by permission from Peter Newman, *The Distemper of Our Times*. Toronto: McLelland & Stewart, 1968.

Canada to regulate all banking carried on in Canada. However, there is nothing in the operations of American-owned banks in Canada which would appear to justify the adoption of regulations that discriminate against them. In view of the important interrelationships of capital markets in the two countries and the substantial benefits derived by Canadian banks from operations in the United States, it is hoped that the Government of Canada would agree that it is desirable to avoid placing unnecessary restrictions on such mutually beneficial activities.

✳ *Appendix C*

**CABLE TO THE CANADIAN EXTERNAL AFFAIRS
DEPARTMENT BY A.E. RITCHIE, CANADIAN
AMBASSADOR TO THE UNITED STATES, ON
NOVERMBER 11, 1966**

I am reproducing below text of USA note on this subject which Under-Sec. Katzenbach gave to me this afternoon.* He indicated that he in fact had this note in his possession when he saw me on another matter the other day but that he had decided to go into the matter more thoroughly himself before giving it to me, as he realized that it was a rather severe communication. He hoped that we would appreciate from note just how serious USA Govt. regarded matter. They were concerned about many aspects of situation including strong political criticism which would be expressed in this country if present Cdn. measures were to go ahead. They were also disturbed at use that might be made by other countries of our action as a precedent. Katzenbach hoped it might be possible to meet our needs without raising all problems and emotions that were bound to be aroused by proceeding with provision now in bill.

2. I replied that his was indeed a very rough note. I asked him if he had really read our June note. I thought this reply contained numerous inaccuracies and some lines of reasoning which seemed highly questionable on a first reading. I thought it also sounded very threatening. Moreover authors still seemed unable to grasp fundamental differences between USA and Cdn. situations. If no rpt. no

---

*Reprinted by permission from Peter Newman, *Distemper of Our Times.* Toronto: McClelland & Stewart, 1968.

189

limitations were to be imposed on size of a foreign-controlled bank with vast resources behind it Cdn. monetary policy could be all too easily frustrated. Cdn. financial system was relatively small in size and a big foreign-owned bank which did not rpt. not necessarily accept same guidance or discipline as domestic banks could make it very difficult for Cdn. financial and monetary authorities to carry out their policies effectively in interests of Cdn. economy. Cdn. agencies in NY were in a different category and incidentally brought substantial benefits to USA financial position.

3. I asked Mr. Katzenbach whether he really thought we could accept a complete absence of any limitation on size of an outside bank. He replied that he hoped that whatever needed to be done could be done in a manner which would not rpt. not provoke criticisms which were bound to accompany our present measure. I mentioned practical flexibility provided by Treasury Board authority.

4. On factual inaccuracies in USA draft I questioned retroactivity and noted that according to our records reps. of USA banks in Cda. had been fairly warned when they were in process of acquiring Mercantile Bank. Katzenbach interrupted to say that their version of these earlier exchanges was obviously rather different from ours. I agreed that accounts seemed to be divergent but I thought he would recognize that Cdn. authorities had to proceed on basis of their own direct knowledge of what had happened or what had been said. I also questioned accuracy of suggestions in note that only an American bank would likely be affected. I thought it was clear that other banks with concentrated ownership could be involved and I mentioned case of Bank of Western Cda. Another inaccuracy seemed to me to be indication halfway through note that Cdn. banking operations in USA are "many times larger" than Mercantile's operations in Cda. I thought that on basis which we would normally make comparison they were roughly same.

5. Katzenbach said that if of course there were any inaccuracies in their note he would welcome any info that might make it possible to correct them.

6. I reverted to point in note about our not rpt. not taking any action when Mercantile Bank had been under other foreign ownership. I thought there was a substantial difference on one hand between a bank owned by a Dutch institution and operating on kind of scale contemplated when its charter was secured and on other hand a bank owned by an institution as large and aggressive as National City. On matter of "discrimination" I referred to limitations on nationality of directors of federally incorporated USA banks including National City.

7. At several points in conversation Katzenbach referred to "political" problem. I said that we were aware of interest of Senator Javits and some others in case. I

emphasized however that there was an extremely political problem on Cdn. side as well which tended to reinforce other arguments for maintaining provision now in bill. Mr. Rufus Smith who was also present remarked that according to his info Cdn. Bankers' Association were critical of this provision in act. I replied that Cda. had a variety of views on this and other provisions of legislation. I knew that at least some of larger banks strongly supported proposed provision.

8. I concluded by saying that I would report contents of note to Cdn. Govt.

Following is text of note:

Govt. of USA refers Govt. of Cda. to note No. 340 April 7 from USA Emb. in Ottawa and Dept. of External Affairs note No. E-270 of June 29 in reply concerning discriminatory treatment of USA banks in Cda. Govt. of USA cannot agree with contention in Dept. of External Affairs note that Bank Act Bill of 1966 will not rpt. not discriminate against USA-owned banks. While it is true that provisions of bill imposing a limitation on growth of only USA-owned bank in Cda. could apply in theory to other banks that either residents or non-residents might wish to establish in future, in fact only existing bank to which they would apply is USA-owned Mercantile Bank. USA Govt. is particularly recognizant of fact that Cdn. Govt. did not rpt. not attempt to impose discriminatory restrs. on Mercantile Bank until its acquisition by American interests, even though its previous ownership was also foreign, and, of course, it was chartered by act of Parliament.

Previous US note pointed out that Cdn. banks are not rpt. not subject to discrimination in their USA operations. In reply to this statement of fact, Dept. of External Affairs asserted that agencies of Cdn. banks in USA are generally precluded by state banking legislation and regs. from receiving deposits. This appears in part to be a ref. to conditions under which agencies of Cdn. banks operate in state of NY. It should be pointed out that this condition obtains owing to their status as agencies and would not rpt. not apply if they were chartered as branches, as they could be under NY law on basis of reciprocity. Moreover, two of Cdn. banks with agencies in NY also have banking subsidiaries in state which are now allowed to accept deposits. In addition there are Cdn.-owned banks in California, Washington, Oregon, Puerto Rico and USA Virgin Islands, all of which are permitted to accept deposits. Cdn. banking operations in USA are many times larger than Mercantile bank operation in Cda. Five Cdn. agencies in NY alone are estimated to account for over $2 billion in assets, or ten times asset ceiling Govt. of Cda. proposes to impose on Mercantile Bank. In all, five Cdn. banks operating in USA have upward of 35 offices. Counting only states in which they are now operating, they have access to a market for banking services in USA which is substantially larger than their home market. USA Govt. considers that it has made clear its view that retroactive discrimination in Bank Act Bill violates a fundamental principle that has heretofore guided both govts. in their conduct with respect to foreign-owned enterprises within their borders; namely, that an enterprise established in accordance with law is henceforth entitled to equal protection of law and to equality of treatment with other like or similar enterprises organized under same law, and should not rpt. not be subjected to discrimination because of its foreign ownership.

While USA Govt. appreciates that Govt. of Cda. has given careful consideration to its views, it cannot accept suggestion in Cdn. note that it consider discriminatory proposals under discussion as reasonable in special circumstances of Cda.

USA Govt. understands that Govt. of Cda. is considering possibility of allowing establishment of foreign bank agencies in Cda. While USA Govt. in principle would welcome such a development, it would in no rpt. no way change retroactive and discriminatory aspect of proposed legislation affecting Mercantile Bank. For its part, USA Govt. continues to hold view that it is not rpt. not reasonable to expect that privileged position now enjoyed by Cnd. banks in USA would continue unimpaired if only USA-owned bank in Cda. is subjected to retroactive and discriminatory treatment.

In this connection, Govt. of Cda. will be aware of legislation which has been introduced before USA Congress which would provide means of giving practical effect to principle of reciprocity through federal control of foreign-owned banks. In addition, since action contemplated by Cdn. Govt. will not rpt. not only adversely affect Mercantile Bank but will also undermine ground rules on which all American-owned firms operating in Cda. must rely, USA Govt. has under exam. a number of other courses of action consistent with very serious view it takes of issue.

Dept. of State, Wash DC Nov. 11, 1966

**EXCERPTS FROM SUBMISSION TO HOUSE
OF COMMONS COMMITTEE ON FINANCE,
TRADE AND ECONOMIC AFFAIRS BY
THE MERCANTILE BANK**

The Mercantile Bank of Canada urges deletion of Section 75(2)(g) from Bill C-222 because:

. . . . .

A. *Section 75(2)(g) is discriminatory because it is directed specifically to the Mercantile Bank.* The Mercantile is the only Canadian bank more than 25 percent of whose shares are held by "any one resident or non-resident shareholder." The section places, or attempts to place, a limitation on the growth of the Mercantile Bank.

This section would preclude a bank, in circumstances that can apply only to the Mercantile Bank, from having outstanding "total liabilities . . . exceeding 20 times its authorized capital stock. . . ." The attention of this Committee is directed to Attachment A, and particularly to column 5 thereof. There it will be seen that liabilities of all chartered Canadian banks are in excess of 20 times, and range up to 70 times, authorized capital. . . . To impose such a limitation on one bank and not on the others is discriminatory and harsh.

The discriminatory feature of Section 75(2)(g) is further emphasized by the fact that it is directed against the present owners of the Mercantile Bank. Historically there has been no restriction on foreign ownership of chartered banks. In the case of the Mercantile, foreign ownership was specifically approved at the time the Bank was chartered. The present proposal was not put forward until ownership of the Mercantile Bank was transferred from Dutch to U.S. hands.

. . . . .

B. *Section 75 (2)(g), in addition to being discriminatory, is also retroactive.* It is submitted that retroactive legislation, especially when aimed at a specific target, is not in keeping with the best Canadian legislative traditions. The section is retroactive because it would alter the terms under which the Canadian Government will treat ownership of a Canadian bank after that ownership has been acquired. . . .

. . . . .

The original acquisition by Dutch interests of all the Mercantile Bank shares and the subsequent transfer of that ownership to United States interests was entirely in accordance with Canadian law. It is hard to conceive of a more egregious example of retroactivity than the proposed section which, more than three years later, seeks to deprive the present owners of the Mercantile of the benefits of a purchase which they made openly and lawfully in reliance on Canadian law.

. . . . .

Some proponents of Section 75(2)(g) have attempted to justify it on the ground that such a provision is necessary to protect the Canadian financial community from the threat of foreign encroachment. If there were such a threat, there are other more equitable means available to deal with it.

. . . . .

Further, however, though foreign owned, the Mercantile is still a Canadian chartered bank and, like all Canadian banks, is subject to all provisions of the Bank Act. This gives the Canadian government precisely the same measure of control over the Mercantile that it has over other Canadian chartered banks. Authorized capital can not be increased or decreased without government approval. Interest rates and reserve requirements are subject to government control, and the Mercantile has the same reporting responsibilities that all other Canadian banks have.

C. *Section 75(2)(g) seeks also to punish the Mercantile Bank, although Mercantile has violated no law.* Of all the Canadian chartered banks, Mercantile is the only one singled out in Bill C-222 for punitive measures in the form of a limitation on its growth. Furthermore, if even by inadvertence Mercantile were to exceed the limitation placed upon it, the penalty which would be assessed is harsher than penalties assessed for violating other parts of the Bank Act. Anyone looking at Section 75(2)(g) for the first time, aside from noting the obviously discriminatory and retroactive features of the paragraph, could certainly also conclude that Mercantile had been singled out for special punishment for some past wrong-doing.

It is submitted that the Committee consider the extent to which Section 75(2)(g) may circumscribe growth opportunities for Canadian Business at home and abroad.

Limiting Canada's only foreign owned bank may also handicap Canadian business. To assess this possibility it is necessary to describe briefly the role Mercantile plays in the Canadian business community.

In contrast to other Canadian banks which operate hundreds of branches, Mercantile has only seven. For example, each of the three largest Canadian banks has more than 1,000 branches in Canada.

It is unrealistic for Mercantile to try to match its competitors' branch networks. That would require an enormous investment and also would hold small promise of any return because the branch systems of other Canadian banks occupy an overwhelming market position.

Mercantile renders a particularly valuable service to Canada's business community in two ways: by encouraging and developing Canadian exports, and by offering lending techniques designed to serve the special requirements of highly technical industries.

How Mercantile Aids Canadian Export Development

Mercantile gives important assistance to the development of Canadian exports because of its direct access to 183 branch offices and affiliates of First National City Bank in 60 countries on six continents. The extent of this foreign banking network is unsurpassed by any other bank in the world.

Other Canadian banks have also established strong overseas branch and agency systems. It is worth noting, though, that the overseas branches available to Canadian business because of Mercantile Bank's foreign ownership complement more than they duplicate the overseas coverage of other Canadian banks. For example, Canadian banks, not including the Mercantile, operate in 42 countries abroad. With the addition of the facilities of the Mercantile, this jumps to a total of 77 countries. So, while Mercantile is small at home, it makes, we believe, a substantial contribution to the coverage of foreign markets rounding out in a special way the broad coverage of other Canadian banks.

With a phone call to the Mercantile Bank, a Canadian businessman can obtain prompt information about markets for his merchandise at points as distant as Milan and Singapore. This information is detailed, current, and based upon on-the-scene reports. Canadian customers of the Mercantile Bank also may receive, if they wish, a monthly worldwide economic summary called the Foreign Information Service. It has recently been rated by those who receive it as the most useful service of its kind.

Export development has always been basic to the health of Canada's economy. Improved access to world markets can be especially significant to Canadian businessmen now, because world markets are more competitive than ever before. Mercantile is qualified and proud to serve Canadian business abroad.

How Mercantile Serves Special
Technical Needs of Canadian Business

Canadian business, like that of all highly industrialized nations, is becoming increasingly technical and specialized, and with the growth in technology has come the need for lending techniques and financing plans to match it. For example, financing petroleum production must be arranged in a totally different way from financing computer production. Mercantile turns to such specialists as geologists, petroleum engineers, and electronic engineers to tailor financing plans to the special needs of Canada's highly technical industries. Through close relationships with the large institutional lenders, access to medium and long-term funds can be made readily available when needed.

An analysis of 1966 borrowings from the Mercantile Bank shows that 86.5 per cent of the borrowers are companies that are wholly Canadian owned or are Canadian controlled. Only 8.8 per cent of the borrowers are United States companies. By total dollars, less than a quarter of Mercantile's outstanding loans are to United States customers. Mercantile's Canadian dollar deposits at August 31 amounted to 0.42 of one per cent of such deposits in all the chartered banks.

Conclusion

We have attempted here to describe the objectionable features of Section 75(2)(g) in terms of the interests of both Mercantile and its customers. We have suggested that measures such as this are contrary to the Canadian legislative tradition of not changing the rules in the middle of the game, and not discriminating against one competitor to favor others. We have no quarrel with the right of any government to regulate bank operations, but we urge strongly that it be done on a prospective, not a retroactive basis. When the Canadian government decided to limit foreign ownership of other financial institutions, insurance and trust companies, it did not even suggest any measure such as Section 75(2)(g). (See Chapter 40, Statutes of Canada 1964-65.) Instead, it enacted legislation limiting foreign ownership from that date forward, and did not persecute existing companies, attempt to limit their growth, nor try to force foreign owners to divest. There is nothing to warrant treating banks worse than other kinds of financial institutions.

Schedule A
Figures as at August 31, 1966 in Millions of Dollars

	Authorized Capital	20 Times Authorized Capital	Liabilities Including Paid Up Capital, Rest and Undivided Profits	Difference	Liabilities Times Capital
Bank of Montreal	100	2,000	5,274.6	−3,274.6	52.7
Banque Canadieano Nationale	25	500	1,075.5	−575.5	43.0
Canadian Imperial Bank of Commerce	125	2,500	6,373.6	−3,873.6	50.9
The Bank of Nova Scotia	50	1,000	3,537.1	−2,537.1	70.7
The Provincial Bank of Canada	20	400	562.1	−162.1	23.1
The Royal Bank of Canada	100	2,000	6,434.6	−4,424.6	64.2
The Toronto Dominion Bank	50	1,000	2,996.0	−1,995.0	59.9
The Mercantile Bank of Canada	10	200	224.5	−24.5	22.4
Bank of Western Canada	25	500			

Bayer Industrial SA

NEGOTIATIONS ABOUT CONTROL OF A
NEW ACRYLIC FIBER PLANT IN PERU

In the summer of 1970 Bayer Industrial SA, a 75 percent owned Bayer of Germany subsidiary, faced the difficult question concerning the status of its acrylic fiber plant in Peru which was in the early stages of construction. The issuance by the Peruvian government of its Industrial Law in July with requirements for the transfer of ownership to the workers substantially changed the basis on which the investment had been initially planned. Furthermore, there were prospects for other changes in treatment of foreign investment coming out of a meeting of the Andean Common Market countries planned for later in the year.

BACKGROUND

Bayer Industrial was an affiliate of Bayer Chemical Company of Germany. The parent company had developed extensive international operations since World War II in a variety of chemical fields. It had become the fourth largest chemical group in the world by 1970, with some $3 billion in sales world-wide. It had plants in 20 countries in 1970. Earlier it had opened a 100 percent owned company in Peru, Laboratories Bayer SA, to make aspirin and a few other products. The laboratory made some 80 percent of the Bayer pharmaceuticals sold in Peru. Bayer also had a 75 percent owned subsidiary, Bayer Quimicas Unidas, producing insecticides and leather dyes.

Written in conjunction with Ralph Diaz, Business International, and published through the cooperation of Bayer, AG and Business International.

THE ACRYLIC FIBER PLANT

The idea of building an acrylic fiber plant originated from discussions among the Andean region countries. These discussions had resulted in the Andean Petrochemical Agreement (LAFTA Complementation Agreement #6) signed in 1969 by Bolivia, Chile, Colombia and Peru. The agreement gave Peru preferential access to acrylic fiber markets in Bolivia and Chile. Any Peruvian producer would be able to sell duty free while third-country sources would be hit with a 50 percent duty in the two countries. Colombia was also allocated production rights for the same product and was already talking to at least one other international company in 1970 about investment prospects.

Bayer felt it had a strong position in the Andean market for its acrylic fiber, Dralon.® It had an estimated 60 percent of the Peruvian market and 70 percent of that in Chile. The market was growing quite rapidly. A 1968 company market study anticipated total demand of 7,000 metric tons by 1973 (3,700 tons in Peru, 3,000 in Chile and 300 in Bolivia). With this prospect, the company felt there was ample demand to justify setting up a 6,000 metric ton per year acrylic fiber plant. Accordingly, the company moved ahead rapidly during 1969 and completed plans for a $16 million operation. No competitive firm had an interest in establishing such a plant in Peru. The government was quite satisfied with the proposals set forth by Bayer. An agreement that gave Bayer considerable tax benefits under Peru's petrochemical law and a guarantee that no competitor would be given similar benefits during the period of validity of LAFTA's Complementary Agreement No. 6 was signed May 1969 by the government. Velasco Alvarado, as customary for the President, only endorsed the Decreto Supremo which allowed the competent government authorities to sign the contract on behalf of the state.

The plant would use imported raw materials, mainly acrylonitrile, to be substituted at a later date from a projected Peruvian government plant source. With the exception of some 25 technical and managerial people brought from the parent firm for training purposes, the full employment of 450 would be local nationals. Assuming exclusive rights to the three-country market under the Ancom Agreement, they estimated total sales of $10 million yearly when operations started in 1971.

The company, aware of growing pressure for joint ventures throughout Latin America, set out to hold 70 percent of the equity (64 percent through its Canadian holding company and 6 percent by Quimicas Unidas) with 19 percent going into the hands of the government-run Banco Industrial and 11 percent into the control of local private investors.

THE PERUVIAN SITUATION

The situation in the summer of 1970 had its immediate origins in the recent major change in the Peruvian government. In 1968, a military group seized control and made radical changes in the direction of national policies. Guided by

General Velasco, the military junta set about a program of social reform and nationalism designed to build what it felt would be an economy more responsive to the needs of the Peruvian population. The nationalistic thrust of the program involved a deemphasis of private enterprise and the role of foreign investment and considerable participation of the government and workers in the economy. The objectives were not completely socialistic. Rather, the concept was one of a mixed economy with active public and private investment, the latter to include foreign investment on terms considered appropriate for national interest.

The nationalistic government policy found immediate manifestation in the expropriation of the International Petroleum Corporation, a fully-owned subsidiary of the Standard Oil Company of New Jersey. There was a long-standing conflict between the Peruvian government and IPC over the legality of IPC's subsoil rights which dated back to the Spanish crown. What actually triggered expropriation of the company by the government in 1969 was the inadequacy of tax payments. The government did not offer significant compensation for the IPC properties as it contended that most of their value was necessary to satisfy the taxes it felt were due to the government. This position was not acceptable to the owners of IPC, nor to the US government which supported the IPC claims. This situation resulted in a severe strain in relations with the US government, including the cessation of economic aid. Furthermore, it resulted in a rather adverse image for Peru among multinational firms. There was a sharp decline, therefore, in interest in investing in Peru. Through 1969 and 1970 no proposals were put forward by foreign firms to invest in that country (except Bayer's) despite earnest expressions by government officials that firms would be treated fairly and that the IPC situation was a special problem not indicative of a general policy of harsh treatment of foreign investors.

Peru's international trade situation further complicated the government's attempt to create a new socioeconomic order. Exports in the late 1960s had grown stagnant, in part due to lower anchovy catches—used as raw material for Peru's fishmeal exports which accounted for 30 percent of total exports. For example, the volume of fishmeal exports had fallen 20 percent between 1968 and 1969, just at a time when average world prices were climbing from $99 per ton to $122 per ton. The balance of payments was suffering.

The balance of payments situation was a significant detriment to Peru in its efforts to build its economy. With unemployment running at 20 percent or more, the government was anxious to expand industrial output. For this purpose, it was actively seeking substantial loans from international or from foreign sources (either international institutions or foreign countries). In this quest, it was considerably handicapped by the consequences of the IPC expropriation including the adverse position of the US government and the unfavorable image conveyed to capital markets in general.

THE INDUSTRIAL LAW

The Industrial Law issued in July 1970 was the first formal implementation of the national industrial policies of the government. The basic concepts underlying it were that control of the main elements of industry should lie in Peruvian hands, and to a substantial degree, in the hands of the workers. Specifically, it reserved for the government all basic industries (steel, petrochemicals, heavy machinery) though participation by private industry in collaboration with the government was to be permitted. The law provided for certain tariff, tax and credit incentives to stimulate investment including the role of private firms in these industries.

The law established a system whereby 50 percent of the ownership of all firms (local and foreign-owned) in major manufacturing industries were to be transferred to workers over a period of time. Each firm was required to establish a comunidad industrial, a holding group made of all the workers of the firm. Each year a company was required to transfer 15 percent of its pre-tax profits to the comunidad industrial in the form of shares of the firm. This process was to continue until the comunidad owned at least 50 percent of the equity of the firm. The only exceptions were public-sector companies for whom the transfer process was to take the form of bonds without voting rights, thus conveying to the workers ultimately 50 percent of the capital of the company but without any control participation. The law did not define the percentage of government percentage in ownership required to qualify for this provision. The law further provided that the workers should be represented on the board of directors of the company in proportion to the ratio of their stock control.

There was little basis for predicting the effects of the labor participation provisions. The financial facts were clear. Since Peruvian law already required that 10 percent of profits be paid to workers, in total, the company would be giving up 25 percent of profits per year. Assuming there was no change in the proportional holdings of the participants in the investments, Bayer's share of the equity would ultimately be reduced to 35 percent.

From the managerial point of view, however, there were no precedents of worker participation from which to predict the effects of a transfer of ownership. Among the leadership of Peruvian labor unions, there were a number of relatively well educated accountants, lawyers and the like. It was possible that the board of directors participation by the workers might be drawn from such people, or from factory workers themselves. The effects of worker participation might range from their simply using it as a vehicle for obtaining information about the company's sales, profits and plans, to efforts to influence substantially management decisions, both for the immediate operations and for the longer term. Likewise, it was not clear what the overall implications of the goals of the government in seeking national control might be, though the implications of reserving industries to the public sector appeared to be a desire to exercise greater government control over investments and other major economic decisions.

THE ANCOM PROSPECTS

In addition to considering the immediate effects of the Peruvian act, there was concern about the possible outcome of meetings to be held in late 1970 among the Andean Common Market governments. A conference was set for September of ANCOM technical experts. There were active rumors in Peruvian circles that the experts were considering plans to achieve nationalization of considerable foreign investment. The rumors were encouraged by knowledge that a small group of academicians from the United States, including Profs. Rosenstein-Rodan and Stephen Hymer, would attend the conference. These men were known to be advocates of progressive reduction of foreign control of industry, advocating, in particular, what was known as the "fade out" formula whereby ownership would be transferred to local stockholders over a period of years.

Some further concrete indication of the intentions of the Peruvian government was also provided by the purchase of control of three commercial banks in 1970, two of which were foreign controlled: the Banco Continental, 51 percent owned by Chase Manhattan Bank, and the Banco Nationale which included 20 percent ownership by Chemical Bank, 5 percent by W.R. Grace and 15 percent by an Argentine group. In this case the government provided compensation for the foreign owners which was considered quite adequate.

BAYER'S SITUATION

The Peruvian Industrial Law and the prospects for further action by the ANCOM governments posed a significant problem for Bayer. Having in hand a contract signed by President Velasco, the company felt that it was in a strong legal position to argue its rights to pursue its operation according to the economic and control conditions existing at the time the contract was completed. The plant at this time was already under construction with about $2 million of investment already committed. On the other hand, the company had been advised by several government ministers that it could expect to be brought under the provisions of the new law despite the existence of its contract.

Esso Fertilizer and Agricultural Chemicals, Inc. (The Philippines)

INTERNATIONAL BUSINESS
DIVESTMENT/INVESTMENT
NEGOTIATION

Esso Fertilizer and Agricultural Chemicals Company, Inc. (ESFAC) was incorporated in the Philippines in September 1962. Plant construction started in January 1964 in the town of Limay and the plant became operational in 1966. The company was capitalized at P150 million, and the plant had a rated capacity of 1,000 MTD (metric tons per day) of different grades of fertilizer with a peak annual capacity of 390,000 metric tons. The plant was the largest in the Philippines, and its entry more than doubled the fertilizer manufacturing capacity.

From the beginning, ESFAC faced many serious problems resulting in heavy financial losses, which by the end of 1968 had accumulated to P28,906,251. As part of a global strategy of divestment from the fertilizer industry, senior management of Esso decided in 1968 to divest itself of ESFAC. On November 25, 1970 Esso sold the operation to International Mineral and Chemicals which later sold it to the Sugar Producers Cooperative Marketing Association.

This study deals with the negotiations among Filipino, US and Japanese businessmen and with various bodies of the Philippine government resulting in divestment by Esso and acquisition by IMC and SPCMA.

BACKGROUND

In the early 1960s many chemical and petroleum companies forecasted tremendous growth of global demand for fertilizers especially in the developing

This case was written by A. Kapoor and is based on a more detailed study by A. Kapoor and F. Alfonso in A. Kapoor *Planning for International Business Negotiations*. Cambridge, Mass., Ballinger, 1975.

countries. The significant growth in population, the critical role of fertilizers in achieving much higher foodgrain yields, the promising prospects of major aid and assistance by the USA and other developed countries to developing countries—these and other considerations encouraged companies to invest in the fashionable fertilizer industry. Oil executives believed that their knowledge of petroleum technology, marketing, international shipping and access to raw materials used in fertilizer manufacturing (natural gas and ammonia derived from petroleum refining) could be profitably used in fertilizer production.

In 1962 Esso Standard Eastern established the Esso Fertilizer and Agricultural Chemicals (ESFAC) plant in the Philippines as part of its worldwide strategy for investments in fertilizer manufacturing. Two considerations encouraged Esso to establish a fertilizer plant in the Philippines. First, the newly established administration of President Diosado Macapagal was championing free enterprise, attempting to create a favorable foreign investment climate and encouraging the establishment of a urea plant in the country. Second, forecasts by different organizations in the Philippines indicated an important increase in demand for fertilizer (see Exhibit 1).

In January 1964, construction of the fertilizer plant was started in a 50-hectare site adjacent to the Bataan (Esso) Refinery (source of refinery gas which is the basic raw material for fertilizer production). The rated daily capacity of the plant was to be approximately 1,000 metric tons of different grades of fertilizer, and at peak capacity operation the plant was designed to produce 390,000 metric tons of fertilizer annually, the largest capacity among the local fertilizer production facilities (see Exhibit 2).

The company's authorized capital was P150 million divided into 15 million common shares with a par value of P10 each. Esso Standard Eastern, New York, provided initial capitalization by purchasing 6 million common shares, while 2

Exhibit 1. Market Forecasts for 1970-1971—Philippine Nitrogen (1000 metric tons nitrogen)

Year	Program Implementation Agency	Farmers Fertilizers Company
1962	—	58.0
1963	58.3	75.0
1964	64.3	81.0
1965	71.0	103.0
1966	78.2	130.0
1967	86.4	164.0
1968	95.3	215.0
1969	105.1	275.0
1970	108.2	350.0

Exhibit 2. Aggregate Rated Annual Capacity, 1966

Name of Firm	Aggregate Rated Annual Capacity (as of 1966)	Plant Site	Start of Operation
Atlas Fertilizer Corp.	162,000	Toledo, Cebu	1958
Maria Christina Fertilizer & Chemical Corp. (Marcelo)	86,624	Iligan City	1958
Chemical Industries of the Philippines (ChemPhil)	81,000	Taguig, Rizal	1960
ESFAC (Esso)	390,000	Limay, Bataan	1966

million common shares (equivalent to 25 percent of the equity) were offered for sale to local investors. However, in spite of a vigorous sales campaign, only 607,758 shares, representing a little over 7.5 percent of the equity, were absorbed by the public.

Pyrites, refinery gas, and petroleum products were obtained locally from Esso Standard Eastern, Inc. Phosphate rock and potash were purchased from abroad from International Minerals and Chemical Company (IMC), a Chicago-based firm reputed to be the largest miner and refiner of basic agricultural minerals and producer of 15 percent of the world's potash and phosphate.

The fertilizer products of ESFAC were marketed under the brand name ENGRO, coined from the phrase, "ENergy for GROwth." The backbone of the company's marketing efforts was a strong network of independent dealers who operated Agroservice stores which were strategically located to allow the dealers direct contact with the farmers. According to a market survey conducted by ESFAC in 1964, only 30 percent of the approximately 2.4 million farmers were using fertilizers; the rest did not, mainly because of lack of knowledge of the benefits that could be derived from using fertilizers. To overcome this problem, a continuing series of farm demonstrations was sponsored by ESFAC starting in December 1964.

These farm demonstrations were joint-effort projects with farmer-cooperatives who agreed to plant their crops in their usual way on one plot; on an adjoining plot, they planted the same crop but used fertilizer according to ESFAC's specifications. When the two plots were ready for harvest, a field day was organized and the neighborhood farmers were invited to see the results for themselves. The company was confident that these farm demonstrations, supplemented by advertising, were most effective in convincing farmers to use fertilizers.

As early as 1966, in its annual report, ESFAC stated that the plant was "experiencing design and equipment deficiencies," and by year's end, they had not been resolved. Power failures were regarded as the major cause of the problems. Breakdown of the plant's ammonia equipment was cited as a reason for the plant's low production. According to ESFAC's 1967 annual report, the "plant's high degree of integration, which brings economies of operations when a plant is producing satisfactorily, led to loss of production in other units when one unit suffered an upset."

THE DECISION TO DIVEST

During the latter part of 1967 and early 1968, the executives of many companies began to realize that the great fertilizer boom was not going to materialize. Consumption increases had failed to keep up with expanded capacities. The Philippines was no exception to this worldwide phenomenon. From 1966 to 1969 actual production of fertilizer was never more than 35 percent of total rated capacity. Approximate rated capacities of the four fertilizer plants were: ESFAC—390,000 MT per year; Atals Fertilizers—200,000 MT per year; Farmers Fertilizers—100,000 MT per year; and Chemical Industries of the Philippines—below 100,000 MT per year. While their rated annual capacities totaled 790,000 MT per year, these four companies produced only about 267,000 MT in 1968. Atlas operated at 47 percent of capacity, ESFAC at 36 percent; Chemical Industries of the Philippines at 22 percent and Farmers Fertilizers at 7 percent.

Two reasons explained why the actual demand for fertilizer continued to run below expected demand: low usage by farmers and heavy importation of fertilizers by agricultural cooperatives. The low usage of fertilizer by farmers in the Philippines, according to a study done by the Presidential Economic Staff, can be attributed to the following factors: (1) lack of sufficient knowledge on the part of farmers regarding intelligent use of fertilizer. The farmers often saw no need to apply fertilizer (where it was needed) or applied less than recommended levels; (2) lack of credit facilities to assist the farmers in the purchase of fertilizers; (3) inadequate irrigation and drainage facilities to make fertilizer application effective; (4) inadequate credit facilities for capital equipment to boost agricultural production.

In addition to the foregoing reasons, of course, was the fact that the intensive use of fertilizer in the cultivation of land required a basic change in habits and attitudes of the farmers. The proper use of fertilizer involved the use of new and scientific methods of farming hitherto untried by the farmers. Changes of this nature take place very slowly.

The sugar planters were an exception to this general trend among farmers in the Philippines. For the most part they were better educated than the other farmers and they also recognized the need for increased efficiency to become competitive in world markets. Their cooperatives, among which Sugar Producers Cooperative Marketing Association (SPCMA) was the acknowledged giant, made arrangements to finance a supply of fertilizer. The sugar cooperatives accounted for almost 50 percent of the fertilizer consumption in the country. The marketing system introduced and implemented by ESFAC sought to bypass this system used by the sugar cooperatives and therefore was viewed as a serious threat by SPCMA and other sugar cooperatives.

In 1968 the actual demand for fertilizers was 406,000 metric tons. However, about 266,000 MT of this amount was provided by fertilizers imported by the agricultural cooperatives and through Japanese reparations in the form of fertilizers in the stock of the Agricultural Credit Administration. Figures for the first half of 1968 revealed that agricultural cooperatives imported about 19,085 MT of fertilizers, worth approximately P3,266,000 of which P2,996,000 or 15,000 MT were imported by the SPCMA.

This heavy importation was attributed to two factors: first, the "dumping" of fertilizers in the Philippines by Germany and Japan, and second, the privilege of cooperatives to import fertilizers tax free.*

Three of the country's local fertilizer manufacturers reported losses in 1968: ESFAC lost some P27,081,403; Farmers Fertilizer Corporation (FFC) was in the red by P403,352; and Chemical Industries of the Philippines lost P180,000. Only Atlas Fertilizers reported a net income of P453,518. ESFAC had lowered fertilizer prices in order to sell fertilizers to SPCMA, but the sugar cooperative was not interested because it could secure even cheaper imported fertilizer, it did not have good rapport with ESFAC management and it was not pleased with ESFAC's marketing system.

The foreign exchange shortage reached crisis proportions in 1970. Deficits began to be serious in 1967 when the shortfall amounted to $64 million. In 1968, the deficit was a more manageable $48 million, but in 1969 it rose to $136 million.

Foreign borrowings complicated the picture further. Increased foreign borrowing, mostly short term, was necessary to finance foreign obligations. The government and government-guaranteed foreign debt of the Philippines rose from $738 million at the end of 1968 to $823 million by the end of November 1969. Because more than half of the foreign debt was short term, the problem of managing it became more difficult.

Faced with this foreign exchange crisis, the Marcos Administration (reinstated after the elections of November 1969) initiated a series of measures designed to alleviate the dollar crisis. Particularly affecting ESFAC was the need to secure dollar allocation of $750,000 to import raw materials. However, the dollar budget prepared and approved for the year 1970 did not include importation of raw materials for fertilizer as a top priority item, and ESFAC was faced with the possibility of closing production.

The ESFAC plant was of an uneconomic size. By the time it became operational in 1966, there had been new breakthroughs in technology to permit bigger and more economical plants. This, plus the fertilizer glut, made it

*Under Republic Act No. 3425, agricultural marketing cooperatives were exempt from "income tax, sales tax and all other percentage tax of whatever nature and description."

increasingly more attractive for consumers to import fertilizers. In order to sell its product, ESFAC was forced to make its prices competitive with those of more economic plants.

ESFAC was predicting that the market demand for fertilizer in the Philippines would not increase significantly. In spite of the massive promotional and educational efforts undertaken by the company, no marked change in the consumption of fertilizer had been discernible.

Those in the fertilizer business in the Philippines felt that in addition to the economic and technical factors already cited, noneconomic considerations contributed to ESFAC's failure to realize profits. For one, its marketing system constituted a direct threat to cooperatives, particularly the sugar cooperatives. The industry, therefore, did not buy the company's products even when it lowered its prices to be competitive with world prices. In addition, because the government wanted to encourage cooperatives, it granted certain tax privileges, particularly the exemption from the 7 percent advanced sales tax that local manufacturers had to pay.

Some "internal" factors also probably contributed to the poor performance. Some high ranking company officials expressed the view that the project had a dim prospect right from the start because it had been oversold to the New York office by those who had promoted the project. They further observed that the situation was compounded by the fact that the personalities of the executives sent to the Philippines were not right for the effective delivery of the project.

ESFAC had no tariff or other protection from the government, and as the situation worsened, it did not seek any. The company felt that since it had sought no such protection when it decided to invest in the Philippines, it could not rightly seek it when it realized that its economic viability was being threatened by imports. They probably felt, too, that it was doubtful that they could have secured such protections because it would have run counter to the interests of the politically powerful sugar bloc.

The fundamental consideration for Esso in its decision on ESFAC was the return on investment. Cash flow projections by the country level managers clearly indicated that the return on investment from ESFAC would not be of a level acceptable to Esso. ESFAC would be attractive for a company that sought integrated operations (from supply of raw materials to manufacturing and marketing) and could achieve an affiliation with a local cooperative to gain tax advantages. ESFAC was neither, and had no intention of moving in these directions.

The decision to divest was reached some time in mid-1968. It was not an overnight decision but was the result of long deliberations and analysis involving a wide range of people. Gradually over time the questions, the alternatives and the objectives of the company became more sharply defined.

The main task faced by Esso management was how to implement its decision to divest most effectively. Some of its main considerations were:

1. The divestment should not hurt the company's name and image in the Philippines and elsewhere.
2. The divestment should not have an adverse effect on the company's much larger operations in petroleum refining and marketing in the Philippines.
3. The divestment should not establish undesirable precedents for the company in other parts of the world where divestments already were under way or might be negotiated in the future.
4. There were only a handful of indigenous potential buyers of the plant—but would they have the financial, technical and managerial resources?
5. The divestment negotiations must be very low key so as not to adversely affect the viability of the ongoing operation.
6. Any terms of divestment negotiated with a buyer should be final and binding. Therefore, the selection of a buyer should be heavily weighted in favor of an organization that would not renege on agreed terms and expose Esso to the necessity of having to renegotiate terms. A US firm was preferred to a firm indigenous to the Philippines.
7. Securing a fair price for ESFAC was an objective; however, price alone was not the major or determining factor.
8. The divestment should be negotiated in a manner and at a location (in the United States between two US companies) in order to achieve benefits of tax loss.
9. The careers and terms of employment of ESFAC employees, particularly expatriates, should be recognized and safeguarded.

These considerations and objectives were generally recognized. However, the major task facing the management was to emerge with a program of action to achieve its objectives.

IMPLEMENTING THE DECISION TO DIVEST

Approach by Esso

The planned disinvestment by Esso of ESFAC was a closely guarded secret through 1968 and the early part of 1969. Only a select group of high ranking company officials (all US citizens) in the Philippines were informed about it during the latter part of 1968. Corporate-level management wanted to keep the decision and the specific moves for divestment a closely guarded secret for several reasons.

1. There was no assurance that the plant could be sold on terms acceptable to Esso.
2. Premature disclosure of divestment negotiations would seriously undermine the morale of ESFAC employees, thereby having an adverse effect on the viability of the organization, which would then become less attractive to a potential buyer.

3. Public disclosure of intent to divest would result in a great deal of publicity that would prevent Esso and the prospective buyer(s) from engaging in considered and private negotiations.
4. Esso did not want its plans for divestment from the fertilizer industry on a worldwide or countrywide basis publicized, as it would have a negative effect on the morale of the worldwide fertilizer organization established by the company.
5. Premature publicity would be embarrassing because management was not sure of what might be involved in accomplishing the divestment.

Although rumors of the proposed sale started to float in mid-1969 among the company's employees and other people "in the know," no official written notice of the same was made to lower-level employees until 24 hours before the transaction took place.

This secrecy, while necessitated by the nature of the negotiations, resulted in adverse comments from employees of ESFAC, particularly Filipinos at senior management levels. They accused corporate level management of using dual standards in dealing with their executives: US nationals were considered more loyal and trustworthy than Filipinos, regardless of their length of service with the company.

Searching for Buyers

A "clean" divestment with no lingering involvements and the protection of the company's image were among the more important objectives of corporate management. Soon after the decision was made in 1968, Esso officials in New York informed International Minerals and Chemical Corporation (IMC) officials in Chicago of the planned divestment in the Philippines and in other countries in the thought that IMC might be interested in buying the ESFAC and other fertilizer plants. At that time (1968) nothing significant developed with IMC.

IMC was an attractive buyer of the ESFAC plant from Esso's viewpoint for several reasons.

1. It was an established company and a leader in its industry. If IMC were to become the successor to Esso, then Esso could not be accused of selling ESFAC to some third-rate company. In other words, the interests of the country would be protected.
2. IMC was well known to Esso and was physically close to Esso's executive offices and therefore would be easier to deal with.
3. IMC might wish to extend its operations to include fertilizer manufacturing, which would offer an assured market for its raw materials such as phosphate rock.
4. Esso was planning major divestments on a global basis. IMC was an organization that might well be interested in acquiring ESFAC and other

fertilizer plants owned by Esso. Therefore, economies of scale in terms of negotiation time could be achieved.

5. IMC was a US-based company that would honor terms of sale agreed upon. However, if differences were to arise, Esso could litigate in US courts rather than in foreign courts.

6. IMC could be expected to go along with the low profile, no publicity approach adopted by Esso in implementing the decision to divest.

7. IMC possessed the financial resources to offer a "clean" divestment.

8. IMC, through its subsidiary Continental Fertilizer Corporation (CFC), was familiar with the Philippines and had dealt with SPCMA and other parties which might become IMC's partners in acquiring ESFAC.

There were several reasons why IMC considered Esso a desirable party to deal with: knowledge of the company and existing relationships, potential for acquiring more than one plant, and securing a bargain basement price under distress sale circumstances on the part of Esso. In brief, Esso and IMC seemed to possess a large commonality of interests.

Buyback of Shares

After the decision to divest had been made in New York, it was also decided to buy back the 7.5 percent of the company's shares then owned by the Filipino public. Corporate management also decided to convert into shares a major portion of the advances made by Esso Chemical, Inc., in order to keep ESFAC in operation in spite of the heavy financial losses it had sustained.

The move to buy back the shares was taken because the ESFAC executives in Manila were worried about the possible reaction of the Filipino stockholders if and when the divestment took place. They were quite sure that the local investors put money into ESFAC not because they had any particular faith in the fertilizer industry but because of the Esso name. If Esso was supporting a project, local investors felt they simply could not lose. The company felt something had to be done to regain the faith and to protect the economic interest of these stockholders and partially to redeem the Esso name. People from important opinion-forming groups (executives, government officials, etc.) were the major subscribers.

In addition to the important public relations considerations, Esso also recognized another important benefit. It would be simpler to sell ESFAC if Esso owned all the shares. A potential buyer such as IMC would view it as an "unencumbered purchase." Filipino shareholders were a very small minority but they could pose embarrassing questions during and after the divestment. Therefore, management decided that the divestment could be made "cleaner" if it was 100 percent owned by Esso.

Change of Executives

In addition to the negotiations with IMC and the offer to buy back the outstanding local shares, corporate management took a third step to prepare for the divestment of ESFAC. It effected a change in the leadership of ESFAC during the first and second quarters of 1969. A new president and executive officer was appointed and the company's Filipino vice president and treasurer was replaced. Both of the new executives were Americans who were sent to the Philippines with specific instructions to prepare the company for divestment and to assist corporate level management in planning, negotiating and implementing the divestment decision.

The new vice president and treasurer in particular had prior experience in the company's global divestment program and therefore possessed expertise in this area. Also, the treasurer's functions would be very important in valuation of assets, financial arrangements for payments and in understanding the particular financial requirements of Filipino banks and financial authorities.

The change of personnel was also motivated by other considerations. The divestment process was sensitive and could be explosive if not properly handled. Therefore, the individuals charged with responsibility in the country of divestment must be well known to and have the trust of top management in addition to possessing the functional expertise. Corporate management would be making the major decisions and conducting negotiations on the terms and conditions of divestment and the company to which the plant would be sold. Because of a combination of reasons including tax considerations, the situs of the sale had to be in the United States, and since IMC appeared to be the most likely purchaser, corporate level management would be handling the negotiations in the United States. The role of the country level managers would then be to "hold the fort," serve as the eyes and ears of corporate management in the country, especially as it related to potential local participants in the transaction, retain the good will of the host government, and above all, offer clear communications to corporate management in a form and manner that would be relevant to the needs of corporate management.

There would be almost daily communications between New York and ESFAC executives as events unfolded over the coming months. Overall corporate plans, strategies and postures in various parts of the world would be part of the discussion relating to ESFAC. Reactions of corporate executives in New York would need to be conveyed often on an informal basis without fear of being misunderstood or misquoted. The issues involved in the divestment negotiations would expose a Filipino to charges of loyalty conflict—was he more loyal to the company or to the country? Of course, these considerations meant that only Americans well versed in company mores and knowing the ambiance could be appointed as top executives of ESFAC at the time of divestment.

Besides, assignment of new American executives at this stage was deemed desirable because of the need for interacting with Filipino groups. A new executive would not have built a set of personal relationships with Filipinos, would not be obliged to the government in any particular way and could afford to adopt a tough stance because his duration of stay in the country would be limited.

Esso had undertaken a series of moves for the implementation of the divestment. However, there were important developments within the Filipino fertilizer industry involving powerful economic and political forces which were to influence the manner and the approach of Esso's divestment of ESFAC. The groups involved were Marcelo, Garcia and SPCMA.

Prospective Filipino Buyers

In 1962, when ESFAC was being planned, Marcelo's proposal to establish a nitrogen plant was one of the alternatives considered by the Philippine government. He dropped his plans when the ESFAC project was approved. In 1967 Marcelo saw the prospect for the establishment of a larger and integrated plant to produce ammonia and urea. To tap this opportunity, he incorporated the Farmers' Fertilizer Corporation and became its first president. During the fourth quarter of 1967, plans for the new plant were commissioned and negotiations were initiated with possible suppliers. These plans, however, were aborted when government approval was denied. The rejection of FFC's application was one of the events that led to the fertilizer controversy of 1970. Although this controversy, more popularly known as the Marubeni-Iida deal, had no direct bearing on the ESFAC divestment process, indirectly it had a significant effect on the final outcome of the ESFAC negotiations. Appendix A narrates the events of the fertilizer controversy.

SPCMA was organized in 1948 as a sister organization of the National Federation of Sugarcane Planters in the Philippines. It was a stock corporation organized under the Agricultural Cooperatives Act and was owned by 23 sugar planters' associations. It had 27,000 members representing more than 90 percent of the sugar cane planters in the Philippines. Its principal objectives were to assist its members in selling their products and in purchasing their requirements, principally fertilizer.

The sugar planters, often referred to as the "sugar bloc," were an economically and politically influential group. Unlike other industrial groups, they were able to exercise considerable influence because they were well organized.

During their national convention in February 1968 the sugar planters approved a project to establish a fertilizer plant to supply their needs and constituted Mr. Alfredo Montelibano as a committee of one to pursue the project. The plan envisioned the establishment of a plant to be owned and operated by SPCMA. The fact that SPCMA as a cooperative was exempted from paying certain taxes, particularly the 7 percent advanced sales tax on the sale of fertilizer, was a clear advantage. SPCMA's pursuit of this project is covered in the Marubeni-Iida controversy in Appendix A.

Chemical Industries of the Philippines, Inc. (Chemphil) was one of three companies manufacturing fertilizer in the Philippines prior to the entry of

ESFAC. Its principal stockholders were members of the Garcia family, headed by Dr. Eusebio Garcia. During the last quarter of 1968 and early part of 1969, Chemphil management closely watched developments in the fertilizer business worldwide. When they saw large multinational companies like Esso starting to unload their investment in other parts of the world, they decided to prepare for the eventuality that ESFAC might be sold.

DIVESTMENT NEGOTIATIONS ACKNOWLEDGED

This section deals with the negotiations directly related to the sale of the ESFAC plant, covering the period from March to June 1970, ending with the selection of the Philippine group that would eventually buy the plant.

Esso was more convinced than ever that the divestment must be a "clean" one, and this would require selling to a US company. The SPCMA-FFC-Marubeni controversy was a good example of what Esso might get entangled in if it sold to a Filipino company. Also, Esso realized that SPCMA would now undertake steps to actually develop a fertilizer plant. But in Esso's view, SPCMA lacked the managerial and technological know-how to evaluate the viability of the hastily construed project proposal with Marubeni-Iida. Informal and preliminary feelers to SPCMA had been extended by ESFAC but without an obvious and positive response by SPCMA. There are conflicting recollections within the Esso and ESFAC organizations on this point. One recollection is that an informal but serious inquiry was made of SPCMA by ESFAC. Another recollection is that ESFAC was under strict instructions from corporate headquarters not to deal directly in any manner whatsoever with SPCMA. SPCMA executives recall the second approach.

The three key parties at this stage—Esso, IMC and SPCMA—were exploring an important policy decision. Esso had almost reached agreement in principle with IMC on sale of ESFAC. However, Esso realized that IMC would have to associate itself with a Filipino cooperative because of tax advantages to the new owners and the promise of markets. SPCMA was the most viable choice.

SPCMA, on its side, realized that ESFAC was a most sensible compromise between the size of project it had proposed and the size deemed economical by the BOI. Also, ESFAC was an existing and on-going operation which was attractive to SPCMA, which lacked in managerial and technical know-how of the fertilizer industry.

The Marcelo Group

Marcelo came to know that ESFAC was for sale on April 30, 1969 when he received a letter from a friend in Canada, a former employee of ESFAC who was quite familiar with its operation. The Canadian friend informed Marcelo that he had received news that the ESFAC plant was for sale. However, he noted that Esso would not advertise the fact but was trying quietly to get rid of it. The

Canadian added that the entire investment in ESFAC was $27 million. An acquisition price of $15 million would make ESFAC an attractive purchase. After technical and organizational changes costing $2.5 million, the plant could contribute a minimum yearly profit of $5 million. But he cautioned that ESFAC was having difficulties in selling the production of the 200 MTD urea plant. The Canadian advised Marcelo that if he was interested in investigating the ESFAC acquisition further, Marcelo should write directly to New York, as the company executives in Manila would not make any decision without referring matters to their principals in Standard Oil of New Jersey.

After Marcelo received this letter, he went to see the president of ESFAC in his Manila office. In this meeting, Marcelo expressed his interest in acquiring the plant provided the price was right. Apparently ESFAC managers could not give Marcelo any definite answers. After this meeting Marcelo informed his friend in Canada on May 13, 1969 that his preliminary talks with senior ESFAC executives indicated they were awaiting additional instructions from New York on the manner of selling the plant. Marcelo promised to keep the Canadian informed of developments. In early June the Canadian was asked for more information on the proposed ESFAC sale and specifically the thinking of corporate level management on the nature of the offer they would like to receive and what they were likely to accept.

After over three months of delay while he was making inquiries, the Canadian informed Marcelo, toward the third week of September, that after several unsuccessful tries, he had been able to contact by telephone a week earlier, the senior vice president of Esso Chemicals, Inc. in New York, who was in charge of liquidating the fertilizer plants. The senior vice president stated that as far as ESFAC was concerned, the company had not yet made up its mind whether to sell. This statement did not agree with other unofficial information the Canadian had received from other sources. Because of the conflicting statements and the need for a firm response as soon as possible, the Canadian suggested that Marcelo should write directly to the new president of Standard Oil Company.

Other evidence indicates that at the time the Canadian contacted the senior vice president in New York, the decision to sell ESFAC had already been reached by the company and advanced negotiations with IMC were underway. It is highly probable that Esso was hesitant to reveal any definite information to the Canadian to promote and protect the ongoing and any future negotiations. Both New York- and Philippines-based Esso executives were careful not to leak out any news on the proposed sale. Nor did Marcelo get any clarifications from the president of ESFAC regarding his queries until after the IMC-sponsored food conference in Manila.

At the time the Canadian wrote to Marcelo regarding the availability of the ESFAC plant, Marcelo and his group were very much occupied with pursuing their earlier proposal to set up an ammonia and urea plant. Understandably, therefore, they did not pursue their interest in the ESFAC plant with vigor. Only after the food conference did Marcelo take very definite steps to make a bid for the plant.

During the food conference Marcelo learned from the president of ESFAC that the plant was definitely for sale. Arrangements were immediately made for him and some members of his staff to visit the plant in Limay, Bataan. During his visit Marcelo inspected the plant and obtained operational and other data to assist him and his staff in making a financial evaluation of the plant.

Subsequently, Marcelo went to Canada and visited Hudson Bay Company in order to secure its financial backing. In exchange, he offered to sign with Hudson Bay a long-term contract for the supply of potash and phosphate, the basic raw materials used by the ESFAC plant. He also tried to secure financial assistance from Huguenot in exchange for using their vessels in transporting the materials to be imported from Canada. Both organizations agreed to support Marcelo in his bid for the ESFAC plant.

After negotiating with Hudson Bay and Huguenot, Marcelo proceeded to New York to meet with senior Esso executives. At first Marcelo suggested a price of $10 million. When this was found unacceptable, he revised his offer to $12 million. The latter offer was likewise unable to meet the expectations of Esso. While he was in New York, Marcelo was also informed that other parties, including a cooperative from the Philippines, had expressed interest in buying the ESFAC plant. He immediately associated the cooperative with SPCMA. Marcelo desisted from pursuing his bid further when he learned that SPCMA was about to close the deal for the ESFAC plant.

In this whole process all the negotiations were personally conducted by Marcelo himself. His staff were involved only insofar as he needed their assistance in conducting studies that were required in connection with the actual negotiations.

Marcelo did not approach IMC because he was aware of IMC's relationship with SPCMA. But Esso had already engaged in discussions with IMC and therefore preferred to proceed with it instead of starting afresh with another US or Canadian organization. Esso was aware of IMC's explorations with SPCMA. Encouragement to Marcelo at this stage could add to complexities for the ongoing negotiation. Also, Marcelo was structuring a proposal whereby Esso would sell to Marcelo and not to a US group. This would violate some of the key objectives Esso had set itself in the divestment negotiations.

Chemphil

During the food conference, Antonio Garcia, vice-president of Chemphil, learned that ESFAC was for sale. He also met the President of Central Farmers Fertilizer Company who was in Manila for the food conference organized by IMC.

Central was a cooperative engaged in the manufacture and distribution of fertilizer in the United States. During the decade of the sixties, when the fertilizer industry was at a low ebb, Central showed a remarkable resiliency and ability to withstand the crisis. *Fortune* magazine attributed this to Central's substantial investment in a network of distribution outlets throughout the country.

During the food conference Garcia explored the possibility of having Northern Negroes Farmers' Cooperative (NNFC) and Central join forces in order to place a bid for the ESFAC plant. NNFC was organized by Garcia in 1969. Garcia's proposal was for Central to assist in raising the financing required for the project and to supply the raw material for the plant. NNFC would be the vehicle for making the bid in place of Chemphil because the former could obtain the benefits of tax savings available to cooperatives in the Philippines. The plan likewise envisioned gradually bringing in SPCMA after the acquisition.

Garcia's plan seemed to have obtained a sympathetic hearing from Central. As soon as he returned to the United States, on request of Garcia, Central immediately tried to verify whether the ESFAC plant was indeed for sale. A series of cables and letters ensued detailing the negotiation.

In the meantime, Garcia sought the assistance of Mitsubishi through its Philippine representatives to modernize the plant should Chemphil acquire it. Chemphil had previously dealt with Mitsubishi in relation to fertilizer and raw material imports. In the course of these meetings Garcia disclosed his plans and strategies for the acquisition of the ESFAC plant to the Mitsubishi representative in Manila. The latter, however, leaked the information to Montelibano so that SPCMA was kept abreast of Garcia's plans.

On April 16 the President of Central met with the Senior Vice President of Esso Chemical in New York and relayed a message to Garcia to the effect that Esso was willing to negotiate a considerably lower price than their investment, and that two other Philippine as well as US and Canadian companies were also interested.

The President of Central also met with IMC officials while in New York and on April 21, wrote to Garcia to apprise the latter of the results of his meetings. This letter was very factual and indicated that Esso would not be willing to settle for less than $15 million, as this was the value of ESFAC's working capital.

On May 5 Garcia arrived in Chicago for a short meeting with Central. He then proceeded to New York and met with Esso executives. He asked for an option of first refusal, but Esso's reaction was negative. Garcia was requesting time to put together a viable proposal but Esso was anxious to unload the plant within a specified time because it wanted to take advantage of the tax benefits emanating from the transaction. Moreover, Garcia later discovered that SPCMA had by then secured an option to buy the plant.

SPCMA

Alfredo Montelibano, the committee of one commissioned by the sugar group to implement its plan of setting up a fertilizer plant, had always thought that the sugar industry should have its own plant. There were three stages in the pursuit of his objective. During the first stage Montelibano seriously pursued the establishment of a plant in cooperation with Marubeni-Iida (see Appendix A). The second stage started with the availability of ESFAC. In the third stage, SPCMA found ESFAC increasingly more attractive and decided to buy it. This stage was subdivided into the negotiations with IMC and the negotiations with the government.

IMC first made SPCMA the offer of joint ownership of the ESFAC plant at the time of the food conference during the height of the fertilizer controversy in the Philippines. The offer was probably made because SPCMA was a major consumer of fertilizer in the Philippines and marketing was a critical problem for ESFAC. In addition, IMC and Esso most likely thought that SPCMA was indeed serious about putting up a plant of its own. If the Marubeni project were to materialize, ESFAC would have difficulty in selling its plant, and even if it did sell it, the price would be nominal.

SPCMA consulted its lawyers on the offer of joint ownership, especially on the question of the tax benefits enjoyed by cooperatives. The lawyers gave the opinion that if ESFAC became a joint venture project, it could not, under the Cooperative Law and other special legislations, enjoy the benefits provided for. From the point of view of SPCMA, this was a vital issue, since the viability of the project would depend in large measure on the exemption from the 7 percent advanced sales tax ordinarily imposed on the sale of fertilizer.

On the other hand, the issue of ownership was not crucial for IMC. Its primary objective was to secure outlets for its products. IMC was flexible on this issue. What was more critical in the transaction was the cash payment required by Esso.

Some time in late May or early June, IMC technicians and staff came to Manila to look over the ESFAC plant. Although Montelibano regularly met with the IMC representatives, at no time during the negotiations did he directly deal with ESFAC. All the operational data that SPCMA needed were secured through IMC. The reason for this mode of conducting the negotiations was that the relationship between ESFAC and SPCMA, and in particular Montelibano, had not been cordial, and the ESFAC officials in the Philippines could not make any commitments on behalf of Esso.

Montelibano, on the other hand, had full powers to commit SPCMA. Therefore, he preferred to deal only with people who could bind their organization. There had been instances when Montelibano had embarrassed ranking ESFAC executives because the latter could not even commit the company on the pricing of its products without referring the matter to New York. ESFAC executives, however, were under instructions not to engage in direct negotiations with SPCMA.

During the succeeding months a series of negotiations were held between SPCMA and IMC, with all the meetings held in the United States. SPCMA relied heavily on a panel of lawyers and consultants. The main negotiations were carried on by the panel of lawyers while another group negotiated the financial and still another the technical aspects of the deal. These groups received instructions from and were coordinated by Montclibano.

SPCMA had emerged as the victor in the long struggle of various Filipino interests to engage in the fertilizer industry. It had stopped FFC, its most serious rival, from either building a new plant or acquiring ESFAC. But before the transaction could be completed, SPCMA still had to reconcile other issues.

The monetary and International Monetary Fund constraints were part of the fiscal and monetary austerity plans adopted by the Philippine government early in 1970. The country's foreign debt load had become unmanageable and reserves were strained to the breaking point. The problem was caused by a number of things: too many short-term debts, overspending by the government, lower world prices for some basic exports and the wide-ranging effect of a series of devastating typhoons that had caused considerable damage to the crop areas. To solve these mounting problems many decisions had to be made, one of which was the devaluation of the peso. On February 21, 1970 the value of the peso, which had been fixed at P3.90 to a dollar, was permitted to float to allow itself to find its level. Significant measures affecting the monetary situation were taken by the Central Bank.

DIVESTMENT NEGOTIATIONS CONCLUDED

This section covers the period from late June to November 1970, when the terms and conditions of the contract and process of obtaining government approval for the contract were concluded.

SPCMA-IMC Agreement

By late September or early October, IMC and SPCMA had worked out the mechanics of the transaction. IMC, through its lone subsidiary, Continental Fertilizer Corporation (CFC), would buy the ESFAC plant and in turn would sell it to SPCMA for a total price of $29,278 million, payable in five years. At the same time IMC would manage the plant, and provide technical expertise and program for training Filipinos for the duration of SPCMA's obligations to IMC. Also, IMC would supply the necessary raw materials.

Before the transaction could be completed, one more roadblock remained: approval of the Philippine government for the terms of payment had to be obtained. In order to pay for the plant, SPCMA needed to secure from the PNB a letter of credit, which could not be issued without prior approval from the Central Bank. Technically speaking, only Central Bank and PNB approvals were required. But because of the previous controversy regarding the Marubeni-Iida transaction, other government agencies were consulted. This resulted in delays. Esso was eager to dispose of the plant at an early date and had given a deadline for SPCMA to make up its mind about the sale. This deadline was moved four times before government approval was eventually secured.

Marubeni also had to consent to the cancellation of the letter of credit issued in its favor the previous year. IMC required this cancellation because it felt that SPCMA would be unable to secure two letters of credit at the same time.

The process of getting approval of the government was a joint effort of ESFAC, IMC and, of course, SPCMA. The first move to inform the government of the proposed disinvestment was made around the first quarter of 1970 by the president of ESFAC. He went to see Secretary Virata (the former chairman of the BOI who had by then assumed the Finance portfolio) and told him of Esso's intention to disinvest. The main objective of this meeting with Virata was to explore the question of whether the government would allow the buyer to remit to Esso New York the dollars necessary for the purchase of ESFAC. Also, however, rumors had started to surface about the negotiations, and ESFAC management thought it should inform the government about its decision to move out of the fertilizer business in the Philippines. At that time, Virata gave no negative reactions toward Esso's decision to divest.

Around late April or early May 1970, ESFAC management (upon insistence of its public affairs advisers) held informal chats with President Marcos regarding the proposed sale. In the communication with President Marcos the approach adopted by ESFAC was not to ask him whether the company should divest but rather to tell him of the decision to sell the company.

At the same time ESFAC assured the President that the negotiations under way would not be detrimental to the company or to the country. The ESFAC executives pointed out that the party wanting to buy the company was a responsible one, that Esso had no plans of leaving the country and in fact had undertaken an expansion of its refinery operations, and that Esso was following a course of action it felt would be mutually beneficial to the country and the company. The President was also apprised of the contributions ESFAC had made to the economy, particularly in educating farmers in modern methods of cultivation and in the use of fertilizer.

Continental Fertilizer Company's option to purchase the ESFAC plant was submitted to the Monetary Board of the Central Bank and was approved by virtue of Resolution No. 1639 dated October 8, 1970. Subsequently, SPCMA filed an application with the PNB for the issuance of a letter of credit for the amount of $29,278,500 in favor of Continental Fertilizer Corporation (Continental). The type of letter of credit sought was a deferred payment letter of credit providing for payments by means of sight drafts similar to promissory notes. A unique feature of this L/C was a time enforcement clause. Whereas ordinary L/Cs provided for a single payment within a range of time, the L/C sought by SPCMA provided for several disbursements spread over a long period of time. Each payment was to be covered by a separate draft due to mature on a specific future date. These drafts were designed to cover the installment payment for the plants over a period of five years. On the basis of studies undertaken by IMC, SPCMA anticipated that with a change in product mix, the plant could generate the cash required to pay the notes within the specified period.

SPCMA was highly dependent upon IMC for know-how relating to the fertilizer industry. IMC was a well established and internationally known company in the industry. SPCMA, on the other hand, had limited knowledge of the technical and even marketing aspects of the industry. The ESFAC plant was the largest in the Philippines and people with know-how in operations of plants of such size were all with ESFAC. SPCMA, therefore, relied heavily on IMC for guiding SPCMA on what it should do. IMC did a study for SPCMA to suggest modification of product mix of the ESFAC plant. The modifications, IMC stated, would permit ESFAC to generate sales and cash flow to permit repayment in a short period of time. SPCMA accepted this conclusion on IMC's part without challenge, a decision which SPCMA regretted at a later stage. Seeking longer payment terms would have been more acceptable to SPCMA.

The PNB considered SPCMA's application for letters of credit three times and finally, on October 15, approved the application in principle in its Resolution No. 541. Subsequently, the bank reviewed the entire transaction and gave final approval in its Resolution No. 848, dated October 28, 1970. Thereafter, the application was submitted to the Central Bank, and Monetary Board Resolution No. 1774 approved the transaction on November 3. Upon receipt of the CB approval, PNB had full authority to negotiate the terms and conditions of the L/C with the parties. On November 13, the PNB Board gave final authorization for letters of credit.

In approving the loan, the CB had imposed five conditions, only three of which were disclosed. They were:

1. PNB should insure that the loan would be within the lending ratio allowed by the General Banking Act. A bank's allowable lending ratio to any single borrower was 15 percent of the unimpaired capital and surplus. This condition was subsequently dropped.
2. SPCMA's capitalization should be able to support the amount being applied for, in order to insure that the PNB was not assuming too much risk.
3. SPCMA should execute a waiver of its right to import fertilizer tax-free.

For its part PNB imposed twenty-five conditions for the issuance of the letters of credit, of which the following were the principal ones:

1. SPCMA should renounce its rights to import fertilizer tax-free. This was identical to the condition imposed by the CB.
2. SPCMA and its members should sign joint and several guarantees for the payment of the amount being applied for.

3. Sinking funds should be established to guarantee payment of the letter of credit based on piculs of sugar produced by the members.
4. A chattel mortgage on the plant should be executed in favor of PNB.

The cancellation of the $92 million letter of credit in favor of Marubeni-Iida presented no problem to SPCMA because of the previous relationship between Marubeni and the sugar bloc. Marubeni had supplied a number of the new sugar centrals that had recently been established in the Philippines. SPCMA offered to reimburse Marubeni for the expenses that the latter had incurred. Marubeni declined this offer. Instead, SPCMA agreed to grant Marubeni priority in the supply of any equipment that might be needed in case of expansion.

However, other considerations affecting Japanese-Filipino relations also figured in Marubeni's decision, encouraged by the Japanese government. Of course, Marubeni could not have supplied the equipment without securing the approval of the Japanese government. The cancellation of the L/C would result in significant foreign exchange saving for the Philippines because the ESFAC price would be far lower than the one contained in the original SPCMA-Marubeni version. Of course, this would contribute toward good will for Japan in the Philippines. The good will could help in securing Senate ratification of the Philippine-Japanese Treaty of Amity, Commerce and Navigation, which was signed in 1960, ratified by the Japanese Diet in 1961, and submitted by President Marcos to the Senate for ratification in 1970. Also, Japan viewed the Philippines as an attractive country for investment, especially as US companies reduced their investment by 1974, when the Laurel-Langley Agreement (giving US citizens parity rights with Filipinos) expired.

As things turned out, however, one more hurdle remained. The transaction had been forwarded to President Marcos for his endorsement. The President passed the project on to the Presidential Economic Staff (PES) for study and would not take any action until after he had received its recommendations.

As the project started to gain publicity, President Marcos invited the president of ESFAC and Montelibano to visit him sometime during the third week of November. During this meeting President Marcos said that because of the publicity on the project, it was essential that full and free public hearings be held in order to avoid any charges of wrongdoing by the government. The President suggested that these hearings be held within the next three succeeding months.

ESFAC's president, however, reminded President Marcos that the company did not wish to have any further delay. The November deadline set for the consummation of the contract was the third extension of the target date that had originally been set. It was explained that in order for Esso to gain from the tax benefits in the United States, the sale had to be concluded before the end of 1970. The President was not very pleased with this pressure put upon him, but because of Esso's view that the transaction could not be delayed further, he concurred with a suggestion to hold the hearings as soon as possible.

It is unlikely that SPCMA preferred long and extended hearings on the ESFAC transaction. SPCMA had achieved its objectives. Extended hearings would result in additional charges and countercharges. Marcelo and other fertilizer manufacturers might create new and unexpected pressures and objections. Therefore, public hearings of a brief duration would preclude any surprises while also fulfilling the President's objectives of "public disclosure."

Esso also encouraged brief public hearings. One key objective of management was to bring the terms of the transaction into the open and thereby prevent any subsequent charges of secret deals having been made by Esso in selling ESFAC. This would be an important feature of a "clean" divestment sought by Esso, especially because it would still have extensive investments in petroleum refining and marketing operations in the Philippines.

The Presidential Economic Staff Hearings
Accordingly, the PES called for a hearing on November 18 in order to sound out the views—particularly the objections—of interested parties about the project. Present at the hearings were Jose P. Marcelo, Dr. Uesebio Garcia, Senator Benigno Aquino, who had exposed the Marubeni-Iida deal, Crispin D. Reves, a representative of the Anti-Graft League of the Philippines, ESFAC representatives and Alfredo Montelibano of SPCMA.

During the hearings, Aquino expressed fears that SPCMA might monopolize the supply and production of fertilizer to the detriment of the industry and the consumers. Marcelo and Garcia, on the other hand, were seeking confirmation of the commitment required of the SPCMA that it no longer import fertilizer tax-free. They also recommended that a lower selling price be negotiated for the ESFAC plant following the precedent set by Esso when it sold its Aruba plant to W.R. Grace in 1969. They claimed that the selling price was net current assets plus $1 million and therefore the selling price of the ESFAC plant should be much lower than $22.6 million.

In response, Montelibano assured those present that fertilizer prices would not increase once SPCMA owned the ESFAC plant. He confirmed that SPCMA had signed a waiver of its right to import fertilizer tax-free. He disclosed the following information on the ESFAC purchase: (1) SPCMA had already contracted for the technical services of IMC for the operation of the plant; and (2) the amount involved in the transaction was $29,278 million, which included the selling price of $22.6 million plus interest charges. However, the selling price included working capital of $8,471 million, resulting in a net price for the plant of $20,807 million. (It was believed by informed sources that Esso would sell the plant for about $15 million excluding working capital. This offers an estimate of the profit IMC might have made.) The payment would be made in five years in 20 quarterly installments.

He also emphasized that the transaction had been previously approved by the CB and PNB after serious deliberation. Finally, he stressed the need for an early approval of the project because of the tax implications for Esso if the sale was delayed.

At the close of the hearings, those present expressed their approval of the project. Almost immediately after the hearing, the PES recommended to the President that the project be approved. However, it laid three conditions to be complied with by SPCMA:

1. SPCMA should follow and comply with the conditions set by the CB and PNB.
2. Sugar cooperatives affiliated with SPCMA should build up their equity holdings over a five-year period by mortgaging sugar proceeds for additional credit coverage.
3. In the selling price, the principal should be segregated from the interest to be paid so that the Bureau of Internal Revenue would know of the taxes due from the selling company.

Appendix A

The Fertilizer Controversy

Although this controversy, more popularly known as the Marubeni-Iida deal (Marubeni being the prospective supplier), had no direct bearing on the ESFAC divestment process, indirectly it had a significant effect on the final outcome of the ESFAC negotiations.

Board of Investments

To channel and encourage investments in productive areas, the Congress of the Philippines passed Republic Act No. 5186 (Investment Incentives Act) and created the Board of Investments (BOI) as its organic body to implement the intent and provisions of the Act; the BOI was organized on November 16, 1967.

The BOI was expected to channel investments into preferred areas through a system of incentives for companies registered with it. Every year it came out with a list of preferred areas, better known as the Investment Priorities Plan (IPP), which designated economic activities where the flow of investments was to be encouraged. The IPP was prepared by the Board and was submitted to the National Economic Council (NEC), another government body, for review. The NEC in turn recommended it to the President for approval. The NEC could delete but could not add to the listing submitted by the Board.

Among the incentives given to BOI-registered firms were protection of patents and other proprietary rights, capital gains, tax exemptions, tax exemption on sale of stock dividends, deduction of organizational and pre-operating expenses, accelerated depreciation, net operating loss carry-over, tax exemption on imported capital equipment and others. To be eligible for these incentives, a company needed to be engaged in a project registered with the BOI. Projects submitted for registration were evaluated according to certain criteria which the Board had prepared to help select projects with characteristics considered essential to the Philippine economy.

227

The BOI had no power to prevent any investor from entering into any of the priority areas without the benefit of registration. The only effect on non-registration was that the company could not avail itself of the incentives offered under the Investment Incentives Act.

Applications Submitted to BOI

On May 2, 1969 the second IPP was approved by the President of the Philippines. The production of urea was included among the priority areas of investment. The BOI recommended a plant with a capacity of 330,000 MT per year and estimated the cost at P159 million.

The inclusion of urea in the second IPP had originally been proposed by Jose P. Marcelo in his letter to the BOI on May 13, 1968. In the same letter Marcelo informed the BOI of FFC's plan to put up an ammonia and urea plant. In order to gather data to assist in the making of an assessment of the fertilizer industry, the BOI decided to conduct a hearing on June 1, 1968 and invited all the companies in the industry to send their representatives. The hearing was intended to gather information regarding (1) market size, measured in terms of actual demand at a given price; (2) the expansion plans of the various companies in the industry; and (3) alternative production methods.

At the hearing Marcelo took the opportunity to discuss FFC's plans to set up ammonia and urea plants. Two of the other three companies in the industry, namely, Atlas and Chemphil, interposed no objection to FFC's proposal provided they were assured that they could secure ammonia from FFC at prices competitive with world prices. Only ESFAC interposed an objection. ESFAC stated that it was against the inclusion of urea in the second IPP and was therefore objecting to the plan of FFC. The two reasons advanced by ESFAC were as follows:

1. Figures compiled by the Fertilizer Institute of the Philippines consistently indicated an overcapacity in the fertilizer industry. In 1967 the industry operated at only one-third of normal capacity.
2. The plants existing at that time could be modified easily to expand their capacities. It was stated that ESFAC, for example, could increase its urea capacity by about 30 percent through minor debottle-necking and enlargement of its facilities with minor additional investments.

One final point discussed at the hearing was the feasibility of a joint enterprise among the fertilizer plants so they could pool their resources to put up an ammonia or urea plant. Discussion of this issue was initiated by Chairman Cesar Virata of the BOI. Those present, however, did not seem to be enthusiastic about the idea.

This hearing and other studies conducted by the BOI had led to the inclusion of urea in the second IPP. On May 12, 1969, ten days after the approval of the second IPP, Marcelo formally submitted his application to the BOI for pioneer status for the FFC-integrated ammonia/urea/bag project. The ammonia plant had a daily rated capacity of 600 MTD and the urea plant 1,034 MTD; the bag plant was rated at 12.5 M bags per annum.

On May 19, 1969 FFC followed up on its requests for modification of the DBP guarantees. In spite of the adverse recommendations of the Manager of the Investment Banking and Economic Research Department of the DBP, as earlier discussed, the FFC request was granted on June 11, 1969. As amended, the bank's guarantees extended in favor of Farmers Fertilizer Corporation amounted to $42,025,000. Among the more significant conditions imposed by the DBP were the following:

1. Submission to the DBP of a registration certificate from the Board of Investments, considering that the exemption privileges assumed for FFC in the study affected to a great extent the viability of the project.
2. Submission to the DBP of a four-year export contract for the sale of FFC urea abroad.
3. Submission to the DBP of a ten-year contract for the supply of its naphtha requirements at an assured price throughout the contract period.
4. Submission to the DBP of the contract between the supplier and FFC and the foreign financing institution in whose favor the DBP guarantee would be issued.

During the succeeding weeks, Marcelo and the Japanese contractors for the plant took a series of moves towards the implementation of the project. Toyo Engineering, the Japanese firm, contracted to build the FFC plant, started to work on its end for the issuance of an export license and financing of the project by the Japan Export-Import Bank (EXIM-Bank). It also submitted its application to the MITI for approval. On July 1, 1969 Toyo assured Marcelo that the FFC project was being given top priority by MITI. However, MITI did not want to take any specific action until the total amount of loans to be allocated to the Philippines was fixed.

For his part, Marcelo in June and July held several conferences with Chairman Virata of the BOI and Chairman Licaros of the DBP. Marcelo was given the impression both by the BOI and DBP that they were both of the belief that the Philippines needed only one fertilizer project to meet immediate requirements. Hence, any other project other than FFC's would likely be denied.

Meanwhile, SPCMA was pursuing a series of moves designed to effectively block the final approval of the FFC project by both the MITI and BOI.

SPCMA Pursues Its Project

On August 4, 1969 SPCMA wrote BOI expressing its intent to register an integrated fertilizer plant. One week later Chairman Virata wrote and informed

SPCMA that the BOI had already received a completed application for a larger integrated fertilizer plant. Virata observed that although the proposed plant of the SPCMA was geared toward the requirement of the sugar planters, it was below the minimum economic size required by the BOI. Virata, therefore, recommended a joint venture between SPCMA and FFC since the country could support only one fertilizer project.

Around this time SPCMA concluded its negotiations for the construction of the plant with Marubeni-Iida although a contract was not signed until September 5, 1969. Like Toyo Engineering, Marubeni applied for an export license with the MITI. At the same time both Marubeni and SPCMA submitted to the MITI a letter of guarantee which SPCMA had secured earlier from the Philippine National Bank. The PNB letter of guarantee was much simpler than the letter of undertaking secured by Marcelo from the DBP on June 11, 1969. With the submission of the SPCMA project, MITI had two applications pending before it.

Developments at the BOI

On September 4, 1969 the BOI evaluation team presented a memo to its Board of Governors outlining several problem areas with the FFC project. Primarily, they raised doubts on the ability of the Marcelo group to raise the equity required by the project.

While the Board found it objectionable to place its stamp of approval on the FFC project officially, it could not even consider the SPCMA project, because no formal application had been submitted to the Board. It was only 90 days later on December 15, 1969 that SPCMA completed the documents required by the BOI with the submission of the financial, technical and marketing study for its project.

SPCMA and PNB

In the meantime on September 23, SPCMA requested PNB to grant letters of credit to support its September 5, 1969 contract with Marubeni-Iida for the supply and construction of the fertilizer complex. The letter of SPCMA informed PNB that the project had been submitted to the BOI for registration.

This request was approved on October 9, 1969 as embodied in PNB Board Resolution No. 493. The following day PNB opened four letters of credit in favor of SPCMA in the total amount of $90,277,362, which included interest on the principal.

For some time after the issuance of the letters of credit, there was little indication that either Marcelo or the SPCMA made any significant moves toward implementing their projects. Marcelo, it appears, learned of the PNB action in favor of SPCMA only from Toyo Engineering who sent Marcelo a telegram.

Events after Elections

During the four months that followed the presidential election, a number of events related to the Marubeni-Iida deal took place: the Fertilizer Institute of the Philippines protested the issuance of the letters of credit; DBP suspended the FFC guarantee; BOI returned both the SPCMA and FFC application without any action; the Marubeni-Iida deal was exposed to Congress and a congressional investigation ensued.

The FIP Protest

The Fertilizer Institute of the Philippines was an association of all the fertilizer manufacturers in the Philippines organized in 1966 at about the time when the ESFAC plant went into operation. Jose P. Marcelo was the President of the Institute in 1969.

On December 3, 1969 the FIP sent a telegram to President Marcos protesting the action taken by the PNB. The other fertilizer companies including ESFAC decided to join Marcelo in protesting the PNB action. Since SPCMA accounted for about 50 percent of the fertilizer consumption in the Philippines, establishment of the plant would in fact be fatal to the other plants which were then running at only about 30 percent of rated capacity. Furthermore, there was a feeling that there was some irregularity in the manner in which the letters of credit were issued by the PNB.

Return of SPCMA and FFC Application

As stated in an earlier section, after the MITI deferred action on either project, the focus of attention centered on the BOI. Due to the mounting publicity surrounding the controversy, however, the BOI found it difficult to take any action. Whichever project it approved or denied, the BOI was susceptible to public attack by whoever was prejudiced. Moreover, rumors started to circulate that should the BOI be pressured to any course of action, Chairman Virata was ready and willing to resign his post. Virata, therefore, had to choose a course of action whereby he could preserve his integrity without at the same time opening himself to a public attack. Accordingly, on January 28, 1970 Virata returned the applications of both SPCMA and FFC.

In a letter dated February 9, 1970 Marcelo vehemently contested the action taken by the BOI on the following grounds: the letters of credit issued by the PNB were subject to the condition that SPCMA should obtain BOI approval for its project; the PNB letters of credit were subject to MITI approval and MITI would not approve the same without prior registration of the project with the BOI. As a final appeal, Marcelo threatened to expose the whole deal.

The Marubeni-Iida Deal Exposed

On February 23, 1970 Senator Benigno Aquino, Jr., who was the most vocal critic of the Marcos administration, exposed the deal on the floor of the Senate. A senate investigation followed although the senate committee that investigated the deal never came out with its final recommendations. On April 8, 1970 the Anti-Graft League of the Philippines took the cudgels for Marcelo and filed a criminal case against the PNB officials, SPCMA officers and officers of Marubeni-Iida. These persons were charged with violation of the Anti-Graft and Corrupt Practices Act in connection with the irregularities accompanying the issuance of the letter of credit by PNB. Finally, from December 1969 until the latter part of March 1970, the leading dailies almost continuously carried stories regarding the controversy.

These series of moves undertaken by Marcelo resulted in the following:

1. On February 4, 1970 President Marcos sent a diplomatic representative to Japan with a mission of having the letter of credit cancelled.
2. On February 24, 1970, the day after the Aquino exposé, PNB suspended the implementation of the letter of credit.
3. BOI denied FFC's request for reconsideration on March 4, 1970.
4. On March 6, SPCMA directed PNB-New York to return to Marubeni-Iida New York the amount of US $5,579,553 deposited by Marubeni the previous day in the account of SPCMA.

PNB officials, however, stated categorically before the senate investigating committee that, although the implementation of the letters of credit was suspended, these continued to be effective, having been availed of previously. In order to cancel them, the consent of the three parties involved had to be obtained. PNB and SPCMA could not agree unilaterally to cancel their effectivity without approval from Marubeni-Iida.

Cases

Part B

Shave-all Company

BREAKDOWN IN RELATIONS WITH
AN INDIAN PARTNER

John Macy sat in his room on a hot June evening and wondered what he could do about the sales of his company's products in India.

Mr. Macy was Far Eastern manager for the export division of Shave-all Company. He had been sent to India because the sales of Shave-all products which had been taken over by an Indian firm had fallen off sharply in the last two years. Mr. Macy felt he knew what should be done to increase the sales but he was at a loss as to how to get the program under way.

THE SHAVE-ALL COMPANY

The Shave-all Company manufactured safety razors, razor blades, shaving cream, brushes, lotions and a few other related products. The company's line could be classified as medium grade. There was one US company that manufactured products which sold at higher prices and whose quality was accepted as superior to Shave-all items. There were two other companies which manufactured lines of the same grade as Shave-all and several whose products fell in a lower grade in both price and quality. The company had succeeded in obtaining a substantial portion of the United States and export markets through its low prices and an active promotion program which included extensive field sales activity and a steady flow of advertising in the press, radio and television, supported by special promotions every couple of months for one of the products. The promotions included price cuts, advertising splurges, premiums and point-of-sale displays. Shave-all had sales offices in various foreign countries, but until the Indian venture, the company had not been involved in any foreign manufacture. Foreign sales were supervised by the export manager, Mr. Rainey, who was 50 and had been with the company for 25 years. There were five sales managers. John Macy, who handled the Far East, was 41. He had been with the company for about 15 years, including service in both domestic and foreign sales.

SALES IN INDIA

Shave-all had started selling in India through a local distributor. A few years later the company's leading competitor had established its own sales organization in India and intensified its efforts. Shave-all had felt compelled to counter this move and had set up its own sales office. A man from the United States was sent to Calcutta to serve as sales manager and he employed an average of 10 Indian salesmen. The actual distribution was still handled through the former distributor.

The staff served as missionary salesmen, visiting merchants throughout the country, pointing out the low prices of Shave-all products and their other advantages, giving out samples and setting up point-of-sale displays. The sales manager kept close tabs on these salesmen and brought them together every four or five months in Calcutta for meetings in which he explained sales techniques and encouraged them in their efforts. The company also did extensive advertising by posters, newspapers and other media.

After two years, sales had been built up to about $550,000 a year, and the company's sales promotion program was the most aggressive in its industry. At this point, however, the company began to have difficulty obtaining import licenses for a few of its products. The items affected were minor ones, but it appeared that in view of the Indian Government policy and foreign exchange difficulties, products such as Shave-all's might at any time become very difficult to import. Consideration was therefore given to establishing local manufacture. After some study, the management concluded that political conditions in the country were too uncertain to justify any investment.

ASSOCIATION WITH RAMA BROTHERS

At the same time that Shave-all was considering local manufacture, Vishnu and Patel Rama were looking into the same possibility from a different angle. The Rama brothers, who were 59 and 61 respectively, were the leaders of a family which had amassed a large fortune in the manufacture of steel products (chiefly basic forms like sheet and work tools such as shovels). They were leading members of Indian society and influential in government circles. The Rama factories were located in Calcutta, and there were warehouses and sales offices throughout India.

As the Rama family's wealth expanded, they considered extending their activity into other product lines. One which appealed to them was the manufacture of razors and razor blades. After some investigation they concluded that setting up business independently would not be satisfactory because it would take too long to establish themselves in the market. It was observed that there were two Indian factories already, and that both of these had remained fairly small and ineffective. Therefore, they decided that the best possibility lay in taking over the manufacture of some line which was currently being imported.

The Rama brothers made discreet inquiries of all the companies currently importing, and when they found that Shave-all had been thinking about local manufacture, direct negotiations were opened. Within a short time an agreement was reached which both parties felt was mutually beneficial. A new company, Shave-all of India, was set up and the full capitalization of $550,000 was supplied by the Ramas. Shave-all received a 10 percent interest in return for assigning all manufacture and sales rights for Shave-all products to the company. The Rama brothers agreed to commence production of the Shave-all line within two years. All products would be sold under the Shave-all name. Rama also agreed to "maintain the quality of all products according to standards applied to Shave-all manufacture in the United States," and "to promote sales actively." The agreement was for a 20-year term.

Vishnu Rama was made chairman of the board of directors. Shave-all was given one seat on the board. Patel Rama and other members of the family filled out the board membership. Vishnu Rama's son, Shanti, was made president. Shanti was a metallurgist who had been trained in England and Germany and was considered quite brilliant. He had been working for several years as a supervisor of production in one of the company's steel plants.

Shave-all of India immediately took over full distribution of Shave-all products imported from the United States. The former Shave-all sales manager was assigned to another country and the salesmen were absorbed by the new concern.

Work on the factory proceeded rapidly. The Rama brothers purchased the best available equipment and the Shave-all technical advisors on the spot reported that the production setup was excellent. The technical advisors were supplied at the request of the Rama brothers, and their expenses were paid by them. Some difficulties were experienced when production started because the grinding was a more precise process than the Rama production personnel had previously experienced. When inspection by the Shave-all advisors showed the first runs of razor blades were below standard, they told Shanti Rama that the complete lot would have to be destroyed. He and his father objected considerably because an investment of several thousand dollars was involved. However, after a brief discussion emphasizing the necessity for maintaining quality to assure market acceptance the Ramas agreed.

In the sales end of the business, however, results were far from satisfactory. After only about one year of Rama management Shave-all executives became aware of a gradual decline. Mr. Macy visited India and discussed the problem with Shanti Rama. He observed that Mr. Rama was little interested in promotion so he gave him a lengthy description of how the company operated in the United States. Mr. Rama showed considerable interest and told Mr. Macy he would certainly look into the application of such ideas in his program. Mr. Macy left with the impression that Mr. Rama was in agreement with his point of view. He realized that it would take a little time for promotion to get under way and sales to start increasing again, so he did not give much thought to the problem for several months. However, when sales continued to fall, reaching 50 percent of the pre-Rama level a year later, he consulted with the Shave-all export manager and they agreed that Mr. Macy should go to India and get the sales program in hand. They obtained authorization from the president of Shave-all to take whatever action seemed necessary, with the qualification that any drastic action should be checked first with the top management.

When Mr. Macy arrived in India, his first objective was to familiarize himself thoroughly with the sales situation so that he could make sound recommendations for a program. He spent three months traveling throughout the land observing sales operations. He found that Shave-all products were being distributed through the sales system used for other products manufactured by the Rama brothers. For the most part, this consisted of warehouses in all cities of substantial size. In the larger cities one man spent full time supervising the distribution of Shave-all products while in the smaller cities this was a part-time job for one of the men handling other Rama products.

Each warehouse had a stock of Shave-all products which was allowed to vary from about one month's supply down to close to zero, at which point a new stock was reordered. All sales were made at the warehouse for cash regardless of the nature of the buyer or the volume of his purchases. The only other sales personnel were two men who traveled about as missionary salesmen—one in the North and the other in the South. These men visited stores in the cities. They were instructed to make a minimum of 60 calls per day. They had samples and posters which they were expected to give to the retailers.

Mr. Macy spent several days with these men. The visits to the stores were all virtually identical. The salesman went into the store and looked around for a clerk. When he found one, he explained who he was and gave him a sample of a Shave-all product and a poster. The clerk expressed his appreciation and told him what fine products Shave-all had and then the salesman departed.

Mr. Macy very rapidly came to the conclusion that the decline in sales was attributable to the lack of an adequate sales promotion program. Specifically, he felt that more salesmen with better training were required. Special sales and promotion campaigns such as were used in the United States would help. Service to the merchants should be improved by more adequate stocking at supply points, and devices such as delivery, credit sales and quantity discounts should be adopted to encourage stocking by the independent distribution system.

As soon as he returned to Calcutta, Mr. Macy reported to Shanti Rama what he had seen, the conclusions he had drawn and the program which he felt was required. He elaborated to the point of detailing the costs which would be involved and the sales which would be expected to result from this activity. Mr. Rama was much impressed and told Mr. Macy that he would certainly give serious consideration to applying the ideas he proposed. Mr. Macy said that this assurance was not sufficient for him. He demanded that the company immediately start applying at least some of his programs because the sales situation was too serious for further delay. Mr. Rama said that he would take the matter up with his father. The next day he reported that his father had rejected the recommendations and he was sorry that nothing further could be done about the matter.

Mr. Macy was quite disturbed by this development and asked if he could talk directly with Vishnu Rama to state his case to him. This was arranged and Mr. Macy made the same presentation to him as he had made to his son. At the end of the presentation Mr. Rama said he was much impressed by the work Mr. Macy had done and he greatly appreciated his desire to help the company. He regretted, however, that he could not accept the proposals. He pointed out that he had been in business for a long time and had been quite successful. He knew that a good product was its own best advertisement. Rama tools, for example, were widely accepted in India even though he had never advertised them. If Shave-all products were good, as he believed they were, then they would surely sell themselves. He insisted that his son maintain high-quality standards in production and this was the best possible way to build up sales. Mr. Rama was quite satisfied with the current operation. He pointed out that the company was making a profit. Therefore, he had no intention of investing in substantial sales promotion activities which would result in the company operating at a loss for the time being with no assurance that sales would increase sufficiently to make up for the loss in the long run.

For several days thereafter, Mr. Macy spent more time with Mr. Rama going into further detail on possible programs which were very similar to those previously used in India. He argued that if they had worked once, they would work again and the company would have to make some effort if it was ever to raise sales above the present low level. He also noted that Shave-all's leading competitor did more promotion than Rama and was doing well. Mr. Rama, however, was unconvinced. He felt that circumstances had changed to some degree, but his basic reasons were faith in his management approach and the fact that the company was now making a profit so that no change was necessary. He pointed out that even though he was uncertain of its value, he had done some newspaper advertising and had authorized the giving out of samples and posters. In his opinion, he had carried out fully the agreement to promote Shave-all products actively. As to the activity of competitors, he observed that Shave-all's earlier program and Mr. Macy's plans were (as Mr. Macy agreed) much greater than those of the leading competitor. In any case, this was a United States concern, and if it chose to spend money advertising, that did not prove it was sound business in India. The other competitors were English firms with long experience in India, and the fact that they did no more promotion than he endorsed reinforced Mr. Rama's faith in his conclusion.

MR. MACY'S DILEMMA

It was this situation which Mr. Macy was pondering in his room in Calcutta. In the process of his meetings and various social engagements, Mr. Macy had acquired a great respect for Vishnu Rama as a person. He was sure he had a brilliant mind and a friendly personality. He was convinced that if he could ever really demonstrate to Mr. Rama that his ideas were sound, Mr. Rama would be his strongest supporter. He was at a loss, however, to conceive an approach to the solution of this dilemma.

General Foods Corporation—
International Division (A)

In September 1964, various members of the International Division of General Foods were scheduled to visit Gellini, S.p.A., GF's Italian subsidiary, to assess the company's plans for the future. The group would include Robert Howell, Vice President of GFID and Area Director of Europe, members of the GFID engineering and marketing staffs and Walter Connell. Mr. Connell was one of four European area directors reporting to Mr. Howell. He was responsible for Scandinavia, Benelux, Switzerland and Italy. In late April 1964, Mr. Connell had commented:

Although I have had problems in four countries, our operations in Sweden and Holland are going well, and I think we have definitely turned the corner on our major problems in Denmark. But we have yet to solve our big problems in Italy. We acquired Jules Jorgensen, a biscuit manufacturer in Denmark, in 1961. The Jorgensen plant had burned down two years before, during which time the Jorgensen's products were off the market. Our people became fascinated with Jorgensen's new plant and the opportunity in the market and so bought the company. By that time the Jorgensen name had lost its consumer franchise, and on sales in 1962 of $890,000 the company lost $267,000. So, we added several products to the operation, including rice-boiled-in-a-bag (purchased locally); Minute-

Financial data which are not publicly available, the name of the Italian company and names of people have been disguised. This case was prepared by Prof. John Fayerweather, New York University, by condensing material in General Foods Corporation (H1)(ICCH 9-365-002) and (H2)(ICCH 9-365-003). The original cases were made possible by the cooperation of the General Foods Corporation and prepared by Christopher Gale, Research Associate, under the direction of the Advanced Management Program faculty of the Harvard Graduate School of Business Administration. Copyright by the President and Fellows of Harvard College. Reproduced by permission.

Rice (shipped from Canada); and coffee (from our plant in England). In 1963, sales were up 38 percent. This year we are adding Jell-O production and so 1965 should be our breakeven year for Jorgensen.

In February 1963, we acquired a Swedish business. We have done very well with it. It's one of the few smaller operations which hasn't run into the red. It was large enough to cope with the systems and overhead which General Foods requires. The products had all been well managed. Sales are $9.5 million, of which more than $8.5 million are in regular coffee. Our parent company also exports Certo, Jell-O, and Minute-Rice to an agent in Sweden. His contract expires in December and will not be renewed. We hired a noncoffee products manager in Sweden whom we're now training, so that we will eventually manage our manufacturing and importing in Sweden through one division.

In Italy, it's a story similar to Jorgensen in Denmark, except it is one which hasn't been solved yet.

GELLINI, S.p.A.

The International Division's Italian subsidiary was Gellini, S.p.A., located in Bologna in Northern Italy. Gellini was founded in 1882, originally as a small shop selling pastas. In 1885 Gellini became a manufacturer as well as a seller of pastas. After considerable searching in Italy, GFID had located a promising venture: a large food processor in Parma which was interested in selling out. At the same time, the staff also became interested in Gellini, an apparently sound but considerably smaller company. Each of the two companies was considered to possess strengths which complemented the other ideally. Gellini was then owned jointly by the founder's two sons, Mario and Vittorio Gellini. In 1952 Vittorio, who owned 25 percent of the company, left Italy to establish a factory in Rio de Janeiro, and by 1961 he wanted to sell out his interest in Gellini. Mario considered the remaining quarter interest a good buy, but he did not have enough cash to buy out his brother.

The Gellini plant had been built in 1957. Its equipment, though second-hand, was reconditioned, and was found to be in good operating condition. However, the equipment was of pre-World War II design, of limited capacity, with limited flexibility as to types of products that could be handled. Nevertheless, GFID was enough attracted by the possibilities in merging Gellini and the company in Parma to offer to buy 75 percent of the Gellini company, leaving Mario and Vittorio 25 percent. Mario, who would own 75 percent of the brothers' interests, was to remain as the general manager. Meanwhile, a purchase offer made to the larger concern was not accepted. By this time in the negotiations, however, GFID's management felt committed to purchasing Gellini. Moreover, since it was obvious that there would probably be significant difficulties in adapting to the Italian business climate, it was just as well to gain experience first in a small company while establishing a foothold in Italy. GFID consequently paid $420,000 in cash for 75 percent of Gellini's capital stock. The purchase was recorded on the Division's books as $180,000 paid for net tangible assets and $240,000 paid for Goodwill.

GELLINI AND THE PASTA INDUSTRY

Pasta is the generic name in Italy for the flour product used in the manufacture of many food products, including spaghetti and macaroni noodles; the ravioli "wrapper," etc. Since the water used in the flour dough was virtually eliminated at the end of the process, the quality of the finished pasta depended on the egg content in the dough and on the quality of the flour.

In Italy, the heaviest meal came normally at mid-day, a lighter dinner being eaten later in the evening; breakfast often consisted only of Expresso coffee and rolls. The two larger meals usually consisted of three main courses plus an optional hors d'oeuvre (antipasto). The first and usually most important course always involved pasta, either in a soup or "dry." The very fact that pasta was a major part of almost every meal was given as the explanation for the hundreds of different shapes and varieties which were demanded by an Italian consumer. Moreover, certain shapes could be properly used with some condiments and not with others, and similarly for special events and occasions in the home. In addition, there were regional preferences throughout Italy, with some sections creating a unique demand for certain types of pasta.

In addition to regular pasta, Gellini manufactured various specialty pasta: (1) one type was of higher quality with eggs added to the flour; (2) another was a green colored pasta made with spinach and eggs; and (3) a third was an important specialty item, "tortellini," which was pasta filled with meat, like ravioli, but had a distinctive shape. Tortellini tended to be a seasonal product, used mainly during holiday seasons, such as Christmas and Lent and for special occasions in the home. In 1961 58 percent of tortellini sales were in November and December and 13 percent in March. Gellini's tortellini had an exclusive shape (three small points), and was considered to be of very high quality. Both Mr. Connell and the Gellini executives believed that the Gellini name had achieved an excellent reputation in Northern Italy. The executives further believed that this good name had been built largely through the superior quality of the Gellini tortellini. Furthermore, Bologna was known as the "gourmet center of Italy," which added to the reputation of the Gellini products in Italy.

It was estimated that there were about 2,000 mass producers of pasta. The largest by far was Barilla, which still was not thought to have more than 7 percent of the market. Hence, the pasta market was fragmented and highly competitive. Gellini's share in nonspecialty pastas was about 0.4 percent. Its production capacity in 1964 was 900 quintals a week, or $1.8 million in sales. Barilla, which had an almost entirely automated production process achieved a production of 4,000 quintals a day.

In tortellini, Gellini's was the oldest and most respected name, and it maintained the leading share of the market. Gellini manufactured a completely dehydrated tortellini; in this field there were only two other manufacturers of any importance. Of lesser but growing importance were two manufacturers which made a "half-dry/half-fresh" tortellini, through a newer oil and water process. Although this tortellini was often considered better tasting, it was still difficult in 1964 to judge how competitive these manufacturers would prove to be in the future. Finally, there were numerous fresh tortellini manufacturers, but because of problems in preservation, these manufacturers could serve only a limited local area. Gellini sales executives believed that their advertising program had increased total demand for tortellini, which the small local manufacturers were trying to exploit by converting to a new, vacuum-packed-in-a-cellophane-bag packaging process. It was also still too early to determine the potential competitive threat posed by these companies.

Sales for Gellini's tortellini were we seen below.

Fiscal Year	Sales in Quintals*	Fiscal Year	Sales in Quintals*
1956	1,076	1961	1,784
1957	1,325	1962	1,900
1958	1,530	1963	2,800
1959	1,762	1964	3,600
1960	1,722		

When Gellini was acquired in 1961, another Gellini line consisting of two meat sauces was dropped because the products lost their best flavors when sterilized to American standards. However, Gellini had in 1964 a co-packing arrangement with another company to package that company's "bread sticks."

RESTRUCTURING OF GELLINI

In April 1964, Mr. Connell commented:

> When I first visited Gellini in September 1963, we had owned the company for 15 months. Up to then, the Internàtional Division seemed to have made a calculated effort not to burden the company with extra overhead, but to let it run pretty much as it had prior to the purchase. However, we invoiced all of our orders, eliminated any deals with the Italian government, and paid all of our Italian taxes. These steps, which are customary in the United States but not in Italy, turned a previous profit of $45,000 on $1.4 million sales in fiscal year 1963 (April 1962 to March 1963) to a loss of $145,000. When I visited Gellini, I kept asking questions about the profitability of different lines and operations, but there apparently was no way of finding out.
>
> I started spending money to improve the management. Mario Gellini

*1 quintal = 100 kilograms or 220 pounds.

himself is actually a very able, intelligent, and honest man by anyone's standards. He was 54 years old then, with 40 years experience in the business, but his had been a one-man show. I brought in a new plant manager, a new marketing manager—who didn't work out—and a Swiss controller. Our sales went up 27 percent in FY 1964 to $1.8 million, but we lost $267,000. We are still paying taxes to the Italian government for years prior to our acquisition, because the government doesn't believe we were losing money and we didn't have the figures to prove otherwise.

We finally got hold of product costs at the end of January 1964 through a new cost-accounting procedure which we introduced. In March, at the end of Fiscal 1964, Price-Waterhouse came in to take our first physical inventory. We are going to IBM in June with the sales statistics on our approximately 150 different items so we'll know what we are selling and to whom. We hope this year to find out what is going wrong; before we couldn't tell what was happening.

The question is whether Mario will be capable of absorbing the change as we expand our operations in Italy. So far he has been trying to get things down on paper, and trying to communicate with his people. In Italy the boss is all-wise and all-powerful, and what he says is accepted, even if it's obviously incorrect. Mario has the title of "Commendatore," a decoration in Italy of official status and distinction. There is no question that he has been trying to adapt to our ways. I see him about one week in every two months. He speaks no English, and I no Italian—we communicate in poor French—but he is trying to learn English. There are moments, however, when he shows outward signs of strain.

In 1963 Mr. Connell persuaded Mr. Gellini and his brother to sell their remaining 25 percent in the company to General Foods for $105,000. Mr. Gellini was not wealthy enough to maintain his share in the investments which Mr. Connell foresaw being made in the company as General Foods expanded in Italy. In March 1964, when year-end statements for FY 1964 were prepared, Gellini was technically bankrupt according to Italian law, since accumulated losses were over one-third of the capital invested. The government could have closed the company down, so there was a hurried injection of fresh capital in the form of new equity. However, the Corporate Treasurer of General Foods was reluctant to put any more equity into Gellini, so the management was instructed to increase its overdraft facilities with the Italian banks. General Foods couldn't simply loan the money, since government capital restrictions would tax any GF notes to equalize the current 8 percent interest rate in Italy. The Corporate Treasurer's office thought that the required $1 million spread over four banks would be easy to obtain, but the Italian banks did not understand GF's position. Therefore the overdrafts had to be guaranteed by General Foods with a promissory note; these notes cost an extra 1.5 percent in interest on the amounts of the overdraft.

ORGANIZATION AND PERSONNEL

Prior to the acquisition, Mr. Gellini's staff in the headquarters had numbered fourteen. Besides Mr. Gellini, there was Mr. Marini, the Controller; three functional heads—a Sales Chief, a Cashier and a payroll/personnel head—and eight persons in administrative/staff functions. All had worked for the company for periods of 15 to 30 years. None of the executives had a secretary. In the plant, there were four foremen but no plant manager.

By 1964, the staff had increased to 37. Besides Mr. Gellini, there were five executives: Werner Speidel, Controller; Dr. Guido Dentone, Plant Manager; Mr. Giovani, a former plant manager who was hired after the acquisition but now reported to Dr. Dentone; Dr. Crespi, Office Sales Manager; and Daniele Civitali, Field Sales Manager. Under Mr. Speidel (besides a secretary), there were two assistants and 13 clerks. Dr. Crespi had a secretary and had reporting to him a traffic clerk and his assistant and three salaried field sales representatives (who also worked for Mr. Civitali). Besides Mr. Giovani eight other staff employees, including a chemist, reported to Dr. Dentone. All of the staff had been hired by Mr. Gellini.

Mr. Speidel had worked as controller for GF's European office, and in this capacity he had visited Gellini once every three months to close the books. In 1963 he was hired as Gellini's full-time controller. Mr. Speidel did much of the paper work himself, and with the increasing volume of work which had to be done, coordination between his control staff and the sales departments was occasionally subject to strain.

Dr. Dentone, the plant manager, a Canadian-Italian, arrived in November 1963 and, according to some employees, started under a definite handicap, which was that "the new American Marketing Manager had already been working for a few months." This Marketing Manager had not fitted in very well with the rest of the organization, and consequently there was some fear that Dr. Dentone would be "another of those know-it-all American-trained executives who would make those stupid mistakes." However, by working very slowly, by taking an active part in the company, and by showing a willingness to work and cooperate with the other departments, Dr. Dentone won deep respect and the confidence of his associates.

Dr. Crespi and Mr. Civitali were hired by Mr. Gellini to assist him in sales; neither of these men had had experience outside of Italy and neither spoke English. Dr. Crespi had worked in another food industry, while Mr. Civitali had once worked for Gellini before the acquisition. In 1964 Dr. Crespi had spent some of his evenings learning English, since he felt it was important to be able to communicate directly in English with the GFID personnel. Like Mr. Speidel, Dr. Crespi kept very informed of all the details under his management; for example, he believed that it was important for him to maintain close personal contact with all of his 90 agents. Like Mr. Speidel, he worked long and active hours.

Mr. Civitali was also studying English in his spare time. He was described by one GFID executive as a:

> strong and deceptively aggressive field sales manager who would be an asset to any field sales organization. He stands up to his largest and most indispensable agents and, despite their justified complaints, manages to keep them working for Gellini. Civitali and Crespi work well together and with approximately 90 agents and wholesalers to control, they have almost more to do than they can handle. Both are heavily sales-oriented and have had little, if any, experience with either advertising or new product development. They would have no objection to reporting to a competent marketing manager.

ITALIAN TAXES AND CONTROL

The taxes levied on companies in Italy included (1) a "turnover" tax, (2) various income taxes, (3) social insurance contributions and withholding taxes based on employees' salaries, and (4) miscellaneous stamp taxes. The turnover or "I.G.E." (pronounced "ee'jay") was levied not only on the company's turnover—i.e., gross sales—but on almost every other external transaction the company made, except for salaries. Gellini had to send each week to Rome the details of each invoice, including its number, the name and address of the client, his province, the amount of the invoice and the I.G.E. taxes.

Wages and salaries were subject to a special tax for which there were several different categories and structures. The total tax on wages paid to "workers" (blue-collar) usually amounted to 80 percent of the wages; the tax on wages paid to "employees" (white-collar) usually amounted to about 65 percent and to top executives about 35 percent. The salary taxes were calculated each week, since the base tax rates were adjusted weekly by the government according to the Cost of Living Index. Finally, there was also an Italian tax on net income. The official income tax rate was 44 percent, but in practice this had little relation to the amounts actually paid to the government. According to Mr. Speidel, 96 percent of the firms in Italy kept two sets of books, known regularly as "white cash" and "black cash," the white cash being the set shown to the government and the general public.

The common practice of carrying two sets of books was generally attributed to the stiff taxes, other than those on income, to which a company was subject, especially the I.G.E. and salary taxes. Therefore, it a company were officially to record only a fraction of the sales invoices and wage payments, it could realize substantial savings. The unofficial sales would be recorded in the "black cash," on which no taxes were paid. From this black cash, moreover, the company would (under prior agreements), pay its employees the difference between the official wages and the normal going wages. These agreements were not usually difficult to make since the employees would then have less officially-taxable income. The double set of books required an elaborate chain of mutual understanding across all of Italian commerce to avoid being detected by tax officials. This system seemed secure since outside of the relatively few United States and British subsidiaries in Italy, there existed virtually no practice in public accounting.

The Italian tax officials were not unaware of the usual accounting practices. They applied strict controls, such as the recording of invoices mentioned earlier. But more important, the amount paid by a company for income tax became, in practice, a negotiated amount which characteristically had little relation to the published income statements and to the official schedule of tax rates. The tax officials had a period of five years after the end of a given reporting year to review the company's situation and statements. At some point, the tax officials would submit a tax bill for a given year. If a company objected to the amount rendered, then the figure was renegotiated and paid.

"By Italian standards," Mr. Connell said, "Gellini's bookkeeping prior to the acquisition was almost white. When we started invoicing all our sales and recording all our salaries, our total lawful taxes would have amounted to about 105 percent of any profits. Our situation is this: the Italian officials consider American companies as rigid and stupid. They feel that in negotiating the tax bill (whether we're losing money or not) they are being reasonable." Company executives estimated that perhaps only 50 to 60 percent of Gellini's invoices had been registered before the acquisition. There was also reported to be some reaction among the workers in the plant when all salaries were recorded officially. Apparently they thought Americans were supposed to be good businessmen, but when they were faced with increased officially taxable incomes, they greeted this event with astonishment and dismay.

After acquiring Gellini in 1961, the International Division brought in Price-Waterhouse, public accountants, to value the assets. Price-Waterhouse reported that the plant and assets had been carried at "arbitrary costs," and only at about 50 percent of their actual value. Mr. Speidel commented on the situation:

> Only this year (February 1964) has Price-Waterhouse given us an unqualified statement on Gellini. The problem arises when an American firm comes in and pays an unconcealed price for a firm; then the tax people have a good idea of what that firm is worth in profits and sales. I can't tell from the books, but I'm convinced that the company wasn't making a profit before. We're still paying income taxes on the years prior to our acquisition. However, we have not paid taxes on losses in the years since the acquisition, nor are we going to. Some day in the next year or so, we will be presented with a tax bill on our earnings since the acquisition. We're not going to pay it. Then we will face being in court for one, two, maybe even eight years. Then there will finally be a meeting of the minds, and we'll get this thing settled. Maybe already they realize that American

companies operate this way, and an unqualified Price-Waterhouse statement on the Gellini financial statements will help.

For control purposes, Mr. Speidel was responsible for submitting at least six major reports to the International Division headquarters. These reports were (1) Balance Sheet and Income Statements, (2) Weekly Gross Sales, (3) Cash Report and Borrowings, (4) Inventory Report, (5) Quarterly Profit Estimate and (6) Capital Expenditure Report. Details of these reports and their use are given in General Foods (B).

MANUFACTURING AND COST CONTROLS

The Gellini plant consisted of three main areas: the flour "dumping" room, the tortellini room, and the production-packaging-finished-inventory section. The dumping room was partially filled with bags of wheat which was delivered by truck three or four times a week. It also contained six dumping hoppers which in turn fed into six pasta presses. In the presses the flour was mixed with water, pressed into the proper shape, and dropped onto drying trays which were placed into drying ovens for a day or more. Once the pasta dried on the trays, it was moved to the packing section where it was either packed in large bulk bags or into small boxes or bags.

On each of the six dumping/pressing lines it was possible to make only certain kinds of "formati," or shapes of pasta, which could be made on no other line. Gellini offered about 96 different pasta formati. Some other formati not shown in the catalog were still sold because of customer requests, although some of these were in the process of being eliminated from the product line. In addition to the different formati, the pasta was also made in four different flour formulas differing in wheat quality and egg content. Not all formati were made in all formulas and consumer package sizes, but the total line, including formati, formulas and different package weights, numbered about 200 items.

Only one of the six production lines was fully automated from raw materials up to the packaging operation, and in one weighing and filling the pasta and the sealing process had been automated in 1964. The materials-handling and packaging for the majority of the products were done by hand. The tortellini was a self-contained operation. At one end of the tortellini room the superpasta "wrapper" and the meat filling were prepared. The materials were carried by hand to one of the 14 tortellini machines, which automatically filled the pasta, twisted it into the familiar shapes and deposited these shapes onto drying trays.

INSTALLING THE COST CONTROL SYSTEM

In October 1963, Mr. Connell sent Joseph Romero, staff analyst in the GFID controller's department, to Italy for seven months to set up a cost system in the

Gellini plant. Mr. Romero, a New Yorker of Italian parents, could readily understand spoken Italian and was able to speak it with some facility. In November, Franco Torno, a Sicilian with a four-year degree in economics, was hired as cost accountant to run the newly established control system. According to Mr. Romero:

> We wanted to impress the need on local management for obtaining cost by package size. It was a battle against tradition. The Italians are individualists—it is difficult to put them under the same system. The first thing I tried to do was to establish a dumping report. I tried one day to explain to the dumpers where I had provided different spaces on the form to be marked, depending on the type of wheat dumped. It quickly became obvious that a problem to be overcome was illiteracy. This was resolved by having the dumpers deposit the tickets attached to each sack into receptacles placed in front of each production line.

Similarly, by working with the press-machine foreman and the packaging forelady, Mr. Romero was able to install in four months a system which recorded key data on work time by product. Mr. Romero observed about the system:

> You have to be firm. You've got to watch out for passive resistance or sabotage. The Italians are enthusiastic and want to work hard—but in their own traditional way. I kept hearing—"But no other pasta factory does things this way." It was fortunate I could understand Italian since I was able at crucial points to detect trouble and establish my authority before things got out of hand.

During a plant tour in August, Mr. Torno commented that the finished inventory "warehouse" was too small, which meant that goods were often out of stock and had to be repacked from other sizes. Later, when asked why his control system could not be used to predict shortages, he said:

> We tried to do this for a week and gave it up. We found it was just too difficult. This meant that we had to keep filing through our Cardex file for 200 stocked items and it just took too much time on top of the other bookkeeping work we have to do. I have tried to ask for all of this to be put on IBM, but they haven't been able to put our sales records on IBM yet. Writing a program for the computer [which was being done in the Bologna IBM offices] is proving very difficult. Our forelady has been as much as three weeks behind in her production reports. She tries but when I notice variations it's too late to go back and ask why, because no one can remember what happened. I'm getting discouraged with my status here. I don't really use my training on the job, since I only collect figures and don't calculate costs. I'm applying for a scholarship to Pittsburgh.

PRODUCTION PROBLEMS

Dr. Dentone had an Italian degree in chemistry and had received a Ph.D. in Food Technology from the University of California. He recalled his first problems in the plant as being mainly ones of shortening delivery times, mechanizing where he could afford to, and introducing the concept of "scheduling orders through production." In recalling his experiences, Dr. Dentone's first comments were these:

> The personnel problem is easier here than it was in Canada (although I feel they are more aware of personnel problems in the United States than in either Canada or Italy). The people in the plant have been easy to work with. In Italy, the unions are run by the political parties, and most workers' strikes are national. Here they are not wealthy enough to afford a strike against just one company like Gellini. If the party calls for a national strike, then they will strike against us, but they are usually only protest strikes lasting a half hour or half a day. I respect my contacts with the unions, so there are no problems among the workers here. There are two shop stewards, but they never come to my office and except for financial matters about vacation pay, etc., there are few grievances.

In order to meet the company's budgeted sales requirements, in the last year, Dr. Dentone found it necessary to increase production in all lines. In increasing production his biggest bottleneck was in packaging since, as he pointed out, the trend in retail consumption of pastas was from buying it in bulk sacks to buying it in the smaller consumer boxes and cellophane bags. He estimated that whereas a few years ago 85 percent of all production was in the bulk packages (6 kilograms, 8 kgs., 10 kgs. and 15 kgs.), now 45 percent of it was sold in the 200-gram and 400-gram packages.

To speed up the packaging process, Dr. Dentone put some idle equipment into use. In October 1963 he submitted a report to GFID headquarters recommending the purchase of certain new packaging machines. The division's request was approved, and the recommendation, with further back-up calculations, was resubmitted to the division in March. In May the funds were approved, and the orders were placed among Italian manufacturers for the machinery. However, Dr. Dentone guessed that about 2,000 other pasta plants in Italy were also in the process of increasing their packaged production so he did not expect delivery on his order until the end of September. Until recently, packaging machinery could not be designed for formati representing about 50 percent of the company's pasta production. Even with the new machinery, about 25 percent would still have to be hand-packed because certain formati didn't lend themselves to automation.

A particular problem existed with tortellini, since it combined a highly seasonal sales pattern with a limited shelf life. In slack periods, Dr. Dentone tried to run the department one or two days a week and then use the tortellini production force for packing other pastas the remaining four days. Since the shelf life of tortellini was increased by cold storage, he hoped to rent outside cold storage facilities in order to prevent scheduling overtime work and excess temporary staff.

Hiring temporary staff in Italy was complicated by the fact that any nonseasonal industry could not hire temporary staff; that is, no employee could be legally dismissed under normal circumstances. Whereas packing fruit was considered to be seasonal, tortellini making was not. It was possible, legally, to lay workers off when sales and production fell off, but not to fire them. Dr. Dentone had recently dismissed 10 workers (eight women and two men) but, as he said:

> They were nice about it and there were no complications. I promised them that when we expanded, as I hope we shall soon, we would hire them back. I also introduced the idea of seniority, since I let those go who had been most recently hired by the company. This actually boosted morale in the plant by giving the older workers more confidence. With the temporary workers, I have them sign papers, and the union doesn't get too involved in it.

One of the innovations Dr. Dentone introduced was to establish a quality control department at the plant, which included a small lab, a chemist and a technician. The chemist was given full authority in the plant to "freeze" any shipment which did not meet specifications. Shipments which the chemist "froze"—perhaps because moisture content was too high or because of defective manufacture—were either rectified and repacked, or destroyed. Although this would be expensive to the company, Dr. Dentone thought this policy would eventually pay dividends, since in the first place, damp pasta could get moldy, damaging Gellini's reputation, and second, the Italian government was becoming increasingly strict on all producers.

Another important service which the quality control department performed, in Dr. Dentone's opinion, was to test supplier's materials:

> Until a few months ago, Mr. Gellini used to buy everything, and he usually bought from the same few suppliers. Now in this service alone the quality lab pays for itself since we discovered that 90 percent of the raw materials being delivered to us were not up to our specifications. Now we are in a position to ask for reduced prices or to refuse the shipment. We are also now open to bidding from any supplier who can give us the required quality. This means we are buying at the lowest prices. It was difficult for Mr. Gellini to accept our specifications and system, especially since he had been so involved in the buying before. I could understand both sides, however, because I have been away from Italy for 12 years. Of

course, Mario's first reaction to me is that I speak the language. Then I explained that the American company likes the specification procedure. Now we have the proof that it works, and he is usually open-minded if he sees the advantage. It took him two or three months but now on the whole he doesn't bother with purchasing any more. Three truck loads were rejected the other day from an old supplier, but he didn't seem to mind.

IMPLEMENTING CHANGES

In implementing each of several changes, Dr. Dentone said he was able to get Mr. Gellini's agreement and cooperation. Dr. Dentone would "always try to discuss any changes with him, because he does have invaluable experience." Dr. Dentone continued:

> Italians do tend to be conservative. They sometimes don't look far enough into the future as Americans and Canadians have learned to do. They are easily discouraged by early failures, and become very pessimistic. They are mostly concerned with fixing up problems so they are all right for the present. I am changing the arrangement in the tortellini drying room. Even though we've been on holiday now, I called in our tortellini drying foreman to discuss the change with him. If I hadn't consulted with him before making it, he would have resisted us for a long time. The people here are nice. When the last sales forecast was made last week, half our staff was on vacation. But the sales forecast went way up and if it is true, we'll have to change our plans and cancel vacations. The employees have indicated their willingness to cooperate. Shifting the vacations once more will not be easy, but we'll probably be able to do it. Bologna is the center of Communism in Italy, and the union and many of the workers are Communist, but we still haven't had any trouble. Maybe we will later. But I do try to stay aloof, and try not to get too close to the workers . . .

THE GELLINI SALES FORCE

The sales force was managed by Dr. Crespi with a field sales manager, Daniele Civitali. The remainder of the salaried sales force consisted of three supervisors. Their job was to call on outlets six to seven times a year to observe problems and to perform missionary selling. There was also one supervisor on salary and commission responsible for an area within a radius of 90 miles from Bologna.

Gellini sold through about 60 agents and 30 wholesalers. None of them handled directly competing products, and 35 just sold the Gellini line. Some agents handled Gellini tortellini and other specialty pastas but also sold competitors' non-specialty pastas. All wholesalers had warehouses but not all of the normal agents did. The agents' commissions varied by product, being highest for tortellini and lowest for regular pasta. For tortellini, many of the agents used "route selling" (selling directly from small trucks). Besides getting immediate payment on sales, route selling also (1) was an effective method for securing and maintaining widespread, "capillary" distribution; (2) helped to prevent out-of-stock, particularly on high turnover items; (3) enabled the retailer with limited shelf space and limited funds to buy in small quantities; and (4) assured the dealer of fresh product, this being a particularly distinct advantage. Route selling was not suitable for all products: fresh tortellini was especially suited to this method, but other pasta specialties, which were bulkier and came in a variety of shapes and packages, were not well suited. Some route salesmen sold products off their trucks while at the same time taking orders to be delivered later. In all circumstances route selling was more costly than the traditional methods, yet it was still a firmly entrenched institution, especially for selling fresh products to small stores.

Since the accounting section of the Gellini clerical staff was not always able to produce sales statistics which were less than three months old, Dr. Crespi asked his agents to submit weekly (or in some cases daily) reports on sales which were compared to reports for the same periods in prior years. In some cases remedial action would have to be taken, including extra promotions or special trips by the supervisors. Because Dr. Crespi and Mr. Civitali were mostly occupied by trips into the field, it had taken two years to devise and to implement this heavy but, they believed, very important flow of paper work.

FOOD DISTRIBUTION

The distribution of food in Italy was still largely a "Mom-and-Pop" operation with about 180,000 retail stores selling various types of food products. Many of these also sold toiletries. A significant feature was that the stores were mostly specialty shops, selling certain items but not others. The reason for this was that retailers had to apply to their Comunes for licenses to sell each different type of food product. Clearly defined distinctions between different types of food outlets really did not exist, but a few important classifications were possible: (1) *Drogherie* (about 14,500) sold canned goods (meats and vegetables), confections, toiletries, oil, spices, soft drinks, beer, wine and liquors. Most of them sold packaged tortellini; (2) *Salumeric* (about 19,000) were similar to delicatessens (without the lunch counter). These sold cheeses, sausage meats, some canned goods, and were an important outlet for loose and packaged tortellini; (3) *General Alimentari* (about 115,000) were a general combination of the drogherie and salumeric, that is, sold the products of both. They were particularly important in areas too small to support a variety of specialty shops; (4) *Tabacchi-Alimentari* (about 14,000) sold such products as tobacco, gum, candy, stamps, postcards and souvenirs; they were often connected with bars; (5) *Panetterie* (about 4,000) were an important outlet for pasta, bread, flour and biscuits; and (6) *Latterie* (about 1,000) sold all dairy products, biscuits and candies. About 3,000 stores belonged to "comparatives"—organizations of independent retailers which bought as a group.

There were about 206 supermarkets with 19 more in progress, which all dated since 1959. It was estimated that the number might be doubled by 1970. The reasons given for the small number of supermarkets was the low population increase, the fact that few people commuted to work, low disposable income precluded large one-time purchases, and "convenience" was relatively unimportant as a consumer motivation. Also, 40 percent of the population lived in scattered homes (not even in villages), meaning that in many areas there wouldn't be sufficient volume.

Because of the food outlet pattern, almost every food company of any importance in Italy sold directly to retailers. This pattern was expected to continue for at least another five years. One exception to this was a large processed food manufacturer which had little competition and advertised heavily; this company sold at the wholesale/direct account level, using its own salesmen to obtain orders for the wholesalers. This company would, however, resort to direct retail merchandising and delivery in order to meet occasional competitive threats. Wholesalers did exist, however, to cover those areas for a company where volume did not justify direct selling. Whereas the customers of an agent were normally billed by the manufacturer, the wholesaler did his own billing. This meant that two I.G.E. taxes were involved.

MARKETING PROBLEMS

Dr. Crespi recalled some of the problems he faced:

> Every company in the food industry is economically strapped and so they find it difficult to modernize. About 80 percent of the companies are family-owned, so the human elements in management determine company policies more than pure market competition. Real "marketing" doesn't exist in the mentality of the industry—market research is rarely done, simply because the companies don't have the financial strength to support it. We have a small plant with a small capacity. Therefore, in order to cover our costs, we have to have higher prices for the same product. Our problem is to sell an identical product at a higher price, so we stress "quality," always "quality." We do have a quality product, which we really didn't have before, but selling it at our prices is still a problem we have to face every day. Gellini agents have to really "market" the product; it's not a matter of a customer preferring a different box pattern or some other small difference—the product must really be marketed. We are one of the few companies which declare the truth on the exact content of our ingredients. Also, because of a new law which has been passed but not signed into actual enforcement, we have to package our products in 400-gram packages, but the competition is waiting until the law becomes effective and so is still selling in the old 454-gram package. Here is a table I prepared for a June 22nd report on representative competitive prices: [see below]

	Gellini	*Barilla**	*Riccardi**	*Santipasta**
Normal Pasta (bulk 1 kg.) L	194	182	180	182
Normal Pasta 400 grams	92	98(454g)	92(454g)	95(454g)
Egg Pasta (bulk 1 kg.)	325	308	305	310
Egg Pasta 400 grams	170	173(454g)	170(454g)	165(454g)

*Barilla, Riccardi and Santipasta are granting higher discounts per minimum purchase than we do; they also make promotional sales with 10 to 15 percent discount.

Here's a good example to show how good our salesmen are: they sell the smaller packages by telling the pasta shop to buy our package so that when the new law is finally enforced and all manufacturers then will have to sell in 400-gram bags, their customers will already be used to our product and won't have to endure such a shock in getting used to the new size. We have been working like this for two years now and the agents have been keeping our sales going only through sheer human effort. And we have been keeping the interests of our agents alive by promising that General Foods will do something, like giving them more products, higher margin products, etc. But we have all about reached the limit.

Dr. Crespi explained that a further difficulty was created by the geography of the country, which was long (840 miles) and split down the middle by a "backbone" of mountains from the Alps in the north to the Appennines in the center. Because of the geography, markets were small, isolated and far between, and it was difficult to find good people in each self-contained area or to hire salesmen to cover larger areas. The same geography hindered delivery to all parts of the country also.

Dr. Crespi described some of the problems the company had encountered with their product line:

With the continuing problem of low margins, we faced two possibilities: either (1) eliminate normal pasta and devote all our sales effort to selling a full production of the higher margin pasta specialties, or (2) limit our normal pasta to that radius around Bologna in which we could deliver directly from our plant in one day. Discontinuing our normal pasta altogether was not the best solution since the company had second-hand machinery which had just been completely reconditioned and in perfect shape, but still so obsolete as to have no resale market. Also, in order to sell our specialties, we needed normal pasta in our line as an entry for our tortellini into the retail shops. The other possibility seemed more feasible, since our normal pasta never had too strong a market in the South anyway (because that is where the best pasta is made, both in the home and in local factories). We decided to contain our sales of the normal pasta to a zone with a 90-mile radius from Bologna, which is flat land and easily covered by our own trucks in one day from the plant.

Agents were encouraged to handle other companies' bulk pasta while handling Gellini's specialties and packaged pasta. Distribution was tripled, so that the number of shops carrying the line by 1964 was increased to 9,000. Dr. Crespi continued:

> Finally, some months ago, we in the Sales Department were asked to establish a five-year sales plan. We planned that over this period we would increase our sales of tortellini to $2.0 million from a current level of $535,000. Eventually, as we added new products such as canned meat sauces or canned tortellini, we planned to eliminate normal pasta altogether. And in fact, during the first year we doubled our tortellini sales. But last year we had problems in tortellini production at the peak season—they were coming out bad because something was going wrong in the production process, and also the line was slowed by insufficient electric power. At the same time that we were irrevocably committed to placing advertising on T.V., with heavy emphasis being placed on quality and the Gellini name (and incidentally some of our T.V. ads displayed the wrong package!) we had to cut customers' orders by 50 percent, and even then 50 percent of the delivered orders were proving defective. Customers came complaining into stores with cooked tortellini on their plates. It was a disaster, as can be pointed up by one figure: our tortellini returns in 1963 were $24,000.

The final profit plan for FY 1965, which had been completed in August 1963 showed a sales/production budget as shown below, toegther with actual sales for FY 1965 as projected in September 1964. This compared to total production of 43,000 quintals in fiscal 1964 and sales of $1.8 million, thus reflecting the company's anticipated ability to increase both production capacity and sales.

	Budget		*Anticipated*	
	Quintals	*$ Millions*	*Quintals*	*$ Millions*
Normal Pasta	27,000	0.98	29,310	1.09
Specialties Pasta	23,000	0.98	10,960	0.70
Tortellini	4,500	0.71	4,720	0.89
GFC Products	–	–	90	0.02
Condiments & Misc.	–	–	620	0.06
Total Sales	54,500	2.67	45,700	2.76

The sales estimate was significant inasmuch as Italy had by the middle of 1964 been feeling the effects of a protracted economic recession. In April 1964 total national pasta sales had dropped by 30 percent. Competitive reactions in the industry had consisted of "massive" promotions and price reductions by almost all of the companies. Gellini executives pointed out that an almost fully automated company such as Barilla could more easily absorb price cuts, since its major costs were not in labor but in raw materials. There seemed to be a discernible trend among consumers away from specialty food items toward the more standard items including regular pastas. However, even though the per capita consumption of all pastas—both regular and specialty—had declined, there was evidence that the shoppers were refusing to buy the poorer grades of pasta in favor of the higher quality grades. The explanation seemed to be that over the last five to ten years, the general standard of living had improved so dramatically that consumers were now reluctant to buy inferior products, even when their incomes declined. Gellini executives pointed out that, despite this decline in pasta sales in Italy as a whole, Gellini had been able to increase its own sales, especially in its pasta specialty lines. For this reason a prior decision to budget 30,000 quintals of normal pasta and 20,000 of specialties was changed, just before the budget was submitted to GFID, to 27,000 quintals of normal pasta and 23,000 quintals of specialty pasta, while still utilizing full capacity of 50,000 quintals.

Moreover, the Gellini sales department expected to increase sales even further in calendar 1965 by increasing distribution and by extending its sales of normal pasta outside of the "pasta zone." This increase would be achieved by improving the number and quality of its agents and by "capitalizing on Gellini's higher quality to meet the gradual improvements in the standard of living." New promotional tools were also planned, including new package designs, dealer display racks, "one-free-in-sixteen" deals, prizes, point-of-purchase display materials, sales flip charts and a revamped sales catalog.

EXPORTS

Dr. Crespi had made a modest move toward developing an export program. Export sales in FY 1964 had been $27,000 and were limited mainly by the fact that Gellini prices were generally too high and that foreigners, being relatively insensitive to pasta quality, were unwilling to pay more. However, the sales department was building relations with importers in various foreign countries in anticipation of an estimated heavy demand for canned meat sauces, canned tortellini and canned ravioli.

GELLINI'S ADVERTISING PROGRAM

In Italy, the radio and television services were administered by the government through a sole agency, the RAI (Radio Televisione Italiana). There were three radio networks, the National Program, the Second Program and the Third Program. Advertising was allowed only on the first two programs consisting of three types: normal "spot" announcements, special spots, and spots inserted in "Zig-Zag," a special five-minute program of advertisements heard either once in the afternoon or evening. The government controlled the content of the advertisements; consequently there were specific restrictions on the format of the ads and on the types of products which could be offered in them. Prices for the spots ranged from $100 for a normal spot up to $250 for a 50-second insertion in Zig-Zag. In 1964 there were about 9 million radio owners in Italy.

There were two television networks, the National Program and the Second Program, for which advertising was again carefully controlled by the government. Television advertisements became part of a three- to five-minute program consisting only of commercials. During this miniature show, a cartoon sketch, a dance routine or some other entertaining theme was used to connect the various advertisements together. There were five advertising programs on the National Program with commercials of 35 seconds costing about $3,000 to $5,000 apiece in the evening. Intermezzo, the sole advertising program presented on the Second network beginning at 9:10 p.m., consisted of four commercials up to 40 seconds long, costing up to $2,000. In 1963 there were about 3 million television sets in Italy, about half of which were capable of receiving the Second Program.

There were about 10,400 cinema houses, although the houses covered by the major advertising production companies numbered only about 5,000. Because of higher ticket prices, cinema attendance had been dropping slightly. There were three different types of advertising programs and rates, depending on the type of cinema house in which the films were displayed (from "extra" and "first" classes down to "fifth" class). The general rate for a top class cinema house was $44 for each showing of a ten-minute film, down to $8 for the same film in a fifth class house. The films could range up to 100 minutes of advertising, each additional minute beyond 20 minutes costing about $1.

In both television and cinema advertising, regulation required that the same film could be repeated only after an interval from a week between showings up to an interval of several months.

The Gellini advertising agency had evaluated the various advertising media and concluded that for tortellini—the only product which the company felt was worth advertising—the best impact per dollar spent would be in television, given a shortened selling season and limited advertising funds.

Prior to 1962 the company had advertised only in newspapers and in weekly magazines. Only three competitors advertised, spending a total of about $400,000 a year in newspapers. By late 1964, one competitor was reportedly going to use T.V., but not much information was available on this rumor. A difficulty in broadcast advertising was that time had to be purchased from the government agency the preceding year for the entire next year's requirement, which then became an inflexible and final commitment. The government usually granted an advertiser time on better or poorer commercial programs depending on how much the company had advertised the year before and how much it had advertised in all media. Gellini's policy was, therefore, to put as much of its advertising budget into television as it could afford in order to establish a good television advertising record.

For FY 1965, Gellini budgeted $87,000 for advertising tortellini: $69,000 in T.V., $12,000 in radio, $3,600 in cinema and $2,600 in a nationally published radio/TV "guide." The T.V. advertising consisted of 21 forty-second advertisements running from July 12 to November 11 shown about 8:00 p.m. Because of government regulations concerning repetition of the same ad, four films had to be made for this schedule. The radio spots ran from October to December, the cinema for three weeks beginning in late November and the program guide for September and November.

In late 1962 the former marketing manager and the Gellini advertising agency commissioned an independent market research firm to explore the "Italian Market for Tortellini"; the instructions to the researchers were to determine the overall extent of the tortellini market and to assess Gellini's relative position in it. The report, which cost nearly one million lire ($1,400) was the analysis of 3,100 interviews with grocers and restaurateurs. However, because Gellini executives had many questions and doubts about the report, arising out of the research firm's sampling techniques and its interpretation of the data, the results of the project were considered inconclusive and the report failed to provide any guidelines for action. Some of the general findings were: (1) the total market for tortellini was about 46,000 quintals a year; (2) the average annual tortellini sales for a pasta dealer were 55 Kilograms (0.55 quintals); (3) pasta stores and delicatessens accounted for about 76 percent of tortellini sales, whereas the demand by restaurants and other food stores was low and was usually highly seasonal.

The research firm concluded that restaurants constituted a poor potential market, and that the major potential lay rather in convincing food stores to switch from selling fresh tortellini to selling the dry variety and in persuading non-consumers to try it. There did seem to be a resistance at the store level to trusting the quality and flavor of factory-made, dry tortellini and, moreover, the figures seemed to indicate that 46 percent of the shops had not bought any of the Gellini tortellini.

"THE AMERICAN MARKETING MANAGER"

In describing the Marketing Manager who hadn't worked out in Gellini, Mr. Connell recalled:

> He was a nice guy, really. He was personable, bright, about 42, with a long agency background. He was also highly creative. In Italy he got along well with Gellini at first and got along well with the agency. However, he was a very poor administrator and his communication with others was almost non-existent. Soon he and the Sales Manager were at sword's point, the program was getting fouled up. Gellini was getting fouled up with the

agency, and the sales department was getting fouled up with the Controller. I'm looking now for a good marketing manager—an Italian with U.S. experience and who knows the Italian market—one who will go about it in a different way. I can afford to look for a qualified Italian rather than an American because I have other General Foods people in the company who know the ropes.

MR. GELLINI

Mr. Gellini was held officially accountable to the International Division for the performance of the company. In 1961/62 GFID proposed that the company should institute a system of cost controls. Mr. Gellini, however, strongly believed that the company simply "couldn't afford increased staff." He pointed to the Barilla Company, which reportedly had 23 times greater sales than Gellini with an administration staff of only 20 people.* It was not until a personal visit to General Foods' headquarters in 1962 that Mr. Gellini really began to feel that he could understand the need for figures and cost accounting. After returning he told his staff:

> Now I understand! . . . Now I can know what General Foods means. We are just a tiny company in comparison. It's understandable why they can't always pay attention to us, and yet keep asking for all those figures.

Many different members of the staff remarked that Mario Gellini was "a very clever man, and he knows his business." However, while he tended to be very enthusiastic about General Foods and his business after his visits, it was commented that he did become frustrated and discouraged by the various delays encountered from the GFID headquarters in the fulfillment of the programs which had been discussed and promised during his trips to New York. One example of such a delay was the time it took between requesting and receiving the tortellini drying equipment—more than a year—mentioned earlier in the case. Consequently, Mr. Gellini's usual enthusiasm would wane in a few months.

Mr. Gellini made these comments about changes in the firm:

> Going back to 1961, the planned expansion in Gellini didn't materialize. There was just an increase in expenses for the new accounting, but it wasn't compensated by an increase in production or sales. As for normal pasta, our budget for FY 1965 is set at the maximum which the plant will produce, so we can't consider expansion in that area—the gross margins in

---

*In one interview, Mr. Gellini pulled out a recent article in an Italian newspaper which he considered "very interesting." The article reported total sales and number of employees of major Italian companies, one of which was Barilla. Whereas Gellini had sales in 1964 of 1,225,000,000 lire with 140 employees, Barilla had sales in 1964 of 21,253,000,000 lire and had 1,211 employees (mostly production workers).

pasta are too low. Therefore we need other products in order to reach the
$8 million goal, and so Gellini can be in the position it should have the
right to be in, because of the Gellini name, and General Foods' name. So
the sacrifice we have made from 1961 to 1965 has created a base of good
men, a good organization, and a good system for Gellini, and we are ready
to go. Those years of sacrifice were not wasted and we are in a position to
realize the aims set in 1961.

Now here's a very interesting development we've come up with. It's a
new process for cooking tortellini before they're dried: the process
pasteurizes the product, gives a richer color, and increases its preservation
characteristics so it has a longer storage life. It also means that we can add
parmesan cheese, which we couldn't do under the old process because it
deteriorated too quickly. We will have a unique product for which we will
charge 1250 lire per kilo as opposed to 1050 lire per kilo for the present
product. We have added a machine which will cost $2,000 and, although
we haven't been given the official authority yet, we will come out with it
soon. It really is a very interesting product. As I said, we're ready and
waiting to go.

FUTURE OUTLOOK

Financial data for Gellini appear in Exhibits 1 and 2. When asked at one point to
supply approximate margin and expense percentages, Mr. Speidel had produced
these figures:

Income and Expense Percentages			
Present Net Sales			100%
Cost of Goods			
Materials		62	
Labor			
Direct	14		
Overhead	7	21	83%
Gross Profit			17%
Sales expense			
Variable		5	
Fixed		8	13%
Media			6
G&A			5
Interest			2
Net Profit (Loss)			(9%)

These figures were based on the current fiscal 1965 annual production of about
3,600 quintals of tortellini and about 43,000 quintals of pasta. Tortellini sales

**Exhibit 1. Gellini S.p.A., Balance Sheet as of March 31, 1964 and 1965[1]
(U.S. Dollars)**

		FY 1964	*Est.* *FY 1965*
			$000
Cash	$	$ 202,526	3
Marketable Securities		1,215	—
Accounts Receivable—Customers		338,367	363
Accounts Receivable—Other		12,448	—
Inventories:			
Raw Materials	48,848		
Packaging Materials	113,082		
Finished and Semi-Finished Goods	120,832		
Supplies	2,842		
Total Inventories		285,606	228
Prepaid & Deferred Expense (Supply			
Qtrly. Analysis)		15,770	23
Total Current Assets		856,702	617
Notes Receivable	7,268		
Invest. & Advances-Subsid. (Cons.)			
(G.F. Corp.)	38,652		
Total Investments & Other Assets		45,920	—
Machinery, Equipment, Motor Veh., etc.	579,501		
Construction Work in Progress	5,428		
Total Property, Plants &			
Equipment (Gross)		584,929	822
Less: Reserves for Depreciation		223,346	294
Total Property, Plants &			
Equipment (Net)		361,583	528
TOTAL ASSETS		1,264,205	1,145
Notes Payable—Current		787,933	849
Accounts Payable		257,157	120
Federal & Foreign Income Taxes Accrued		34,206	30
Other Accrued Liabilities		193,725	40
Total Current Liabilities		1,273,021	1,039
Common Stock 360,000 Shares		516,424	227
Retained Earnings Prior to Acquisition		(23,680)	—
Retained Earnings Since Acquisition			
(At beginning of Year)	(209,948)		
Net Profit Year to Date	(291,612)		
Retained Earnings Since Acquisition to Date		(501,560)	(121)
Total Capital Stock & Retained Earnings		(8,816)	106
Total Liabilities, Capital Stock &			
Retained Earnings		1,264,205	1,145

1. The report sent to GFID headquarters included local currency figures.

Exhibit 2.   Gellini S.p.A., Profit and Loss Statement for Periods Ending March 31, 1964 and 1965[1] (U.S. Dollars)

		FY 1964	Est. FY 1965
			$000
Sales–Customers		$1,931,637	2,753
Allowances	$ 16,207		30
Transportation	85,125		100
Warehousing	41,519		43
Cash Discount	1,642		2
Total Deductions		$ 144,492	175
Net Sales–Customers		1,787,145	2,578
Cost of Goods Sold–Customers		1,568,216	2,060
Gross Profit–Customer Sales		218,929	518
Advertising Expense		87,867	106
Deals		27	–
Selling–Field	206,431		233
–Admin. & Prod. Management	25,528		–
–Market Research	578		11
–Sales Accounting	29,009		54
Total Selling Expense		261,549	298
Total Marketing Expense		349,441	404
Merchandising Profit		(130,512)	114
Research Expense	2,242		7
General and Administrative Expense	102,868		113
Total Research Gen. & Admin. Exp.		105,110	120
Operating Profit–Customers		(235,622)	(6)
Interest Expense (exclude intercompany)	45,641		68
Other Expense	9,509		14
Interest Income	110		–
Other Income	37		–
Net (Other Expense)–Other Income		(55,003)	(82)
Profit Before Technical Service Fee & Interco Interest		(290,625)	(88)
Profit Before Income Taxes		(290,625)	(88)
Provision for Foreign Income Taxes (Prior years)	987		–
Total Income Taxes		987	–
Net Profit–G.F. Corp.		(291,612)	(88)

1. The report sent to GFID headquarters included the current month's profit and loss figures, as well as month and year–to date figures in local currency.

and specialty sales each comprised about 33 percent of the total sales. Asked if he could foresee a profit in the future, Mr. Speidel said:

In pasta, no. If we were fully automated both in our packaging and production lines, from raw material to packaged product, and if we had a potential market like Barilla, then we might make a profit. But this would require a tremendous investment in new equipment, which is expensive. To go to sales of $10 million or $15 million would require—I'm not sure—but about $5 million to $6 million in machinery. We need more volume to make a profit. Given our present marketing set-up, we might be able to increase our sales by 100 percent; this is leaving aside the fact that we're at full production capacity now. The profit margin on tortellini is about 35 percent but only about 13 percent on pasta and 15 percent on specialty pasta. If we are given some new higher-margin products to sell which are as important as pasta, and if the supermarket appears as a major outlet for pasta, then we could make money.

When asked who was responsible for making new investment and new product decisions, Mr. Speidel said:

That's up in the area of Mr. Connell and Mr. Sorenson (GFID president). We are constantly on the search for new products both locally and at headquarters. Mr. Sorenson would not accept a statement such as "This product won't go in Italy." His philosophy is that you simply cannot be sure in respect to the success of any product until a market test has actually proved otherwise.

For two years after it was bought, the development of this company has been slow, for two reasons, I think: First, a tremendous effort was needed to put the house in order and to establish a sound base on which to build, and second, there were other acquisitions made at the same time requiring full attention. Most of the $180,000 invested in plant and equipment since then has been in the tortellini segment. For example, of the $83,000 spent in fiscal 1964, 85 percent was spent in tortellini.

In August 1964, Joseph Romero, staff financial analyst for GFID, returned to Italy to check on the production control system which he had installed on an earlier trip, and to help Mr. Speidel in the preparation of the September Profit Plan. Mr. Romero commented:

I have a theory about international operations: the further away you are, the more follow-through you need. The situation is different in the U.S.: General Foods had built itself on marketing know-how, although you will notice that a significant part of its growth has come from acquisitions made throughout the years.

But it's different abroad. The further away you are, with strange laws and a different language, the more your assets are in jeopardy, and the more you need financial control. And financial people—because a "credit" is always a "credit" and a "debit" is always a "debit"—tend to be more conservative and down to earth.

In the U.S., it's easy to find a good financial manager to back up the marketers. But I strongly believe that when you're far away, and disaster is too close for the overenthusiastic marketer, you need to have a general manager who's financially rather than marketing oriented. Since good financial people are hard to find abroad, he will have to be domestically trained. But you have to make sure that your overseas company won't move into disaster before you have a chance to stop it.

PRODUCT LINE PLANS

A variety of plans for changes in Gellini's product line were being developed. Canned tortellini which Dr. Dentone had helped to perfect in early 1964 was submitted to General Foods in New York for testing of its flavor, quality, consistency and safety, after which it had received official approval for marketing. However, when in May 1964 the plans for Gellini FY 1965 budget were being reviewed in New York, it was decided to postpone the introduction of any new products in FY 1965, although it was agreed that 900 quintals of production in addition to the 54,500 quintals of the current production would be budgeted for "development production" and test marketing. Gellini had manufactured canned tortellini once before, but General Foods still classified it as a "new" product, which meant it had to follow all the steps required before a new product was introduced.

It had also been previously planned to develop a canned meat sauce (which Gellini had also once manufactured but had discontinued at the time of the acquisition) and to manufacture dry soups packaged in an envelope. Gellini still had the necessary canning equipment to produce these items on a limited basis. However, the manufacture and packaging of dry soup ingredients—a "dry mix operation"—required a sophisticated quality control for the ingredients and completely different packaging procedures from pasta. The decision to postpone these two products was based on two factors. First, Gellini was heading into the peak December quarter when all the plant efforts would be devoted to producing at capacity, and second, the company was already committed to producing the test market quantities of condiments and sauces. It was therefore decided to wait until after the end of FY 1965 before beginning development of a soup line.

Mr. Gellini explained that these particular products were selected for development and introduction because they were either complementary to the pasta line (such as condiments) or were similar to the present manufacturing process and, just as important, they appeared to be highly profitable items. Mr. Gellini also believed that normal pasta could be more profitable if the company bought completely automated machines capable of putting out 200 quintals a day. He believed that ten of these machines could easily supply the $8 million volume which he felt the company needed to: (1) match the Barilla competition, and (2) provide the volume to cover the present overhead. Ten machines, however, would require an investment of $3.0 million. On the other hand, since only about $42,000 would be needed to buy the equipment and introduce the higher profit condiment and soup items, the pasta investment was clearly out of the question.

Mr. Gellini was also intrigued by the high profit potential in pasta baby food, a market which was currently dominated by two Italian food companies. The basic pasta product was practically the same as Gellini's present line, he contended, but could demand as much as 2-1/3 times the price per pound as normal pasta. However, it was difficult and time-consuming to establish a market position since success in this market required the doctors' support and public endorsement of the product. At least five years would be required, Mr. Gellini estimated, and even then success was not automatic—in fact, Barilla had tried twice and failed in its effort to enter the pasta baby foods market.

Mr. Gellini was also looking forward to the time when, along with its regular Gellini line of products, his sales force would also carry the General Foods brand of products. He was mainly interested in General Foods' Maxwell House coffee, since "General Foods means coffee." There had never been a large market for coffee in Italy, since import duties almost doubled its normal price; nevertheless, Mr. Gellini believed there was no reason why a good market for instant coffee could not be easily developed. General Foods did some importing to Italy, using the services of an import agent. Mr. Gellini believed that his sales force should be allowed to handle any General Foods import business which could be developed since it was "embarrassing when the Gellini name is so widely associated in Italy with General Foods not to be able to handle General Foods business."

Mr. Connell made these comments on product development:

> The total General Foods export business to Italy is only $60,000. We have an Italian agent in Bologna handling our coffee and some other of our products, but it's in only about 20 stores—you couldn't find it if you looked. This agent is due to be discontinued in November, but not everyone in the GFID staff believes Gellini can handle the import business. If we are serious about coffee, we must buy a coffee roaster or a plant, both of which are major investments. There was some question whether we could use Gellini as a platform to build our coffee sales, but Jim Davis visited Italy in March and says we can. And Gellini is expecting it. There are a whole host of problems connected with coffee. In Italy, the main product is Expresso [a quick-brewed coffee with a powerful flavor]—it's supposed to be a jolt, not a beverage. The market for U.S. coffee in Italy is mainly accounted for by the wealthy as a form of conspicuous consumption. As far as Jell-O, SOS scouring pads, Post-Toasties and other products are concerned, there just isn't the volume yet for any of them. We have the plant facilities in other European countries, and some day it will make sense to begin to develop the Italian market.

Mr. Jim Davis, former Marketing Director for GFID, spent a month in Italy in early 1964. In his report, Mr. Davis concluded:

> Without question, any new products to be introduced in Italy—including coffee—should be given to the Gellini sales organization. This organization

is already far better than it has any right to be. The organization has great flexibility and can be tailored to meet the needs of either a large and demanding "new products" program or a modest one. While condiments and canned tortellini are natural additions to the Gellini line, it is doubtful whether either of them can be expected to contribute important volume. The market for canned tortellini does not exist at present (although some canned ravioli is sold) and with limited marketing funds available, may be slow in developing.

Dried soups containing pasta are another fine idea, assuming the right product can be developed. At present, the dry soup market is dominated by Knorr, who have an 80 percent share. Other major brands are Star (6 percent share) and Liebig and Maggi (5 percent share each). In order to stand a chance against this kind of competition, Gellini soups will have to meet several specifications: (1) they will have to be top quality; (2) they should be heavily pasta-oriented, i.e., pasta should be major and essential ingredients (otherwise, what excuse does Gellini have for being in the soup business?); and (3) to the extent possible, Gellini soups should be exclusive. (This isn't going to be easy since a number of pasta soups have already been introduced by competition.) Development work on these soups has just started and is being handled by Dr. Dentone.

Italy's biggest new product opportunity is coffee. The coffee business is large ($113 million in home consumption in 1963) and one that can be expected to grow as national income increases (hence the estimated decline in the coffee substitute market). Coffee is also a highly competitive business with competition coming from several directions. In the first place, an estimated 60 percent of coffee consumption takes place in bars—a business of no immediate interest to General Foods. Competing for the home consumption are more than 2,000 local roasters, together with the large, well-established coffee companies such as Lavazza and Bourbon whose products are widely distributed and aggressively sold and promoted. Figures show that 62.8 percent of the total coffee for home consumption is still sold in loose bean form. (In dollar sales, however, loose beans represent a smaller per cent of the total—$69 million vs. $44 million for packaged coffee.) Nevertheless, the trend is definitely toward packaged coffee and the large, well-managed, aggressive companies will inevitably supplant most of the local roasters in the long run.

Mr. Davis indicated several requirements for General Foods to be successful in the coffee business in Italy.

(1) A high quality blend developed specifically for the Italian market; (2) Packs including whole beans and ground coffee; (3) A minimum of two and preferably three different roasts for different parts of the country, i.e., a lighter roast for the North, a darker roast for the South, and a medium roast for Central Italy; (4) Only packaged coffee should be sold and to support a quality image and a high price, all coffee should be vacuum-packed; (5) Before deciding upon tins or cartons, vacuum-packed glass jars

should also be considered. They enable the customer to see the product, have reuse value, and would be different from any other coffee pack on the market; (6) There is a tendency for retailers to favor loose coffee over packaged, one reason being that they can weigh and charge for the paper on which the beans are weighed. Therefore, to gain retailer support, margins should be adequate. This would also apply to agents' commissions; (7) A heavy and continuing advertising program (preferably TV) will be mandatory; and (8) Route selling—used by all the leading coffee brands—will be needed for the launching of any GF coffee products and for an indefinite period of time thereafter. The Gellini sales organization is well-equipped to provide this type of sales operation.

It would probably be quicker (although no less difficult and complicated) to get into the coffee business by buying a company that already has its equipment, its established brands, franchises, etc. However, while they should be pursued further, the acquisition possibilities appear to be limited.

Consideration should be given to assigning one or more of the export products to the Gellini sales organization—if only on a trial basis. Mario Gellini has expressed interest in cake mixes. Other possibilities might be dog foods and Jell-O desserts. There is every reason to believe that the Gellini sales organization could and would do as good—or better—a job with any food products, as either the present agency or [the agency the Export Director was investigating] —and at lower cost. . . .

Canton Drug Company

Late in 1969 Thomas Phillips, the Middle Eastern manager of Canton Drug Company, was concerned about how he should handle a difference of opinion with Abdul Baba, President of the Wadi Drug Company with which Canton was associated in its operations in Zardin, a leading Middle Eastern country. The two men disagreed over whether the company should follow a liberal dividend policy in view of a need for funds for plant expansion.

The Canton Drug Company was one of the outstanding concerns in the pharmaceutical field. As a result of extensive research it had developed several important new drugs, and its line of products was constantly being improved, giving the company a strong competitive position. Canton had extensive international operations. In Zardin it had sold through a local distributor, the Wadi Trading Company, since the mid-1930s. In the Zardinian market it had active competition from several other United States companies and some European concerns.

In 1963 the Zardinian government issued a decree requiring that certain of the simpler drug products be manufactured within the country by 1965. Companies which wished to manufacture the products had to apply for approval from the government, as only a limited number of factories would be approved. The Canton management immediately initiated discussions with Abdul Baba,

The real company name, product line and some other facts have been disguised. Written in conjunction with Richard Nolte, Director, Institute of Current World Affairs, while he was a member of the American Universities Field Staff.

owner of the Wadi Trading Company, as to how they should adjust to this new development. They had great respect for Mr. Baba's abilities and position. He was generally considered an extremely able man. As a member of Parliament in the majority party, he was a rising political force and widely recognized as a potential prime minister. This position gave him strong political influence which he used effectively.

As a result of the discussions with Mr. Baba, it was agreed that the Wadi Drug Company should be organized to undertake manufacture of those products which were to be restricted from importation. The Wadi Trading Company would continue the distribution of imported products. Mr. Baba immediately applied to the government for approval for the plan, and authorization was received within a few days. The new company was set up later in 1963, with 7,000 shares of stock issued at 100 Zardinian pounds per share (one Zardinian pound equals 40 cents US). The Canton Drug Company received 3,000 shares in return for equipment and cash investment. Mr. Baba subscribed to 3,000 shares and the remaining 1,000 were purchased by Ali Tabrizi, an associate of Mr. Baba. Mr. Tabrizi was also a member of Parliament in the majority party. He was a prominent Zardinian attorney employed by a number of foreign companies and local concerns.

The board of directors of the Wadi Drug Company was composed of Mr. Baba, two of Mr. Baba's friends who had participated in his share of the investment, Mr. Tabrizi and three representatives of Canton Drug Company: the company's local attorney, Hamid Nezak; the Eastern Hemisphere Director, Mr. Jones; and the Middle Eastern Manager, Thomas Phillips. Mr. Phillips made his headquarters in Tor, the capital of Zardin, where the Wadi plant was located and served as immediate liaison representative between Canton and the Wadi Drug Company. Mr. Baba was elected president of the company.

It was decided that operations should be started with the minimum investment feasible, and plans proceeded on this basis during 1964. An old warehouse was purchased and converted to a small factory. Canton equipped the factory largely from machinery out of its US plants, which had been replaced by more automatic equipment but which was still serviceable. It was considered quite satisfactory for the simple mixing, tablet-making and bottling operations proposed for the Wadi plant. In addition, Canton sent technical experts who supervised the installation of the machinery, training of personnel and the initial operations of the plant.

In April 1965 the factory started production, and at the same time the government import restrictions went into effect. Several other companies had applied for manufacturing permits, and two had received approval. One was entirely owned by a US concern and the other was a joint partnership between Zardinian and European capital. Their factories also opened in 1965. Other firms continued to import a wide range of drug products but were excluded from the sale of those which were manufactured locally.

Operations proceeded satisfactorily during 1965, the year closing with a profit of 275,000 Zardinian pounds. A dividend of the full amount of the profits was declared at a meeting of the board of directors in early 1966. Mr. Phillips expressed some doubts at the wisdom of this action, but as there was no immediate need for funds he did not feel that he had a basis for arguing his point. At a board meeting in August 1966, an interim dividend of 344,000 pounds was proposed. Mr. Phillips said that he felt it would be wise to retain profits and defer a dividend until the end of the year. But there was still no evident need for cash, and it appeared that the profits for the year would be substantially in excess of this amount. Therefore, he went along with the Zardinian members of the board who advocated the dividend.

The final accounting for 1966 showed that the company's net undistributed profits, after deducting statutory reserves, were about 180,000 pounds (see Exhibits 1 and 2). Strong pressure developed in the board to pay out this full amount as a final dividend At a board meeting Wadi's local auditor, Bulus Iktisat, expressed approval of the dividend proposal as being a sound action for the company. Mr. Nezak felt that it might be advisable to proceed cautiously but agreed to go along with the position of the auditor.

Mr. Phillips, feeling some concern about the matter, discussed it privately with Mr. Iktisat. In this conversation Mr. Iktisat said that he was actually inclined to agree with Mr. Phillips. He said it was not just a matter of general policy, but that the company had to consider its situation with regard to its equipment which would fairly soon have to be replaced. Mr. Phillips asked Mr. Iktisat to put his views in writing, and Mr. Iktisat gave him the following statement:

"The Wadi Drug Company's chief investment is in production equipment. The present equipment was fairly old when it was installed and it is rapidly wearing out. An expected life of about five years is reasonable on the average. The company has followed a policy of charging 20 percent depreciation per year, so this equipment will have been paid for at the end of that time. However, even if it were replaced with identical equipment, the cost in Zardinian pounds would exceed the initial cost substantially, in view of the inflation in this country which has been running about 20 percent per year. Accordingly, it would seem sound practice for the company to retain a portion of the earnings each year as a reserve for re-equipment, and on this basis I believe that no further dividend should be paid out of the 1966 profits."

Mr. Phillips talked to Mr. Baba after his session with Mr. Iktisat. He said that he was now completely opposed to a further dividend payment. He said that a further analysis of reserves and future requirements made that policy seem extremely undesirable. He observed that he was supported in his position by Mr. Iktisat. Mr. Baba was quite upset and remonstrated strongly against Mr. Phillips' position. Mr. Phillips said that he was sure he was acting in the best interests of the company. He offered to refer the whole matter back to his home office and abide by its decision, but Mr. Baba declined this offer.

Exhibit 1.   Wadi Drug Company Condensed Statement of Profit & Loss (In thousands of Zardinian pounds)

	1966		Pro forma estimate 1967
Sales		2,593	3,600
Depreciation	115		130
Wages and salaries	841		1,120
Materials	1,070		1,700
Total expenses		2,026	2,950
Net operating income		567	650
Income taxes*		10	100
Net profit		557	550

*1966 taxes were reduced by certain exemptions allowed in the first year of operation.

The following day Mr. Baba proposed to Mr. Phillips that Wadi issue a limited dividend of 75,000 pounds. He showed Mr. Phillips a paper which he said was written by Mr. Iktisat suggesting a dividend of that amount. Mr. Baba was not aware that Mr. Iktisat had given a written statement to Mr. Phillips opposing any further dividend for 1966.

Mr. Phillips deferred a decision saying that he would like to think further about it. He immediately went to Mr. Iktisat and asked him how it was possible that he could have written such a statement. Mr. Iktisat said he had not taken the position Mr. Baba claimed. He said that when Mr. Baba had consulted him he had told him exactly what he had told Mr. Phillips. Mr. Baba then had asked what procedure should be followed if Wadi decided to issue a limited dividend and the paper Mr. Phillips had seen was the result of this hypothetical question.

Mr. Phillips and Mr. Iktisat went to see Mr. Baba the same day and asked him to explain his position. Mr. Baba said that Mr. Phillips had misunderstood him; that he had said, "If! If Wadi were to declare a dividend, Mr. Iktisat suggested one of 75,000 pounds." Mr. Phillips then said that in view of all the facts available he would definitely vote against any further dividends for 1966. Mr. Baba did not agree to this position, but he did not pursue the matter further and no dividend was declared.

During early 1967 the matter of new equipment was given considerable study. There had been some intimations that the government might restrict the importation of additional drug products so that expansion of production facilities might be required. Furthermore, competitive pressures were encouraging additional investment. The two other factories in Zardin had also been operating on a fairly shoestring basis, but it was known that they had definite plans to build new factories and install new equipment. It was the consensus that

Exhibit 2. Wadi Drug Company Balance Sheet December 31st
(In thousands of Zardinian pounds)

	1966		Pro forma estimate 1967
Current Assets			
Cash	212		1,266
Accounts receivable	446		680
Materials and supplies	337		410
Total current assets		995	2,356
Fixed Assets	690		747
Less reserve for depreciation	207		337
Net fixed assets		483	410
Deferred charges			83
Total assets		1,478	2,849
Current Liabilities			
Accounts payable	376		588
Accrued salaries and wages	72		142
Accrued taxes	12		–
Other current and accrued liabilities	104		655
Total liabilities		564	1,385
Capital Stock			
Common stock–par value			
£100/share 7,000 shares	700		700
Surplus (includes full 1967 profit)	180		674
General statutory reserve	34		90
Net worth		914	1,464
Total		1,478	2,849

these facilities would give them a significant competitive advantage if they were not countered by Wadi. Customers of drug products would probably be impressed by the cleanliness and the efficiency of the bright new plants proposed by the companies and would purchase their products in preference to those produced in the relatively unimpressive facilities of Wadi.

A team of technical experts from the Canton Drug Company visited the Wadi plant, and they recommended that the old equipment be replaced quite soon by machinery of improved design which would provide some cost saving in addition to the prestige value. As a result of these considerations a facilities plan was developed which would call for construction of a new plant by 1970 capable of producing products with a total value 25 percent in excess of the current volume with the same size labor force. This new program would cost 2,500,000 pounds of which about 250,000 might be recovered from the sale of the existing plant and equipment. It was expected that per unit labor costs of the new plant might be about 20 percent lower than in the present facilities.

There was some reluctance among the Zardinian members of the board of directors to undertake this major investment, but on the whole they felt that it was a sound move. There was considerable difference of opinion, however, as to the methods of financing it. Mr. Baba took the position that it should be financed by the sale of additional stock. He proposed that 4,000 new shares be sold for 100 pounds each plus a premium of 500 pounds. He said he could sell them at that amount to some of the emirs and sheiks of the Persian Gulf area who had become wealthy through oil royalties. In order to attract these buyers, he proposed that a 1967 interim dividend of 50 percent of capital be declared.

Mr. Phillips argued that this proposal was unsound. He felt that Wadi should retain its full 1967 profits to use in financing the new facilities. He did not think that a high dividend policy was necessary to attract new investors, that the financial advisers of these men would base their decisions on net profits earned and not on the basis of profits distributed. In fact, he felt that an excessive dividend policy might well discourage investors rather than attract them. Furthermore, he felt that a premium of even 200 pounds was uncertain.

Discussions along these lines continued during the fall and in early November Mr. Baba announced that a meeting of the board would be held on November 30th to make a decision on the dividend, the proposal for new stock and the new facilities plan.

The Canadian-United States Automotive Products Trade Agreement

BACKGROUND AND ISSUES FOR NEGOTIATION

In early 1976 renegotiation of the 1965 Canadian-United States Automotive Products Trade Agreement was being strongly advocated by groups in both Canada and the United States. A study initiated by the US Senate Finance Committee, proposals by an organization of Canadian parts manufacturers and a 1975 imbalance in automotive products trade of $1.7 billion were among the major elements encouraging renegotiation. While it was generally agreed that the development of the industry under the Auto Pact was beneficial for both countries, major controversy had surrounded the pact throughout most of its existence.

HISTORY OF THE AUTO PACT

The conditions which led to establishing the Auto Pact originated in policies adopted by Canada to foster manufacturing. Tariff rates of 17.5 percent for automotive vehicles and up to 20 percent for parts were established, along with exemption for imports of parts of up to 40 percent of the total value of cars assembled in Canada. These barriers were an effective block to the importation of most complete automobiles from the United States, as it was economically more profitable to import parts and assemble them. Thus the major US automobile companies established Canadian factories and assembled a full line of automobiles there.

The tariff also provided some incentive to purchase parts made in Canada. However, the 40 percent exemption and other considerations led to a large flow of parts into the country. As the Canadian parts manufacturers had relatively smaller volume than producers in the United States, their prices tended to be higher than those in the United States, and there was relatively little export to US factories. These conditions combined to result in significantly higher costs and prices of cars in Canada compared to the United States and a growing deficit in trade in automotive products between the countries.

By the early sixties the trade deficit had grown so large that it was a matter of very serious concern to the Canadian government. An official study concluded that Canadian production had to be shifted from a domestic to an international orientation if the inefficiencies of small scale and excessively diversified output were to be overcome. In October 1963 this concept was applied. Thereafter automotive manufacturers in Canada were allowed to earn remission of duties on any amount of new vehicles or original equipment parts imported equivalent to the amount of vehicles or parts exported in excess of a base level which was set as the amount they had exported between November 1, 1961 and October 31, 1962.

This action evoked a counteraction from the US side. US tariff legislation provided that a countervailing duty should be imposed whenever the Treasury Department determined that exports to the United States were being subsidized by a "bounty or grant." There was no requirement under the legislation to demonstrate that harm or injury to US industry had been caused. On April 15, 1964 the Modine Manufacturing Co. filed a petition arguing that the Canadian program resulted in a subsidy to automotive exporters. No final action was taken on the Modine complaint, however, because the general concern aroused by the Canadian action set in motion government negotiations which ultimately resulted in the Auto Pact. Essentially, the US government, recognizing that the Canadians were determined to solve the problem of the balance of trade by one means or another, decided that a bilateral approach was preferable to the unilateral action being taken from north of the border.

The essence of the concept underlying the Auto Pact was to eliminate the effects of the border between the two countries so far as manufacturing of automotive products was concerned, subject to sufficient safeguards to assure that a reasonable portion of manufacturing was undertaken in Canada. At the time it was perceived that this concept was on balance beneficial to Canada but that it was acceptable to the United States in preference to the unilateral action by Canada or the prospect of a conflictual relationship in which unilateral Canadian actions were countered by countervailing US duties.

The sense that the United States made some concession in the matter was conveyed by Walter Gordon, the Canadian minister of finance, in a later book in which he alleged that Canadian concessions in a tax act which would have been adverse to the *Reader's Digest* and *Time* were made in part as a price of US acceptance of the automotive agreement.[1] Opposition to the Auto Pact was expressed in Congressional hearings primarily by some US auto parts manufac-

1. Walter Gordon, *A Choice for Canada*. Toronto: McClelland & Stewart, 1966.

turers and by organizations generally opposing tariff reductions. The adverse arguments included fears that US parts manufacturers would suffer, a charge that the agreement involved a "neat little cartel" among the auto manufacturers and opposition to the increased US investment in Canada that it would produce at the expense of US manufacturing.

The treaty is reproduced in full in Appendix A. It provided for complete freedom of trade of new motor vehicles and original automotive equipment parts by manufacturing firms. Tires were excluded from the pact except when mounted on new vehicles. In 1971 the pact was extended to cover snowmobiles. The provisions excluded replacement parts and trade among individuals or firms which were not manufacturers. Trade of this sort remained subject to the regular duties which, as a result of subsequent general tariff reductions, stood in 1976 at 15 percent for Canada and 3 percent for the United States.

The safeguards for Canadian manufacturing were embodied in the agreement and in letters of undertaking from the automobile companies to the Canadian government. The Chrysler letter is reproduced in Appendix B, those from the other two companies being of essentially similar character except for detailed amounts involved. The safeguards in the agreement provided in effect that: (1) each manufacturer would maintain a ratio of production of completed vehicles in Canada to vehicles sold in Canada at least as high as that achieved for the 1964 model year; (for the industry as a whole these ratios were 1.081 to 1 for cars and 1.036 to 1 for trucks) and (2) that the dollar value of Canadian value added (CVA) in Canadian-assembled vehicles would be at least as great as that of the 1964 model year. The letters provided that the companies would raise the CVA in each model year by 60 percent of the incremental growth in net sales value of cars and 50 percent of the growth of net sales of commercial vehicles sold in Canada. A minimum base for this growth was also established by the letters which committed the companies to specific increases in production in Canada totalling $260 million by the end of the 1968 model year.

The automotive pact was technically inconsistent with Article 1 of the General Agreement on Tariffs and Trade (GATT) which provided for extension of unconditional most favored nation treatment in respect to customs duties levied on products imported from GATT contracting parties. It was therefore necessary for the United States to obtain a waiver from the GATT obligations to permit it to allow duty-free entry for products from Canada and not other countries. This waiver was approved on December 20, 1965 without opposition. The GATT agreement provided for opportunities for subsequent complaints by other countries if they believed there had been a significant diversion of trade into US-Canadian relations at their expense because of the agreement. No request of this nature had occurred as of early 1976.

The US legislation for the Auto Pact provided for special adjustment assistance for firms or workers suffering dislocations because of the operation of the agreement. These provisions expired June 30, 1968. Prior to the expiration there had been no request from firms for aid. There were petitions from 21 worker groups. Certification of injury on account of the pact was issued in fourteen of these cases, and weekly payments extending as long as 52 weeks for lost employment were made to approximately 1,950 workers in a total amount of $4.1 million. Assistance to workers in relocation in new employment was provided, and for the most part new jobs were found by workers in less than the 52-week maximum period. Canada also had an assistance program under the Auto Pact. Through 1968, 8,000 workers had been declared eligible for help, 11.6 percent of the 69,000 workers in all Canadian auto plants in 1964. In addition, 70 loans totaling $52 million were authorized to help Canadian firms adjust to the impact of the pact.

EFFECTS OF THE AUTO PACT

The basic expectations from the Auto Pact were that the production in the North American area would be rationalized and the balance of payments situation between the two countries would stabilize with a balance favorable to the United States but at a tolerable level for Canada. In operation major effects were realized in these two areas and a number of other effects resulted as the managerial and economic impact of the new arrangement evolved.

Rationalization

Rationalization of manufacturing proceeded rapidly under the impetus of the pact. By 1968 all factories in Canada were specialized in the production of models or components for the full North American market. For example, in 1974 General Motors made one-third of all Vegas for the North American market in three of its Canadian plants, St. Catherines and Oshawa in Ontario and Ste. Therese in Quebec. The St. Catherines plant made 175,000 V-8 engines, many of them for use in the United States, and the Windsor plant made trim which was used in ten US factories. The rationalization was accompanied by substantial investment in Canada by the auto companies in 1965-66 followed by lesser and fluctuating amounts in later years (see Exhibit 1).

Balance of Trade

As a consequence of the rationalization, the cross flow of trade between the two countries had grown tremendously, reaching a total of over $10 billion per year (see Exhibit 2). The balance in this trade shifted at first in the favor of Canada. The deficit which had stood at $563 million in 1964 declined steadily and Canada had a surplus in automotive vehicles and parts of $197 million for 1971. At least two factors contributed importantly to this result.

First, there was the undertaking of the manufacturing firms to expand production in Canada and increase Canadian content. Apparently the firms had gone substantially beyond the specified undertakings by 1968. The ratios of

Exhibit 1. Selected Statistics on the Canadian-US Automotive Industry

| | Investments in New Plant & Equipment by Major Automobile Firms (Millions of dollars) | | Production (1000 units) | | Retail Sales . . . (1000 units) | | | | Employment (1000 workers) Annual Average | | Consumer Price Index for New Passenger Cars 1967 = 100 | |
| | | | | | U.S. | | Canada | | | | | |
	US	Canada	US	Canada	North American Type	Overseas Import Type	North American Type	Overseas Import Type	US SIC-371	Canada SIC-323-5	US	Canada
1965	$3,382	$334	9,335.2	706.8	8,763	569	634	75	842.7	81.9	100.3	100.0
1966	1,245	90	8,604.7	684.5	8,377	651	627	68	861.6	85.7	98.3	99.1
1967	1,330	81	7,412.7	708.3	7,568	769	605	74	815.8	84.1	100.0	100.0
1968	1,507	78	8,848.6	889.4	8,625	1,031	637	105	873.7	84.8	101.8	102.8
1969	1,303	122	8,224.4	1,026.0	8,464	1,118	638	123	911.4	92.1	102.4	104.4
1970	1,200	60	6,550.1	923.4	7,120	1,285	497	143	797.3	83.4	104.2	107.6
1971	1,260	59	8,583.7	1,083.2	8,681	1,570	592	188	842.6	93.4	107.9	112.0
1972	1,690	86	8,828.2	1,154.5	9,327	1,623	654	205	862.8	98.7	110.0	111.0
1973	1,949	107	9,667.6	1,227.5	9,676	1,781	783	188	944.5	110.2	110.5	111.1
1974			7,324.5	1,165.6	7,454	1,417	799	144	860.6	108.1	118.4	117.5

Exhibit 2.   United States-Canada Trade in Automotive Products (Millions of US Dollars)

	1964	1967	1968	1969	1970	1971	1972	1973	1974
US exports[1]									
Cars	34	544	748	732	631	985	1,075	1,437	1,657
Trucks	23	122	175	244	263	334	504	643	916
Parts	577	1,216	1,684	2,134	2,019	2,448	2,866	3,484	3,980
Sub-total	634	1,882	2,607	3,110	2,913	3,767	4,445	5,564	6,553
Tires and tubes	6	7	27	34	23	36	51	92	na
Total exports	640	1,889	2,634	3,144	2,936	3,803	4,496	5,656	
US imports									
Cars	18	692	1,114	1,537	1,474	1,924	2,065	2,272	2,595
Trucks	4	228	369	560	564	587	713	789	887
Parts	49	474	783	959	1,080	1,481	1,795	2,172	1,997
Sub-total	71	1,394	2,266	3,056	3,118	3,992	4,573	5,233	5,479
Tires and tubes	5	12	8	5	14	8	22	68	na
Total imports	76	1,406	2,274	3,061	3,132	4,000	4,595	5,301	
Net balance	+563	+483	+360	+83	-196	-197	-99	+355	
Snowmobiles included									
in truck exports above	—	—	—	6	12	22	33	30	33
in truck imports above	—	36	61	111	141	124	104	66	35

1. Canadian import data. Parts exports (Canadian imports) adjusted to exclude tooling charges in millions of US dollars as follows: 1966-$29; 1967-$44; 1968-$47; 1969-$75; 1970-$98; 1971-$68; 1972-$84.9; 1973-$56.

Note: Data exclude US-Canadian trade in materials for use in the manufacture of automotive parts. Data are adjusted to reflect transaction values for vehicles.

$1.00 Canadian = $0.925 US, 1964-69; $0.958 US, 1970; $0.990 US, 1971; $1.009 US, 1972; $0.9997 US, 1973.

Source: U.S. Department of Commerce.

production to sales in dollars (the basis specified in the agreement) were not publicly known because dollar figures were not released. However, unit figures for production and new registrations indicated substantial increases in the production to sales ratios for all firms from 1964 to 1968, the firms having evidently expanded assembly operations in Canada proportionately relative to the United States (see Exhibit 1). The increase in CVA was also not precisely determinable from public data. However, estimates by Carl Beigie indicated that the companies had overfulfilled their undertakings by about $396 million.[2]

Several factors were believed to have contributed to the excess in the companies' performances: (1) there were aspects of the statistical reporting system relating to transfer prices which might have inflated the results. Beigie estimated that $175 million of the excess might be due to this cause; (2) the manufacturers probably provided a safety factor in their planning in light of the severe penalty of having to pay full tariff if they fell short of their undertakings; (3) the "lumpiness" of investment based on optimal size for cost economies might be a factor leading to some units being built in Canada that were larger than strictly necessary to meet the commitments; (4) Beigie concluded that Canada's initial cost disadvantage had largely disappeared as a result of the working of the agreement so that investment in new plants in Canada was economically attractive compared to US facilities.

Second, the improvement of Canada's balance of trade received a further boost from the evolution of the automobile market. The models assigned to Canadian factories were generally smaller cars and, with the rise in popularity of them, the output in Canada tended to expand more rapidly than that of the United States.

Despite the overall satisfactory shift of production to Canada, there were many complications for the companies. One of these caused very adverse publicity when the Auditors General's report of 1967-8 included the statement that a company had failed to meet the safeguard obligations of the pact. Minister of Industry, Jean Luc Pepin, explained the situation thoroughly to the House of Commons. "It was recognized and understood at the outset that in several cases the companies could not achieve this overall obligation placed upon them without encountering some difficulties in respect to some of the specific conditions . . . I have only praise for the Ford Motor Company which has been identified and singled out for attention in the public accounts committee . . . Being on the verge of modifying its engine factory in Windsor, it was faced with the necessity of substantially changing its plans on an impractical basis and at great cost to meet the new conditions which had suddenly been established by the agreement or alternatively to seek a modification of the new conditions on a short-term basis. The Ford Motor Company has acted openly, honestly and quite sincerely through Mr. Scott and his executives, in all its dealing with the

2. Carl E. Beigie, *The Canadian-U.S. Automotive Agreement: An Evaluation.* Washington: National Planning Association, 1970, p. 93.

government on this matter. The company did indeed offset its shortfall of 'in vehicle content' and also generated an additional $200 million Canadian content." Mr. Pepin's remarks made it clear that the government and companies had been working very closely and openly to implement the difficult aspects of the agreement to mutual satisfaction.

Subsequent to 1971 the trade relations shifted in the other direction and for 1975 Canada had a deficit of $1.9 billion in the automotive account. Differences in conditions in the two countries in 1973-74 accounted for the major portion of this change. After registering record sales in 1972, the US automotive market entered a cyclical decline reinforced by the energy crisis. In Canada, on the other hand, with ample oil supplies, the energy crisis had little impact on demand for automobiles and the general economy was stronger. The net effect of these conditions was a 1.5 percent increase of Canadian car sales in 1974 over 1973 while US sales fell 30 percent. Thus the Canadian share of the continental sales total increased and with production rationalized, the balance of trade shifted substantially in favor of the United States.

In the background of the changes caused by the Auto Pact was the trend of Canadian car imports from other countries. They rose from 75,000 units in 1965 to 187,000 in 1971, the latter composing 26 percent of total Canadian sales. Thereafter the trend reversed, imports falling, especially after the currency revaluations in 1973. In 1973, they accounted for 21 percent of sales, and in 1974, 16 percent. In early 1975 the auto importers' association launched a drive to get the import duty reduced from 15 percent to 3 percent (equal to the US rate) to bolster their sales.

While the initial direct effect of the Auto Pact on Canada's balance of payments was favorable, some economists observed that it had indirect effects which reduced its benefits. The net change of trade balance of $760 million from 1965 to 1971 was a major factor in strengthening the Canadian dollar which rose about 8 percent relative to the US dollar after the exchange rate was allowed to float in 1970. This change reduced the international competitiveness of other Canadian industries and thus presumably lowered their exports. The rise of auto worker wages noted below also contributed in this direction by adding to pressures for wage increases in other industries.

A longer-term indirect effect lay in the complications to other trade negotiations created by the Auto Pact. The pact was viewed adversely by many people in the United States and other countries. For example, Senator Albert Gore was quoted as saying that the pact was "probably the most disastrous bilateral agreement in US history." Such views were adverse to the prospect of continental free trade agreements for other industries and were perceived by some as a drag on the general progress of trade negotiations. On the other hand, there were those who, believing strongly in broad, multi-industry, multinational approaches to trade negotiations rather than sectoral deals, found in the shortcomings of the Auto Pact an illustration to support their case.

Employment

Although there was an overall trend of increased production subsequent to the start of the Auto Pact, employment in the industry did not increase proportionately during the early years, particularly in Canada (see Exhibit 1). The basic factor at work in this respect was the notable increase in efficiency of production in the Canadian plants as they shifted from assembly of varied models to specialization in a single model. It was therefore possible to accomplish the increase in production without a proportionate increase in employment.

Wages

In 1965, wages in the Canadian automobile factories were roughly 30 percent lower than those of comparable jobs in the United States. A primary goal of the United Automobile Workers, which represented labor in both countries, was the achievement of wage parity. This objective assumed greater importance in the minds of workers in both countries with the establishment of the automotive agreement. Those in the United States feared that with an open market and lower wages in Canada, the companies would shift production into Canadian factories. The Canadian workers wished to raise their standard of living and felt that equity called for equal wages in an integrated continental industry. As a consequence of this pressure the differential steadily narrowed and the agreements signed by the UAW with the companies in 1973 established full nominal parity in wages for the two countries.

In 1975, the Canadian government established an anti-inflation program including guidelines restricting pay increases to 12 percent. UAW leaders in both Canada and the United States made strong statements warning the government that they would not be restricted by the limits nor would they allow them to break the wage parity system. They anticipated that the agreements to be negotiated with the auto companies in mid-1976 would result in increases greater than the guidelines permitted and they would expect the settlements to be implemented regardless of the wage restraint program.

Labor Costs and Quality

While no concrete data were available to determine the exact difference in labor costs and quality between factories in Canada and the United States, there were indications that a difference favorable to Canada continued even after wage parity was established. Because the overall Canadian wage scale was lower than that of the United States, Canadian auto workers had a relatively higher status in the total national scheme than that of their US counterparts. That is, a job in an automobile plant in Canada was a higher paid position in relation to available alternative jobs as compared to the relationship in the United States. Thus the auto companies in Canada tended to attract a somewhat higher quality of worker than those in the United States. These people appeared to be more productive and to produce with higher quality standards. Substantive support for this general supposition was found in the companies' experience that cars produced in the Canadian factories were of higher quality. Distributors in the United States receiving models from both Canadian and US sources reported consistently that the former had fewer defects and were less troublesome. According to a report in a Detroit paper, "Even employees of the auto companies try to buy cars made in Canadian plants because the workmanship is far superior in those 'foreign models' than in home-made models." The differences in labor performance were, however, discounted, at least in part, by some people who attributed the superior quality to newer plants.

On the other hand, data in the 1976 International Trade Commission report (see below) in Canada indicated that the same models required from 1 to 6 percent more man-hours when assembled in Canada compared to the United States.

Prices

The higher costs of production in the diversified assembly plants in Canada prior to the Auto Pact had resulted in substantially higher prices to the Canadian consumer protected behind the tariff wall (see Exhibit 3). Price differentials varied according to models with the weighted average in 1965 about 8 percent. Rationalization resulted in a steady decrease in Canadian costs and prices relative to US trends. By 1970 the differential was down to an average of about 3.5 percent. The subsequent changes in the US-Canadian exchange rate adversely affected comparisons so that by 1973 the differential was back again in the 9 to 15 percent range. The price to the consumer was further adversely affected by the 12 percent excise tax in Canada in contrast to the excise tax in the United States which had been eliminated by that time.

The manufacturing companies stated that full price equality was not practical because of differences between conditions in the two countries. The lower population density in Canada resulted in higher distribution costs. The colder climate increased production costs slightly, and it also worked adversely to the companies' total cost-profit situation by reducing the sale of air conditioners which were profitable extras. In general the Canadians were inclined to buy fewer of the high margin extras on cars, which had a further adverse effect. The cost of parts was in some instances higher because of higher manufacturing costs of Canadian producers or the transportation costs for imports from the United States. GM's Canadian president also observed that despite rationalization and substantial investment, the productivity in Canadian factories still lagged, that the capital investment per man was sufficiently below that in the United States, so that with equal wages, total costs were somewhat higher.[3] The president of Ford of Canada predicted a long run price gap of 3 to 4 percent and observed

---

3. "G.M.'s New Man up North," *Dun's*, July 1974, p. 61.

that complete free trade would work a hardship on dealers and possibly tip the balance toward more production in US plants.[4]

Allegations appeared regularly in the Canadian press charging that the higher Canadian prices were due to higher profits protected by the provisions of the Auto Pact excluding individual imports. Publicly available information on this count was conflicting. For example, the annual reports of General Motors showed a profit margin of 3.7 percent on sales of $3.1 billion of goods for 1973 in Canada compared to a margin of 6.7 percent on sales in the United States of $35.8 billion. On the other hand, Stephen Lewis, leader of the New Democratic Party in Ontario, claimed Ford made 26.5 percent on investment in Canada compared to 14.6 percent in the United States.[5] The 1976 ITC report indicated that the big three auto companies all had a higher return on equity for 1970-74 in Canada than in the US though Ford and GM had a lower profit as a percent of sales.

Control

Rationalization of production resulted in a substantial shift of management control functions to Detroit. Basic production allocation and planning was necessarily centralized there to coordinate plants for the continental industry. Research and development functions also shifted in that direction. Ford and Chrysler moved all parts procurement from Canada to Detroit while General Motors kept a substantial portion of procurement in the Canadian offices.

The control effects were a source of general adverse reactions among Canadian nationalists as a prime example of the power of US firms to direct Canadian industry. The only major auto company with any local ownership was Ford of Canada, 12.2 percent of whose stock was in Canadian hands, and even it had been buying up portions of local equity in recent years, raising its control from 80 percent in 1967. Ford had four outside Canadian directors and the company said that any decisions involving conflict of interest between Canadian and US operations were left to their decisions. The shift of management decision making was seen as a further significant loss to Canadian economic sovereignty. Other Canadians, however, felt that as long as the industry was foreign owned, the effect of the shift to Detroit had only minor real effect on the outcome of industrial decisions.

ENVIRONMENTAL CONDITIONS

Discussions of the Auto Pact between Canada and the United States were substantially influenced by conditions in the two countries and relations between them.

---

4. Toronto *Star*, April 13, 1972.

5. Toronto *Globe & Mail*, June 4, 1974.

Exhibit 3.   Prices of Typical Popular Model, 4-Door Sedans, 8 Cylinder with Comparable Standard Equipment in the United States and Canada, Model Years 1965 and 1975

Item	Price in United States (US dollars)	Price in Canada		Canadian Price Differential Over (under) US Price	
		Canadian dollars	United States dollars[3]	Amount US dollars[3]	Percent[3]
1965 Model Introduction					
Factory List Price[1]	4,103	5,815	5,946	1,843	44.9
Sales/Excise Tax[1]	333	442	452	119	—
Dealers Delivery & Handling	50	40	41	(9)	—
Manufacturer's suggested retail price[2]	4,486	6,297	6,438	1,952	43.5
1975 Model Introduction					
Factory List Price[1]	7,633	8,355	8,543	910	11.9
Sales/Excise Tax[1]	18[4]	713	729	711	—
Dealers Delivery & Handling	50	40	41	(9)	—
Manufacturer's suggested retail price[2]	7,701	9,108	9,313	1,612	20.9
1965 Model Introduction					
Factory List Price[1]	2,565	3,040	3,108	543	21.2
Sales/Excise Tax[1]	149	256	262	113	—
Dealers Delivery & Handling	40	40	41	—	—
Manufacturer's suggested retail price[2]	2,754	3,336	3,411	657	23.9

1975 Model Introduction

Factory List Price	4,702	5,005	5,117	415	8.8
Sales/Excise Tax[1]	19	429	439	420	—
Dealers Delivery & Handling	40	0	—	(40)	—
Manufacturer's suggested retail price[2]	4,761	5,434	5,556	795	16.7

1. Canadian sales tax 11 percent 1964-67, 12 percent 1968; US excise tax 10 percent 1964-65, 7 percent 1966-Aug. 1971. US excise tax on passenger cars and light trucks repealed as of Aug. 15, 1971.

2. Manufacturer's suggested retail price includes factory list price, sales tax or excise tax and dealer delivery and handling, but excludes destination charges, state and local taxes, license and title fees.

3. Based on the conversion rate of 1.02246 = $C1.00 the exchange rate in Dec. 1974.

4. Excise tax on tires and tubes.

Canadian Conditions

Most prominent from the Canadian point of view were the influences of labor conditions, political affairs and nationalism.

In the early 1970s Canada had the largest rate of increase of labor force in the world as a result of a unique combination of the postwar baby boom and immigration. The labor force was increasing at a rate of as much as 3 percent a year, creating great pressure for the generation of new jobs. Industrial expansion and employment growth had lagged during the 60s behind the rate of labor force growth. As a consequence unemployment grew and was relatively high in the early 1970s (in the 6 to 7 percent range). Canadians were sensitive to the employment effects of the automotive agreement as the big companies and parts suppliers were the largest employer group in Canadian manufacturing.

The political situation in Canada changed considerably during the first ten years of the auto agreement. Throughout the period the Liberal party was the leading factor in the country. However, from the outset of the agreement until 1968 and again from July 1973 to July 1974 the Liberals did not have a clear majority in the House of Commons and maintained control only through the support of the New Democratic Party (NDP). The NDP was quite socialist and nationalist in its outlook and closely allied to labor groups. While it held the balance of power, it exerted a strong pressure for its viewpoint on the Liberal government. Having achieved a clear majority in 1974, the Trudeau government was more independent of the NDP pressure.

Throughout the 1960s and early 1970s nationalism was growing in Canada, particularly as manifest in feelings that the role and influence of foreign firms should be restricted. As compared to other parts of the world, specific nationalist actions had been relatively mild. The strongest ones were directed at key sectors of the economy such as banking, publications and the like in which measures had been enacted to achieve Canadian majority ownership of companies. After much discussion the government had enacted in 1973 a Foreign Investment Review Act which provided at the outset for screening takeovers of Canadian companies by foreign firms to assure that the results were beneficial for Canada by various stated criteria. In 1975 screening was extended to new firms entering Canada or established firms entering new fields. No restraints had as yet been placed on the large body of existing investment or expansion by it in its established fields of operation.

These and other factors resulted in mixed feelings in Canada about the Auto Pact. In the period when the balance of payments was moving in Canada's favor, the general consensus was supportive of the pact despite nationalist misgivings on the shift of control to the United States and worries lest the control combined with the rationalized structure result in long run evolution to the disadvantage of Canada. When the trade balance shifted, however, public opinion became quite adverse to the pact. In early 1976 with the deficit close to $2 million and strong adverse public views, Finance Minister Donald Macdonald reported to Commons that the government was seriously considering the question of revision of the pact.

United States Conditions

The primary influences from the United States point of view were the balance of payments situation and labor pressure. Governmental thinking throughout the period of operation of the pact was heavily preoccupied with the adverse balance of payments. The Canadian auto trade was a big enough factor to be quite significant in this picture. As the auto trade shifted to the favor of Canada, therefore, the US government was increasingly dissatisfied with its operation.

At the same time labor in the United States was becoming increasingly protectionist as it suffered the adverse consequences of growing imports of manufactured goods. While the main thrust of this resistance was directed at imports from low wage areas, notably Asian and to a lesser degree European products, the Canadian situation fitted into the mood of the times with the desire of US auto workers to limit the expansion of manufacturing in Canada to keep in the United States a larger portion of automotive jobs.

Increasing US labor pressure during 1975 resulted in action by three government bodies. The Senate Finance Committee instructed the US International Trade Commission to make a full study of the effects of the Auto Pact, preparatory to considering action on its part. The ITC report was published in early 1976, containing extensive factual data and proposals made to it during hearings. It did not make any recommendations but expressed the views that Canada had "not fully complied with the agreement" in failing to phase out the provisions viewed as transitional by the US government that the only true concessions made under the agreement were by the US since Canada had already prior to it allowed US autos duty free entry, and that the agreement had "primarily benefited the Canadian economy." Among the proposals reported was one by the UAW that the North American content requirement for autos be raised from 50 percent to 75 percent. This proposal arose from the fact that Canada allowed duty free import of parts from many countries. Such imports could then be used in assembly of cars and shipped to the United States whose tariffs would not allow direct import duty-free from the source countries. The UAW was concerned at the possibility of large scale imports from LDCs undercutting US production.

In July 1975 the United Auto Workers initiated complaints to two departments. It filed a claim for aid under the Foreign Trade Act of 1974 to the Labor Department on behalf of 39,000 Chrysler workers whose jobs it claimed were cut off because of Canadian plants. The Labor Department ruled in favor of the union claim in this case, saying "for the products there were no significant losses to domestic competition and Canadian imports increased substantially." At about the same time the UAW filed a general complaint with the Treasury Department claiming that foreign cars were being dumped in the US and should be subject to extra duties to protect the US industry and jobs. The UAW cited cases in which European, Canadian and Japanese cars were sold in the United States at prices lower than retail prices in their home markets. As the first stage in the investigative process the International Trade Commission studied the situation and determined that it could not rule out conclusively that imports were a factor in the depressed state of the domestic industry in September. The Treasury Department then continued the study to determine whether the charges of dumping were valid.

In the totality of US international relations, the Auto Pact was a very small piece. Thus it received only minor attention. There were occasional articles in the press, and once a year or so politicians with a particular interest in the subject would make statements about the matter, notably Senator Long, chairman of the finance committee which was responsible for the subject and Senator Griffin of Michigan whose constituency was notably affected by it. Their comments were often strong, threatening, for example, that Congress would abrogate the agreement unless the administration succeeded in negotiating a favorable revision.

Canada-US Relations

In the background of the Auto Pact negotiations were important elements in the overall relationship between the two countries. Two aspects of the relationship were particularly significant: the basic attitude of the United States toward Canada and the key areas of conflict between them.

For many years Canada-US relations were based on the fundamental concept of the "special relationship." The concept meant in effect that the United States looked upon Canada as a distinctly different country from other nations because of its geographic, economic and cultural closeness. Thus it was the normal expectation that, when general international actions were taken, special consideration would be given to the Canadian situation. Throughout the 1960s there was some evidence of movement away from the special relationship concept, but by and large it continued. On August 15, 1971, however, it came to an abrupt end when the emergency balance of payments actions taken by President Nixon, including the 10 percent import surtax, were universally applied with no exception provided for Canada. Subsequently US officials confirmed in many ways their view that henceforth Canada should be treated like all other nations with no special considerations given to it. While this situation was painful in some ways to the Canadians, it also to some degree fitted their own objectives. The Canadian government had frequently stated as a matter of basic policy that it wished to move away from its strong bilateral dependence on economic relations with the United States and to seek greater economic ties with other countries and to achieve policy goals through multinational negotiations rather than bilateral deals.

While the Auto Pact was a discrete agreement which in principle could be negotiated on its own merits, in fact the priorities given to it and its outcome were influenced to some degree by other issues in relations between the countries. The importance and character of other issues varied over the course of time. In the late 1960s and early 1970s a substantial issue subject to regular debate was the division of expenditures on defense between the two countries. A mutual defense procurement agreement had been worked out between them (based on somewhat the same philosophy as the auto agreement) to develop a rationalized continental industry and to assure that each country had a fair share of the economic benefits of that industry in employment and balance of payments. In operation, however, the United States had consistently purchased somewhat more in Canada than the Canadians procured in the United States, and a cumulative deficit to Canada's advantage of some $500 million had been built up by 1975 which was the subject of substantial dissatisfaction on the part of the US government.

In the meantime issues in the energy area, notably petroleum and natural gas, had been growing during the period and became a dominant element in the energy crisis. The United States had obtained about 5 percent of its oil requirements from Canada in 1970. Expert estimates, based on the maturity of the US industry and promising prospects in Canada, had projected an increase of imports during the 1970s to provide about 10 percent of US requirements by 1980. The Canadians, on the other hand, were reluctant to deplete their reserves to serve the United States and sought rather to build a strong petrochemical industry and to use the energy from their resources to expand their own manufacturing capability.

These issues of the allocation of Canadian energy supplies were aggravated in the energy crisis by the increases in prices charged by Canadian sources to the United States. Canada in this instance generally followed the pattern set by the other oil-producing countries rather than taking the initiative. Nonetheless the US suffered in its balance of payments on account of the Canadian actions, so it added to the aggravation of the situation. The US deficit in trade in energy products between the two nations for 1974 was $3 million greater than in 1972. A further major development was the announcement by the Canadian government in 1975 that all exports of natural gas would end by 1980.

Along with these major issues there were a number of questions of varying prominence during the period. For example, in 1972-73 there was much debate about the allocation of air routes between Canada and the United States and the use of advance customs clearance which placed US customs officials in Canadian airports. These issues were resolved by an agreement in late 1973 to the apparent satisfaction of all concerned, though while they were being debated there was considerable tension. Likewise during 1973-1975 a complex set of issues arose over beef trade between the two countries.

NEGOTIATION ISSUES

A clause in the Auto Pact called for review of its terms in 1968. From that year on negotiations between Canada and the United States took place from time to time.

In the early stages of negotiations the US government assumed a quite critical position reinforced first by a resolution by the Senate Finance Committee recommending that the agreement be terminated and then by a letter from the Committee to the President in 1970 directing him to "take whatever action was necessary to assure that complete freedom in trade in automobiles between the US and Canada is achieved by January 1, 1973." Bargaining was not pursued strongly at first. In 1971, however, under Secretary of Treasury John Connally, the US position became quite tough. Connally became a personal symbol of this US stance in Canada evoking considerable nationalistic reaction and affecting thereby the approach of the Canadian negotiators. When George Schultz took over Connally's position, the negotiations assumed a more moderate tenor. However, little real progress was made. During 1974 attention was distracted by the US presidential situation and Canada's general election. Subsequently the severe recession in the auto industry discouraged the governments from considering what might be disruptive changes.

In the negotiations several interrelated issues were at work, revolving essentially around the allocation of production, balance of payments effects and the price differences between the two countries. Attention tended to be focused on the safeguard provisions affecting the allocation of production, the exclusion from tariff exemptions of individual sales, used cars and replacement parts and certain actions outside the terms of the agreement itself.

It was the official US position that the safeguard provisions were transitional measures which were intended to run only to 1968. The Canadians did not accept this position, viewing all of the provisions as of permanent force until revised. On both sides by 1976 there was a sense that the safeguards were no longer effective in light of the wide balance of trade swings which had been experienced.

The basic US government stance was to seek a fully open market system with the elimination of the exclusion of individual, used car and replacement part sales and reliance on free market forces to develop the structure of the industry. For their part Canadians were concerned particularly lest the long-run evolution be in the direction of a greater portion of manufacturing taking place in the United States. This had been the experience in a free market structuring of agricultural equipment trade established after World War II. Under it there had been a steady shift toward a greater proportion of manufacture in the United States. Given the pressures existing in the United States, the Canadians were apprehensive that the next round of investment in new plant for the industry as a whole would favor the United States. At an early stage in the negotiations

Minister of Industry Pepin had met with the automobile companies in order to seek long-range forecasts assuring more Canadian production. He was disappointed to find that the companies could not give him such predictions.

The safeguard provisions had acquired considerable political aura in Canada which substantially deterred any government action to drop them. For example, the UAW and the NDP had organized massive letter campaigns to support their continuance. Likewise provincial and municipal politicians had made frequent strong public statements counseling against abandonment of them. Thus any public reversal of policy on this count was politically difficult.

Some alternatives had, however, been put forward. During negotiations in 1972 it was reported that Canada offered to (1) suspend or ignore the ratio and CVA provisions and (2) refer to a joint committee questions of duty-free imports of cars and trucks into Canada from the US by individuals. Carl Beigie had proposed maximum as well as minimum limits on Canada's share of North American automotive production. The *Financial Post* suggested a minimum of 80 percent would be a reasonable guarantee.

A possible further deterrent to eliminating tariffs on individual sales lay in the necessity to obtain GATT approval and the prospect that foreign auto makers might object. Whereas the free trade for manufacturers could be justified as a production rationalization scheme comparable to rationales of other regional economic blocs, a bilateral individual free trade provision would be more questionable. It was quite possible that it would have to be extended to all countries, thus aiding imports from Europe and Japan.

A major component of this picture was the outlook for parts production. A large portion of the parts were made by independent firms, and about 80 percent of the production of parts in Canada was by foreign-owned firms. The Canadians believed there was already substantial evidence of a trend toward a greater portion of parts production taking place in the United States. In part this was structurally induced due to the shift of research and development and procurement to the Detroit headquarters of the auto firms. The Canadians felt that purchasing officials, for reasons of convenience and economics, perhaps supported by cultural and national affinity, had a tendency to favor US firms. Some Canadian firms had noted that they had shifted the general orientation of their operations toward the United States so as to be close to the Detroit organizations.

Canadian parts manufacturers suffered also from a competitive disadvantage with US firms because of the requirement in the auto pact that they use 50 percent Canadian or US content in all automotive parts shipped to the United States. A company whose production consisted for example very substantially of simple processing of steel products, was forced to use largely North American steel, whereas US stamping plants, not subject to this restriction, could use cheaper Japanese steel and underprice the Canadian firms. Other influences included the US job development tax credit and DISC described below. It was noted that investment in the Canadian parts industry had dropped by 50 percent from 1973 to 1975, while the trade deficit in parts had reached $2.6 billion in 1975.

Thus the possibility of freeing replacement parts from duty was particularly significant to the Canadians who saw in this a change in the structure which might well push a larger portion of parts production into the United States. Since in the total trade picture the balance of parts flow was already very favorable to the United States, the prospect of further change in this direction was quite disturbing. The Canadian Automotive Parts Manufacturers Association in 1975 and again in 1976 had formally petitioned the government to renegotiate the terms of the pact to help the industry. The association proposed that a joint Canadian-US commission be established to supervise trade under the Auto Pact. Specifically, it was proposed that the deficit in trade between the countries be controlled by agreement with the commission empowered to take measures to achieve a balance in trade averaged over a number of years. A regularly functioning agency was seen as preferable to dealing with questions under the pact by irregular government negotiations. It was also proposed that protection be based on employment, investment, and research and development rather than exclusively on the basis of trade balance.

The parts situation had been further complicated in early 1972 by reports that US and Canadian customs officials were imposing extra delays and red tape on parts shipments into their respective countries. Canadian newspapers suggested that the US officials were engaging in deliberate harassment. As their operations fell under the Treasury Department, this practice was readily related to Secretary Connally who had acquired an image of toughness in the Auto Pact negotiations.

Notably affecting this aspect of the situation, but outside the trade agreement, were the tax moves of the two governments. The first major move was the establishment of the Domestic International Sales Corporation (DISC) by the US government in 1971. The DISC was designed as a device to foster US exports to help the balance of payments situation. Income taxes on 50 percent of the profits earned by a DISC could be deferred until the profits were paid to the parent corporation. Thus by channeling exports through a DISC a firm could achieve substantial economic benefit. The DISC system came under immediate attack in Canada as it was perceived to be a thinly veiled subsidy of exports. The government made a formal protest to this effect during GATT discussions and strong criticism, especially related to the auto companies, was expressed in House of Commons debates.[6] There was no way for the Canadians to directly counteract the effect of DISC, but some general offsetting effect was achieved by the reduction of the corporate income tax to 46 percent in 1973. By this means US firms were given an incentive to expand Canadian output rather than increase imports from the United States to take advantage of DISC tax privileges.

6. *Debates*, House of Commons, April 22 and May 11, 1975.

Sensitive to the adverse Canadian views toward DISC, the US auto companies initially were reluctant to use DISCs and played them down in public statements. In due course, however, they started to employ them as the large volume of exports of automobiles provided too great a financial benefit to avoid. Also sensitive to this Canadian concern, the US government offered the Canadians a special agreement which would have closed off the DISC option to companies functioning under the auto agreement. The Canadians declined this offer. However, as a direct counter-measure, the Canadians did impose, in 1974, a special excise tax of $20 per 100 pounds of weight in excess of 4,000 pounds. Since the auto companies specialized their Canadian plants in small cars and therefore imported virtually all large cars, this resulted in a special tax applicable mainly to imports.

Much discussion about the auto agreement focuses on the remaining price gap between Canadian and US cars. It was a source of continuing annoyance to Canadian consumers, expressed frequently in the press, that people in Buffalo could buy a Vega made in an Ontario factory for less than a car made in the same factory when sold in Toronto. The apparently easy solution to this problem was the elimination of the exclusion of individual sales from the Auto Pact. Presumably if an individual could go to Buffalo and buy the car there without paying the 15 percent duty this would force prices down in Toronto substantially, though presumably not quite as far as the Buffalo price because of the added cost and inconvenience of going to Buffalo.

Nonetheless, the Canadian government consistently held to continuance of the exclusion of individual sales from the pact. It was supported in this position by the auto dealers of Canada who feared that the companies would not lower the prices to them sufficiently to match the price pressure placed upon them by open competition with US dealers. They were also worried over the capital loss they would face on their inventory of cars if prices were reduced. The government and the dealers were both in effect concurring in the position of the companies that Canadian costs could not be brought down to an equal level with those in the United States. Canadian consumer groups on the other hand advocated free trade as a means to force prices down. The US government for its part consistently worked for the elimination of the exclusions, presumably believing that it would increase exports because US sources of production would be at a relative advantage in a completely free market structure. The force of US opinion on this point was not clear, though it was reported in 1972 that Treasury Secretary Connally was threatening to reimpose the 7 percent excise tax on Canadian-made autos. The tax had been eliminated previously for the industry as a whole. UAW leaders in both Canada and the United States expressed displeasure at the higher Canadian prices. They were in agreement, however, on maintenance of the exclusion of private car sales from terms of the agreement, calling for direct government pressure on the companies in Canada to reduce their prices.

The Canadian government was not insensitive to the price differential problem as it affected consumers. Therefore it attempted, by direct pressure on the companies, to exhort them to lower prices. In 1973 Minister of Industry, Trade and Commerce, Alistair Gillespie, went through a strong round of negotiations with the companies with this objective. Mr. Gillespie was reported to have threatened to remove the tariff on imports of cars by individuals if the price gap was not narrowed. While the discussions in part were secret, substantial publicity was given to them as the leverage of the government in this case was dependent to a considerable degree on public support. Mr. Gillespie made claims at one stage that the companies had agreed to certain reductions in prices. The companies indicated that the statements were inaccurate. Mr. Gillespie claimed they had reneged on agreements. This interplay between the government and the companies did not, however, apparently result in significant change in the price relationships. A new round of pressures on the companies appeared to be in the offing as Mr. Gillespie's successor, Don Jamieson expressed concern publicly about the price differentials in January 1976 and indicated that he was going to make inquiries with the companies about the matter.

GENERAL REFERENCES

Carl E. Beigie, *The Canadian-U.S. Automotive Agreement: An Evaluation.* Washington: National Planning Association, 1970.

Carl E. Beigie and Moyra Sinclair, "The Canadian-U.S. Auto Pact," *Journal of Contemporary Business,* Autumn 1972, pp. 67-69.

John Fayerweather, *Foreign Investment in Canada.* White Plains, N.Y.: International Arts and Sciences Press and Toronto: Oxford University Press, 1973.

Canadian Automobile Agreement, Annual Reports of the President to the Congress, 1967 and subsequent years. Washington: Government Printing Office.

Background on the Canada-U.S. Automotive Products Trade Agreement. Toronto: Motor Vehicle Manufacturers' Association, 1973.

U.S. International Trade Commission, *Report on the United States-Canadian Automobile Agreement for the Committee on Finance, U.S. Senate.* Washington: Government Printing Office, 1976.

※ *Appendix A*

**Agreement Concerning Automotive Products
between the Government of the United States of America
and the Government of Canada**

The Government of the United States of America and the Government of Canada,

Determined to strengthen the economic relations between their two countries;

Recognizing that this can best be achieved through the stimulation of economic growth and through the expansion of markets available to producers in both countries within the framework of the established policy of both countries of promoting multilateral trade;

Recognizing that an expansion of trade can best be achieved through the reduction or elimination of tariff and all other barriers to trade operating to impede or distort the full and efficient development of each country's trade and industrial potential;

Recognizing the important place that the automotive industry occupies in the industrial economy of the two countries and the interests of industry, labor and consumers in sustaining high levels of efficient production and continued growth in the automotive industry;

Agree as follows:

Article I

The Governments of the United States and Canada, pursuant to the above principles, shall seek the early achievement of the following objectives:

a) The creation of a broader market for automotive products within which the full benefits of specialization and large-scale production can be achieved;

b) The liberalization of United States and Canadian automotive trade in respect of tariff barriers and other factors tending to impede it, with a view to enabling the industries of both countries to participate on a fair and equitable basis in the expanding total market of the two countries;

c) The development of conditions in which market forces may operate effectively to attain the most economic pattern of investment, production and trade.

It shall be the policy of each Government to avoid actions which would frustrate the achievement of these objectives.

Article II

a) The Government of Canada, not later than the entry into force of the legislation contemplated in paragraph (b) of this Article, shall accord duty-free treatment to imports of the products of the United States described in Annex A.

b) The Government of the United States, during the session of the United States Congress commencing on January 4, 1965, shall seek enactment of legislation authorizing duty-free treatment of imports of the products of Canada described in Annex B. In seeking such legislation, the Government of the United States shall also seek authority permitting the implementation of such duty-free treatment retroactively to the earliest date administratively possible following the date upon which the Government of Canada has accorded duty-free treatment. Promptly after the entry into force of such legislation, the Government of the United States shall accord duty-free treatment to the products of Canada described in Annex B.

Article III

The commitments made by the two Governments in this Agreement shall not preclude action by either Government consistent with its obligations under Part II of the General Agreement on Tariffs and Trade.

Article IV

a) At any time, at the request of either Government, the two Governments shall consult with respect to any matter relating to this Agreement.

b) Without limiting the foregoing, the two Governments shall, at the request of either Government, consult with respect to any problems which may arise concerning automotive producers in the United States which do not at present have facilities in Canada for the manufacture of motor vehicles, and with respect to the implications for the operation of this Agreement of new automotive porducers becoming established in Canada.

c) No later than January 1, 1968, the two Governments shall jointly undertake a comprehensive review of the progress made towards achieving the objectives set forth in Article I. During this review the Governments shall consider such further steps as may be necessary or desirable for the full achievement of these objectives.

Article V

Access to the United States and Canadian markets provided for under this Agreement may by agreement be accorded on similar terms to other countries.

Article VI

This Agreement shall enter into force provisionally on the date of signature and definitively on the date upon which notes are exchanged between the two Governments giving notice that appropriate action in their respective legislatures has been completed.

Article VII

This Agreement shall be of unlimited duration. Each Government shall however have the right to terminate this Agreement twelve months from the date on which that Government gives written notice to the other Government of its intention to terminate the Agreement.

Annex A

1. 1) Automobiles; when imported by a manufacturer of automobiles.
   2) All parts, and accessories and parts thereof, except tires and tubes, when imported for use as original equipment in automobiles to be produced in Canada by a manufacturer of automobiles.
   3) Buses, when imported by a manufacturer of buses.
   4) All parts, and accessories and parts thereof, except tires and tubes, when imported for use as original equipment in buses to be produced in Canada by a manufacturer of buses.
   5) Specified commercial vehicles, when imported by a manufacturer of specified commercial vehicles.
   6) All parts and accessories and parts thereof, except tires, tubes and any machines or other articles required under Canadian tariff item 438a to be valued separately under the tariff items regularly applicable thereto, when imported for use as original equipment in specified commercial vehicles to

be produced in Canada by a manufacturer of specified commercial vehicles.

2. 1) "Automobile" means a four-wheeled passenger automobile having a seating capacity for not more than ten persons;

2) "Base year" means the period of twelve months commencing on the 1st day of August, 1963 and ending on the 31st day of July, 1964;

3) "Bus" means a passenger motor vehicle having a seating capacity for more than 10 persons, or a chassis therefor, namely an electric trackless trolley bus, amphibious vehicle, tracked or half-tracked vehicle or motor vehicle designed primarily for off-highway use;

4) "Canadian value added" has the meaning assigned by regulations, made under section 273 of the Canadian Customs Act;

5) "Manufacturer" of vehicles of any following class, namely automobiles, buses or specified commercial vehicles, means, in relation to any importation of goods in respect of which the description is relevant, a manufacturer that

   i) produced vehicles of that class in Canada in each of the four consecutive three months' periods in the base year, and

   ii) produced vehicles of that class in Canada in the period of twelve months ending on the 31st day of July in which the importation is made,

   (A) the ratio of the net sales value of which to the net sales value of all vehicles of that class sold for consumption in Canada by the manufacturer in that period is equal to or higher than the ratio of the net sales value of all vehicles of that class produced in Canada by the manufacturer in the base year to the net sales value of all vehicles of that class sold for consumption in Canada by the manufacturer, in the base year, and is not in any case lower than seventy-five to one hundred; and

   (B) the Canadian value added of which is equal to or greater than the Canadian value added of all vehicles of that class produced in Canada by the manufacturer in the base year;

6) "Net sales value" has the meaning assigned by regulations made under section 273 of the Canadian Customs Act; and

7) "Specified commercial vehicle" means a motor truck, motor truck chassis, ambulance or chassis therefor, or hearse or chassis therefor, but does not include:

   a) any following vehicle or a chassis designed primarily therefor, namely a bus, electric trackless trolley bus, amphibious vehicle, tracked or half-tracked vehicle, golf or invalid cart, straddle carrier, motor vehicle designed primarily for off-highway use, or motor vehicle specially constructed and equipped to perform special services or functions, such as, but not limited to, a fire engine, mobile crane, wrecker, concrete mixer or mobile clinic, or

b) any machine or other article required under Canadian tariff item 438a to be valued separately under the tariff item regularly applicable thereto.
3. The Government of Canada may designate a manufacturer not falling within the categories set out above as being entitled to the benefit of duty-free treatment in respect to the goods described in this annex.

Annex B

(1) Motor vehicles for the transport of persons or articles as provided for in items 692.05 and 692.10 of the Tariff Schedules of the United States and chassis therefor, but not including electric trolley buses, three-wheeled vehicles, or trailers accompanying truck tractors, or chassis therefor.

(2) Fabricated components, not including trailers, tires, or tubes for tires, for use as original equipment in the manufacture of motor vehicles of the kinds described in paragraph (1) above.

(3) Articles of the kinds described in paragraphs (1) and (2) above include such articles whether finished or unfinished but do not include any article produced with the use of materials imported into Canada which are products of any foreign country (except materials produced within the customs territory of the United States), if the aggregate value of such imported materials when landed at the Canadian port of entry, exclusive of any landing cost and Canadian duty was—

(a) with regard to articles of the kinds described in paragraph (1), not including chassis, more than 60 percent until January 1, 1968, and thereafter more than 50 percent of the appraised customs value of the article imported into the customs territory of the United States; and

(b) with regard to chassis of the kinds described in paragraph (1), and articles of the kinds described in paragraph (2), more than 50 percent of the appraised customs value of the article imported into the customs territory of the United States.

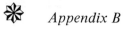 *Appendix B*

Sample "Letter of Undertaking"

Chrysler Canada, Ltd.
Windsor, Ontario, January 13, 1965

Hon. C.M. Drury
Minister of Industry,
Ottawa, Canada

Dear Mr. Minister:

I am writing with respect to the agreement between the Governments of Canada and the United States concerning production and trade in automotive products.

Chrysler Canada, Ltd. welcomes the agreement and supports its objectives. In this regard, our company notes that the Governments of Canada and the United States have agreed "***that any expansion of trade can best be achieved through the reduction or elimination of tariff and all other barriers to trade operating to impede or distort the full and efficient development of each country's trade and industrial potential***." In addition, we note that the Governments of Canada and the United States "***shall seek the early achievement of the following objectives:

a) The creation of a broader market for automotive products within which the full benefits of specialization and large-scale production can be achieved;

b) The liberalization of United States and Canadian automotive trade in respect to tariff barriers and other factors tending to impede it, with a view to enabling the industries of both countries to participate on a fair and equitable basis in the expanding total market of the two countries;

c) The development of conditions in which market forces may operate effectively to attain the most economic pattern of investment, production and trade."

Our company also notes that the right to import motor vehicles and original equipment parts into Canada under the agreement is available to motor manufacturers in Canada who meet the conditions stipulated in the Motor Vehicles Tariff Order 1965.

These conditions are, in brief, that vehicle manufacturers shall maintain in each model year their domestic production of motor vehicles in the same ratio to their domestic sales of motor vehicles and the same dollar value of Canadian value added in the production of motor vehicles in Canada, as in the period August 1, 1963, to July 31, 1964.

In addition to meeting these stipulated conditions, and in order to contribute to meeting the objectives of the agreement, Chrysler Canada, Ltd. undertakes:

1. To increase in each model year over the preceding model year, the dollar value of Canadian value added in the production of vehicles and original equipment parts by an amount equal to 60 percent of the growth in the market for automobiles sold by our company for consumption in Canada and by an amount equal to 50 percent of the growth in the market for the commercial vehicles specified in tariff item 950 sold by our company for consumption in Canada, it being understood that in the event of a decline in the market a decrease in such dollar value of Canadian value added in the above percentages is acceptable. For this purpose, growth or decline in the market shall be measured as the difference between the cost to our company of vehicles sold in Canada during the current model year and the cost to our company of vehicles sold in Canada during the preceding model year net of Federal sales taxes in both cases, and

2. To increase the dollar value of Canadian value added in the production of vehicles and original equipment parts over and above the amount that we achieved in the period August 1, 1963 to July 31, 1964 and that which we undertake to achieve in (1) above by an amount of $33 million during the period August 1, 1967 to July 31, 1968.

Chrysler, Canada, Ltd. also agrees to report to the Minister of Industry, every 3 months beginning April 1, 1965, such information as the Minister of Industry requires pertaining to progress achieved by our company, as well as plans to fulfill our obligations under this letter. In addition, Chrysler, Canada, Ltd. understands that the Government will conduct an audit each year with respect to the matters described in this letter.

I understand that before the end of model year 1968 we will need to discuss together the prospects for the Canadian automotive industry and our company's program.

Yours sincerely,   Ron W. Todgham.

Singer Company (B)

GLOBAL LOGISTIC STRATEGY

Through the first century of its existence Singer was the dominant factor in the sewing machine industry, virtually unchallenged as market leader throughout the world. After World War II, substantial competition developed to which the company responded with varied changes in strategy and organization. This case summarizes those changes and describes the global status of the company in 1975. Key financial statistics for the company are given in Exhibit 1.

The first Singer Company was established in 1851. Exports commenced almost immediately and within a few years accounted for more than 50 percent of sales. The company expanded rapidly, establishing itself as the leading sewing machine producer both at home and abroad. Its strength was based upon its product and its sales organization. The sturdy black Singer sewing machine met a basic need of housewives, small dressmakers and other buyers in every country. The sales organization consisting of thousands of company-owned sewing centers brought instruction, service and financing within their reach. A large portion of customers could not afford to buy except on the installment plan, many did not initially know enough to operate their machines effectively, and to all of them the assurance of good repair facilities was an important purchasing consideration.

Until the 1950s Singer concentrated almost exclusively on sewing machines. In 1958, 94 percent of its sales were in that basic product area. In the next few years, the company undertook an energetic diversification effort and by 1973 only 30 percent of sales were in sewing machines. The distribution of sales among the main product areas and related data are given in Exhibit 1. This case

Exhibit 1. The Singer Company Selected Operating and Financial Data (Amounts in millions)

	Year Ended December 31				
	1975	1974	1973	1972	1971
Sales by Major Product Areas:					
Consumer sewing machines and related products	$1,069.5	$ 969.5	$ 917.2	$ 800.6	$ 794.1
Aerospace systems	360.6	371.0	335.6	323.3	337.5
Industrial sewing and textile machinery	166.9	179.0	188.3	166.5	152.5
Housing	151.2	122.8	157.1	136.0	109.4
Metering and controls equipment	138.6	154.9	148.1	128.9	116.8
Furniture	102.3	178.5	166.1	85.2	72.2
Other	222.7	250.1	255.9	272.8	275.1
	2,211.7	2,225.8	2,168.3	1,913.3	1,857.6
Less sales of unconsolidated housing subsidiary	151.2	122.8	157.1	136.0	109.4
Total sales from continuing operations	$2,060.5	$2,103.0	$2,011.2	$1,777.3	$1,748.2
Operating Income (loss) by Major Product Areas:					
Consumer sewing machines and related products	$ 79.0	$ 65.8	$ 44.4	$ 49.9	$ 62.4
Aerospace systems	16.5	17.3	23.1	22.9	26.9
Industrial sewing and textile machinery	(17.1)	14.1	22.2	19.5	19.8
Housing	12.6	4.4	16.5	18.2	14.6
Metering and controls equipment	9.4	17.1	20.9	19.4	17.1
Furniture	(7.3)	11.1	17.9	10.2	10.3
Other	.9	10.0	21.9	22.5	21.6
	94.0	139.8	166.9	162.6	172.7
Less operating income of unconsolidated housing subsidiary	12.6	4.4	16.5	18.2	14.6
Operating income	81.4	135.4	150.4	144.4	158.1
Income before tax of unconsolidated subsidiaries	25.5	13.9	29.8	29.8	27.3
Interest	(50.5)	(45.3)	(31.8)	(23.4)	(28.5)
Foreign exchange adjustments	(24.3)	(23.0)	4.1	(5.9)	(4.9)

Other income and expense	.3	12.7	9.5	9.2	10.2
Provisions for facility closings and other items	(63.7)	–	–	–	–
Provision for income taxes	(10.0)	(33.0)	(67.1)	(65.8)	(71.0)
Income (loss) from continuing operations	$ (41.3)	$ 60.7	$ 94.9	$ 88.3	$ 91.2
Financial Position					
Working capital	$1,125.1	$1,246.1	$1,234.3	$1,138.8	$1,154.6
Property, plant and equipment—net	532.6	494.3	467.2	385.3	355.2
Long-term debt	189.4	164.3	146.0	122.5	124.5
Retained earnings	213.4	198.3	163.7	130.7	113.9
Shareholders' equity	$2,060.5	$2,103.0	$2,011.2	$1,777.3	$1,748.2
Sales by Major Geographical Areas:					
United States	$ 280.3	$ 562.8	$ 457.7	$ 457.1	$ 459.2
Europe and Canada	309.7	331.1	331.2	294.9	277.5
Latin America	450.1	405.0	254.9	241.0	238.0
Other International	127.0	589.7	646.3	603.6	562.8
	306.2	768.9	817.8	763.2	769.3

deals only with the consumer sewing machine field. Statistics for Singer's sewing machine business are given in Exhibit 2. For 1975 worldwide unit sales remained about 3 million with significant growth experienced chiefly in parts of Asia and Latin America. The competitive situation and key aspects of operations including products, marketing and organization will be described in subsequent sections.

THE INTERNATIONAL COMPETITIVE SITUATION

For many years Singer sold more sewing machines than all of its competitors combined. After World War II, however, foreign producers made major inroads into Singer's position. The first challenge came from European producers who developed substantial sales of zig-zag machines in the United States. Singer had been selling zig-zag machines to small artisans in Europe since 1937, but had never felt that there was a market for them among United States housewives. The European manufacturers also came out with designs which were more appealing than Singer models, and the prices of many European machines were below those of Singer.

Stirred by this competition, Singer imported its own zig-zag machine into the United States and improved its styling. Having its own European factories, it was able to hold close to the prices of its competitors there, the difference in prices being largely caused by the cost of greater service provided by Singer. The cost of maintaining the sales-service centers ran as high as 50 percent of retail prices. The company found the competition from European firms along with a few producers in India and communist China stimulating but not alarming. In total, these companies sold about 2,500,000 machines in 1957 against Singer's 1,900,000.

The second wave of competition came from the Japanese, and it was a major threat to Singer. The evolution of the Japanese industry is described in the Singer (A) case. Starting from virtually nothing after World War II, 300 companies were by 1957 producing 2,300,000 machines per year. Exports amounted to 1,630,000—880,000 to the United States and Canada, 120,000 to Europe and the Middle East, 340,000 to Asia and Africa and 290,000 to Latin America. The prices of the Japanese machines were substantially below those of

Exhibit 2.   Singer Sales of Home Sewing Machines (Thousands of Units)

	1957	1967	1970	1972	1973	1974
North America	600	875	1,075	950	1,125	900
South America, Africa, Middle East, Asia & Australia	700	1,000	1,100	1,000	1,100	1,100
Europe	600	625	800	825	875	900

Singer, their costs being considerably less than those of United States or even European factories. Labor composed about 40 to 50 percent of the cost of company-made and procured components and machine assembly, so the low Japanese wage scale was a key factor. To meet this threat, Singer developed various sites for lower cost manufacturing which will be described below, seeking to utilize economies of scale and low wage levels as far as possible. By this means it had by the mid-sixties essentially matched the cost capabilities of the Japanese. In the early 1970s, in fact, Singer's lowest cost production sources like Taiwan had an advantage over factories in Japan because of the steady rise of wages there.

In the immediate post-World War II period, Singer had strong competition from European firms like Pfaff in Germany and Necchi in Italy. However, by 1975 these firms had ceased to be strong factors in the field. Necchi was technically bankrupt, operating under government subsidy, and other European firms were financially weak. They had failed to develop significant international operations and could compete effectively only in the European market where they were protected by tariffs and import restrictions from low-cost foreign producers.

On the international level, the large Japanese firms, notably Brother, Janome and Marutzen (Sears Roebuck's supplier for the US market) were Singer's strongest competition. The smaller Japanese firms were significant factors, but with rising domestic labor costs and insufficient capital to undertake manufacture abroad, their position was weakening. Small producers in Taiwan had come on since the mid-1960s to fill much of the unbranded market for low-cost machines which the small Japanese firms had previously served. But these small firms did not have the capacity to directly counter Singer's financial and marketing strength. The big Japanese firms did have the financial capability, and they had established factories in Korea and Taiwan indicating an intent to maintain cost parity with Singer in production bases. However, they had undertaken only limited other foreign manufacturing ventures, i.e., one plant in Brazil.

PRODUCT LINE

For many years Singer's consumer product line was essentially limited to its simple straight-stitch sewing machine. The introduction of zig-zag machines, often modernistic in design and color, started a process of relatively rapid product evolution which was being maintained in the early 1970s. In 1975 the company had a wide range of products with US retail prices running from $99.95 to $900.00. Each year the company introduced at least one new model, so the whole product line changed steadily. The basic straight-stitch model #15 continued to be a strong seller, especially in the less developed countries where it was sold either with a motor or for manual operation. The greater portion of world-wide sales though were of zig-zag models which gave the user substantially greater flexibility in sewing operations. As income rose in the LDCs the demand for the more sophisticated machines increased rapidly. For example, in Africa, Asia and Latin America zig-zag models composed 25 percent of sales in 1968 and 50 percent in 1970.

Among the zig-zag machines there were important variations in operating mechanisms and housings. For many years all home sewing machines employed a moving shuttle as their basic operating mechanism. In the early sixties, Singer adopted the rotating hook system for its more sophisticated machines because of its quiet operation and greater flexibility in adapting new features. The hook system had been employed in industrial machines for many years. Subsequently competitors had also introduced it in their machines. In the mid-sixties Singer introduced the touch-and-sew system in its top-of-the-line machines. Until then the basic system for all machines required both a spool of thread feeding down from the top through the needle and a bobbin of thread in the housing below the needle. The new system required only a spool on the top and threading was completely automatic. This system was patented, so it gave Singer a unique competitive advantage in the highly sophisticated machines in which it was used.

The housing differences were related to other product characteristics. Cast iron housings had been used historically for sewing machines because of their low cost. For simple machines, they were entirely satisfactory. However, as the complexity of machines increased, the size of the housing grew and thus its weight. In the most sophisticated machines, a cast iron housing resulted in an excessively heavy machine. For the many customers who desired a degree of portability in machines, this characteristic became a substantial drawback. Therefore, Singer started making die cast housings which were considerably lighter, although somewhat more expensive.

Because of the severe competition which it experienced from Japanese producers on the bottom end of the product range, Singer had explored means to produce lower cost models. It was not possible to produce a simpler machine, as the basic model #15 performed no more functions than the lowest priced Japanese models. The company experimented with less expensive materials. For example, it tried using a plastic housing. However, the results were not entirely satisfactory. Some of the difference in the costs of competitors was attributable to lower quality standards, notably in the tolerances of working parts. Singer did not feel that reduction of quality in this respect was sound in light of the importance of the reputation of the Singer brand for high performance standards. Thus the company had essentially concluded that it could not expect to match the lowest prices of competitors and that it had to rely on its quality, marketing and financing strengths to offset the price factor.

MANUFACTURING OPERATIONS

Singer's manufacturing operations developed over time according to a pattern influenced by environmental and market conditions. In the early years of the company, manufacture was concentrated in two major plants: Elizabeth, New Jersey and Clydebank, Scotland. As demand in the major European countries grew and tariff barriers appeared protecting local firms, Singer built plants in France, Italy and Germany.

After World War II the number of foreign plants multiplied steadily under the influence of two factors: competition from low cost producers and restrictions by less developed countries favoring local production. The pressure to reduce costs fostered a succession of production moves, notably operations in Japan, Italy, Taiwan and Brazil.

In 1955, Singer entered into a 50-50 joint venture in Japan, partly to give it access to the Japanese market but also to provide a base from which to supply markets in South East Asia and Africa on a cost basis comparable to Japanese competitors. This move had met with substantial opposition in Japan as described in the (A) case. Despite the opposition Singer went ahead with the agreement without government validation. In 1960 the government had validated Singer's agreements with Pine. Significant changes in the circumstances in the Japanese industry apparently contributed to the willingness to give approval. Whereas the sewing machine industry had been in a recession in 1954, its sales had moved ahead sharply by 1960. In the meantime Singer had been present in the Japanese market for five years, and the industry had a more accurate picture of the impact of its presence. While Pine's output had increased by 1960, it still represented only a minor portion of the industry, and the Japanese could see that Singer's presence did not have a devastating effect on the industry. Thus the resistance by 1960 was moderate. At the same time the Japanese government with a constant problem of maintaining a sound balance of payments was impressed by the contribution to exports which Singer could provide. Production at the Japanese plant was increased substantially over the course of time. By 1968 the output for local consumption was about 90,000 units per year, and about half of the production went into export markets. Most of the exports were to South East Asia. The only other significant amounts were to the United States, and these were limited to irregular shipments to meet particular shortages, not on a continuous basis.

A new plant was built in Monza, Italy in 1968 where the bottom-of-the-line machines were turned out on a high-volume basis with consequent efficiency and low cost. The plant was intended to provide a low-cost source of supply for markets in any part of the world, especially the less developed countries. In practice the Italian and Japanese plants were both used to serve LDC markets in the late 1960s. Their costs were essentially similar. In 1968 the cost of labor per hour was running about 85¢ in Japan compared to around $1.30 in Italy. However, the Italian plant benefited from substantial economies of scale because its output of each model was in the order of five times greater than that of the Japanese plant. The latter had to serve the full range of needs of the Japanese market, so it produced a great variety of both die cast and cast iron consumer products as well as industrial sewing machines. The Italian plant, on the other hand, concentrated entirely on a limited line of cast-iron consumer units, with total output of about 500,000 units per year. The Japanese plant was also not altogether satisfactory as a source, because of the complications of operating on a partial ownership basis. The volume of exports to South East Asia was motivated in large measure by concern for the Japanese government interests.

The two major European export plants were subject to further development in the early 1970s influenced by manufacturing and market considerations. In Scotland, the company's oldest foreign plant had been extensively modernized to lower costs. At the same time output was reduced by about a quarter to roughly equal that of the Italian plant. Singer had experienced the difficulties among its roughly 1,700 workers common to firms in the United Kingdom, including wildcat strikes and the legal unenforceability of labor agreements resulting in losses of productivity and unreliability of production. Costs relative to plants in other major industrial countries had tended to rise in the preceding years. The cost status was also affected by devaluations. The Clydebank plant was used for production of middle range machines, about 85 percent for export, mostly to Europe and the United States with modest portions shipped to Latin America and Asia.

In Italy, Singer had experienced a steady rise in wages, the level at Monza by 1975 standing close to that in the company's South Carolina plant. To offset this factor, the Monza plant was re-equipped in 1972 with a high degree of automation. In 1975, 80 percent of its output was basic cast-iron zig-zag machines with the balance straight-stitch machines. About 85 percent of production was for export to Europe, Canada and the United States with some sales to Latin America and Asia. Labor conditions had become progressively less favorable in Italy. National work stoppages for political purposes were quite frequent. Government labor regulations were also quite strong, including requirement of official approval to discharge workers.

Singer was invited to establish a plant by the government of Taiwan in the early 1960s. A substantial local sewing machine industry had evolved out of the initiative of local entrepreneurs. Aided by a wage scale much lower than that of Japan, they had expanded exports to about 100,000 units per year. However, the industry was poorly organized with little standardization of components and erratic quality control. The government asked Singer to come in with the mission of establishing standardization of components procured from local manufacturers and quality standards for them. This initiative of the government was resisted by the guild of local parts makers and assemblers. However, the government went ahead with its invitation to Singer, and its plant opened in 1964. Within the next few years Singer was fully accepted by the local firms as its efforts proved highly beneficial to the industry. With improved quality and lower costs through parts standardization and quality standards, exports had increased to 1,100,000 in 1970, of which Singer's share was only 150,000. The Singer exports were all to Africa and South East Asia.

As an incentive to establish the Taiwan plant, the government gave Singer a 5 percent rebate on taxes for goods exported. However, the basic incentive for the company lay in the utility of the plant as a sourcing point. The chief deterrent was that the Taiwan industry was not as fully developed as that in Japan so it was not possible to procure a full range of satisfactory components. At the outset about two-thirds of the content was purchased locally. By 1975 the portion had been brought up to over 90 percent. All major manufacturing operations, including foundry work, machining and plating, could be performed by the plant for most Singer models. The quality standards were not fully up to those of the most advanced Singer plants, but they were adequate for the export markets it served. The Taiwan industry was not, however, capable of supplying parts for the more sophisticated machines, nor was the Singer plant equipped to make die-cast housings. In 1974 Singer had decided to double the capacity of the Taiwan plant in anticipation of its expansion as an export source.

The differences in the production capabilities, costs and market conditions of the Singer plants in Japan and Taiwan resulted in an evolution of different roles for them. From 1967 to 1973 total national exports from Japan fell from about 2.6 to 2.2 million units while Taiwan's exports rose from 0.1 to 1.1 million. The Singer shipments had followed similar trends. In the mid-sixties the Japanese plant had been exporting a full line of straight-stitch and zig-zag machines, largely to South East Asia. Over time the cost advantages of the Taiwan plant led to shifting to it the sourcing of the simpler machines including some zig-zag models, thus increasing its export volume substantially while that of the Japanese plant declined and was specialized heavily in more sophisticated zig-zag machines, especially the die-cast models. The latter by 1975 made up 50 percent of domestic Japanese sales for Singer while they were still in quite limited demand for export, there being, for example, no sales of them in Thailand. There was some overlap in the production lines of the Japanese and Taiwan plants because of the transition process, the value of alternative sources and their use in supplying their local markets.

Over the long term Singer's supply system showed a steady movement toward use of new lower-cost sources as the production capabilities and cost relationships among countries evolved. However, the flexibility and rate of change in this process were substantially tempered by product and marketing conditions. Despite a continuing effort toward global standardization of products, there were, for historical reasons, considerable differences among the products available from export plants. When a given market had been supplied from one source, a change to a new source would therefore usually require adding a complete new complement of parts with consequent increase in inventory costs. The parts for the previously sold model would have to be kept in stock for many years because of the durability of Singer machines and the importance to the company's image of being able to provide good repair service. A further deterrent to changes was the large scale and fixed costs in the major export plants. Their efficiency was essentially dependent upon maintaining large volume output, so shifting any significant percentage of volume to another supply source might cost more in loss of total plant efficiency than would be gained by utilizing the lower cost plant. For this reason, changes in sourcing in many cases had to be by major steps, e.g., dropping one model completely at a given plant at one time phased to the start-up at another rather than gradually shifting over an extended period. Such major shifts required large investments and had serious labor and other consequences, so they were made only after very careful consideration.

While the company attempted as far as possible to serve markets from high-volume, low-cost factories, pressures from many countries led it to undertake varying degrees of manufacture in many places. Less-developed countries perceived sewing machines as logical candidates for local manufacture. With substantial local demand and a high proportion of labor costs, local production seemed a good way to save foreign exchange and increase local employment. There were significant opposing considerations. Manufacture of sewing machine parts required considerable technical skill and materials of adequate quality. Even the demand in the larger LDCs was relatively small so that economies of large-scale output could not be achieved. And, from Singer's viewpoint, the risks of investment in many countries were deterrents. These considerations led Singer to decline to undertake production in some countries, despite government pressures, in early post-war years. However, as the company observed that the countries were determined to achieve local production and the price of resistance might be complete exclusion from markets, it acceded to the local desires to varying degrees.

The pattern of manufacture in the LDCs was governed by the nature of sewing machine manufacture. It did not lend itself to a process of gradual increase of locally procured parts. Packing and shipping separately the many individual parts in a sewing machine was excessively expensive. Also locally manufacturing just a few of the parts at the volume required for a plant geared to local requirements only would be quite inefficient, and in smaller countries, lacking machinery industries, it was scarcely practical at all.

Therefore the manufacturing undertaken tended to be of certain limited types. In some cases, it consisted simply of assembly of major components with the "head" (containing all the working parts) imported fully assembled and local work limited to assembling it to the cabinet and stand. In some instances the cabinet and stand might be procured locally. Likewise, only in unusual cases were a few components other than the cabinet or stand made locally. When the market was big enough and the technical capabilities of the host country sufficient, the typical pattern was for full manufacturing to be undertaken, rather than importing progressively greater portions of the parts.

Following this pattern, Singer had undertaken full manufacture in Argentina, Brazil, Mexico, Pakistan and Turkey, while in smaller markets operations were essentially limited to assembly work. In 1976 such assembly plants were located in Colombia, Peru, Thailand, Sri Lanka, Bangladesh, Malaysia, Indonesia, Morocco, Ghana, Nigeria, Zaire, Malagasy, Kenya and Tunisia. The full manufacturing operations generally produced in the 30-60,000 units per year range while the assembly plants had outputs in the 2-35,000 per year range. For the most part, the operations that evolved out of this pattern had relatively high costs by international competitive standards, and they were largely confined to serving their local markets.

The exception to this generalization was the Brazilian plant which, through a combination of a large internal market and low wages, had become the lowest cost plant in the world. Labor productivity and relations with the roughly 2000 workers were good. The government was supportive and provided tax incentives for exports. As a consequence the Brazilian plant had become an important source of supply for assembly plants and sales offices in a number of countries in both Latin America and South East Asia. Because of its effectiveness, the plant had been designated as the first LDC production source for heads of rotating hooks, and in 1975 they were being exported to a number of countries. In this role the operation had expanded steadily so that its output in 1975 was approaching the level of the company's other major export plants in Italy and Scotland. Singer had also invested in planting a large number of trees for future cabinet production under a tax-incentive program for development of the Brazilian interior.

Singer had a good position in the domestic Brazilian market. The only other foreign firms had smaller operations. The largest competitor was a subsidiary of the Italian firm, Vigerelli. Vigerelli was not a major international competitor, the Brazilian plant being its only foreign venture, going back to special ties at an earlier period. The Japanese firm, Brother, had bought an interest in a Brazilian firm in 1972. There were also a handful of locally owned companies.

The evolution of the limited manufacturing operations engaged essentially in assembly work is illustrated by two operations in South East Asia: the Philippines and Thailand. Philippine production started in 1955 with the manufacture of wooden cabinets. In 1960 a foundry to make cast-iron housings was built, and assembly of straight-stitch machines commenced. Up to that point completed heads were being imported from the Scottish factory. Considerable price competition had developed, especially from a Philippine company which was making housings locally and importing Japanese parts. By switching to assembly, Singer improved its cost position in two respects. The parts imported from Japan and later from Taiwan had lower production costs and tariffs on parts were only 40 percent compared to 80 percent for completed machines.

In the mid-sixties, Singer took a further step by starting to manufacture shuttles and some other cast-iron parts. This endeavor was not, however, satisfactory. The new operations required considerable additional skills, for example, in the hardening process, and quality control was hard to maintain. It also appeared that the volume required was too low for an economically efficient operation. Therefore, this phase of production was dropped in 1969. While the reversion to importation of the parts had some adverse balance-of-payments effect for the Philippines, it was cushioned by Singer's export efforts. The company had exported wooden cabinets since the late 1950s to several other assembly plants (e.g., Singapore and Indonesia). Subsequently it had started exporting stands made partly from steel legs bought from a Philippine firm and partly from cast-iron parts made by its own foundry.

The tone of the Philippine operations in 1975 was related to the competitive situation. The chief competition was from the local Philippine firm, Japanese imports being a weak factor due to the high tariff. No Japanese firms had undertaken assembly within the country. The local firm did not have a source of supply of rotating hook models, so Singer was able to compete satisfactorily with continued reliance on shuttle straight-stitch models from Taiwan and zig-zag machines from Japan. All management personnel in the unit were local nationals which facilitated relations with the government.

Singer established an assembly plant in Thailand in 1967. The company had a strong position in the Thai market. In the post-World War II period it had been able to import machines freely building on its prewar status. The subsequent influx of Japanese machines had made inroads in its market position. However, in the early sixties it still held a strong market position against the efforts of 50 or so importers and it was maintaining that position in 1975.

The assembly plant was set up at the urging of the Thai government which was anxious to foster industrialization. Initially it did not appear that the operation would be economically viable, so the company was given status as a pioneer industry. It received a 50 percent reduction in tariffs for a period of up to five years subject to fulfillment of a planned program of increases in locally purchased content. The program was terminated after about four years because Singer found it was not economical to achieve the full 50 percent level of locally purchased input. Somewhat less than 50 percent was achieved, about half in labor and half in the cost of cabinets purchased from a local manufacturer. By 1971 the company was paying full tariff on its imported content but did have some continuing advantage in having no tariff on its locally procured share. No competitors had assembly operations in the country.

Three models were assembled in the Thai plant. Parts for the #15 model were imported from Japan and Taiwan, chiefly the latter because of the lower costs. Parts for two zig-zag models were imported from the Brazilian factory. The source in this case was based on the fact that the Brazilian models were of a more modern design, i.e., rotating hook models, than comparable units available from Taiwan and Japan. The FOB costs from Brazil and Taiwan were about equal. The Brazilians provided a larger export bonus, offsetting the greater transportation as compared to Taiwan.

The product mix in Thailand had changed substantially as the market became more sophisticated. When production started in 1967, the full output was limited to the simple straight-stitch (#15) model. By 1971 the mix had changed to roughly half straight-stitch and half zig-zag. In addition, about 5,000 more sophisticated zig-zag machines were imported complete from Japan.

The Thai factory employed about 100 workers. The assembly operations were relatively simple, but still considerable care was required to achieve precision in putting the machines together, finishing and some other operations. About two years were required to bring the quality performance of the workers up to consistently high standards. The turnover in the plant was relatively low.

In the early 1970s a new type of situation influencing manufacturing plans was emerging in the Andean Pact countries (ANCOM): Bolivia, Chile, Colombia, Ecuador, Peru and Venezuela. A central objective of the Andean group was to foster industrialization by establishing a free market area, with manufacture of products allocated to one or in some cases two countries so that an economical scale of production could be achieved. The first Sectorial Program of Industrial Development was agreed to among the countries in 1972. It covered about 200 products in metalworking operations. Among them were sewing machines, production of which was assigned to Colombia and Chile. In order to receive the free trade benefits of the ANCOM program, a foreign company had to declare its intention to reduce its foreign equity share to 49 percent and to achieve that goal within 15 years.

In 1975 Singer had manufacturing facilities with ownership as noted in Colombia (100 percent), Chile (100 percent) and Peru (85 percent). The Colombian plant was essentially an assembly unit. It did, however, manufacture motors for its own use and export to Brazil. This activity had been undertaken because Colombia allowed repatriation of earnings only to the extent companies exported goods. In Peru Singer had an assembly operation. The Chilean subsidiary owned a warehouse which was equipped for machining castings for housings and for assembly. However, it was not at the time in use because local conditions had discouraged company operations. The company was maintaining its organization in Chile in the early 1970s with a modest import program. The only other manufacturers in the Andean region were two small firms, one in Colombia and one in Chile, which assembled parts imported from Far East sources. These local firms automatically qualified for ANCOM trade benefits. In 1975 it was not clear what further developments might result from the sectorial development plan.

The expansion of foreign factories had been motivated by the general corporate view that Singer should maintain its market position in every country, undertaking at least assembly when government pressures to that end became strong enough to suggest possible exclusion. By 1968 the management felt that this policy had been carried further than was necessary or wise in some cases. The risk to the company's position upon which it was based assumed that, if Singer did not set up plants, competitors would do so. Since European firms were not moving at all in this direction and only the bigger Japanese firms were prepared to do it on a limited scale, the risks of market loss seemed small. In the larger countries, local firms were capable of developing manufacture, but in most of these Singer was satisfied that the demand justified establishing its own plants. The issue concerned smaller countries, or those presenting greater political and foreign exchange risks or other cases in which competitive pressures or various factors made the need or value of establishing factories debatable. Contributing to management thinking was an observation about the general balance of risks and profits in the world situation. In earlier years, while risks of adverse conditions existed in many countries, there were also enough favorable situations in which good profits could be made to offset the losses in others. By the late 1960s, however, there were few really favorable situations and many in which risks were high.

A somewhat different situation occurred in Australia where a plant was set up with government assurances that protection would be given against imports. When this protection did not materialize and imports gave Singer tough competition, the plant was closed in 1967. Likewise a plant had been closed in South Africa because the sophisticated market there required a full line of machines but the demand was too small for economical production and effective protection from imports was not provided. The general policy in 1975 was that further expansion of foreign production should be viewed quite critically.

Yet another aspect of the manufacturing evolution was the role of the US plants. With stiff competition, first from Europe and then from Japan, Singer's US sewing machine production contracted greatly by the late 1950s, and all production by other firms in the United States ceased. Singer continued to produce its top-of-the-line machines in the United States but imported the balance of its requirements from its lower cost European plants. In 1973, a highly automated plant had been built in South Carolina which, in conjunction with the Elizabeth plant, was supplying all of the US requirements of the company's most sophisticated product, the Futura model, as well as some other lines, and doing some exporting to Europe and Canada. Its costs were slightly higher than those at the European plants which were competent to make such a sophisticated model. However, the company was satisfied that, given the risks, the trend in costs and other factors, it was sound to rely to this degree on US manufacturing.

A further development took place in 1974 when an entry was made into the Eastern European area. Singer made an agreement to provide know-how for the production of sewing machines in a factory to be built and owned by the Polish government. The machines would be sold under the Singer label primarily in Eastern European countries (not Russia) by the Poles with Singer contracting to take a small share of the production for sale in Western Europe. The models produced would be in the lower to middle price range, comparable to those made in Italy. They would carry the Singer label, and a system was established to permit Singer to monitor the quality control. Singer would receive a royalty for all machines produced.

MARKETING

Singer's traditional marketing system was based on its sewing centers. Singer was the only firm which had developed an extensive system of company-owned retail stores, so it had a unique advantage in this respect.

The role of the sewing centers is illustrated by the situation in Thailand. There were roughly 100 retail shops throughout the country, bringing training, service and financing within easy reach of the greater portion of the population. With 80 percent of sales made on time, the company's large resources gave it a further competitive advantage, and the Singer name had a reputation unapproached by other makers. The company also had some 2,000 sales people engaged in door-to-door canvassing. These people were paid on a commission basis. Some were full-time workers while others sold very little, but the aggregate effect provided a large amount of customer contact.

Singer's competitors all sold through independent distributors. As the Japanese firms typically had limited financial resources, the distributors had to provide their own financing for installment sales. Distributors would provide some training for customers in the use of sewing machines but not as much as the Singer centers. The distributors also tended to sell two or more competing brands of sewing machines.

While in 1975 the company continued to give primary emphasis to the sewing center system, variations in the pattern had developed out of assorted conditions. In Europe the company made its own appliances (e.g., refrigerators) which were sold by the centers. In a number of cases the centers had broadened their lines to non-Singer products. For example, beds were sold in the Philippines and refrigerators in Thailand. In this manner they were able to increase their market contacts and spread their overheads over a greater volume.

The other significant variations were in the extent of use of independent dealers, the practice employed by competitors. In general, Singer felt this was a less satisfactory system partly because independent dealers often handled competing lines or at least other products which diverted their main attention from Singer products. However, the use of independent outlets was undertaken in many cases because of prevailing marketing conditions and in others because of local requirements. In the United States, the largest portion of sales was made in 1975 through 1,200 company sewing centers; but an equal number of dealers were contributing a large and expanding volume of business. In Europe, there were 1,400 sewing centers and about 2,500 dealers, a large portion of them in Italy. To assure close control and effective promotion by dealers, the company employed a staff of salesmen-inspectors who visited the outlets regularly.

Requirements affecting the retail system originated in the desire of some host governments to foster the status of local merchants. Singer's first experience in this respect was in the Philippines. A law was passed in 1954 restricting retailing to local nationals starting in 1964. The law was directed mainly at the large portion of Philippine retailing controlled by Chinese, but it covered all aliens. US firms were exempt from immediate application of the law under the Laurel-Langley Act which gave them status equal to Philippine firms until 1975. By the end of 1975 therefore all retailing had been transferred to local dealers. Singer provided strong support for the dealerships by guaranteeing their consumer financing paper as it was taken over by banks. A similar situation developed in Turkey in 1974 when a law excluding foreign nationals from retailing was passed, and comparable experiences might be expected in other countries where non-nationals were major factors in retailing. More broadly Singer was conscious of general nationalistic sentiment in less developed countries against its company-owned retail system. Host nationals felt that retailing was an area of business in which local merchants should be given preference because less capital and fewer special skills were required, as compared to manufacturing in which the special technological and large capital inputs for foreign firms were considered more acceptable and often essential.

OWNERSHIP

As a matter of general policy Singer preferred full ownership and control of its foreign units. Product management, sourcing decisions, financial arrangements and other aspects of operations were more readily handled in a fully integrated system. Besides the Japanese arrangement described earlier, Singer had joint ventures in 1975 in India, Nigeria, Peru and Morocco. The Indian joint venture had been formed essentially as a means of maintaining the Singer retail sales organization. When India pressed Singer to undertake local manufacture in the early 1950s, it decided not to do so and it was subsequently not allowed to import machines. In order to maintain its marketing organization Singer started to buy machines made to its specifications in 1960 from Mahabir, the second largest local manufacturer. Usha, the largest firm, had over 50 percent of the market. In 1972 Singer purchased a 49 percent interest in Mahabir. The government, wishing to give the fully-owned local firms a stronger market position, required that Singer not be used as a primary brand name in local marketing. Thus the Mahabir products were sold under the name Merritt, with the Singer name appearing in small print on the machines. For export sales the Singer name was allowed, but the Indian plant was not used appreciably for exports because of quality and cost considerations. Another Indian joint venture to manufacture needles was established in 1962. The Indian situation was complicated by the general policy of the Indian government to seek greater local ownership and the pressures on all firms to increase exports, especially in light of the critical balance-of-payments situation created by the energy crisis and the rise of oil prices.

In Nigeria, in accordance with a change in the foreign investment law, Singer sold a 40 percent interest in its subsidiary in 1973 to local investors, but still retained management control of the operation. Similar legislation led to the sale of 50 percent of the Moroccan subsidiary in 1974.

The extent to which some governments were pressing for majority ownership by local businesses was illustrated by Peru. The foreign investment code agreed to among the Andean countries endorsed a general policy of gradual divestment by all foreign manufacturing subsidiaries. Peru had implemented this policy most actively requiring all companies to sell 15 percent of equity, which Singer did in 1974. The Peruvians in addition had enacted a law in 1970 which required the gradual transfer of ownership of all plants to their workers. Companies were required to turn over shares in their firms equivalent to 15 percent of profits each year to a trust owned by the workers until 51 percent was owned by labor. As the portion owned by the workers increased, they were to be allotted proportionate representation on the board of directors. Such conditions would be in marked contrast to Singer's historical pattern of operations, and management was doubtful if it could maintain satisfactory quality control and other standards under those circumstances. The possibility of such problems was present in all six of the Andean Pact countries where Singer had operations.

A further complication in the ownership situation was the difficulty of finding suitable local investors in countries where divestment was required. These countries were often at a low level of industrial development, so there was limited capital available, and conditions were often not such as to encourage new investors. Singer's preference was for businessmen as partners, if possible people whose businesses were related to Singer's, for example, a large supplier. But with the sizeable investment required to buy a large share of a subsidiary with an established plant, it was not easy to find a good partner.

ORGANIZATION

Up until the late 1950s Singer was organized on a functional basis. A manufacturing division supervised all of the factories. The central management decided on the pattern of distribution of their products which were sold through sales organizations in each country. In the early 1960s the company was reorganized to provide greater autonomy for operating units. The major manufacturing plants in Europe and the United States remained under the central control of the manufacturing division. Six geographic areas were set up encompassing control of marketing and smaller factories within their boundaries and functioning as profit centers. The units within each area were at the outset relatively free to make trading arrangements among themselves. For example, the African division sought bids to supply its market from the Italian, Japanese, Brazilian and Canadian plants. The autonomy to make sourcing decisions was monitored by a man in the president's office. In the interests of assuring concern for overall corporate considerations, the influence of this monitoring process grew steadily stronger.

In 1967, the system was reorganized with the establishment of three geographic units—Europe, North America and International (including Africa, Asia and Latin America). Each unit controlled all manufacturing and marketing in its territory. While there was some interchange between the units, by and large they were independent in their operations and sourcing arrangements between them were left to the three units. Product development was coordinated among the units through a newly created corporate staff called the Office of Product Policy. This staff office was created primarily to increase the standardization of products globally and to reduce the number of models which had previously tended to proliferate.

A further reorganization occurred in 1973 in which all manufacturing was centralized under a unified management with marketing continuing in a geographic structure. These operations were part of the overall responsibility of a group vice-president for consumer products. Under this organization efforts toward global rationalization of products and production strategy were given new emphasis.

REGIONAL MARKET CONDITIONS

Singer's position in a number of markets has already been described in previous sections. A general summary of other market conditions is given below.

In the fifteen years following World War II Singer's share of the US market shrank steadily from two-thirds to one-third under pressure from European and then Japanese imports. Thereafter its position more or less stabilized as it achieved reasonable cost competitiveness with foreign products using its European plants as major supply sources. While the ownership ratio of sewing machines in the United States was quite high, total demand had grown steadily, assisted particularly by new home formation and replacement sales. The company noted that the number of people sewing was increasing and that their reasons for sewing had broadened from strict economy to include more emphasis on fashion and style, sewing as an enjoyable hobby, and sewing to achieve a better wardrobe, wider choice of fabrics, better quality and better fit. To serve this market the company placed emphasis on product improvements. The Futura model introduced in 1973 generated more sales in its introductory period than any previous top-of-the-line machine. It offered distinctive new convenience features and was attractive to a number of buyers as a replacement for machines they already owned.

The European market was partially isolated from low-cost international competition by import restrictions. France and Italy excluded imports of Japanese sewing machines. Imports were permitted by Germany, and Japanese machines sold well there. In the United Kingdom, Brother had bought a large British sewing manufacturer. It closed down the company's plant, but used the British brand name on machines imported from Japan. It provided Singer's strongest competition. With the European firms in relatively weak financial condition, Singer was able to maintain its traditional strong position. Its factories in France, Germany and Italy had been specialized by product lines to benefit effectively from the creation of the Common Market. While there was some slackening of European economies in the early 1970s, Singer's sales were strong.

The fastest growth of sales in the early 1970s came in less developed countries of Latin America, Middle East, Africa and Asia along with Australia. Conditions in some individual countries, as noted earlier, were difficult but in general these markets offered large opportunities because of the still limited degree of ownership of sewing machines. Singer, having adjusted its production system to meet the low costs of Asian producers, was well positioned to gain a large share of the growth of sales.

Data on production and foreign trade in sewing machines for various countries are given in Exhibits 3, 4 and 5.

Exhibit 3.   Sewing Machine Production in Selected Countries (Thousand Units)

Country	Footnotes	1963	1964	1965	1966	1967	1968	1969	1970	1971	1972
Africa											
Egypt		11	12	11	10	14	13	27	6	11	..
Tunisia		..	..	..	–	..	1	2	2	2	2
America, North											
Canada		..	119	85	78	72	136	..	..	..	..
Mexico		..	..	162	172	186	..	..	..	..	..
America, South											
Argentina		60	75	85	67	60	63	68	59	56	61
Brazil		306	341	311	368	162	458	461	409	..	..
Chile		..	..	..	..	24	41	24	27	25	..
Columbia		29	25	29	36	24	19	20	..	..	..
Peru		..	..	..	31	24	..	..	..	..	..
Asia (Excl. USSR)											
India	1/	346	255	421	411	358	423	408	204	329	315
Israel		8	9	8	7	5	7	8	6	5	6
Japan		3,565	4,010	4,218	4,053	4,150	4,564	4,752	4,281	4,666	4,461
Korea, Republic of		..	..	82	74	111	112	114	118	129	112
Pakistan	2/	..	5	58	43	39	57	80	88	85	..
Philippines		..	76	80	75	56	37	31	25	49	38
Sri Lanka		..	..	20	44	27	29	34	39	34	..
Turkey		..	..	..	..	..	104	118	75	135	..
South Viet-Nam	3/	..	20	36	47	88	17	48	8	6	49
Europe (Excl. USSR)											
European Econ. Comm.											
Belgium		..	..	..	17	13	3	4	3	..	..
Denmark		..	..	..	8	9	11	13	7	3	5
France		139	135	158	163	89	64	57	42	41	23
West Germany		597	650	694	635	579	646	671	693	594	591
Italy		537	540	477	650	807	844	862	1,005	900	818

United Kingdom		549	...	...	...	...	...	473	...	...	...
EFTA											
Austria	4/	31	23	35	26	30	25	25	31	33	35
Finland		33	7	3	6	3	1	—	...	...	...
Sweden	5/	96	104	111	110	118	122	117	131	145	...
Eastern Europe											
Czechoslovakia	6/	158	161	132	77	67	47	31	30	33	35
East Germany		259	195	217	214	208	206	192	217	229	215
Hungary		27	24	11	2	2	3	2	2	2	2
Poland	5/	218	180	178	135	144	175	210	235	249	264
Romania		74	79	81	69	74	85	88	87	89	95
Other Europe											
Spain		349	364	349	261	233	228	295	386	357	494
Yugoslavia		56	83	98	108	94	113	108	117	116	113
USSR											
Byelorussian SSR	7/	2,717	1,664	905	1,146	1,323	1,431	1,462	1,529	1,565	1,605
Ukrainian SSR		4	5	4	4	4	4	4	5	5	5
Total		10,874	10,145	9,761	9,791	9,818	10,758	11,147	10,693	11,152	11,036

Note: All types of sewing machines, whether operated by hand or fitted with a built-in electric motor, for household use or for industrial use (tailors, dressmakers, shoe industry, etc.).

1. Marketed local production.
2. Twelve months ended 30 June of year stated.
3. Data refer to assembly.
4. Beginning 1967, source, organisation for economic co-operation and development (OECD).
5. Beginning 1966, for household use only.
6. For household use only.
7. For industrial use only.

Source: *The Growth of World Industry*, United Nations, Vol. II, 1972 edition.

Exhibit 4. Sewing Machine Imports of Selected Countries by Source

January-December 1973

	Quantity Metric Tons	Value Thousand US Dollars
Canada TOT		32901
Untd States		12388
Brazil		89
Japan		6637
Korea Rep.		145
Oth Asia Nes		266
Belgium-Lux		243
France		764
Germany Fed.		2562
Italy		2303
Netherlands		77
Untd Kingdom		5500
Sweden		225
Switzerland		1538
Poland		116
Untd States TOT		192,422
Canada		9819
Brazil		2947
Colombia		57
Japan		80370
Hong Kong		1185
Korea Rep.		1613
Oth Asia Nes		6053
Belgium-Lux		1480
Denmark		76
France		2871
Germany Fed.		30989
Italy		13325
Netherlands		903
Untd Kingdom		23295
Norway		428
Portugal		831
Sweden		5380
Switzerland		10550
Yugoslavia		66
Israel TOT		5224
Untd States		394
Japan		1632
Belgium-Lux		299
Germany Fed.		1247
Italy		601
Switzerland		160
Not Spec.		722
Japan TOT	2590	22566
Untd States	275	6385
Hong Kong	8	69

	Quantity Metric Tons	Value Thousand US Dollars
Korea Rep.	330	448
Oth Asia Nes	1034	1080
France	275	2008
Germany Fed.	443	9369
Italy	127	2203
Netherlands	2	56
Untd Kingdom	29	306
Sweden	5	72
Switzerland	17	203
Czechoslovak	19	213
Hungary	1	51
Belgium-Lux TOT	1944	16987
Untd States	48	1237
Japan	216	1382
Oth Asia Nes	157	286
France	123	807
Germany Fed.	418	6411
Italy	265	1343
Netherlands	459	2829
Untd Kingdom	33	425
Portugal	9	466
Sweden	33	267
Switzerland	117	1261
Spain	18	102
Denmark TOT	785	6992
Untd States	23	683
Japan	173	1137
Belgium-Lux	7	85
France	41	217
Germany Fed.	213	2267
Italy	86	465
Netherlands	15	67
Untd Kingdom	28	215
Sweden	78	770
Switzerland	59	680
Spain	6	55
Czechoslovak	46	309
France TOT	6425	56747
Untd States	128	3238
Brazil	38	130
Japan	811	5163
Korea Rep.	44	102
Oth Asia Nes	26	51
Belgium-Lux	38	668
Denmark	6	72
Germany Fed.	2141	28709

Exhibit 4. (cont.)

	Quantity Metric Tons	Value Thousand US Dollars		Quantity Metric Tons	Value Thousand US Dollars
Italy	2175	9888	Czechoslovak	8	59
Netherlands	99	922	Netherlands TOT	2743	19154
Untd Kingdom	363	3487	Untd States	121	1451
Sweden	17	133	Japan	691	3214
Switzerland	251	3299	Oth Asia Nes	125	336
Spain	143	388	Belgium-Lux	47	334
Czechoslovak	13	91	France	94	749
Poland	114	303	Germany Fed.	1008	8429
Germany Fed TOT	7502	48003	Italy	275	1377
Untd States	207	4560	Untd Kingdom	43	335
Brazil	26	71	Portugal	12	85
Japan	2678	17007	Sweden	178	1518
Korean Rep.	160	382	Switzerland	88	1088
Oth Asia Nes	982	1998	Untd Kingdom TOT	8866	55559
Belgium-Lux	94	2074	Untd States	291	6965
Denmark	11	78	Brazil	246	704
France	605	2535	Japan	2934	12896
Italy	1602	8605	Hong Kong	22	81
Netherlands	208	2216	India	113	140
Untd Kingdom	299	3483	Korea Rep.	269	652
Austria	33	145	Thailand	22	65
Portugal	3	240	Oth Asia Nes	795	1826
Sweden	87	731	China	56	105
Switzerland	246	2662	Belgium-Lux	18	624
Czechoslovak	36	269	Denmark	72	679
Hungary	4	174	France	973	3591
Poland	205	678	Germany Fed.	952	14188
Ireland TOT	684	3796	Ireland	148	1170
Untd States	43	463	Italy	547	3973
Japan	250	959	Netherlands	251	553
Oth Asia Nes	42	50	Portugal	46	93
France	15	146	Sweden	169	1338
Germany Fed.	83	653	Switzerland	402	4786
Italy	16	147	Spain	362	654
Untd Kingdom	187	1242	German DM RP	20	106
Italy TOT	4202	36805	Poland	94	186
Untd States	117	2711	Austria TOT	1575	12895
Brazil	57	149	Untd States	12	315
Japan	9	70	Brazil	27	50
Belgium-Lux	17	614	Japan	222	1484
Denmark	6	121	Korea Rep.	33	94
France	91	1024	Belgium-Lux	2	66
Germany Fed.	2417	26068	France	33	171
Netherlands	25	433	Germany Fed.	704	6298
Untd Kingdom	341	2880	Italy	101	593
Switzerland	46	591	Netherlands	9	55
Spain	338	1049	Untd Kingdom	158	1314
Yugoslavia	720	930	Sweden	73	670

Exhibit 4. (cont.)

	Quantity Metric Tons	Value Thousand US Dollars		Quantity Metric Tons	Value Thousand US Dollars
Switzerland	120	1434	Untd Kingdom	56	365
Czechoslovak	18	118	Switzerland	103	1194
Poland	28	87	Switzerland TOT	783	8183
			Untd States	29	716
Finland TOT	848	7684	Japan	49	489
Untd States	21	482	Belgium-Lux	2	85
Japan	134	1008	France	10	74
France	16	114	Germany Fed.	435	4860
Germany Fed.	202	2579	Italy	131	775
Italy	217	1298	Untd Kingdom	12	99
Netherlands	14	76	Sweden	82	832
Untd Kingdom	36	299	Czechoslovak	17	131
Sweden	163	1317			
Switzerland	39	435	Greece TOT	1774	8550
			Untd States	28	387
Iceland TOT	56	567	Japan	360	1966
Germany Fed.	23	223	Oth Asia Nes	87	109
Italy	9	86	Belgium-Lux	4	125
Sweden	11	123	France	23	79
Switzerland	4	56	Germany Fed.	227	3209
			Italy	716	1685
Norway TOT		6734	Untd Kingdom	53	305
Untd States		165	Switzerland	16	167
Japan		66	Spain	99	249
Denmark		67	USSR	150	165
France		209			
Germany Fed.		1568	Spain TOT	1000	15483
Italy		445	Untd States	65	1511
Untd Kingdom		225	Japan	239	2403
Sweden		2275	Belgium-Lux	10	396
Switzerland		1637	Denmark	15	153
			France	37	306
Portugal TOT	966	8405	Germany Fed.	328	6371
Untd States	43	609	Italy	188	2948
Japan	94	679	Netherlands	11	273
Belgium-Lux	4	106	Untd Kingdom	65	565
France	18	228	Switzerland	28	399
Germany Fed.	239	3257	German DM RP	1	56
Ireland	19	93			
Italy	117	1112	Yugoslavia TOT	867	11761
Netherlands	7	71	Untd States	1	307
Untd Kingdom	110	836	Japan	56	591
Sweden	12	88	Belgium-Lux	1	62
Switzerland	18	303	Denmark	2	54
Spain	278	985	Germany Fed.	446	6892
			Italy	235	2123
Sweden TOT	543	6100	Netherlands	3	54
Untd States	15	363	Untd Kingdom	35	774
Japan	58	485	Austria	32	299
Denmark	8	69	Switzerland	8	76
France	21	137	Czechoslovak	7	59
Germany Fed.	213	2969	German DM RP	23	236
Italy	49	377	Hungary	12	178

Exhibit 4. (cont.)

	Quantity Metric Tons	Value Thousand US Dollars		Quantity Metric Tons	Value Thousand US Dollars
Australia TOT		23244	Sweden		1948
Untd States		1750	Switzerland		6122
Brazil		637	New Zealand TOT		7943
Japan		5471	Untd States		422
Korea Rep.		217	Brazil		173
Philippines		76	Japan		1816
Oth Asia Nes		995	Germany Fed.		1042
France		121	Italy		362
Germany Fed.		3229	Untd Kingdom		698
Italy		547	Sweden		293
Untd Kingdom		2007	Switzerland		2987

Exhibit 5.   Sewing Machine Exports of Selected Countries by Destination

	Quantity Metric Tons	Value Thousand US Dollars		Quantity Metric Tons	Value Thousand US Dollars
Canada TOT		5066	Netherlands		1581
Untd States		4809	Untd Kingdom		7125
Brazil		128	Austria		213
Untd States TOT		67252	Finland		321
S. Afr. Cus. Un.		1052	Norway		124
Algeria		297	Portugal		540
Morocco		91	Sweden		446
Egypt		66	Switzerland		697
Canada		10074	Greece		466
Argentina		438	Malta		136
Brazil		4453	Spain		1266
Chile		262	Yugoslavia		468
Colombia		1078	Australia		1688
Ecuador		149	New Zealand		357
Mexico		4911			
Peru		421	Japan TOT	46383	220795
Uruguay		141	S. Afr. Cus. Un.	548	2518
Venezuela		1321	Algeria	9	76
Costa Rica		499	Liby Arab Rp	52	152
El Salvador		308	Morocco	31	120
Guatemala		200	Sudan	16	111
Honduras		229	Tunisia	35	96
Nicaragua		258	Untd. Rp. Camp.	52	158
Barbados		162	Angola	84	251
Dominican Rp		519	Ethiopia	74	223
Haiti		769	Ghana	34	62
Jamaica		311	Ivory Coast	41	85
St. Kitts Nev		58	Kenya	61	295
Trinidad Tbg		217	Madagascar	68	142
Belize		66	Mauritius	37	157
Guyana		58	Mozambique	53	199
Panama Ex. Cz		223	Nigeria	433	1025
Israel		474	Untd. Rp. Tanz	8	89
Japan		5902	Zambia	25	100
Iran		98	Canada	1390	6078
Lebanon		90	Untd States	16610	75304
Turkey		68	Argentina	121	882
Hong Kong		2166	Brazil	938	6125
Korea Rep.		166	Chile	530	1555
Philippines		435	Colombia	150	785
Singapore		76	Ecuador	228	462
Thailand		85	Mexico	502	2947
Vietnam Rep.		168	Peru	231	714
Oth Asia Nes		302	Venezuela	135	733
Belgium-Lux		1317	Costa Rica	48	210
Denmark		464	El Salvador	102	223
France		2572	Guatemala	81	124
Germany Fed.		5030	Honduras	74	123
Ireland		281	Nicaragua	42	150
Italy		2799	Cuba	27	336

Exhibit 5. (cont.)

	Quantity Metric Tons	Value Thousand US Dollars		Quantity Metric Tons	Value Thousand US Dollars
Dominican Rp	87	169	Switzerland	106	482
Haiti	73	91	Greece	435	2325
Jamaica	24	60	Spain	91	603
Trinidad Tbg	45	198	Yugoslavia	48	630
Panama Ex. Cz	64	289	Bulgaria	9	75
Surinam	27	59	Czechoslovak	48	375
Israel	347	1481	Poland	328	2184
Bahrain	19	67	Romania	38	398
Cyprus	82	300	USSR	52	602
Iran	1304	3204	Australia	1112	5806
Iraq	10	61	New Zealand	273	1749
Jordan	40	160	Belgium-Lux TOT	437	4820
Kuwait	42	134	S. Afr. Cus. Un.	11	135
Lebanon	252	1163	Tunisia	16	189
Qatar	21	66	Angola	1	51
Saudi Arabia	204	688	Untd States	1	58
Yemen Dem.	18	56	Brazil	3	81
Syrn Arab Rp	243	934	Turkey	1	50
Untd Arab Em	40	125	Denmark	3	69
Turkey	312	1909	France	86	675
Yemen	38	78	Germany Fed.	39	582
Afghanistan	44	100	Italy	15	414
Bangladesh	14	76	Netherlands	187	1048
Khmer Rp	31	84	Untd Kingdom	9	269
Sri Lanka	23	95	Portugal	4	86
Hong Kong	987	5736	Greece	3	50
India	50	384	Spain	12	277
Indonesia	265	1363	Yugoslavia	1	82
Korea Rep.	3040	13781	Denmark TOT	170	1989
W. Malaysia	273	1340	Untd States	2	54
Pakistan	195	1361	Germany Fed.	8	120
Philippines	340	2918	Italy	6	132
Singapore	622	3156	Untd Kingdom	38	401
Thailand	1025	3361	Finland	28	177
Vietnam Rep	9	63	Iceland	7	72
Oth Asia Nes	1801	9212	Norway	18	96
China	64	789	Sweden	17	93
Korea D P Rp	9	91	Spain	11	78
Belgium-Lux	194	1150	Yugoslavia	3	99
Denmark	124	612	Czechoslovak	2	80
France	613	3454	German Dm Rp	8	289
Germany Fed.	4024	23649	France TOT	2606	14160
Ireland	196	765	S. Afr. Cus. Un.	6	58
Italy	51	558	Algeria	8	203
Netherlands	679	2755	Tunisia	31	334
Untd Kingdom	2425	12065	Ivory Coast	16	112
Austria	163	936	Canada	80	395
Finland	35	192	Untd States	262	2156
Portugal	88	585	Japan	262	1728
Sweden	20	133			

Exhibit 5. (cont.)

	Quantity Metric Tons	Value Thousand US Dollars		Quantity Metric Tons	Value Thousand US Dollars
Lebanon	4	63	Venezuela	51	822
Hong Kong	9	66	Costa Rica	14	132
Belgium-Lux	132	791	Nicaragua	9	73
Denmark	36	209	Cuba		56
Germany Fed.	486	1941	Trinidad Tbg	7	68
Italy	71	510	Guyana	4	63
Netherlands	85	536	Panama Ex. Cz	17	90
Untd Kingdom	862	2747	Israel	70	1118
Austria	11	89	Japan	520	10011
Finland	16	111	Cyprus	20	295
Norway	34	203	Iran	136	1777
Portugal	17	226	Iraq	18	266
Sweden	29	174	Kuwait	6	65
Switzerland	11	75	Lebanon	62	551
Greece	26	75	Saudi Arabia	2	54
Spain	26	195	Syrn Arab Rp	10	118
Hungary	4	57	Turkey	93	1613
Poland	3	186	Hong Kong	87	1631
Romania	3	97	India	25	346
USSR	4	94	Indonesia	2	63
Germany Fed TOT	14873	211906	Korea Rep.	15	187
S. Afr. Cus. Un.	172	2259	Malaysia	9	61
Algeria	129	1311	Pakistan	13	146
Morocco	23	279	Philippines	3	76
Sudan	2	55	Singapore	13	314
Tunisia	61	809	Thailand	25	261
Egypt	5	91	Oth Asia Nes	47	683
Untd. Rp. Camp.	14	125	China	61	1142
Angola	30	345	Belgium-Lux	389	6302
Zaire	13	182	Denmark	174	2099
Ethiopia	4	89	France	2086	26911
Ivory Coast	4	75	Ireland	74	696
Kenya	9	146	Italy	2407	26761
Madagascar	4	52	Netherlands	931	8408
Mauritius	15	133	Untd Kingdom	882	12544
Mozambique	14	84	Austria	678	6555
Nigeria	4	120	Finland	182	2467
Untd. Rp. Tanz	4	54	Iceland	20	196
Zambia	17	349	Norway	110	1372
Canada	187	2637	Portugal	237	3268
Untd States	1464	30460	Sweden	204	2987
Argentina	46	954	Switzerland	434	4912
Brazil	269	5272	Greece	262	3533
Chile	10	389	Malta	54	529
Colombia	71	895	Spain	309	5855
Ecuador	12	154	Yugoslavia	376	6582
Mexico	86	1256	Bulgaria	7	200
Peru	22	309	Czechoslovak	66	1482
Uruguay	2	54	Hungary	61	1106

Exhibit 5. (cont.)

	Quantity Metric Tons	Value Thousand US Dollars		Quantity Metric Tons	Value Thousand US Dollars
Poland	406	7843	Ireland	12	147
Romania	74	1759	Netherlands	260	1099
USSR	96	2076	Untd Kingdom	535	3350
Australia	203	2856	Austria	87	478
New Zealand	69	992	Finland	192	1017
Ireland TOT	189	1403	Iceland	9	89
Untd Kingdom	125	1052	Norway	67	504
Portugal	37	189	Portugal	141	1294
Italy TOT	11874	66400	Sweden	74	406
S. Afr. Cus. Un.	40	726	Switzerland	135	751
Algeria	196	586	Greece	735	1743
Liby Arab Rp	14	78	Malta	59	216
Morocco	19	127	Spain	172	2739
Tunisia	48	318	Yugoslavia	206	1889
Untd. Rp. Camp.	60	89	Czechoslovak	20	238
Mauritius	12	106	German Dm Rp	37	657
Mozambique	24	140	Hungary	9	130
Canada	781	2879	Poland	68	738
Untd States	2900	14346	Romania	88	874
Argentina	17	344	USSR	16	90
Brazil	40	498	Australia	45	610
Colombia	8	124	New Zealand	38	386
Ecuador	24	186	Netherlands TOT	1237	10220
Mexico	51	536	Belgium-Lux	391	2542
Peru	37	312	Denmark	16	50
Venezuela	32	377	France	98	987
Dominican Rp	9	51	Germany Fed.	219	3027
Jamaica	20	76	Italy	36	477
Panama Ex. Cz	14	59	Untd Kingdom	235	615
Israel	45	545	Austria	17	98
Japan	145	2148	Sweden	11	85
Cyprus	47	165	Spec Cats	197	2242
Iran	67	305	Untd Kingdom TOT	7100	50232
Iraq	22	131	S. Afr. Cus. Un.	35	292
Lebanon	101	356	Angola	8	55
Saudi Arabia	20	102	Kenya	17	70
Syrn Arab Rp	23	110	Nigeria	49	202
Turkey	29	302	Canada	1039	5486
Hong Kong	20	235	Untd States	2651	21242
Korea Rep.	7	92	Brazil	61	888
Malaysia	8	55	Colombia	26	296
Philippines	11	116	Mexico	105	539
Singapore	33	271	Peru	33	156
Oth Asia Nes	10	100	Venezuela	8	85
China	10	142	Cuba	1	54
Belgium-Lux	245	1116	Panama Ex. Cz	15	129
Denmark	103	474	Israel	38	158
France	1948	9160	Japan	44	335
Germany Fed.	1487	8255	Cyprus	29	171

Exhibit 5. (cont.)

	Quantity Metric Tons	Value Thousand US Dollars		Quantity Metric Tons	Value Thousand US Dollars
Iran	29	184	Japan	6	58
Lebanon	18	85	Iran	18	153
Turkey	15	211	Belgium-Lux	36	296
Hong Kong	114	654	Denmark	92	824
India	21	154	France	21	165
Pakistan	14	60	Germany Fed.	103	786
Philippines	8	134	Netherlands	161	1387
Singapore	11	142	Untd Kingdom	135	926
Thailand	6	96	Austria	69	673
Belgium-Lux	21	188	Finland	219	1612
Denmark	28	209	Iceland	9	112
France	435	2926	Norway	240	2396
Germany Fed.	326	2641	Portugal	19	128
Ireland	284	1788	Switzerland	82	784
Italy	318	2423	Greece	4	68
Netherlands	42	269	Australia	150	1756
Austria	164	961	New Zealand	26	290
Finland	42	252			
Norway	40	244	Switzerland TOT	3944	49222
Portugal	122	803	S. Afr. Cus. Un.	162	2090
Sweden	76	445	Algeria	12	166
Switzerland	14	144	Morocco	8	105
Greece	54	306	Zaire	19	266
Malta	34	94	Ivory Coast	8	93
Spain	74	563	Kenya	5	57
Yugoslavia	64	400	Zambia	15	188
Czechoslovak	6	54	Canada	151	1789
USSR	73	508	Untd States	887	11522
Australia	231	1583	Argentina	9	116
New Zealand	80	484	Mexico	17	143
			Venezuela	6	73
Austria TOT	59	480	Israel	13	196
Germany Fed.	34	199	Japan	11	107
Yugoslavia	9	159	Iran	5	77
			Lebanon	5	58
Finland TOT	40	194	Turkey	17	195
Germany Fed.	4	92	Hong Kong	18	239
			Singapore	7	99
Norway TOT		145	Belgium-Lux	115	1333
Sweden		62	Denmark	57	662
			France	267	3373
Portugal TOT	260	2561	Germany Fed.	250	2910
Angola	102	447	Ireland	6	55
Mozambique	102	295	Italy	52	640
Untd States	10	788	Netherlands	103	1246
Belgium-Lux	10	550	Untd Kingdom	358	4318
Germany Fed.	4	251	Austria	137	1751
Netherlands	12	75	Finland	41	482
Sweden TOT	1969	18252	Iceland	5	63
S. Afr. Cus. Un.	16	172	Norway	130	1686
Canada	28	267			
Untd States	508	5169			

Exhibit 5. (cont.)

	Quantity Metric Tons	Value Thousand US Dollars		Quantity Metric Tons	Value Thousand US Dollars
Portugal	20	336	Colombia	51	194
Sweden	112	1393	Mexico	82	328
Greece	22	208	Venezuela	65	121
Malta	6	85	Belgium-Lux	18	104
Spain	30	398	France	138	361
Yugoslavia	3	53	Germany Fed.	9	58
Romania	5	63	Italy	298	904
USSR	32	272	Untd Kingdom	354	552
Australia	503	6247	Portugal	256	683
New Zealand	241	3038	Greece	126	266
New Calednia	4	58	Yugoslavia TOT	443	1035
Spain TOT	2154	4942	Iraq	20	55
Algeria	141	322	Italy	347	844
Morocco	344	410	Australia TOT		570
Mozambique	15	52	New Zealand		305
United States	19	63	Papua N. Guin		139

Source: *World Trade Annual*, United Nations, Vol. V.

Ford Motor Company

LABOR RELATIONS IN BRITAIN

Labor relations in the Ford Motor Company in Great Britain were characterized by continuing tension punctuated by periodic major disputes. In the background of this situation were aspects of the political and economic conditions in Great Britain, the policies and strategy of the company and characteristics of labor relations in the British automotive industry. These background elements will be described in this case followed by a history of major events in the labor relations of Ford.

POLITICAL AND ECONOMIC ENVIRONMENT

Throughout the post-World War II era, Great Britain was plagued by interrelated problems of industrial productivity, balance of payments deficits and inflation. The low productivity problem was attributed by experts both to deficiencies in management skills and investment and to performance of individual workers and organized labor. To compensate for the low productivity there was heavy pressure to keep wages down to assure competitive costs. However, British employment was generally high throughout the period (as distinguished from heavy unemployment in a few depressed sections). As a consequence, pressure for increases in wages was strong with costs tending to push steadily upward and contributing to inflation.

In the late 1960s the government sought entry into the European Common Market. Among the benefits anticipated were improved access to EEC markets for British industry and competitive pressure from European firms to strengthen the productivity of British industry. Many of the labor unions opposed entry into EEC, in large part because of the implications of the productivity pressure. They perceived that a significant consequence would be actions by many companies to cut work forces and require greater performance from their employees. Despite this resistance Britian did join EEC in 1974.

In the early 1970s the heart of the government approach to dealing with inflation was an incomes policy with restraints on wages and prices. In practice the effects of the restraints were limited to moderating the rate of increase of prices and wages. Strong restraints were impossible because of equity considerations and the political necessity of allowing cost of living increments to groups of workers who would otherwise see their real incomes fall behind because of inflation. The power of the government was also severely restricted by the militant strength of some unions which would not conform to the government guidelines. Periodically the government program was restructured to give it new vitality and relate it to the existing economic situation. Thus in March 1973 the government announced a new set of price and pay codes composing Stage Two of its program. In October 1973 Stage Three was announced.

In general, labor accepted the overall concept of these restraints though there were a reasonable number of situations in which individual unions broke with them and companies did not succeed in resisting the pressures. In 1974, the acceptance among workers increased, first, to help the Labor Party in national elections and then to support its governing policies. The Labor Party perceived that its position would be improved if the populace was convinced that it had better control over wage pressures than the Conservative government. In September 1974, the labor leadership was successful in obtaining broad union endorsement for the "Social Contract." The essence of the Social Contract was that for the next two years the unions would not seek any major wage increases in return for support by the government for basic improvements in labor relations and efforts to achieve better income distribution. To the surprise of many observers even some of the very militant unions and labor leaders agreed to support the Social Contract at the annual Trades Union Congress.

The Social Contract was not successful, however. In the subsequent year, unions obtained increases averaging around 30 percent while the cost of living was rising at about 25 percent per year, the highest rate among industrialized nations. The Labor government, viewing this condition as intolerable for England's long-term economic welfare, set forth a program in July 1975 designed to limit pay increases to £6 per week (about 10 percent for the typical worker) in the coming twelve-month period. The wage limit was not mandatory, but companies would not be allowed to increase prices to compensate for wage rises in excess of the limit. The across-the-board amount was set forth in part to overcome a weakness of the Social Contract which had allowed greater increases for low versus high paid workers. The latter had reacted adversely to shrinkage of their pay differentials, resulting in pressure to receive the same rates of increase as lower level workers.

Labor union support of the £6 limit was essential to its success. Key leaders, notably Jack Jones, head of the Transport and General Workers Union, endorsed the program while others, including Ken Gill, leader of the Amalgamated Union of Engineering Workers, opposed it. The subject was the central issue at the annual Trades Union Congress meeting in September with the outcome a two to one majority supporting the government. Although this vote was encouraging to the government, grave doubts existed as to the viability of the restraints, with sizeable unions, e.g., railroad workers, coal miners and government employees, opposing them. If one or more large union forced a wage rise in excess of the ceiling, the whole program would rapidly collapse. A key factor in the outcome was the success of the government in checking unemployment which had risen rapidly to the 5 percent range in 1975, well above the 2 to 3 percent common to Britain in recent years. Key unions indicated they would support wage restraint only if the government was able to increase employment. The government had announced various measures to create jobs and encourage lagging industrial investment. However, rising costs had hurt exports and fostered imports, notably from Japan, whose automobiles, for example, had captured up to 40 percent of domestic British sales during some months of 1975. To check the latter the TUC was advocating import restrictions, a measure strongly opposed by the manufacturers.

While wages were the central labor issue in 1975, industrial democracy came along quite rapidly as a second subject of major interest. Although much progress in this area had occurred on the Continent in the post-war era, there had been only minor developments in Britain. It appeared that, on the whole, unions preferred to fight for their benefits independently of management rather than involve themselves in the management process. However, by 1975 the TUC and the Labor Party were advocating general adoption of worker participation in management decisions. In August, the government set up a committee to propose legislation in 1976-77. The committee was expected to look favorably on the TUC position favoring 50 percent labor membership on boards of directors and groups at lower levels of management. The Confederation of British Industries was critical of the announcement of the committee because it indicated official partiality to the TUC position. However, the CBI was generally receptive to movement toward greater industrial democracy.

In this general context, conditions in the automotive industry were a matter of prime interest. It employed many workers and it was a leading factor in exports as indicated by the data in Exhibit 1. In 1971, vehicles composed 13 percent of all manufactured exports. The data seen below show the distribution of output and exports among the major firms in 1970.

The importance of the industry to the economy was underscored by the decision of the government to rescue British Leyland Motor Company. As a result of several strikes and the decline in sales of vehicles because of the oil situation and economic slump, Leyland suffered a large loss in 1974. It faced

	Thousands of Vehicles					
	Cars			*Commercial Vehicles*		
	Home	*Export*	*Total*	*Home*	*Export*	*Total*
British Leyland	420.4	368.4	788.7	100.7	72.2	173.0
Ford	262.7	185.7	448.4	83.0	57.8	140.8
Chrysler	117.7	101.5	219.2	21.2	10.7	32.0
Vauxhall	112.4	65.7	178.1	53.7	47.9	101.7
Others	5.4	3.4	8.7	8.7	1 4	10.1

severe difficulties in financing a capital investment program of £550 million over the next seven years. Collapse of the company with 59 plants in Britain turning out a variety of lines (Jaguar, Rover, Triumph, Leyland trucks, etc.) would have had serious consequences. Therefore the government provided an estimated £95 million in December 1974, partly in loans and partly in equity to save it. Key management changes were made and strong action taken to improve operations

Exhibit 1.   Selected British Balance of Payments Data (Millions of Pounds)

	Exports		*Imports*		*Net Current Balance of Payments*
	All Commodities	*Cars and Commercial Vehicles*	*All Commodities*	*Cars and Commercial Vehicles*	
1960	3,555	328.9	4,541	20.6	−273
1961	3,682	279.8	4,395	10.5	−14
1962	3,791	329.5	4,487	20.6	+122
1963	4,365	358.6	4,983	20.9	+124
1964	4,565	383.2	5,696	29.4	−382
1965	4,901	388.0	5,751	24.8	−49
1966	5,255	376.5	5,949	29.5	+84
1967	5,300	328.2	6,437	44.3	−301
1968	6,434	415.0	7,898	55.2	−275
1969	7,339	519.4	8,315	60.9	+462
1970	8,061	482.9	9,037	98.4	+735
1971	9,181	577.1	9,821	194.0	+1048
1972	9,746		11,138		+128
1973	12,454		15,840		−835
1974	16,494		23,117		−3,668
1975	19,762		24,028		−1,917

including dropping 21,000 workers in 1975. Another 20,000 were expected to go in the next year.

A government study of the auto industry released in August 1975 identified several key difficulties. In general, the firms were said to have ignored industrial relations, marketing and after-sales service. A low rate of investment was observed, much of that being limited to replacement. The difficulties of Vauxhall and Chrysler were noted particularly, with the conclusion that both "are in a long-term loss-making situation—most probably because of lack of scale." Ford was seen as relatively much stronger because of its size in Britain and ability to spread development costs over bigger European operations.

During 1975 there was regular speculation in the press that Chrysler and General Motors might pull out of Britain. Chrysler might shift UK production to France where it had lower costs and excess capacity with a more tractible labor force. Prime Minister Wilson had taken a special interest in Chrysler and had urged its workers to cease the 1975 strike which threatened the viability of the firm. Mr. Wilson had asserted more generally that the government would not bail out companies to save jobs unless the workers showed responsible conduct in efforts to permit companies to operate satisfactorily. General Motors' situation was not so shaky, but rumors persisted that it would shift its unprofitable car production to Germany. Through 1973-75, around 30,000 workers had been cut from its plants. In September 1975, the company announced plans to import Opels from Germany to fill a gap in its line. The unions expressed great concern at this move, but GM's chairman, Thomas Murphy, said after a meeting of GM's European Advisory Council two days later that, "It is definitely part of General Motors' European strategy to maintain a separate Vauxhall car line, with continuing production of Vauxhall cars in Vauxhall plants." He noted particularly the promising future of the new Vauxhall Chevette. However, his statements did seem to indicate a greater integration of Vauxhall/Opel operations with emphasis on trucks in the former and cars in the latter.

In late 1975, the Chrysler situation reached a critical stage. With the parent company in a severe financial crisis, the management decided that continued operation of the British unit in the face of sustained major losses was unsound. After a tense period of negotiations, the British government agreed to provide a £150 million package of direct aid, loans and loan guarantees to subsidize the company's losses and provide funds for new car development. The primary motivation of the government was to save most of the jobs provided by Chrysler, but the agreement did accept layoff of 8,000 workers to cut Chrysler losses.

FORD OPERATIONS

Ford's operations in Great Britain were a major component of its international production organization. To a degree the operations were integrated with other European plants. In 1974 for example, the UK factory supplied parts to Belgian and German Ford plants. This integration was expected to increase with Britain's joining of the EEC. In addition, a number of components were made in both UK and European plants so that they could be used as interchangeable supply sources.

The nature of the labor relations situation in Britain figured prominently in Ford's production planning. Historically wages in the British industry were lower than those on the Continent, as illustrated by the data in Exhibit 2. Direct wages composed 25 percent of the cost of automobiles and total labor some 30 percent of the cost. Ford management frequently made adverse comparisons between the labor relations situation in Germany and Britain, citing for example, the data on disputes and on productivity shown in Exhibits 3 and 4. Despite these differences, however, the lower wage costs resulted in sufficiently low production costs so that Britain was a satisfactory production site. The data in Exhibit 5 indicate that the Ford plant in Britain had been quite profitable. In 1971 there was a large loss as a result of a prolonged strike. Otherwise the operations had been profitable continuously since 1939. The continuance of the wage differential was generally perceived to be a necessary factor for this satisfactory condition.

Throughout the 1960s the trend of Ford investment had been away from

Exhibit 2. Net Wage Rates per Hour for Identical Task (1969)

Germany		France		United Kingdom	
VW	65-½p	Renault	41-½p	BMC (Longbridge)	78-½p
Ford	60-½p	Citroen	36-½p	Ford	52-½p
Opel	66-½p	Peugeot	45p	Vauxhall	49p
Mercedes	66p			Rootes (Ryton)	86-½p
BMW	62p	*Sweden*			
		Volvo	44p		

Source: Rhys, p. 9.

Exhibit 3. Disputes at Ford Plants

	United Kingdom		Germany	
	Strikes	*Overtime Bans*	*Strikes*	*Overtime Bans*
1967	50	36	0	0
1968	90	59	1	0
1969	63	26	1	0
1970	155	11	1	0

Source: Rhys., p. 20.

Exhibit 4. Labor Productivity (1971)

	Car Production per Employee	Car Sales per Employee (£'000)	Value Added per Employee (£'000)	Fixed Assets per Employee (£'000)
Chrysler (UK)	17.0	7.1	1.4	3.0
Chrysler (France)	15.5	8.8	2.2	2.4
Ford (Germany)	14.0	12.0	4.0	7.8
Ford (UK)	8.0	8.5	2.0	5.4
Opel	14.0	11.0	4.5	3.5
Vauxhall	10.0	5.0	1.8	5.2
Volkswagen	12.0	10.0	3.4	6.0
Renault	11.0	7.2	2.0	3.0
Fiat	10.0	6.5	4.0	6.4
BLMC	5.5	6.3	1.9	2.5

Source: Rhys, p. 20.

Great Britain. In 1964 the German operation had been one-quarter the size of that in Britain, while in 1973 it was just as big as the British operation. On the whole it appeared that this change was essentially due to the German factory serving the rapidly growing EEC market, while the market of the UK plants had not been growing proportionately. Likewise other large Ford investments had been made in Europe, notably a transmission factory placed in Bordeaux and a $1 billion new operation being constructed in Spain for completion in the late 1970s. Henry Ford indicated the relevance of the labor relations situation in a comment in 1971 which received wide publicity in Great Britain. He had lunch at 10 Downing Street with the Prime Minister at a moment when Ford was experiencing particular difficulties with its unions. Emerging from the lunch, he observed to the press that unless labor relations became less difficult, Ford would be forced to shift production away from England.

Subsequent to 1971, however, Ford's thinking shifted. Profits in Germany began to slip as wages rose and exports were impaired by revaluation of the mark. Then a major strike in the Ford Cologne plant in 1973 broke the image of industrial peace compared to Britain. Since in 1974 the company estimated production costs for the same car were 20 to 30 percent lower in Britain than Germany, continued emphasis on the former as a production base was supported. Thus for 1973-74, £132 million was invested in Britain, about a third of it for expansion, including some acquisitions, e.g., a ceramics factory. In 1975 Ford announced it would produce about 100,000 per year of its new minicars (comparable to GM's Chevette) at Dagenham, adding 1,000 jobs. The major European source of the minicar would be the new Spanish plant, with an annual target of 250,000. Some would also be made in Germany including output for

Exhibit 5.   Selected Operating Data for Ford Motor Company Ltd.

	1964	1965	1966	1967	1968	1969	1970	1971	1972	1973
Sales (£ million)										
Export Market	154.0	174.3	194.4	164.2	207.8	266.6	266.2	275.5	309.0	369.3
Home Market	213.5	214.7	226.7	240.9	280.2	271.2	320.5	313.5	488.8	520.9
	367.5	389.0	421.1	405.1	488.0	537.8	586.7	589.0	797.8	890.2
Vehicles Sold										
Export Market	294,000	303,000	286,000	236,000	320,000	342,000	292,000	219,000	207,000	205,000
Home Market	381,000	360,000	344,000	342,000	392,000	339,000	385,000	331,000	500,000	469,000
	675,000	663,000	630,000	578,000	712,000	681,000	677,000	550,000	707,000	674,000
Profit (Loss) before taxes (£m)	24.0	8.9	7.4	2.6	43.0	38.1	25.2	(30.7)	46.8	65.4
Taxes	(10.8)	(1.6)	(2.0)	(2.1)	(15.0)	(17.4)	(9.5)	13.7	(19.1)	(33.6)
Profit after taxes	13.2	10.5	5.4	0.5	28.0	20.7	15.7	(17.0)	27.7	31.8
Net Assets (£m)	175.5	176.5	174.3	166.7	182.3	193.7	217.1	240.6	253.8	277.7
Capital Investment (£m)	47.5	39.4	41.9	37.3	19.2	36.0	67.8	48.5	32.3	41.7
Motor Industry Investment (£m)	67.0	84.0	94.0	90.5	70.0	134.0	173.0	101.5	79.3	93.7
Fords % Share	70.8	46.9	44.6	41.2	27.4	26.8	39.2	47.9	40.8	44.2
Floor Space (million sq. ft.)	18.3	18.8	22.1	22.4	23.0	23.9	22.8	23.4	23.7	23.6
Number of employees	62,000	61,000	64,000	60,000	61,000	65,000	68,000	70,000	70,000	71,000
Production										
Cars	526,041	505,168	465,164	425,222	483,490	524,003	450,636	368,482	537,722	453,448
Commercial	92,170	85,317	113,623	93,860	108,986	134,792	141,517	121,260	143,519	137,209
Tractor	63,542	79,959	77,108	56,165	60,207	61,872	60,993	42,655	63,373	61,027
Total	681,753	670,444	655,895	575,247	652,683	720,667	653,146	532,397	744,614	651,684

sale in the United States to benefit from the quality image of German cars there.

LABOR RELATIONS IN THE AUTOMOBILE INDUSTRY

The automotive companies were the largest single group of employers in the British manufacturing industry. Total employment in the auto companies and in production of components for them among suppliers was estimated at 600,000, composing about 7 percent of the British industrial labor force (2 percent of total employment). Geographically about three-quarters of the jobs were concentrated in the Southeast and in the Midlands, with a slightly larger portion in the latter area. Among the major companies employment in 1973 was approximately as follows:

Leyland	180,000
Ford	70,000
Chrysler	40,000
Vauxhall (GM)	38,000
Others	15,000

Labor relations in the auto industry were chronically troublesome, and the number of disputes had been rising steadily through the 1960s and early 1970s. As the data in Exhibit 6 indicate, the number of days lost through work stoppages was far greater in the auto industry than in British manufacturing in general. In 1973, auto workers accounted for one-third of man hours lost through strikes in Britain. Many of the actual disputes were on a small scale, directly involving only a limited number of workers. However, they tended to be highly disruptive because of the interdependent character of work in the companies. Thus a prolonged stoppage in a small unit could shut down a whole factory or even a complete company.

This disparate pattern of work stoppages was in considerable part due to the pattern of union relations. There were a large number of unions in the industry, Ford workers, for example, being represented by 22 unions. The Transportation and General Workers' Union (TGWU) with 250,000 members was the largest single group and the dominant voice in the field. However, the National Union of Vehicle Builders with 85,000 members was quite strong and other groups, including the Amalgamated Union of Engineering Workers, were fairly large. Even one of the smaller unions was capable of closing down a whole operation at a given moment.

Another contributing factor was the disorganized pattern of negotiating relations, with manufacturers negotiating separately and at different times. Furthermore, there was a degree of competition between and within companies because of differentials in wage rates. As a general matter in Britain, the workers

Exhibit 6.   British Labor Disputes

	1960	1964	1968	1970	1972
Auto Industry					
No. of stoppages	129	165	233	336	216
No. of workers involved	186,300	150,000	402,500	271,400	246,600
Working days lost	515,000	429,000	898,000	1,105,000	1,363,000
Days lost per 1,000 employees	1,000-1,500	500-1,000	1,800	2,000	2,700
All Industries					
Days lost per 1,000 employees	100-250	50-100	200	470	1,100

Source: Rhys., p. 6.

in the Midlands, where labor was tight, were paid substantially more than those in other parts of the country. This sort of regional differential tended to shift over time periods. Thus in 1938 Ford workers at Dagenham near London received slightly more pay than those at Coventry in the Midlands, whereas by 1968 the best Dagenham pay was 56-1/2 p per hour compared to 74 p an hour in Coventry. Likewise there were substantial differences within the scope of a single company where its plants were divided regionally and particularly where these were the result of acquisitions as in the case of Chrysler. The existence of these varied differentials led to a continuing process of jockeying, with some groups seeking to reduce the differentials and others trying to preserve them.

A major factor contributing to work stoppages in the industry was the weak union discipline and responsibility characteristic of British labor relations. All unions in the country were affiliated with the central Trades Union Congress. However, the TUC was a weak federation—only in unusual cases like the 1974 Social Contract situation was it able to bring together a consensus on major controversial issues. The TUC played a relatively minor role in negotiations with companies, the nominal power in this respect lying with the separate unions, but even they had relatively limited discipline within their ranks as compared with the situation in many other countries. The grass-roots level, particularly the shop stewards, wielded a large degree of control over negotiations and the handling of problems. They were traditionally inclined to exercise a high degree of independence and often to act quickly without significant effort to coordinate their activities with the central union organization. Thus wildcart strikes were a major factor in British labor relations, composing some 90 percent of stoppages in recent years.

Contributing to the frequency of wildcat strikes was the lack of legal responsibility in labor relations. Unique among industrial countries was the tradition in Britain that an agreement between a company and a union was simply a statement of present understanding of acceptable terms of work rather than a contract with legal force. Thus a breach of the agreement was not subject to any legal constraint. Public dissatisfaction with the high cost in terms of productivity of a large number of wildcat strikes serving the interest of only very small groups of workers led to the passage of the Industrial Relations Act in 1971 which established the concept of the legal responsibility of workers under labor agreements as well as placing some restrictions on management, for example, in limiting the freedom with which workers could be discharged. The labor unions had strongly resisted the passage of the act and both vocally and in their actions indicated their intent to keep it from being implemented. The government, beset by other problems, was not inclined to enforce its terms rigidly. Therefore the pattern of wildcat strikes continued after the passage of the act, and in 1974 it was repealed. The new Trade Union and Labor Relations Act had no effective provisions against wildcat strikes nor did it contain the concept of legal responsibility under labor contracts.

Also fostering disputes in the auto industry was the presence of a number of militant union leaders. Most vocal but probably least effective were the political militants who sought to use the labor situation to advance their political philosophy. The larger number of militants who were more significant directed their efforts at pragmatic goals affecting workers and their own status. The multiplicity of unions and the preoccupation with differentials in wage levels had fostered a narrow view of the negotiating process. In the opinion of Rhys, the companies had tended to reinforce this pattern, "often management has given in to shopfloor militancy when refusing to concede the same point at the national level. This has undermined official procedure and shown that militancy pays. Buying-off trouble by paying more money solved little; at BMC it led to constant haggling and strife between worker and management, and at Ford it led to continuous attempts by management to suffocate the internal shop stewards' movement."[1]

While the Ford approach was in principle directed at reducing the shop-steward role, in fact Rhys felt that the lack of effective consultation at that level had not led to improvement. "In the factories of the US parent, matters such as seniority, manning scales and work loads are subject to mutual agreement with the stewards who then feel that they are dealing daily with members' problems. In the UK Ford's management regards such matters as their preserve, thereby creating an atmosphere where any issue could blow up into a trial of strength."[2]

Various aspects of auto-industry working conditions influenced the nature of labor relations, including the compensation structure, operating conditions and stability of employment. Traditionally factories in the Midland area had been paid on a piece-work basis. However, this system involved a variety of internal pay differentials, the protection of which became a complex and continuous issue among the workers. Consequently all firms were moving away from the system. Ford, with its operations largely outside the Midland area, had some on an hourly basis for many years, and other major firms, notably BMC, were moving rapidly toward an hourly pay system. Thus by the early 1970s regional and inter-firm differentials were substantially replacing in-plant differentials as the major source of grievances. (See Exhibit 2.)

The overall aspect of working conditions most notable in the auto industry was the monotony associated with continuous work in assembly plant operations. While there was some talk about job enrichment in the industry, little tangible effort in that direction was under way. There were no concrete efforts such as Volvo's program of group rotating tasks in Sweden. The chief concrete questions concerned the character of the assembly line operations and differences among companies as related to wages, profits and work psychology. In 1968 Ford had an investment of £5,285 in fixed assets per worker compared

---

1. D.G. Rhys, "Employment, Efficiency and Labor Relations in the British Motor Industry." *Industrial Relations Journal*, Summer 1974, p. 14.

2. *Ibid.*, p. 15.

with £2,217 at Leyland. The Ford output was 11.7 vehicles worth £8,000 per worker compared with 5.6 vehicles worth £5,180 at Leyland. Likewise Ford consistently showed the highest profits per man. These differences led to substantial debate as to whether Ford's apparent substitution of capital for labor was a basis for higher or lower wages for workers.

A further element in the situation was the speed of the assembly lines. British speeds were relatively slow compared with those in the United States. For example, a General Motors plant in Ohio turned out 101 cars per hour compared with rates around 50 to 52 cars per hour in Britain. However, in some plants the rate of the assembly track had been a source of contention, particularly where compensation was on an hourly rather than on a piece rate system with bonuses tied to the rate of the track. Thus Rhys observed, "The Ford track had led to tremendous animosity. Perhaps Ford's problem was one of attempting to attain BMC output figures on a Vauxhall wage structure."[3]

The employment stability question related both to the history of employment and the general pattern of manning in the British firms. The life style of the auto workers in England was geared to continuance of a steady flow of earnings at their established rate. They were therefore highly sensitive to inflation or other circumstances which threatened their real incomes and inclined to strike quickly to support their maintenance. As Rhys observes, there was also a history of insecurity which underlay their psychology. "Dagenham, for instance, grew out of misery in that much of the original labor force fled from unemployment and poverty in the depressed areas in the 1930s. Any threat, real or imaginary to a person's job can therefore lead to instant and massive strike action."[4]

The manning system differed significantly from that common in the United States. In the latter, companies geared their manning to minimum yearly production levels. Fluctuations were then covered by use of overtime or discharge of workers. In the United Kingdom, the manning was geared to maximum capacity and drops in demand were covered by reducing the work hours but retaining most of the total labor force. This system put a heavy strain on workers whose life styles were geared to pay at a full week's work time. There had been some efforts to introduce the US system, particularly at Leyland. However, this had required reduction in the work force which had a severe impact on morale, and productivity slumped because of restrictive practices and strikes caused by uncertainty.

A final factor in the labor relations situation was the locus of decision-making authority within the firms. In general, it appeared that where the authority was closer to the working level, labor relations were more satisfactory. For the multinational firms, there was a further problem of the role of the parent headquarters. From time to time union leaders in these firms expressed

---

3. *Ibid.*, p. 11.
4. *Ibid.*, p. 2.

dissatisfaction because they felt the local national executives had insufficient authority to deal with them. In general the managements stated that their British managements had essentially full authority. For example, the roles were defined as follows by Ford:

> Ford-US has several unwritten policies regarding collective labor negotiations at foreign subsidiaries. First, no corporate staff personnel attended these negotiations. This would completely undermine the authority of local management. Second, management positions on bargaining issues were not uniformly defined by Dearborn and applied on a worldwide basis. Third, the US line management and the overseas liaison manager are advised when a strike or strike threat develops over a bargaining impasse. Fourth, US labor relations staff approval is required when a subsidiary negotiates major changes in its compensation system or funded benefit programs. Fifth, the US staff will make itself available for consultations on any bargaining issue on which foreign management may request assistance. Sixth, Ford Motor Company expects that subsidiary management will conduct labor relations negotiations in such a manner that positions it takes on certain issues are not prejudicial to Ford management in other parts of the world—i.e., that bargaining positions are defensible in a rational management sense and are related to specific regional or industrial patterns covering conditions of employment. Thus, should a union in one country cite some conditions at a Ford subsidiary in another country in support of a bargaining demand, the Ford management concerned will have a reasonable basis to refute the propriety of the comparison between it and the other subsidiary. Seventh, Ford-US line management and the overseas liaison manager are advised on critical tactics developed by subsidiary personnel during collective negotiations. Two reasons were stated for this practice: (1) US corporate management should be advised of all significant events prior to their announcement to the public, and (2) corporate management should be allowed to comment on such tactics prior to their use.[5]

Given the existence of the parent-subsidiary ties and the suspicions in labor management relations, however, the continuing doubts on this count were inevitable.

A major change in the whole pattern of decision making started to emerge in 1975 with the adoption of industrial democracy schemes in Chrysler and Leyland. Chrysler took the initiative in May, offering its workers two seats on its thirteen-man board of directors and participation in joint committes at other management levels along with a profit-sharing scheme. In return the company required of the unions formation of a single joint bargaining committee with which it could negotiate a single contract (as did Ford) to replace the 54 contracts with individual unions it then had and acceptance of binding

5. Duane Kujawa, *International Labor Relations Management*. New York: Praeger, 1971, pp. 111-112.

arbitration by a third party on certain types of grievances. The company further offered a £50 lump sum per worker if the unions agreed in principal to this package by July 1, and another £50 if a final agreement was reached by the end of the year. At the time of the offer Chrysler was suffering from a prolonged strike in one engine plant, and many people felt that unless a satisfactory system to solve labor troubles was found, the company would shut down its British operations which had been losing money for years. The immediate reaction of the unions to the proposal was unreceptive as the shop stewards felt they would lose much bargaining power if national negotiations were introduced. There were also questions of the role of the unions in selecting representatives and of how the latter would be paid. However, the unions agreed to negotiate on these matters, thus meeting the terms for the first £50 payment.

Subsequently negotiations at Leyland led to agreement on 50 percent worker representation in a three-tier system of management committees concerned with the full range of decisions including production methods, car models, marketing and investment but not wages or working conditions which the unions insisted be left to traditional negotiation. The chief contention in the negotiations was over the manner of selection of worker representatives, with management favoring individual election by secret ballot of all workers while the stewards wished to do the selecting themselves. The latter view ultimately prevailed with agreement in October that shop stewards decide who would sit on the lowest tier committees, the latter in turn to designate members for the highest tiers from their own membership.

RECENT INDUSTRIAL RELATIONS AT FORD

Ford carried on its formal negotiations with labor through a National Joint Negotiating Committee (NJNC) representing fifteen unions. The national automotive secretary of the TGWU, Ford's biggest union, was normally chairman of this committee. The company had experienced a long history of strained relations in its negotiations and ongoing labor management. The major events in the recent history are described briefly here. The historical progression of the wage settlements is shown in Exhibit 7. Cost of living and earnings data are given in Exhibit 8.

In 1969 when its regular contract came up for renegotiation, Ford decided to make a significant effort to reduce the number of wildcat strikes. Sporadic stoppages by small groups of workers were particularly damaging to productivity in automotive operations because of the high degree of interdependence in assembly line plants. As it did not appear practical to impose any workable penalty system, management decided to offer an incentive to workers, namely to guarantee full pay for workers who had not participated in wildcat strikes over the previous six months.

After some negotiations the leaders of the majority of the unions accepted

Exhibit 7.   Ford Base Wage Rates

Effective	Grades				
	I		*II*		*III*

	(Expressed in shillings and pence per hour)				
January 1965[a]	6/4½		8/1		8/9
July 1965[b]					8/11½
December 1965	7/3½		8/5		9/3½

	A	*B*	*C*	*D*	*E*
July 1967[c]	7/6½	8/9½	9/3½	9/9½	10/9½
March 1969	8/3½	9/6½	10/0½	10/8	11/8
	(Expressed in pounds and new pence per hour)				
March 1970[d]	0.515	0.58	0.60	0.635	0.685
March 1971[e]	0.605	0.67	0.695	0.725	0.775
December 1971	0.655	0.72	0.745	0.775	0.825
August 1972	0.705	0.77	0.795	0.825	0.875
April 1973	0.76	0.825	0.85	0.88	0.93
March 1974[f]	0.825	0.89	0.915	0.945	0.995
July 1974[g]	0.885	0.95	0.975	1.005	1.055
October 1974[h]	1.158	1.245	1.281	1.322	1.388
Number of workers in grade, October 1974	890	25,200	16,200	2,730	6,630

[a]Base hourly rate for adult males; excludes merit pay and conditions allowances.

[b]Adjustment for skilled tradesmen only.

[c]Revised wage structure; excludes new service increments; merit pay and conditions allowances discontinued.

[d]Decimal currency.

[e]Applicable to all adults (including females).

[f]Excludes service increments and new cost-of-living allowance.

[g]Service increments integrated into base rates.

[h]Cost-of-living allowance integrated into base rates.

Exhibit 8. British Price and Wage Data

	Retail Price Index (Jan. 1962 = 100)	Average Weekly Earnings of Workers in Vehicle Industry, Men 21 and Over (pounds)
1962	101.6	
1963	103.6	
1964	107.0	
1965	112.1	
1966	116.5	21.97
1967	119.4	24.42
1968	125.0	26.45
1969	131.8	28.67
1970	140.8	32.43
1971	154.2	35.21
1972	164.3	41.63
1973	179.4	45.74
1974	208.2	
1975	258.5	

the company's proposal and signed an agreement to that effect. Subsequently, however, when the agreement was disseminated substantial groups of workers opposed it, and the union leadership felt obligated to reject it. Thereupon Ford took the matter to court, arguing that the leadership had entered into a contract. The court refused to hear the case, ruling along traditional British lines that a labor agreement was not a legal contract.

In 1971 Ford's basic labor agreement again came up for overall negotiation. The union demanded wage increases of about 140 percent. Ford countered by offering increases of roughly 20 percent. The British government expressed the opinion that the union demands were excessive, that they would lead to undue inflation and adverse effects on exports. At the same time Chrysler had accepted substantially larger increases than Ford offered (about 40 percent). Chrysler was a smaller and weaker operation, and it did not feel it could withstand a long strike. Ford, on the other hand, felt that it had the long-term strength to stand up to the unions and that its long-term interests in keeping British costs low justified that stance. It was at this point that Henry Ford made his statement after seeing the Prime Minister. Against this background a strike continued for nine weeks, during which the company lost 150,000 vehicles or about £77 million of production. A small amount of output was made up by shifting sourcing to Germany, but the overall impact on the company was severe, including a loss of £17.0 million for the year.

In December 1972 the Ford unions presented demands in anticipation of the renegotiation of their agrement in early 1973. They asked for "substantial" wage increase (no specific figure was proposed but in the supporting statements 20 percent was mentioned as illustrative of the type of raise expected), and improvements in hours, holidays, lay-off pay and pensions. The union supported this demand with an extensive analytical document, the main burden of the document being that the company's sales and profits were very good while the real earnings of workers had declined as a result of inflation. The unions observed that Ford had increased its prices by about 20 percent over a period of 20 months. It was noted that in the two-year period from April 1970 to April 1972 the retail price index had increased 19.6 percent and the wages of workers had not risen comparably so the true take-home pay had dropped by 8.5 percent. At the same time the company had been making favorable profits. In further support unfavorable comparisons with earnings of workers in other firms and in other countries were cited.[6]

> Thus if we take the most recent major settlement, at Longbridge (Leyland), the pay rate is £46 for direct workers (or 115 p per hour) rising to £48 in November 1973. . . . The slightly earlier Chrysler Ryton agreement (dating from July 1972) gave the direct production worker £44.77. . . . The "indirect" workers' pay rates have clustered around £37 to £38 for semi-skilled grades. . . . If we take the present Ford pay rates, these represent *even after four years* for the same basic 40 hours no more than £33.20 for Grade B and £34.20 for Grade C.
>
> Thirdly, there can be no doubt that Ford workers are not lagging behind the general standards of productivity of the British motor firms. We were able to show in our last negotiations that *Value Added per worker* in Ford's was exceptionally far ahead of the available figures for the other major British companies; so was the cruder figure of *sales per employee*. We have already referred to our own estimates of the rapid increase in *sales per employee* to be expected in 1972 and 1973 for Ford's. If Ford wants to disagree materially with our estimate that *sales per employee* may be around £12,500 in 1973—or about 40 per cent higher than in 1970—we would be interested to hear their reasons. . . . Fourthly, recent detailed international studies have shown that *total wage costs per working hour* for the British motor industry are well below those of the other major European producers. The estimates we wish to use are those made by the Swedish Employers' Confederation and published under the title *Direct and Total Wage Costs for Workers*.

Great Britain	100 (1970)
USA	242
Whole EEC	120
Belgium	116
W. Germany	135

6. *The Ford Claim*, 1973, The Ford National Joint Negotiating Committee Trade Union Side, Dec. 14, 1972, pp. 17-19.

Italy	113
France	99
Sweden	153

In January the company issued its response to the union demand. It observed that price increases were essentially based on increases in costs. In particular materials purchased in this period had risen 25 percent in price and wages and salaries by 28 percent. It noted that if the company were to meet all of the union demands it would cost £80 million per year, three and one-half times the average Ford profit in the reasonably favorable years 1966-1970. The company also questioned the basis upon which wage comparisons in relation to inflation had been computed. Because of the timing of wage increases, it was possible to show what amounted to a wage increase over two years in comparison with a cost of living rise over two years and 11 months. By taking a three-year period from February 1970 to February 1973, the company was able to show that the cost of living had increased only 26 percent while wages increased 58 percent. The company also questioned the union data on increase in productivity, presenting the data in Exhibit 9, showing the high investment provided by Ford to indicate that the share of the rise in productivity due to the workers was limited. In response to the international comparison cited by the union, the company noted that the data were for wage costs not total labor costs, e.g., did not include social security. But it mainly relied upon a quotation from the National Institute Economic Review commenting on the Swedish data:

Exhibit 9. Assets and Value Added per Employee in European Auto Companies

Company	Cost Value of Assets per Employee £			Net Value Added per Employee £		
	1969	*1970*	*1971*	*1969*	*1970*	*1971*
BLMH	2,454	2,626	2,786	1,756	1,721	2,141
Chrysler-Rootes	3,186	3,338	3,304	1,628	1,452	2,048
General Mtrs.-Vauxhall	5,679	5,980	6,379	1,879	1,929	2,467
Ford	5,766	6,269	6,493	2,758	2,782	2,167
Renault	3,160	3,811	4,467	2,265	2,291	2,631
Volvo	5,027	5,244	6,148	3,574	3,429	3,731
Volkswagen	6,197	6,378	7,180	3,419	3,239	3,487
Fiat	5,628	5,823	6,548	2,556	2,986	3,184

Note: Comparisons with non-British companies are expressed at 12 July 1972 exchange rates.

Figures published recently in Sweden illustrate the implications of Britain's failure to improve productivity in the 1960s as quickly as continental Western Europe. Though wage costs per unit of output have risen faster in Britain than in other major industrial countries, employers' total payments per hour of work are now lower here than in almost any industrial country except Japan. The disparity in rates of increase in wages has been far exceeded by the disparity in rates of increase of productivity. . . . While British productivity continues to lag by international standards, so too, in all probability, will British real wages. Between 1960 and 1970 estimated output per man-hour in manufacturing industry increased in the UK by rather under 50 per cent. . . . The corresponding rise in West Germany was about 70 percent, in France 80 percent, in the Netherlands and Italy around 100 percent, while in Japan it was close to 170 percent. It seems probable that British exports, and British real earnings too, will continue to lag behind those of continental European countries unless productivity relationships can be changed for the better.

In response to the unions' demands, the company offered in early February the following: an increase of £2.40 per week, which was the maximum permitted under the Stage II program (1 pound + 4 percent increase), and some changes on other provisions included in the union proposals.

Ford's offer was rejected by the unions. In a few plants there were short walkouts in protest. By mid-February several hundred Ford shop stewards backed an unofficial call for an all-out strike of all Ford workers. However, the main body of workers showed little inclination to support a strike. For the most part, they expressed their opposition by refusing to do overtime work and "working to the rules." These actions at their height reduced output by about one-third. Negotiations continued into the spring and finally in May the workers voted to accept essentially the company's initial offer.

The 1973 agreement was for one year retroactive to the February termination of the prior contract. Thus a new contract was required in February 1974. The union again made strong demands to which the company responded with the maximum offer permitted under the Stage III guidelines. These provided for a 7 percent immediate wage rise (£2.80 per week) with a threshold provision to give cost of living pay increases. The latter stated that after the retail price index had risen 7 percent above the base figure, 189.4, (January 1962 equals 100), incremental payments of 1 p per hour should be made for each subsequent 1 percent rise in the r.p.i. (e.g., 200.2, 202.1, etc.). In conformance with the Stage III guidelines the threshold agreement was limited to twelve months starting October 1973. The company's wage proposal was accepted with only limited opposition, apparently because of the desire of the unions to facilitate the election of the Labor government.

In the months that followed, as the retail price index rose steadily, the 7 percent threshold was passed and the workers received eight increments to payment under the threshold provision (by September, £3.20 per week). Ford workers were becoming dissatisfied with the extent of increases they had received, however, and concerned that no more increments would be possible in the five months after the termination of the threshold provisions and before a new contract could be negotiated in February 1975.

Exhibit 10 shows the settlements at various other companies in the industry. Those at Chrysler and other plants were perceived by the Ford workers to be more favorable than their own. This dissatisfaction led to growing unrest. In early September, 1,800 press shop workers at Dagenham and Halewood walked out in support of requests for increases amounting to £4 and £5 a week respectively. These were claims related to their specific work, including shift allowances and restoration of differentials in other work groups. Technically, therefore, they were independent of the general Ford agreement. However, they were recognized as symptomatic of the general mood of Ford workers. The company at first refused to enter into general negotiations, relying basically on the government guidelines to support its position, supplemented after September 5 by the TUC endorsement of the Social Contract. Because of the disruption of operations by the press shop strikes, the company closed down much of its operations on September 10, indicating that it would not budge from its position. Some 28,000 workers were idled by this process, and by September 26 another 12,000 were threatened with layoffs because of the stoppages in production.

On September 23, the company offered to reopen negotiations on the general pay agreement if the press workers returned to work. At that time the company was losing production at the rate of about 2,000 vehicles a day or £2.5 million in sales at retail prices at a time when automobile demand was high. It was therefore anxious to avoid an extended work stoppage. The company's decision had a mixed reception in Britain. Some felt that it was in violation of the spirit of the Social Contract and came at a most inopportune time in view of the recent almost universal labor support for the contract and the upcoming October 10 national election. Some leading labor spokesmen, however, felt that because of the timing of Ford's contract and the termination of its threshold provisions, the spirit of the Social Contract had not been violated.

The press workers were not immediately satisfied with this offer by the company because they felt their immediate demands should not be related to general contract reopening and might not be corrected in its negotiation. They therefore stayed out and the company refused to enter into general negotiations as long as they continued their strike. By this time some Ford plants in Belgium and Germany had suspended most of their production for lack of parts from Halewood. Finally, on October 3 the workers agreed to suspend their strike, full operations were resumed and general negotiations commenced.

At the commencement of negotiations Ford proposed a general wage increase, integration of the weekly cost of living allowance into the hourly base

Exhibit 10. Major British Motor Industry Labor Settlements in 1974

Company	Stage III Deal		Post-Stage II Deal	Main Production Rate 40 Hours	Cost of Living Supplements
Ford	£2.60	(March)	–	£38.00	£2.80
Vauxhall	£2.60	(April)	–	£38.50	£2.80
Chrysler Coventry	£3.23	(July)	£4.36 including £1.20 in lieu of threshold (Aug.)	£54.77	
Chrysler Linwood	£3.19	(July)	£5.86 including £1.20 in lieu of threshold (Aug.)	£49.18	
Austin-Morris Longbridge	£3	(May)	£4.80 from Nov. includes £1.80 in lieu of threshold	£55.80	
Austin-Morris Cowley	£3.20	(Feb.)	Offered £1.80 in lieu of threshold	£49.40	Extra £1.80 COL on offer
Jaguar	£4	(April)	Offered £1.80 in lieu of threshold	£53	Extra £1.80 COL on offer

wages, liberalized premiums for three-shift operations from 23 percent to 25 percent and an improved skill trades wage differential. The general wage increase would amount to 20 percent for the typical semi-skilled employee, so with the cost of living allowances already given, total base wages would increase about 28 percent. The proposed contract would be for a two-year period with an additional 6 percent wage increase to be given after one year and another 6 percent after 18 months. Ford also proposed that, if the r.p.i. rose 36 percent above the September 1974 level, wage rates would then increase 1 percent for each 1 percent increase in the index.

In return the management sought three concessions by the unions. The first was withdrawal of the union's March 1974 statement that they would be unwilling to cooperate in efficiency improvements. The union at the time had taken the position that the agreement reached in March 1974 was subject to government controls and that they therefore were unwilling to help management in seeking improvements for its benefit. Second, the management repeated a longstanding request for a utility classification. The unions had strongly resisted the request in the past as they regarded a utility man as an agent for the foreman who would simply double the supervisory pressure on employees. Third, Ford requested that the union collaborate with them in seeking permission from the government to employ women on shift work, which the unions had previously declined because of union resolutions against such employment for women.

The union proposed that the agreement be for eighteen months with the various wage increases proposed to be achieved within that time period. Negotiations were complicated by a renewal of the walkout of the press workers at Dagenham who were dissatisfied with the progress of their particular claim. However, when Ford increased its offer for the premium for five-day, three-shift operations to 27.5 percent, the workers returned, though the union was still seeking a 33 percent premium.

On October 19 agreement was reached with the negotiators which was subsequently ratified by the great majority of the workers, only small groups rejecting it because it did not satisfy particular objectives. The general wage agreement was slightly higher than the company's original offer with the initial average step of 22 percent and the two subsequent steps of 8 percent each. The company's cost-of-living proposal was accepted. The union would not concede the company request with respect to women shift-work or the utility classification. They were willing to withdraw their March 1974 statement about non-cooperation in efficiency improvements, but they were not willing to make a positive statement of cooperation in this direction. They were, however, willing to affirm clauses agreed to in earlier years which appeared in the general employment agreement accepting certain broadly stated principles for achieving efficiency in operations and the need for overtime work as a part of efficient planning.

The £6 pay-raise ceiling set by the government in 1975 raised questions about the 1974 Ford agreement. The government indicated its intent to apply the limit vigorously by asking Leyland to renegotiate a pay rise of £6.50 per week which had been negotiated prior to the £6 ceiling but due to go into effect on September 15. Shop stewards, chiefly from the Amalgamated Union of Engineering Workers, initially threatened to strike to enforce the agreement. However, they subsequently decided to postpone action until the national AUEW leadership took a clear position. While the AUEW had opposed the £6 limit at the TUC annual meeting, it was possible that it might accede to the TUC position as had some other dissident union groups.

GENERAL REFERENCES

Duane Kujawa, *International Labor Relations Management in the Automotive Industry. A Comparative Study of Chrysler, Ford and General Motors.* New York: Praeger, 1971.

D.G. Rhys, "Employment, Efficiency and Labor Relations in the British Motor Industry." *Industrial Relations Journal*, Summer 1974, pp. 4-26.

John Gennard, *Multinational Corporations and British Labor.* Washington, D.C.: British-North American Committee, 1972.

Textile Machinery Company
de Mexico, S.A.

LABOR RELATIONS PROBLEM IN MEXICO

Frank Murphy, general manager of the Textile Machinery Company de Mexico, S.A., reacted with surprise and distress when he received a written communication informing him that a majority of his 44 employees had taken steps to legalize the formation of a labor union in accordance with Mexican Labor Law, and that the undersigned requested an appointment in order to hand him their demands for the terms of a collective labor contract. The letter was signed by Roberto Carranza, chief accountant, and Juan Sanchez, a mechanic, as secretary and shop delegate, respectively.

The Textile Machinery Company de Mexico, S.A. (usually designated TMC), had been established in Mexico City 30 years before as a subsidiary of a US company which had been doing business in Latin America for many years. The parent company manufactured a line of highly specialized machinery used in certain textile processes; the greater part of this machinery was leased to textile mills and serviced by TMC. The company also sold a few types of textile machinery and a limited line of supplies used in the textile industry. The parent company carried on a world-wide export trade, largely through semi-autonomous subsidiary companies.

Mr. Murphy had come with his parents to Mexico at an early age and spoke Spanish fluently. He had attended college in the USA, graduating with the degree of B.S. in Business Administration. Within a few months after graduation he joined TMC's international division and had a variety of assignments in the

The real company name and product line in this case are disguised. The case was written by Donald B. Campbell, Executive Director, Instituto Mexicano de Administracion de Negocios, Mexico, D.F. Copyright (©) by IMAN, A.C. Reproduced by permission.

home office and in South America. After a period of US military service he was reemployed by TMC and came to Mexico as assistant to Mr. Campbell, the general manager, who had been in charge of TMC de Mexico for several decades. Three years later Mr. Campbell had retired and Mr. Murphy stepped into his position. At that time the company employed around 40 men.

Official home office policy was "to delegate as much responsibility as possible to local management." Mr. Murphy described this relationship by saying that the home office exercised a tight control on policies but that local management was fairly autonomous within the framework of policies and procedures established by the home office.

To Mr. Murphy, the news of the movement to unionize his employees and demand a collective labor contract came as a complete surprise. He knew that the wages paid by his company were higher than the average paid in Mexico City for similar types of work, and he was not aware of any acute outstanding grievances. He liked to think of TMC de Mexico as a big family, with certain traditions of square dealings with its workers which he was honor-bound to respect. In order to form some idea of what kinds of demands his employees might present to him and to reach a decision as to what action he might take, he mentally reviewed the events of the past several years, as well as what he knew of the personal histories of some of his employees who were, or might be, key factors in the situation as he understood it.

For some years, the company had enjoyed a slow but stable growth, and the activities of most of his staff had revolved around the servicing of the rather antiquated machinery already installed. A year after Mr. Murphy became general manager, the home office announced that plans had been approved to introduce more modern equipment and to liberalize the terms under which the company would lease its machinery. The introduction of the new lease terms in Mexico caused a marked increase in business. Servicemen installed many new machines, and numerous old machines which had been out of service were scheduled for rebuilding and repairs. As the number of leases outside Mexico City increased, it became necessary for the TMC roadmen to perform more services away from home; this raised new problems as to travel and overtime pay.

Mr. Murphy was obligated to spend much of his time outside of Mexico City and began to delegate increased authority to his personnel manager, Fortunato Morfin, and to Henry Thompson, a young American trainee. In addition to his title of personnel manager (*jefe de personal*), Mr. Morfin was the company's cashier and office manager. He had been with TMC for nearly 30 years and enjoyed Mr. Murphy's complete confidence. In practice, Mr. Morfin was second in command, although the title of assistant manager was held by Mr. Thompson. In addition, Mr. Morfin was a member of the Board of Directors.

"Morfin was pretty much the fellow you'd go to as the office manager," Mr. Murphy stated. "Although his understanding of jobs and operations may not have been complete, he was, in what I would consider the chain of command, the chief of staff to the manager if you discounted Thompson. We tried to go through Morfin, in other words, as regards personnel. He seemed to be very proud of his position of intimate contact with the management—perhaps that was one of his failings—he might have leaned over backwards against the employees in order to keep after them or get compliance with a full day's work.

"Basically, I would also say, he might have aspired to be assistant manager if it had been in line with our policy to rely on local people for top management—that simply is a policy that we don't have. It was just that he was the closest most reliable right arm that one had; he probably abused this, and it came out in his treatment of the employees."

Mr. Morfin maintained records on absenteeism and tardiness and had considerable influence on decisions to hire or fire. According to Mexican labor law, an employee fired without just cause (as defined by the law) was entitled either to reinstatement or a cash settlement of three months' pay plus 20 days' salary for each year of service with the company. The same rule governed the amount of severance pay upon retirement. On several occasions employees who had been caught stealing or committing other offenses for which firing was sanctioned by the labor law had been induced by Mr. Morfin to "resign" without severance pay. (It was extremely difficult to prove to the satisfaction of the Federal Arbitration Commission that an offense punishable by discharge without severance pay had been committed, and most companies, native and foreign, found ways of protecting their interest against disloyal employees without incurring the expense and risk of an appeal to federal arbitration.)

Henry Thompson was 26 years old, married with no children. The home office had assigned him to Mexico as a trainee two years previously, very soon after his discharge from the United States Armed Forces. He had an M.B.A. from a leading business school, but he had had no previous business experience. In order to facilitate obtaining his working papers from the Mexican Immigration Department, Mr. Murphy had assigned him the title of assistant manager, but in reality his functions were closer to those of a special assistant to the manager, working on whatever assignments would be most conducive to developing his managerial capacity or most helpful to Mr. Murphy. Most of his experience in Mexico had been in sales and general supervision of the mechanical and service activities. At the time of his arrival in Mexico he had spoken little Spanish, but he had studied and practiced diligently and now had a fair command of the language. His wife, however, spoke but little Spanish, and Mr. Murphy was under the impression that she was unhappy in Mexico. Mr. Murphy considered that Thompson was trying hard to do a good job, but he felt that he still had a great deal to learn about handling Mexican workers.

At that time Thompson was spending most of his time working closely with the men in charge of mechanical and repair operations, including the warehouse foreman, Mr. Gallastegui; Mr. Prado, director of services; and Ernest Paine, a young American mechanic.

Mr. Prado, 63 years old, had worked in Mexico under the supervision of the home office even before the Mexican branch had been organized as a separate company; he had completed over 40 years of service. He was a first-rate mechanic. Despite his age he had plenty of health and stamina. He not only understood the machinery thoroughly, but he also knew a great deal about the special branch of the textile industry which TMC de Mexico serviced.

Mr. Prado's title, director of service, was a new one which, at Mr. Thompson's suggestion, had been conferred upon him only a few months previously with a view to separating the shop function, which involved the repair and rebuilding of machinery on the TMC premises, from the service function, which had to do with the upkeep and repair of TMC machines installed in textile factories. Mr. Prado had formerly acted as shop foreman (*jefe de taller*), an activity which included both the above mentioned functions. In fact Mr. Murphy remembered having seen in old company records several references to a "Management Committee" (*Consejo de Administracion*), of which Mr. Prado had been a member. In those days the company did not have more than six or eight customers, and there was little departmentalization of functions.

Concurrently with the increased workload which followed the new leasing policy, Mr. Prado's department had fallen far behind schedule. Not only were there new machines to be installed and serviced, but there were also many old machines—which in some cases had been out of service for years—which had to be cleaned, rebuilt and repainted.

There were two means of coping with the heavier workload: hiring new mechanics and roadmen and obtaining more efficient work from those already employed. Both methods were tried, but many months of training were required to produce a good mechanic; and as for obtaining higher productivity through more efficient methods, Mr. Prado seemed to have no concept of methods improvement, organization or control. He was well-liked by most of the mechanics and roadmen, who had become used to his easy-going ways and who in turn were loath to change their established methods and existing job responsibilities. Mr. Thompson had reported to Mr. Murphy that he estimated a three-year backlog of machines to be repaired unless the present rate of progress could be increased.

A year earlier Mr. Thompson told Mr. Murphy that he had discovered a competent American mechanic, Ernest Paine, working in a nearby garage. In addition to considerable experience as an automotive mechanic in the United States and Mexico, Paine had previously specialized in motors and compressors in a large petroleum company. Because of the fact that he objected on grounds of conscience to participating in war, there was a disagreement between him and the US Government regarding his military service; this accounted for his presence in Mexico. He was intelligent, quiet and modest in manner, and industrious. He was a high-school graduate. His Spanish was excellent.

Thompson and Murphy both became convinced that Paine would be a valuable addition to the work force and that he might in time be able to replace Mr. Prado, who was already eligible for full retirement benefits under Mexican labor law. They hired Paine at a modest salary, telling him that after a training period of from three to five years he could expect a considerable salary increase and rapid advancement. These three, Murphy, Thompson and Paine, were the only North Americans in TMC de Mexico at that time. Mr. Murphy asked Mr. Thompson to supervise Paine's training and see that he obtained a wide variety of experience both in the shop and on the road.

Paine was first assigned to the warehouse under the direct supervision of Mr. Gallastegui, the warehouse foreman. He took to his new job enthusiastically, and within a few weeks was able to install a new system for checking and storing parts earmarked for the rebuilding of machinery. During this period Paine also accompanied TMC servicemen to numerous factories and was able to learn something of that important part of the business. After Paine had completed about three months' experience in warehousing and servicing, Mr. Thompson arranged his transfer to the shop under Mr. Prado. There he went to work rebuilding machines, and within a short period he produced some excellent ideas for expediting and improving the quality of the work. After a few weeks he suggested to Mr. Thompson that a small work group be formed to specialize in cleaning and painting the reconstructed machinery, a phase of the work which was still far behind schedule. This was done, and Paine was put in charge. At the beginning he had two helpers; some weeks later a young man who had worked with him in the warehouse expressed a desire to work in the shop. Mr. Thompson approved that transfer and assigned him to Paine's work group. When the group completed its mission after six months its members were integrated into the regular shop activities. Mr. Thompson reported to Mr. Murphy that he was more than satisfied with Paine's progress.

Three weeks prior to the union announcement some further reorganization was made. The service and shop functions were separated. Mr. Prado was made service director, although he continued to be active in the shop as well where his intimate knowledge of all the TMC machines was still required. Thompson reported that Paine would be able gradually to take over more and more responsibility in the shop, but that he did not feel that the time was ripe to put him in charge. Some days after this change was made effective, Mr. Prado hinted to Mr. Murphy that he would like to retire. Murphy replied in a joking way that Prado was still a young man and had many years of active service ahead of him. Mr. Prado did not press the matter.

Although considerable progress had been made by this time in catching up on the backlog of repair work, Mr. Murphy considered that many problems remained to be solved. The service to clients was not as prompt as it should be in many cases, and there was an increasing number of complaints from factories because of work stoppages caused by machine breakdowns. Repairmen often lost tools, but instead of reporting the loss immediately, would "make do" with what tools were at hand. Some men would occasionally leave their tool kits at a factory upon completing a repair job; several hours of time might be lost the following morning, because the repairman would have to pick up his tools before being able to start an urgent repair job on the other side of town. There was one instance of an entire kit of tools (worth about 1,500 pesos) being lost when a factory burned down at night. Orders were issued in writing over Mr. Murphy's signature that all tool kits must be turned in at the shop each evening, but efforts made by Thompson and Prado to enforce this order met with little success, and considerable grumbling was heard from men who objected to the loss of their time involved in traveling downtown every afternoon in order to turn in their tool kits. Other orders designed to enforce stricter discipline also met with resistance on the part of mechanics and servicemen.

As he considered the case of his chief accountant, one of the cosigners of the letter which lay before him, Mr. Murphy experienced a strong feeling of indignation. Roberto Carranza had been with the company for over 20 years. He had first been assigned to the sales department, but his record there had not been impressive and he had been transferred to the accounting department. At first he had seemed to resent the transfer, but he displayed a marked ability for bookkeeping and accounting and within a very few years rose to the post of chief accountant. The increased volume of business following the liberalized leasing terms meant an increased workload in the accounting department, as well as throughout the rest of the organization. Mr. Carranza reported to Mr. Morfin, and the latter had stated to Mr. Murphy on several occasions that Carranza was falling behind in his work and that he was putting pressure on him to improve the functioning of his department. Mr. Morfin also stated that Carranza had twice requested an increase in salary, but that he had been told to get the work out on time and then ask for a raise. As chief accountant, Carranza, had access to a considerable amount of company data, including, of course, balance sheets and profit and loss statements which Mr. Murphy regarded as strictly confidential.

Juan Sanchez, who signed as shop delegate, had been hired as a green mechanic some two years previously. Mr. Murphy seemed to recall that he had been recommended by one of the older mechanics in the shop; he positively remembered that he had heard complaints about the quality of his work. The other mechanics referred to him as *"El Ranchero"* (The Farmer).

Gulf Oil Corporation

POLITICAL CONTRIBUTIONS TO THE
SOUTH KOREAN GOVERNMENT

Gulf Oil Corporation disclosed to the United States Senate Subcommittee on Multinational Corporations that it made political contributions in South Korea. The Senate Subcommittee questioned the Chairman of Gulf Oil Corporation and in the process highlighted a wide range of policy considerations faced by multinational corporations and the US Government on the behavior of US multinational corporations. The Senate Subcommittee is particularly concerned about the foreign policy implications for the US Government of political contributions and other payments by US multinationals to foreign governments. This case highlights the reasons and the manner in which Gulf Oil Corporation contributed $4 million to the Democratic Republican Party in South Korea.

OPENING STATEMENT OF SENATOR CHURCH

In the course of the Watergate Committee hearings and the investigation by the Special Prosecutor, it became apparent that major American corporations had made illegal political contributions in the United States. More recently, the Securities Exchange Commission has revealed that several multinational corporations had failed to report to their shareholders millions of dollars of offshore payments in violation of the Securities laws of the United States. The Gulf Oil

This case is based on hearings conducted on May 16, 1975, by the United States Senate Subcommittee on Multinational Corporations of the Committee on Foreign Relations. Washington, D.C.

Corporation, before us today, has admitted making $4.8 million in domestic political contributions and at least $4.3 million in overseas political payments.

The Securities and Exchange Commission is understandably concerned that the disclosure requirements of US laws are complied with. This subcommittee is concerned with the foreign policy consequences of these payments by US-based multinational corporations.

No one has put it more succinctly than Gunnar Myrdal in his brilliant book, *Asian Drama.* Describing what he calls the "soft state," Myrdal writes:

> Generally speaking, the habitual practice of bribery and dishonesty tends to pave the way for an authoritarian regime, whose disclosure of corrupt practices in the preceding government and whose punitive action against offenders provide a basis for its initial acceptance by the articulate strata of the populations. The Communists maintain that corruption is bred by capitalism, and with considerable justification they pride themselves on its eradication under a Communist regime.
>
> The elimination of corrupt practices has also been advanced as the main justification for military takeovers. Should the new regime be unsuccessful in its attempt to eradicate corruption, its failure will prepare the ground for a new putsch of some sort. Thus, it is obvious that the extent of corruption has a direct bearing on the stability of governments.

It follows that, if a substantial number of multinational corporations bribe or attempt to gain influence through huge campaign contributions or agent's fees which find their way into the hands of foreign government officials, these very corporations may, in the long run, be the losers. Eventually, indigenous forces of reform or revolution will turn on these companies and make them the targets of radical measures.

Furthermore, illicit corporate contributions, bribes and payoffs create unfair conditions for scrupulous competitors. Foreign officials looking for money are unconcerned about the quality of the product or service being offered. The company which slips the most under the table will get the most favored treatment.

Under such circumstances, a company which tries to maintain higher ethical standards finds itself up against the unfair competition of companies that resort to large-scale bribery. Ethical corporations will be squeezed out of many foreign markets and even the unethical firms will find their profits diminished.

Thus, we must know from our witnesses here today what were the circumstances which led them to make these payments. In what country were they made? Were they illegal in the country in which they were made? If the corporation was reluctant, did it bring the matter to the attention of the US Embassy? If not, why not? Does the United States have a foreign assistance program in the country in which the payment was made? Was the company's investment in the country guaranteed, in whole or in part, by our Government's

Overseas Private Investment Corporation? Was the US Embassy aware of such payments? If not, why not?

Finally, this subcommittee will consider what legislation, if any, is warranted. Much has been written about codes of conduct governing multinational corporations. Many of the issues—transfer prices, expropriation—are complex and controversial. But there should be no controversy about this issue: if the developing countries are sincere in their desire to define acceptable rules of conduct for multinational corporations, then they should be willing to agree that corporations that do business in their country should be free from extortion. The corporations, if they are serious about wanting the rules of the game defined, should be willing to agree that they will refrain from making questionable payments to obtain competitive advantages. And the administration, if it is genuinely concerned about this problem, ought to take the lead in seeking a consensus around these elementary propositions.

In short, we cannot close our eyes to this problem. It is no longer sufficient to simply sigh and say that is the way business is done. It is time to treat the issue for what it is: a serious foreign policy problem.

TESTIMONY OF B.R. DORSEY, CHAIRMAN OF THE BOARD, GULF OIL CORP., ACCOMPANIED BY FRANK L. SEAMANS, ATTORNEY AT LAW, AND MERLE E. MINKS, GENERAL COUNSEL, GULF OIL CORP.

In July of 1973, the then Special Watergate Prosecutor, Mr. Archibald Cox, called upon all companies which had made illegal contributions in connection with the 1972 US Presidential campaign to come forward in their own and the public's interest and to disclose such contributions. Just about the time of Mr. Cox's statement, I learned, for the first time, that our then Washington Vice-President had made certain contributions to the Committee to Re-Elect the President. I issued instructions that these be reported to the Special Prosecutor and that full cooperation be accorded to him. At the same time, I directed that such contributions be publicly disclosed.

On August 1, 1973 a special meeting of the board of directors of the company was convened to consider the contributions which had been made. At that meeting the board of directors directed the outside law firm of Eckert, Seamans, Cherin and Millott to investigate the facts surrounding those contributions and to report its findings to the board. As this investigation continued, it became apparent that more was involved than simply the contributions made to the 1972 Presidential campaign. As a result of the investigation, the board of directors of the company was subsequently advised that during the period of 1960 to July 1973, approximately $10.3 million of corporate funds had been used for various political contributions or related political purposes, of which approximately $5 million were used abroad.

I should like to note that my fellow directors at Gulf and I have been agonizing about this problem since the initial disclosure in 1973. In my more than 30 years with the company, I know of no issue or circumstance that has caused us more grief, concern and remorse than has the matter of these contributions. I can assure you we take this problem most seriously, and we share the deep concern of our shareholders and the public. Since the summer of 1973, our directors have sought a constructive solution to this problem which would redound to the best interests of the company, its shareholders and the country itself.

From the time of the initial disclosure in July of 1973 we have become involved in a number and variety of investigations. We have been, or are being, investigated by the Special Prosecutor's office, the Securities and Exchange Commission, the Internal Revenue Service, the Eckert, Seamans firm, a special review committee, and by this Senate committee. In addition, third party lawsuits have been filed and are currently pending.

. . .

I will address myself to the $4 million in political contributions. The recipient of those contributions was the Democratic Republican Party of the Republic of Korea.

Before I detail the circumstances and amounts of these remittances, there are certain observations which I feel must be made and placed upon this record and before the American people.

There is no universal ethical absolute.

In the course of your responsibilities as US Senators, most of you have traveled around the world. You know that mores, customs, standards, values, principles and attitudes vary all over the world. What is immoral to some, is perfectly correct to others. What is onerous to one culture, may be perfectly proper and decent to another. What is unacceptable in one society, may be the norm in another.

One truth is uniform. The United States neither exists nor grew to its position of strength by building a wall around its borders and isolating itself from the rest of the world. We depend upon other nations for raw materials and for markets. Both of these are essential to the employment, prosperity, progress and growth of our country. Numerous American companies operate in many foreign countries. We not only function in these countries through the sufferance of the respective leaderships, but we are in constant competition with other technological powers who seek these same resources and markets.

And we are sometimes subject—as we were in the case of the Republic of Korea—to political pressures which we cannot always successfully resist. These pressures were even more intense than those to which many American corporations were subjected in the traumatic and scarring 1972 American Presidental election.

From the vantage of hindsight, and sitting as I am in the witness chair, I seriously question whether my judgment as to these contributions was sound or correct. I felt at the time, and under the pressure applied that I had taken the right course in order to preserve our investment and our shareholders' interests. But irrespective of the propriety of my action, what is done is done. And there remains nothing that I can now do other than to report to you and to the American people exactly what was done and how and why it was done.

The responsibility is mine and I accept it. I regret that these decisions have brought pain to the distinguished board of directors with whom I am privileged to serve; embarrassment to the stockholders of my company for whom I am proud to work, and anguish to the many people whom we employ and with whom we do business all around the world. This is a sorrowful chapter in Gulf's long and otherwise productive and constructive history of achievement.

Let us return, now to the $4 million in political contributions which were made to the Democratic Republican Party of the Republic of Korea. That amount represented two separate political contributions, each in connection with a forthcoming national election. The first contribution was in 1966, in the amount of $1 million and the second, in 1970, in the amount of $3 million.

As you all know, following the Korean conflict, the Republic of Korea went through a period of economic and political strife. This struggle was still continuing when Gulf was asked to participate in the ownership of a substantial industrial facility in Korea, which represented the largest foreign private investment in that country.[1]

This came about with the encouragement of the US Government. Korea was given assistance through AID loans, to participate in joint ventures with Gulf, and our Government, through OPIC, provided insurance for our investments in Korea in order to further encourage our participation.

At the same time, the US Government had urged that Korea fully establish itself as a democratic society by holding national elections similar to the election process in this country. Faced with a multi-party political system, the Koreans either quickly recognized, or took advantage of the need to raise substantial funds in order to conduct national elections. The leaders of the governing political party in South Korea determined that this could be accomplished by exerting severe pressure for campaign contributions on foreign companies operating there.

It was this background that gave rise to the demand, in 1966, that the company make a substantial contribution to the campaign of the Democratic Republican Party, which was then and still is the ruling party in South Korea. Our investigation indicates that the demand was made by high party officials and was accompanied by pressure which left little to the imagination as to what would occur if the company would choose to turn its back on the request. At that time the company had already made a huge investment in Korea. We were

1. See Appendix A for details.

expanding and were faced with a myriad of problems which often confront American corporations in foreign countries. I carefully weighed the demand for a contribution in that light, and my decision to make the contribution of $1 million was based upon what I sincerely considered to be in the best interests of the company and its shareholders.

In connection with the 1971 national election, the pressure for a political contribution intensified considerably. Officials of the Democratic Republican Party insisted that the company contribute $10 million. This request was transmitted to the company's area manager in Korea by Mr. S.K. Kim, who was financial chairman of the Democratic Republican Party, as he had been in 1966. I was advised in Pittsburgh of the request. A short while thereafter I had occasion to be in Korea and witnessed, first hand, the pressure being exerted by officials of the Democratic Republican Party. At that time I had heated discussions with officials of the party and flatly rejected both the intensity of the pressure being applied, and the amount demanded. In response to my position, the $10 million request was subsequently changed to $3 million, to which I acquiesced, believing that the contribution would be in the best interest of the company.

Although each of the contributions came from company funds in the United States, the transfers were recorded as an advance to Bahamas Exploration Co. Ltd., where they reflected on the books and records of Bahamas Exploration Co., as an expense.

I would like to make it clear that insofar as I was concerned, both payments to the Democratic Republican Party of the Republic of Korea represented political contributions to that party. To my knowledge the company never asked for nor received anything in return for the contributions except, perhaps, the unfettered right to continue in business. I believed at the time that such contributions were both proper and legal under both American and Korean law. I have recently been advised that they were, in fact, in violation of a Korean statute.

In addition to the contributions which I have just described, there were several other transactions involving Korea which recently came to light and which the review committee is investigating. There is every indication that these transactions do not even remotely approach the magnitude of $4 million, and may ultimately be determined to be funds paid in connection with perfectly proper and lawful commercial transactions.

In addition, we recently became aware of a small amount of funds that was kept in a special account in Korea during the years 1972 through 1974. These funds represented amounts paid, under a common practice of banks in Korea, as additional interest for the deposits in these banks. Since the banks do not reflect these payments on their books, they require the recipients likewise not to do so. Rather than forgo the payments, the company personnel in Korea apparently maintained the funds in a special off-balance sheet, but fully documented the account. These funds were used, from time to time, for payment to off-duty police to provide needed security for the company's facilities, and for other purposes. This fund will be likewise the subject of investigation by the review committee.

. . .

Gentlemen, you have heard much about the Bahamas Exploration Co. I wish to emphasize that none of the members of the Gulf board had any knowledge that it was used to transmit political contributions and related expenses. The board first learned about it sometime after July 1973, and I will now tell you what that is about and how it worked.

Bahamas Exploration Co. was incorporated in 1944 and was organized to acquire exploration licenses in that area of the world. Although it was determined later that there was little expectation of finding crude oil in the Bahamas, the company continued to hold the exploration licenses.

Our investigation discloses that starting in 1960, Bahamas Exploration Co. was used—for bookkeeping and accounting purposes—to transfer funds for use as contributions, gifts, entertainment and other expenses in the United States. The funds were transmitted to a bank account established in the name of Bahamas Exploration in Nassau, Bahamas. The total amount of funds deposited from 1960 through December 31, 1972 was $5,201,798.96.

The funds transmitted to Bahamas Exploration were deposited in the bank account and entered as deferred charge which was written off as expenses during the current year. The transfers, which initially were in the form of intercompany advances, were treated as capital contributions to Bahamas Exploration by Gulf.

Mr. Chairman and Senators, the special review committee has undertaken to file with the Securities and Exchange Commission and the court, a full report and it will be made available immediately upon its completion. The report, we expect, will fill in the gaps and complete the inquiry. We ask that you bear with us until it is available.

You have our complete assurance that every effort is being made to prevent any recurrences of these activities. We are taking very stringent measures—all possible steps—to assure that this will never happen again. The harsh lessons we have learned are indelibly etched in our minds. They will fortify our determination and commitment. This is the ultimate control.

But you can help us, and many other multinational companies which are confronted with this problem, by enacting legislation which would outlaw any foreign contribution by an American company. Such a statute on our books would make it easier to resist the very intense pressures which are placed upon us from time to time. If we could cite our law which says that we just may not do it, we would be in a better position to resist these pressures and to refuse the requests.

. . .

Senator CHURCH. What I would like to know is, inasmuch as the US Government was then engaged in a very large aid program for the Government of Korea, and inasmuch as some of that aid money furnished Korea by the American Government was to be used in this project, there was a clear Government interest involved.

Furthermore, through OPIC the Government of the United States had undertaken to insure your investment against various hazards, including the hazard of expropriation.

That being the case, did you at any time while the conversations were underway with the Koreans involved, and before any money was paid over to the political party, advise the American Embassy of the Korea demand for money?

Mr. DORSEY. No, sir, I did not.

Senator CHURCH. Why did you not?

Mr. DORSEY. Well, I suppose it goes back to a sort of a lifetime habit of our lifetime experience of having received very little help from the State Department and the American Government in foreign endeavors and very often finding they had very little interest and would just as soon as not talk to us. . . . I suppose it was a lifetime habit or maybe I was basically ashamed of what was going on, I do not know.

Senator CHURCH. (Mr. Dorsey) you say:

The leaders of the governing political party in South Korea determined that this could be accomplished by exerting severe pressure for campaign contributions on foreign companies operating there.

To your knowledge, was such pressure exerted against other foreign companies besides Gulf?

Mr. DORSEY. No, not to my certain knowledge. The only reason I would have to think it might be is that the fundraiser for the party, who was the man with whom I dealt, made it clear to me and made it very clear to other Gulf people with whom he had talked before he talked to me, that this favor was being distributed equally among all investors and surely others would be, and, of course, as always in fundraising there is always a broad implication that the other chap has, whether it is true or not. The rules of the game are you do not ask but the strong implication was they had. These things are not quite that straightforward, they are always veiled.

Senator CHURCH. Yes. But would it be fair to say that, and would it be accurate to say that, in your exchanges with the Koreans involved you were left with the impression that other companies were also making contributions or also being approached for the purpose of soliciting contributions?

Mr. DORSEY. That is correct.

Senator CHURCH. (In) your statement you have testified as follows:

Although each of the contributions came from company funds in the United States, the transfers were recorded as an advance to Bahamas Exploration Company Limited, where they were reflected on the books and records of the Bahamas Exploration Company as an expense.

Now, the accounting purposes is really a way of saying that the funds were handled this way in order to conceal the actual use to which the money was put; is that not true?

Mr. DORSEY. I think that is an accurate statement, yes.

. . .

Senator CHURCH. Having had much experience in dealing with the problem you have described to this committee today, do you believe that had . . . a law been on the books you would have been in a greatly stronger position to resist the demands that were made upon you in Korea?

Mr. DORSEY. There is no doubt of that. No doubt of that.

Senator CHURCH. And do you think that the long-term interests of American-owned multinational corporations would be furthered and their acceptability in foreign lands would be strengthened if such a law were enacted?

Mr. DORSEY. Well, I certainly agree that the long-term interest of American companies that operate abroad, that their interest would be enhanced and their situation would be improved by such legislation. As to their acceptability in foreign countries, I would not have any comment on that. You do not really go into countries based on that; there are other factors that determine.

Senator CHURCH. Would you worry or do you think that the fact that other governments might not impose similar restrictions upon their multinational companies would constitute a serious disadvantage to American companies competitively should the law be changed as you suggested?

Mr. DORSEY. I would only speak for the multinational oil companies. I would doubt it because basically, the competition in worldwide oil has been among seven companies and five of which are US-based companies. And I think that that being so, five out of seven, that if they were all under the same constraints and basically, too, the same philosophical approach to the problem, that it would solve the problem. I do not think that two foreign oil companies, I mean non-US oil companies, would have any particular advantage over us, because there again are many, many things that are determining.

You see, you do not go into a country, at least we do not, and contrary to popular opinion, I doubt if many people do, on the basis of bribes and corruption in the first place. I think you go in because you are invited. I think you go in because there are opportunities for you there, that you go in most of all because you are needed. If you are not needed in the country there is no point in your being there, and you will not make any money anyway.

So you do not go into these situations to make political contributions or to have people request them or to have people request anything, but it sort of flows along as you get more deeply involved and as your investment gets greater you tend to run into these things.

Senator CHURCH. The truth is, is it not, that once the investment is made and a great deal of money is then at stake, the position of the company becomes more vulnerable to pressures of this kind?

Mr. DORSEY. Yes, of course. Our history in Korea would indicate that where we started out with an initial $25 million investment and one time had an investment of as much as, I think $350 million.

Senator CHURCH. And the demands went from $1 million contribution to $3 million and then $10 million, did it not?

Mr. DORSEY. That is true.

Senator CHURCH. The next round?

Mr. DORSEY. That is true.

Senator CHURCH. Senator Symington.

Senator SYMINGTON. Thank you, Mr. Chairman. . . . How would these millions upon millions of dollars (be spent) without your knowledge as president of the corporation?

Mr. DORSEY. I have been asked the question before and I can only say that it appears from the investigation, very thorough investigation that has been made, that in 1960, or maybe the year before, that an arrangement was made by the people that were running the company at that time, to where these funds could be made available for those political purposes, and the authorities were established and the mechanism was established, and it simply was like any other authority that gets established in a company. And there are thousands of authorities, if not hundreds of thousands. And this one kept right on going and everyone that was involved in it, quite apparently from the investigation that has been made since, was acting within his authority and within the authorities that had been given to him, and it simply went on until it was revealed in 1973.

Senator SYMINGTON. . . . In other words, as I understand, it was something set up and never divulged to you until you came in as president?

Mr. DORSEY. That is correct.

Senator SYMINGTON. How was it expressed on the balance sheet you would sign when you put out your earnings statement to your stockholders?

Mr. DORSEY. I presume it was, I do not know that it was, obviously not revealed.

Senator SYMINGTON. Did you put it under the heading of miscellaneous?

Mr. DORSEY. Miscellaneous expense.

Senator SYMINGTON. And there were no questions about what this miscellaneous expense was for?

Mr. DORSEY. Senator, this was a relatively small amount of money. During this period of time I think the company did some $60 or $70 billion worth of business in that fifteen-year period and $10 million is not really a very large amount of money, it does not stand out.

Senator SYMINGTON. . . . As I get it, about 80 percent of the money that you felt necessary to pay off the people in order to get a better corporate position went to Korea; is that about right?

Mr. DORSEY. $4 million out of $5 million.

Senator SYMINGTON. And yet you were doing business with, I think your statement says, 70 different countries?

Mr. DORSEY. Yes.

Senator SYMINGTON. You did not have to pay any money to other people in any amounts in other countries?

Mr. DORSEY. Well, I have revealed in my statement everything I know, everything the investigation has brought out, and I rather think it is basically a complete statement.

I would be more surprised than anyone else if there were any large amounts of money that have not been revealed, although I still say the investigation is ongoing.

Senator SYMINGTON. Well, everybody knows that Gulf is a great corporation and I was wondering what percentage of business did Gulf do with Korea as against its worldwide business?

Mr. DORSEY. In any one year, I would think that it would be basically during that period of time it would have been probably in the nature of $200 million a year out of a total of $6 or $7 billion, something of that magnitude.

Senator SYMINGTON. So you would be paying 80 percent of what you had to pay in holding down these political people for less than, $200 million out of $6 billion?

Mr. DORSEY. That is true.

Senator SYMINGTON. Three percent or something like that of your business it cost out of 80 percent of what you paid out in this fashion. Is that correct?

Mr. DORSEY. Yes, sir, I have not thought about it that way but it is quite correct.

. . .

Senator SYMINGTON. Did you ever appeal to the State Department or any other Government agency to suggest that perhaps they get a few more tanks or perhaps it was not ethical if we were giving them all of the taxpayers' money of the United States to help them defend themselves, or whatever the words would be, to put the bite on you to that extent?

Mr. DORSEY. Well, it is very difficult after these years to create the atmosphere that existed in Korea at that time.

Senator SYMINGTON. Have you ever talked to the State Department about it at all, until it was broken?

Mr. DORSEY. No.

Senator SYMINGTON. Never have?

Mr. DORSEY. No, sir.

Senator SYMINGTON. It was always a bribe situation with you and presumably the head of the Government of Korea, South Korea?

Mr. DORSEY. The head of the political party, not the government. I make that distinction because I was dealing with a man—

Senator SYMINGTON. Who was head of the political party at that time?

Mr. DORSEY. S.K. Kim.

Senator SYMINGTON. I have the greatest respect for South Korea, do not misunderstand me, but I cannot understand why, with the exception of South Vietnam or India or France or Great Britain we have given them aid, military and economic aid, more than any other country in the world except South Vietnam. I do not see why, unless there is something that has not come out, it was necessary for you to give them this additional under-the-table money to do business in that country. I just cannot figure it out.... What do you think this money went for?

Mr. DORSEY. Well, I can tell you exactly how it was put to me. It was put to me that here we are, a struggling young democracy, which is true, we have been encouraged by your country to emulate you—that may not be their words—and we are trying to have democratic processes. As you know, it takes money to run an election. That is the way they put it to me. As you know, we as a party have no real way of raising money as you do in your country and we are, therefore, appealing to the business people, people who are doing business in our country, to raise this money, and without this money, we cannot accomplish the things that we are trying to accomplish. And I had substantial admiration for the government at that time, I thought it was doing a very good job, and they made a very cogent argument, I thought, but I do not see really any relationship between that and military or even other governments.

Senator CHURCH. May I make an observation here, Senator Symington? Would you yield for that purpose?

Senator SYMINGTON. Yes.

Senator CHURCH. If other American companies in Korea did in fact make political contributions, which as you have acknowledged, was contrary to Korean law, in these campaigns, in proportion to what Gulf made, then the American companies would have contributed between $25 and $30 million to these campaigns, which is an awful lot of money for conducting a campaign, even as measured by the contribution of businesses for the conduct of a national election in the United States.

Furthermore, with respect to your comment that with all due credit given the key reasons for what they have done, they pulled themselves up by their bootstraps, over this period the Government of the United States contributed a total of $11,201 million to this small country in military and economic aid. So I suggest that Uncle Sam has handled one of those bootstraps awfully hard. Yet, by your testimony, despite the tremendous aid program that flowed into that country, at about $400 million a year, and despite the direct connection that the American Government had with your particular investment, your aid money that it contributed and through insurance guarantees, Gulf never did tell the Government of the United States what was going on. The Embassy was never informed. Yet, you must have known the high sensitivity of such a matter. You referred to it when you made your testimony to us this morning, severe political repercussions that are associated with any disclosure of this kind of contribution—sooner or later the truth comes out. So do you think it was a matter of national interest to the United States to know that these practices were under way, that they involved amounts of money of this magnitude. Why did you not tell the Government of your own country?

Mr. DORSEY. What you are saying sounds very reasonable today but this is a long time afterward.

Senator SYMINGTON. . . . You say that you visited Korea and there were heated discussions and you flatly rejected both the intensity of the measure being applied and the amount demanded, and in response to my position the $10 million request was subsequently changed to $3 million, to which I acquiesced, believing that the contribution would be in the best interests of the company.

So it was not the nature of the transaction, it was the amount of the transaction that was in your mind, is that correct?

Mr. DORSEY. Well, I do not know that was necessarily true. I would certainly rather hope the thing would never be brought up in the first place or go away, but it did not go away, it was persistent, and the real problem, of course, was the amount of money, but it was more than that.

Senator PERCY. Mr. Dorsey, I would like to start with the broadest type of philosophical question but also one that enables you to assess the damages to date. . . . If you could turn the clock back now, knowing the damages to your company because of this disclosure, would you feel Gulf would have been better off if it had taken a firm position it would not engage in any such illegality or immoral activity, knowing what I know today I would have run whatever the risks were at that time and suffered what business you may have lost?

Mr. DORSEY. Yes, sir.

Senator PERCY. Could you have fought it in another way rather than just caving in? Could you have, through the State Department, through public disclosure, through getting tough yourself and toughing it out with these people who were putting pressure on you, do you think you could have minimized and cut down the damage? Was there any attempt to work with other American companies or other multinationals, whatever their origin, to see together if you could not stamp out this practice, because you are bidding against each other, in a sense?

Mr. DORSEY. No; we did not talk to any other companies and I doubt if we would do that under any circumstances.

As far as the American Government is concerned, you know until very recently, it may be a bit of overstatement, but not too much, to say that most American companies that went abroad and made substantial investments basically did it on their own, and as far as the US Government was concerned, they were sort of like motherless children, they had to make their own way in the world, and I would point out to you the oil companies were encouraged by this Government after World War I to go abroad to get our stake in the Middle East, to do all these things. Immediately after we got there we were entirely overlooked, forgotten, or I could argue discriminated against. And in my own experience of working abroad, I can tell you that the US State Department until very recently, and the US Congress either, had damn little interest in our welfare. All at once everybody is concerned about us, they want to help us, but it is a little bit late. We have lost almost what we have had abroad. What we have not lost we will very shortly.

Senator PERCY. When was the last time you went to the State Department as a company and presented a problem to them and said give us your help in this area? I am talking in the general area of political pressure and individual pressure on you for contributions, illegal or immoral.

Mr. DORSEY. Well, I would say that the first time we have had any encouragement to come to the State Department has been over the period of the last two or three years.

Senator PERCY. When did Gulf Oil or any officer or employee of Gulf go to the State Department and ask for help in this regard?

Mr. DORSEY. The last time?

Senator PERCY. Yes.

Mr. DORSEY. I am sure that it would have been within the last few months.

Senator PERCY. And what kind of help did you get? What kind of position did they take?

Mr. DORSEY. Well, let me go back and answer your first question. Over the past three or four years we have been obviously threatened with a loss of all of our foreign assets or at least our foreign production. The State Department has taken a very active interest in what is going on and has invited us in and we have gone to them on our own many times to seek their help, to talk to them, to do what we could, but I say before that, if I were in a given country around the world and you had an investment there, and you went to the Ambassador of that country with a problem you thought legitimate, I would say over the 20 or 30 years of my foreign experience you were very unlikely to get a very receptive answer or any expression of interest on his part so, therefore, you sort of get in the habit of not going, or when you go you get platitudes. So I would think it has been only in the last three or four years this has changed.

Senator PERCY. . . . When you were pressured for $3 million, $10 million, to start with, would that not have been a significant enough thing to have talked to the ambassador in Korea?

Mr. DORSEY. . . . I do not know, I suppose at first the decision-making process says they have got us and we have got to make the best deal we can, we have got to pay. I suppose I then reasoned that to go to the ambassador of the United States and to acquaint him with the fact that we feel we must, would have been an embarrassment to him, and I would just as soon as not do it.

Senator PERCY. In the 1971 national election in Korea, you indicated that you were advised, when you were in Pittsburgh, of the request for $10 million.

You said, "a short while thereafter I had occasion to be in Korea," implying that there was some other business that was important and while you were there, incidentally you started the bargain process with them on this particular contribution.

What was the nature of your business, Mr. Dorsey, that took you to Korea? When was the request transmitted to you in Pittsburgh, and how soon afterward did you go to Korea, what was the nature of your business in Korea, other than to discuss with the party official this contribution request?

Mr. DORSEY. Well, I do not know precisely at the time but I would guess it probably was within 30 or 40 days from the time I heard about it and was there. As to why I was there, I am not sure. During that period of time, beginning rather early, I had a basic responsibility in Korea and I went rather often. I went several times a year. We always had interests in Japan and Taiwan and Hong Kong, many other places.

Senator PERCY. Was the trip essentially, though, because of this request?

Mr. DORSEY. No.

Senator PERCY. Here you are threatened with possibly losing your whole position there, and a demand, pressing demand for $10 million. That seems to me a rather moral issue, and I wondered whether you could not deduce the real purpose of your trip was to take care of this matter and handle it, was it an incidental part of your trip? Because that is the implication, you say you had occasion to be in Korea and witness first-hand the pressure being exerted.

Mr. DORSEY. Well, these are very difficult things to remember. I can only reason that in 1966 I did not go to Korea. In 1970 I did. I went rather often. Quite honestly, if I had to speculate, my speculation would be that I would have attempted to avoid this kind of pressure because basically, once they get to me on an issue like this it is do or die, there is no buck-passing at this point.

Senator PERCY. That is right.

Mr. DORSEY. So, my normal instinct, I think, would have to be to avoid it and let some other poor devil out there take all the flack and fight it out. So I might have had another very good reason for being there.

Senator PERCY. That is right. And that is why the haziness of your memory on this issue, it seems to me, burned into your memory as to why you would take the initial action when ordinarily these things were done by other officers in the company, to personally intervene on this particular matter.

Mr. DORSEY. Well, I did not intervene. My recollection is I was very surprised that indeed, they came to me. I did not expect to be. Normally, this was not what you would expect.

Senator PERCY. In other words, you were in Pittsburgh, you knew about it, you went to Korea, and they broached it with you before you raised the subject with them?

Mr. DORSEY. Absolutely. I could not have been more shocked and more surprised as to what happened. I got there and this Mr. Kim, who had to be, I suppose, about as tough a man as I have been accosted by in my life, invited me out to his home. He got me in his home, and I tell you I have never suffered the kind of abuse I got from him that day. He left no question, he was a plain rough and tough fundraiser and that is what he does.

Senator PERCY. Did he at any time in that conversation invoke the name of President Park and indicate that he was acting under his direction? After all, he is party chairman but he serves at the will of the President, does he not?

Mr. DORSEY. He was not party chairman, he was the fund-raiser for the party. This is S.K. Kim.

Senator PERCY. He was finance chairman?

Mr. DORSEY. Yes, sir.

Senator PERCY. Did he at any time use the name of President Park or invoke that name to indicate what he was requesting had the full support and backing of President Park, or any top official of the Government of South Korea?

Mr. DORSEY. I cannot recall that. It would not surprise me. If anybody came to me in the United States, they would invoke as high a name as they possibly could under any circumstances, you know. That if he did, it did not mean anything to me.

Senator PERCY. You have knowledge that other American companies did make contributions and that you were not just singled out and being made the target to bear the full brunt of this cost?

Mr. DORSEY. Well, I was told by the fund-raiser that all foreign companies were expected, and I think he told me that some had.

Senator PERCY. But that they did make—

Mr. DORSEY. Yes, sir.

Senator PERCY. He said to you they had made contributions and you were expected to do the same thing?

Mr. DORSEY. Yes, sir.

Senator PERCY. Taking into account the Chair's question and calculation as to how much this might have amounted to, assuming that would be a huge sum here in this country, certainly almost as big in itself as any political campaign before the 1972 campaign, which reached proportions that are new highs, or lows—$25 or $30 million could not possibly be spent, and anyone out there observing it and observing the process, and I have been there a number of times, would know that that money was not spent for the political Democratic Republican process of electing President Park or electing anyone who had the kind of control that he had when he did not even permit opposition.

Did you suspect or feel that pay-offs were being made and part of this money was being used for officials and individual bribes in a sense, or contributions to individuals?

Mr. DORSEY. No, I certainly had no reason to believe that.

Senator PERCY. Has Gulf at any time ever made a monetary contribution to an official of another government or a party official or a wife or spouse, as it is frequently done in some Asian countries? You do it to the wife, not to the principal himself.

Has Gulf ever made a contribution to an individual of that kind of any significance?

Mr. DORSEY. Other than that, to my knowledge, no.

Senator PERCY. No individual contribution. What, Mr. Dorsey, was your feeling as to how much of this $10 million request, $3 million actually paid, went into the party coffers and how much went into someone's pocket? Did you suspect part of the political request was in accordance with the customs and mores of the country?

Mr. DORSEY. I certainly have no way of knowing. I would say this. That, as far as I know, we did not suffer what seems to be the normal sort of harassment of, you have got to do a little something for the custom man to get certain things done. As far as I know, this had not happened in Korea.

Senator PERCY. You said in your testimony you had two discussions with an official of the party and you flatly rejected both the intensity of the pressure being applied and the amount demanded. You bargained them down from $10 million to $3 million.

What reasoning did you use and did you attempt to get it down to zero and take a position during the course of the heated conversation with Mr. Kim that you were not going to pay anything, or was it just a question of bargaining as to how much it was going to be, not whether the contribution was to be made?

Mr. DORSEY. I am afraid I had made up my mind by that time we were damn well going to pay something. I was simply trying to reduce the amount.

Senator PERCY. You were bargaining on the amount.

Senator CLARK. . . . is it fair to say that the Gulf Oil Co. violated the laws in Korea and the United States to make political contributions and laundered it through a Bahamas company? Is that fair?

Mr. DORSEY. Well, I think it is fair they made illegal contributions. Laundering is your phrase. I am not sure what I know—

Senator CLARK. Why did you put it through the Bahamas company rather than make it direct?

Mr. DORSEY. Yes, sir.

Senator CLARK. Now do you think that your multinational corporation is any worse or any different in that practice, or do most of them do it, in your judgment?

Mr. DORSEY. Well, I would like to think that we are a lot worse but I do not have any good reason to think that.

Senator CLARK. I think you are right, it is very common practice.... You ... say:

> But you can help us and many other multinational companies which are confronted with this problem by enacting legislation that would outlaw any foreign contributions by any American company. Such a statute on our books would make it easier to resist the very intensive pressures which are placed upon us from time to time. If we can cite our law which says that we just may not do it, we would be in a better position to resist these pressures and to refuse the requests.

But in point of fact, you have already violated both American law and Korean law. What would one more law mean to you in this respect? Why would that help you?

Mr. DORSEY. I am not speaking to the US matter, I am speaking to the foreign matter.

Senator CLARK: You violated US law in your contribution to the Committee to Re-Elect the President.

Mr. DORSEY. Are you saying I am a rascal and no matter what—

Senator CLARK. I am saying I am curious why one more law would be more effective than the laws that are already on the books, which you openly admit you violated?

Mr. DORSEY. Because there is no law, no US law that says our contribution to Korea was illegal in the United States.

Senator CLARK. You are saying you would be more apt to abide by that law than the law that forbids corporate contributions to American parties?

Mr. DORSEY. We are constrained by many US laws about what we do abroad and as far as I know, we have honored every one of them.

Senator CLARK. You did not honor the Korean law.

Mr. DORSEY. The Korean law, as far as I was concerned at that time, I was under the impression, and it seemed to be a very difficult law to interpret, and that is not only true of Korea, it is very true if you go to Japan or Taiwan. If you try to interpret their laws you can get into some very confused areas.

Senator CLARK. You interpreted it in your testimony to have been a violation of the Korean law?

Mr. SEAMANS. May I interject? I think his testimony, including his executive testimony, was he did not know it then but has since been advised there are opinions that way. And may I help if I say it is not only difficult to interpret, it is difficult to find when you are looking for—

Senator CLARK. Do you have some question about the legality of that contribution under Korean law now?

Mr. SEAMANS. We have been advised by people who are probably closer than we, it is illegal.

Senator CLARK. And you would subscribe to the idea that ignorance of the law is no reason?

Mr. SEAMANS. I am merely pointing to the practical problem. If he had asked for our law office to find the legality of the Korean situation, we would not have known where to look.

Senator CLARK. Do you interpret that payment to have been a contribution or a bribe?

Mr. DORSEY. A political contribution.

Senator CLARK. To the Democratic Republican Party?

Mr. DORSEY. Yes, sir.

Senator CLARK. Now, you discussed with Senator Symington about the democratic development of South Korea and talked about contributing to that, and in fact was not your illegal contribution an interference in that democratic process?

Mr. DORSEY. I would have to admit that now, yes.

Senator CLARK. And I was interested in why you feel that the Democratic Republican Party is more democratic than the New Democratic Party whom they opposed and in a very close election? Why did you support the Democratic Republican Party rather than the New Democratic Party?

Mr. DORSEY. Well, I suppose as a matter of pragmatism this was the party that was in power when we came into the country when we made our investments. There was every indication that they were a powerful party and that they probably would be reelected, but I guess most of all, you have got to understand this—or at least I would ask you to. Against a background of any foreign country, any American company living abroad, working abroad outside of certain areas like most of Western Europe, you really are there by sufference and that is made clear to you in subtle ways. You are made to feel that from the time you got there and as I say, the more investment you make the more you are given subtlety to understand it.

Senator CLARK. Well, as you may know, the Democratic Republican Party won that election by only 51 percent. It is conceivable, it seems to me, that your contribution may have made the difference. Do you think that is possible?

Mr. DORSEY. Statistically I would have to admit you are right.

Senator CLARK. But you do not feel any more strongly, your company or you, or whoever made the determination, that the party you supported was any more democratic or has any better tradition than the party you did not support. You did it, I assume, out of the interest of your stockholders?

Mr. DORSEY. Exactly.

Senator CLARK. . . . You make decisions on these contributions solely on profit motives for the stockholders' interest, is that correct?

Mr. DORSEY. Exactly right.

Senator PERCY. Senator Clark, the last comment you made, if you would not mind, it bothers me a little bit.

Senator CLARK. I really not only made it—

Senator PERCY. I am not a spokesman for multinational corporations but I cannot believe that any board rooms when decisions are made, many times what the national interest is comes up as a paramount consideration and that they many times make decisions based upon the national interest.

I can recall in 1954 debating this with my board as to whether I support the tariff policy of my industry, which was a high tariff, or go for what we wanted as a Nation, reciprocal reductions, including everything that we manufactured, and we decided and the board decided that we could not put the company's interest out ahead of the country's interest. We had to adjust and not ask the country, and I cannot help but believe that same debate goes on many, many times and really should, and I would not want the implication left that we would condone a company not taking into account their own country's national interest in a decision they make and only the profit motive should govern their decision.

I do not think you meant to imply that at all, but I felt that the record might stand that way and I want to give you a chance to just comment on it.

Senator CLARK. I certainly do not question that the shareholders or the board discusses the national interest. I was simply trying to establish it is their job, and I think Mr. Dorsey just confirmed that, to operate their company in the interest of the shareholders, not in the national interest. That is not their responsibility to determine what the national interest is. It is the board of directors' position to determine what the shareholders' interests are, that is their responsibility, and that is the basis, I think Mr. Dorsey has testified upon which this contribution was made. If I am inaccurate in that, Mr. Dorsey, I would like to have you correct me.

Mr. DORSEY. No, no, I quite agree with that, that is precisely what I said, passing no judgment one way or the other about the national interest of the United States.

Senator CLARK. . . . When you talk . . . about the changing moral and cultural standards in the world, is the purpose . . . to point out in part you adjust to the morality of the country that you operate in, you do in Rome as the Romans do?

Mr. DORSEY. Well, that may be putting it a little bit bluntly but actually, that quotation is a pejorative quotation, if I may say so. I think, on the other hand, it can be said if you are going to do business within the ambience that exists there within the culture and mores, and that is right and you had best understand it when you get there, and even then you will be surprised.

Senator CLARK. So multinational corporations, I agree with what you are saying, do adjust their ethical standards and morality to fit the condition in which they operate, just as they do the economies in which they operate, or any other part of that country's operation. You could not operate otherwise, could you?

Mr. DORSEY. I think that is correct, you could not.

Senator CHURCH. Mr. Dorsey, can you briefly describe for the record, the nature and extent of the Gulf investment in Korea?

Mr. DORSEY. We went in in 1963 and invested $25 million in a half interest in a rather small refinery. Our partner was the Government. It was the first refinery built in that country, and it basically satisfied their demand at the time.

They had an increase in GNP that was phenomenal, had an increase in energy requirement that was unbelievable, even more than that of Japan. So that over a matter of six or seven or eight years this had grown, this 25,000 barrels a day of product made, had grown by a factor of ten or eleven. So, between 1963 and 1970 our refining capacity went from—ours and the Government's—went from 25,000 barrels a day to 250,000 barrels, and we increased tenfold.

In the meantime, two other oil companies had come in and built big refineries themselves. We were building, we were involved with the Government in a fertilizer plant so they would not have to import fertilizer, at the strong recommendation of US AID authorities and Agriculture. We had been sort of persuaded to expand into the petrochemicals. We made rather large investments there to help them out as much as anything else, I suppose. We engaged in a large shipbuilding program in Korea. We got competitive prices, but a large shipbuilding program. In another rather common practice, in order to enable other industries and big users of energy to expand we had loaned money in to the cement industry and power industry, a very common practice. So that in about seven or eight years we had gone from an investment of $25 million to an overall investment and exposure in excess of $300 million.

Senator CHURCH. And how much of that $300 million is covered by insurance furnished to you by the Government of the United States?

Mr. DORSEY. I do not know at the moment. It has varied because the United States has varied its policies and rules over the period of time. It could be zero at the moment. I do not know but I would be glad to furnish the information. I know OPIC, I talked with them some two years ago and had the impression we did not have a great deal at that time.

Senator CHURCH. We have partial information but we do not have the complete information about the current risk exposure of the US Government with respect to this investment.

We would appreciate it if your company would furnish us with current and complete information. (See Appendix A.)

. . .

Senator PERCY. I believe you have indicated . . . at any time has your board of directors been advised until the disclosure came out, that these contributions were being made abroad and there was the special fund set up in the Bahamas, or any corporate entity that you might have within the board, an executive committee or a finance committee? Was there any advice given by management of the board prior to the public revelation?

Mr. DORSEY. There was not.

Senator PERCY. So it was entirely kept.

Mr. Dorsey, could you indicate why you felt that that was not a matter that should have been discussed by the board and policy established at that level?

Mr. DORSEY. Well, it would appear that there are two questions. If you asked me about Korea, the thing that I know something about, the thing that I was involved in, the area in which I made the decision, it was within my authority within the corporation to make the expenditure. It was an expenditure of money and my authority for expenditures, for expenses, are greater than the $3 million, so it was not necessary under the company policy that I do so.

If you are asking me why the original fund was set up in the Bahamas, I simply do not know, it was long before my time and I do not know.

Senator PERCY. Because of the irreparable damage to Gulf as a result of these revelations, do you think it would be wise for the boards and board members of multinationals in this country, and abroad, to question management as to whether such practices are being carried on in the company and establish a firm policy where the responsibility would be at the board level then?

Mr. DORSEY. I would recommend it very highly.

. . .

Senator PERCY. . . . the funds transmitted to Bahamas Exploration were deposited in a new bank account and entered as deferred charges and written off as expenses during the current year. Would you care to comment on what tax effect that has then on the write-off? Does it affect the tax returns of the United States of America, or any foreign country, and has it been revealed there was any illegality in the type of expenses incurred and, therefore, the write-off?

Mr. DORSEY. Well, I have been advised, I have every reason to think it is absolutely true that there are no tax consequences on any of these transactions that have been made. They were not claimed for tax purposes as expenses for tax purposes. There was no tax consequences.

Senator PERCY. I am glad to hear that.

. . .

Senator PERCY. You indicated that your investment totaled $300 million. What have been recent earnings from Korea on that investment? Have you broken that out in your financial statements at all, or can you tell the committee what your earnings have been in South Korea after taxes?

Mr. DORSEY. No, not precisely. I can probably give you a measure of it. Our total exposure at one time was $300 million. We have been there for twelve years and I think that we have yet to recover about $150 million. So, one way or another we have recovered over fifteen years about half the money we have invested, which does not suggest a very high rate of return.

Senator PERCY. It is fairly standard practice for contributions to be made for the political process in most of the countries in which you do business?

Mr. DORSEY. It is not my impression that it is.

Senator PERCY. . . . How many people within Gulf knew of the payments? In your view, how many people knew about the payments made and their purpose?

Mr. DORSEY. Talking about Korea again?

Senator PERCY. Yes.

Mr. DORSEY. I presume—

Senator PERCY. I would say that the question should be broad enough to include South Korea as well as all other countries where campaign contributions were made?

Let us take Korea first. Be specific about that.

Mr. DORSEY. I am not trying to evade. It is a very difficult question to answer. You never know who is involved in the decision-making at any one time in the past. I would think that probably four to six people had knowledge of it within the corporation.

Senator PERCY. That is on the South Korean contributions?

Mr. DORSEY. Yes, sir.

Senator PERCY. Then, taking into account all other contributions to other countries as well and, therefore, their political campaign, how many people in Gulf might have known of the existence of such a fund and payments were being made and for what purpose?

Mr. DORSEY. I would think at any one time not more than four to six. For example, I did not know about the Bolivian matter, although I was in the headquarters office at the time.[2] I did not know it was done by other people and I was not asked or consulted, but I would think in the nature of four to six people at any one time.

Senator PERCY. Was it ever stated as a policy any place, so that people had some leeway, that you had to accommodate yourself, you had to do business in accordance with the local mores and customs, habits and so forth, therefore, they had the discretion to go ahead but policy had been established at some higher level that this was, if necessary authorized in advance, or when you discovered the Bolivian contributions, for instance, did you feel that it had been made by officers of the company or employees of the company without specific direction and without, in contravention of any policy of the company?

Mr. DORSEY. Well, it was, unfortunately, not in contravention of the policy because there was no policy, and that is too bad in itself. I would believe that whoever made the decision about the Bolivian contribution, did it under great pressure and because they did believe it to be in the best interests of the corporation.

Senator PERCY. . . . In your estimate, how many individuals in the recipient country were aware of the first payment that was made? Did you deal with the very same people at the time the second payment was made? And I think this applies to South Korea, the first payment in 1966, the second in 1971.

---

2. Gulf provided a helicopter and made cash contributions totalling $350,000 to General Rene Barrientos during and after his Presidential campaign of 1966.

Mr. DORSEY. I have no idea how many people in South Korea would have known it. I suspect like most things, they would not talk about it too much, a rather small and select group. And basically, yes, we dealt with, more than one person talked with us, but only about three at most, and I think basically they were the same people in both years.

Senator PERCY. . . . How were you advised that the big people who did make the decisions above Mr. Kim, would know of your contribution?

Mr. DORSEY. After all these years, I cannot say with any exactness precisely what I was told. Obviously, I was, or whoever was involved, would be alternately cajoled and threatened and in a matter like this, and I am sure that somewhere along the line that such a statement was made to me or to some of our people that were involved, but I do not recall it precisely.

Senator PERCY. There is no question though, that probably President Park and other key Government officials would know very definitely about your contribution?

Mr. DORSEY. Well, I cannot say that I had any reason to think they would but I have every reason to believe that I was told that they would, which may be two different things. At least, it turned out that way in our country.

Senator PERCY. Mr. Dorsey, do you think that these payments would have been made had you been under obligation to inform stockholders of this fact?

Mr. DORSEY. I am sure not.

Senator PERCY. What would be your view of legislation not prohibiting foreign bribes, political contributions or excessive agency fees, but requiring that these be made public to the Security and Exchange Commission and shareholders?

Mr. DORSEY. I think it would serve precisely the same purpose.

. . .

Senator PERCY. . . . I have no reason to believe that your testimony is not the truth, the whole truth, and nothing but the truth, in this case, and your commitment to continue to furnish this committee with information I think is a very, very helpful pledge on your part. I think it has been extraordinarily helpful to us and absolutely the right and wise decision by you and your board that this testimony, painful as it is. I think as you walk out of this room, Mr. Dorsey, you will have a tremendous load off your shoulders, and I think you have done eminently the right thing.

 ✳   *Appendix A*

SECTION A:
GULF'S INVESTMENTS IN KOREA—THOSE
CARRYING AID/OPIC COVERAGE

1. Korea Oil Corp.

A. INVESTMENT

Equity

(1) $4.8 million under Stock Subscription Agreement dated September 23, 1963—for 25 percent equity of KOCO.

(2) $25 million under Second Stock Subscription Agreement dated June 19, 1970 by which Gulf's equity in KOCO increased to 50 percent.

Loans

$20 million under Agreement dated 9/23/63 $30 million under loan Agreements dated August 3, 1967.

$25.1 million under loan Agreements dated June 19, 1970.

Use of funds

Under 1963 agreements—construction of refinery.

Under 1967 agreements—construction of Naphtha cracker, terminal and buoy facilities.

Under 1970 agreements—expansion of refinery.

The maximum coverage was taken during the period 1964 to 1970. The maximum coverage allowable for equity investments was 200 percent for inconvertibility and expropriation and 100 percent for war risk. Gulf reached an understanding with OPIC, which is contained in a letter agreement dated March 1971, whereby OPIC insurance would be available for its investments in the refinery expansion providing a reduction took place in the amount of OPIC insurance for Gulf's existing investments in Korea.

In 1972 and 1973, the maximum amount of OPIC coverage selected by Gulf was substantially reduced in accordance with a new corporate policy. This policy stated that the following amounts of insurance should be purchased:

(1) to cover the risk of incovertibility—three years expected dividends for Gulf's equity investment and the sum of three years payments of principal plus interest on Gulf's loans to Korean companies.

(2) to cover risk of expropriation—a nominal amount which would be sufficient to involve OPIC in any dispute with the Government of Korea.

(3) to cover war risk—In order to cover the risk of sabotage, the amount of current coverage taken corresponded to the cost of the most expensive single piece of equipment in the refinery complex. The maximum amount selected corresponded to the cost of the most expensive single piece of equipment in the refinery complex. The maximum amount selected corresponded to the ceiling established under the OPIC contract.

In 1974/1975, due to the deteriorating balance of payments and economic situation in Korea, the amount of insurance placed under the Current Section of the OPIC contract corresponded to the Maximum amount of insurance that Gulf could obtain. This situation differed to some extent from earlier years, where the maximum insurance was divided between the Current and Standby Sections of the contract. At the beginning of each contract year, we decide internally how much of the maximum insurance should be placed in the Current Section and how much in the Standby Section. The amount of any claim against OPIC is limited to the amount in the Current Section.

2. Chinhae Chemical Company

A. INVESTMENT

Gulf Oil (Great Britain) Ltd. a wholly-owned subsidiary of Gulf Oil Corporation, which is incorporated in the United Kingdom, purchased 50 percent of the shares of Chinhae for $10.5 million under a Stock Subscription Contract dated July 7, 1965. On December 23, 1974, Gulf Oil (Great Britain) (GOGB) sold 50 percent of its 50 percent interest to International Minerals and Chemical Company.

AID made a loan to the Republic of Korea in the amount of $24.6 million under an Agreement dated June 11, 1965. The Republic of Korea, in turn, lent Chinhae an equivalent amount in Korean currency.

B. OPIC COVERAGE

The extent of OPIC coverage taken by GOGB and the rationale behind such coverage corresponds very closely to that of Gulf Oil Corporation's years 1965 through 1970, a substantial reduction in accordance with our agreement with OPIC of March 1971 and a further reduction in 1972/1973 in accordance with the new corporate policy.

In December 1974, the purchaser of GOGB's shares acquired, with the consent of OPIC, 50 percent of GOGB's OPIC coverage.

3. Gulf Oil Corporation Loans to Companies Which Are in No Way Related to Gulf

All the loans mentioned below were made as an incentive for the borrower to enter into long-term fuel oil purchase contracts with Korea Oil Corporation, who in turn purchased the crude oil from Gulf.

i. $8 million to Ssaug Yong Cement Company under an agreement dated July 7, 1969.

ii. $5 million to Tonghae Electric Company under an agreement dated July 30, 1969.

iii. $30 million to Korea Electric Company under an agreement dated February 27, 1969.

OPIC Coverage

In 1969 and 1970 the maximum amount of OPIC insurance was obtained for these loans. This insurance encompassed convertibility, expropriation and war risk coverage. Under the March 1971 agreement with OPIC, the insurance was reduced to cover inconvertibility only. The amounts of insurance taken was reduced in 1973 in accordance with the previously described corporate policy. The amounts included in the Current Section of the contracts were increased to the maximum possible in 1975 as a result of deteriorating balance of payments position of Korea.

SECTION B:
GULF INVESTMENTS/LOANS IN KOREA
WHICH DO NOT CARRY OPIC INSURANCE

1. A-Jin Chemical Company, Ltd.

Under agreement signed May 5, 1966, U-Jin and Gulf Oil agreed to form a joint venture company (A-Jin) to manufacture polyethylene bags. During 1967, Gulf (Gulf Oil Great Britain) purchased a total of 85,350 shares for a total cost of $311,945.

2. Korean Lubricants Company, Ltd.

On December 7, 1968, Korea Oil Corporation (KOCO) and Gulf agreed to form a joint venture company to construct, own and operate a lubricating oil and grease manufacturing plant. This project never reached fruition. As originally structured, Gulf would have put up $5 million in equity, loaned $5 million to KOCO (which KOCO would contribute as equity), and loaned $30 million to the new company.

3. Heung Kuk Sang Sa

Under an agreement dated July 24, 1967, Gulf made an equity contribution of $5 million to KHSS, and loaned an additional $1.5 million. In July, 1969, Gulf contributed an additional $2 million in equity (to increase ownership to 50 percent) and made a $5.8 million loan. HKSS is a marketing company. In 1972, Gulf sold its 50 percent interest in KOCO.

4. Korean Flag Tankers

Gulf currently has two VLCC tankers under long-term charter with a capitalized value of approximately $52 million. The tankers are financed via loans from Gulf.

In addition, Gulf has three vessels, each of less than 50,000 D.W. tons, under charter. The remaining payments under these charters, all of which expire in 1975, will be some $3.6 million.

OPIC—EXISTING CONTRACTS OF GUARANTEE

[Key: C=convertibility; E=expropriation; WR=war risk; E=equity; L=loan]

Contract date	Contract No.	Type of coverage	Equity or loan	Maximum	Current coverage
KOCO:					
Nov. 3	1588 AA	C	E	$7,500,000	$7,500,000
Do	1589 AB	C	L	20,000,000	20,000,000
Do	1590 BA	E	E	3,200,000	3,200,000
Do	1591 BB	E	L	17,000,000	17,000,000
Do	1592 CC	WR	E & L	40,000,000	10,000,000
Old KOCO total				87,700,000	57,000,000
Mar. 9	8031 AA	C	E	10,000,000	10,000,000
Do	8031 BA	C	L	10,800,000	10,800,000
Do	8031 AB	E	E	4,000,000	4,000,000
Do	8031 BB	E	L	4,000,000	4,000,000
Do	8031 AC	WR	E	9,000,000	9,000,000
Do	8031 BC	WR	L	11,000,000	11,000,000
New KOCO total				48,800,000	48,800,000
KOCO total				136,500,000	106,500,000
Korea Electric: Apr. 22	6292 AB	C	L	16,425,000	16,425,000
Ssang Yong: Jan. 16	7018 AB	C	L	3,995,000	3,995,000
Tonghae (New Korea Electric): Jan. 16	7019 AB	C	L	2,497,000	2,497,000
Chinhae:					
Sept. 3	5350 AA	C	E	5,250,000	1,700,000
Do	5350 BA	E	E	1,000,000	250,000
Do	5350 CA	WR	E	1,000,000	1,000,000
Chinhae total				7,250,000	2,950,000
Total Korea				166,667,000	132,367,000

Part C

Racker Company (A)

DEALING WITH A PRODUCTION PROBLEM
IN A MEXICAN SUBSIDIARY

James Cowles spent about a month in the Mexican subsidiary of the Racker Company observing its operations as part of his initial training. During the visit Jim was interested in the way a problem which arose in the factory was worked out. This story is told in the following excerpts from his journal.

July 21: I spent an hour with Mr. Tarback this morning getting an initial picture of the operation. The Mexican company sells the full line of Racker products, most of which are based on a combination of electrical and mechanical components. Sales are made to both consumer channels and to industry. The Mexican subsidiary was set up 20 years ago as a sales organization. Today it continues in large part to be a sales outlet for US manufactured products, but over the course of time manufacture of a number of products has been initiated. The procedure is to undertake the manufacture of one product after an other from the US line. The process of starting up each product is a major project for the subsidiary, and typically they won't undertake more than one each year.

This year they have started manufacture of the Wigitator. Actual production got under way a month ago culminating several months of planning, bringing in new machinery and training workers. The Wigitator is a fairly complex product designed primarily for consumer sales. It includes several mechanical parts and an electrical relay device which activates one phase of the mechanical operation.

It is slightly more complex than the products which have been made but similar to them in most of the manufacturing processes.

July 23: I've been hearing about problems with the Wigitator so I asked Mr. Tarback about it today. He told me they are having some trouble with the quality. The mechanical operation of the ones made so far has not been quite satisfactory, especially that of the electrical timing device. This problem has been receiving much attention from him and others in the plant, including the production manager, Mr. Rodriguez; the chief inspector, Mr. Ramos; and the superintendent of the section which produces the product, Mr. Salas.

Mr. Tarback has been giving a lot of personal effort to trying to pin down the problem. He said that he has taken one or two Wigitators home each night to try out in practice and see if he can figure out what is wrong. The next morning he takes them back into the plant and points out the apparent weaknesses to the production prople.

These problems have been particularly disturbing to the organization because the early stages of starting up production had gone extremely well. The installation of the machinery and the training were accomplished quickly, and the Wigitators went into production ahead of schedule, and the rate of output was rapidly brought up to capacity. The production organization had taken great pride in this accomplishment. Mr. Tarback observed that this pride was a complicating factor in the situation. He explained this to me after we were interrupted by a phone call from Mr. Rodriguez.

Mr. Rodriguez called him about the quality problem, and Mr. Tarback told him that he was becoming very disturbed with the failure of the production organization to solve it. He said that unless some improvement came soon he was going to have to take some drastic action. He said he was considering the possibility of having the chief inspector report directly to the general manager, thereby having a stronger check on work down the line. As he hung up he shook his head and said, "I sure hate to do that. Alfonso is overworked, and he will worry over what I've just said. Sometimes you have to be a little mean, though, to shake a man into action. You see, the production department got to feeling pretty cocky over what a good job they had done in getting the Wigitator into production, and something has to be done to get them to really straighten out this quality problem."

He said he hoped that Rodriguez was on top of the problem though he could not be sure yet. He said that Rodriguez had just called to tell him that he was going to move some inspectors around. He says that he thinks that some of them have been working too long close to the same production people and have gotten too friendly with them. He thinks that if he moves them around they will do a proper job of checking.

I asked him to explain something about what was wrong with the production. He said that it wasn't easy to do because the weaknesses don't actually result in the product not functioning. It functions, and in a sense the functioning is adequate, but Racker products have a reputation for precision and reliability. There is no mechanically objective way to measure these qualities in a product like the Wigitator; therefore it was a matter of personal judgment as to when they were satisfactory.

He went on from this to tell me a little about Mr. Rodriguez. He said that he felt as though he was his own son. He has worked with him for several years, bringing him along up through the organization. When something like this comes up where he has to be hard on him, he apparently feels deeply troubled by it. He said he wasn't sure how this change in inspectors would work, but he was prepared to give it a try.

July 28: While I was walking through the plant this morning, I found Mr. Tarback and Mr. Rodriguez in the shop. Both of them looked pretty serious and I asked Mr. Tarback what was happening. He said that he hoped they had now gotten to the root of the problem with the Wigitators. He said that in his checking samples every night he had found consistently that the brackets around the timing device were improperly aligned. He checked back through the production line this morning and found that the jigs which were used in making the brackets were in many cases slightly bent. He'd gotten Rodriguez on the problem, and they were at that moment supervising the construction of new jigs which would be all right. He said that the jigs had gotten bent because they weren't built strong enough and the workers had taken to throwing them in a pile after they were through using them.

We talked a bit about the problem of getting at the root of something like this. He came up through the production side of the business, so he knows how to find the bugs in a production process. He observed that it would be really tough for a general manager with only a sales background to be faced with such a situation.

July 31: Mr. Tarback told me this afternoon that the quality of the Wigitators is showing some improvement. The better jigs seem to have helped a little. However, some of the Wigitators are still coming through in unsatisfactory condition. He has had some trouble convincing Mr. Ramos that it's necessary to bring the products up to a higher standard. As he mentioned before, it is a matter of personal judgment, but he feels that he must keep after the matter.

August 5: Mr. Tarback told me today that they have made a new move to try to straighten out the quality problem with the Wigitators. He said that Rodriguez had come up to him after lunch yesterday and told him that he was not satisfied with the way the inspection system was functioning and felt that something drastic in the way of reorganization was needed. They have now assigned Mr. Fernandez to make a complete study of the inspection system. Fernandez is currently in the engineering department, but for quite a while was chief inspector. Mr. Tarback described Fernandez as a real "tough cookie" and a man who can really straighten things out. He is to make recommendations for any changes he thinks are needed, then Ramos will be given the job of carrying out those recommendations. They are not sure whether Mr. Ramos himself may be the problem. If things don't work out, they may have to move him.

August 8: Mr. Tarback told me today that they have finally come to the conclusion that a major shake-up is needed to straighten out this quality matter. Fernandez submitted his report. On the basis of that, they have decided that the real problem is at the supervisory level. Mr. Salas has not been putting enough effort into straightening out the problem, so he has been put into another job where he won't have as much administrative responsibility, and Fernandez has taken over the supervision of the production section. They also decided that Ramos doesn't have the judgment necessary to make a good chief inspector, so he has been put into another production supervisory job, and a new man has been brought in as chief inspector.

August 15: Mr. Tarback says that the Wigitator problem is now resolved. Fernandez, he says, is doing a fine job of setting high standards for the organization. He has everybody on their toes, and the products are coming out in good quality.

Racker Company (B)

ATTITUDES OF A MEXICAN EXECUTIVE

As part of his initial training with the international division of the Racker Company, James Cowles spent a month with the company's Mexican subsidiary. During his visit Jim talked with Alfonso Rodriguez, the production manager, a number of times and became quite interested in Mr. Rodriguez' approach to his administrative relationships. The conversation on August twentieth, related below, describes some of the important elements of his approach.

When Jim arrived at Mr. Rodriguez' office, he found him talking with Mr. Farley and Mr. Guerrera about the contract for a new building. Mr. Farley was a contract expert from the home office and Mr. Guerrera, the company lawyer. After a few casual remarks Mr. Rodriguez led Jim into the adjoining conference room.

R: We'll let them talk in there. They're going to go over the contract I drew up this weekend. They can tear it all apart if they want to. It's 20 pages long. It was quite a job to draw it up. I don't think they'll find much wrong with it.

C: You've drawn up contracts before?

R: Yes, I've had experience with these things. I've drawn up lots of contracts before. I'm no lawyer, but I think I know how to draw them up.

C: You've worked with Mr. Farley before, haven't you?

R: Yes, I know him well. We know all these people from the States well now.

That wasn't true before. It used to be they'd send letters out and they were all just put in the general file. When I went up to the States the first time and went in and talked to somebody, they just drew back and said, "Who are you, Mr. Rodriguez from Mexico?" (Here he drew himself back and looked rather imperious and strict.) It didn't take long to get over that, though. In four or five days we were all good friends, and since then that's the way it's always been. Now I go up there and they have the secretaries out to meet me, and everybody gives everybody else the big abrazo and we're all good friends. That's the way it has to be, you know. They're staff people and they're there to help us. The company pays good money for it. We've got two of their men down here to help us now, Ransom and now Farley is here to help on the contract.

C: They help you out with the work?

R: Yes, that's what they're for. We get a lot of help out of them. We invite them down whenever we have something we can use them for.

C: I'd like to ask you something that's an extension of what we were talking about last week. We were talking about finding out what was on people's minds and the worries of a boss in that regard. You spoke of one aspect of the situation which is the man's worries with his family. There's another side of it which is quite a problem with a lot of executives and that is the man's worries about the job itself. That is, things right here in the office which may be on his mind. Is this something that concerns you, and do you have any thoughts about it?

R: Naturally. This is something that I think about very much.

C: Can you elaborate on it?

R: You notice something's wrong with a man. You can see that from the way he works and you want to try to find out what his main worry is. The first thing you do is to start with the family and see whether the problem is there, whether it's with his children or his wife or what. If you don't find anything wrong there, then it must be in his job. So what do you do? The thing to do is to get together with the man, take him downtown and have a drink with him or take him to dinner. You may take him alone or you may take him in a group. The chief thing to do is to get him off away from the job. You don't get right into the subject, of course; you don't touch on the subject until the man gets relaxed. If he thinks that you've taken him out just to get him to talk business, then he's going to be defensive. He's going to get scared and pull into himself, so you have to tell him some jokes and talk about all sorts of things. Once you've got him relaxed, then you're okay. You get him to feeling relaxed and in a position so he's not tight, and then you just encourage him to talk. Encourage him to talk to you as a friend. You don't want him to think of you as a boss, just to think of you as a friend that he can talk to about anything he wishes. The idea isn't that you have a boss and employee having a meeting together. This is just a couple of friends having dinner.

C: You get him relaxed so he'll open up.

R: He'll relax and talk to you. You don't try to fix anything right then. You don't try to make any definite plans. You don't give any instructions. You're just trying to find out what's on his mind. Then the next day when you come into the office, then you get to work on it. You try to fix things up and make the changes you have to.

C: You just want him to talk about what's on the top of his head?

R: That's it. You want to find out if he's got a chip on his shoulder or what's bothering him, get hold of whatever the problem is. Don't make any promises. The chief thing to do is find out what's on his mind, and you'll know what that is if he loosens up and talks to you.

C: Is this something you have to do very often?

R: Yes, it happens at least four times a year. Now there's one little thing that I ought to mention. You might not think this is important. It's a small thing but it's quite important. That's choosing the place that you take the man to dinner. That's a very important thing.

C: Why is that?

R: For this reason. You know a man and you know his way of living. You know about his family. For example, you may have a superintendent out on the line. His standard of living isn't very high. Now, if you take him to the Alffer or the Bamer (two of Mexico City's most deluxe hotels) or some place like that, you might just as well not try at all. He's going to feel out of place, and he'll tighten up and won't talk a bit.

C: You want him in a place where he's physically comfortable?

R: Yes. You want him to feel at home. Take him some place where he'll relax and feel quite comfortable. You don't want to try and show off. There's no point in trying to impress the man. If you're out to impress him, you're wasting your time.

C: You try to put yourself in his shoes?

R: You do something he'll like. You want to do something that'll make him feel at home. Now sometimes, for example, I'll just take a man for a car ride down to Cuernavaca. I know something about a fellow and maybe I know that's something he likes. We just go down there and have a soda. We talk on the way there and on the way back. Maybe another man, you've got to take him to a cabaret where there will be lots of girls and lots of drinks.

C: I think I get the idea. You're trying to get these fellows to talk about their worries. If they can get them off their chests, this must be a big help for both of you. Not knowing what's on a man's mind must be pretty hard for you. Does it usually work out pretty well?

R: It works pretty well. But it doesn't always work. Now if a man's problem is you, that is, if his beef is against you, then he probably won't talk. You get a man loosened up and if you try to get him talking, and then if he doesn't talk, if he won't tell you what's on his mind, then I can usually figure that the problem is with me. There's something that I've done that he doesn't like or there's something that he's misunderstood. Then I know he won't talk to me about it. Then what I've got to do is get a third party in. I get hold of some person who's a friend of his. I'll explain the whole thing to him and give him an expense account so he can take the man out. The chances are that the fellow will talk to him and he can report back to me what he's found out, and I can straighten it out.

C: You mean you get some outsider or somebody else here in the plant?

R: Usually somebody outside. Somebody who is a friend of his.

C: The thing that you have to do is figure out some way to get at the man. In some way or other you have to get the information out of him about how he's feeling.

R: Another thing I may do is invite him to my home. I do that sometimes. And that's particularly if his wife is important. You can't omit the opinion of the wife. The wife is a very important person in some of these problems, so if I think that's important, why I'll invite the man and his wife to our home for dinner. That's particularly in cases where I think the problem is a misinterpretation of something I've done. Then we get the man and his wife, and I'll start to talk in the broadest way about the organization and how we are operating things in the plant. I make the wife listen. You see, the man may have misunderstood something, and he's gone home and told his wife. So if I tell them both, then that'll straighten out the misinterpretation. When they go home, she'll say to him, "Now at dinner, you heard what he said. He's on your side; he's not against you the way you were saying. He sees it the way he said, and he's on your side."

C: You just present the true picture to them?

R: That's it. You make the wife listen. You can't expect anything to happen right there at the dinner. But boy, you watch them when they get home. She'll straighten out the question for you.

C: This is an interesting approach, but it must be mighty tough to figure out what to say exactly if you don't know what the problem is beforehand.

R: You may well not know what the problem is, but the thing to do is to take the whole situation in your organization and describe what you're trying to do. And then you'll cover the important problem.

C: This is a very interesting technique as a way to find out what people are thinking, and that's a pretty important organizational matter.

R: It's all part of communications. Communication is a very important matter in an organization. Some good books have been written on communication. You've got to have ideas and information moving up and down the line.

C: People need to understand each other to get the job done.

R: We have to have an exchange of ideas all the time.

C: It isn't an easy thing to accomplish though. People don't talk easily, do they?

R: They won't talk unless you really prove to them that you are willing to listen to them. You have to make that very clear. I make it clear that my door is open all the time to people who want to come in. Men may come any time. They may come in at five o'clock after work with some problem on their minds. Now one thing you want to do is handle the thing right. If a man comes in, he may want to sit right down and talk about what's on his mind. But that's not the way you want to do it. I want him to bring the subject up the right way. I say, "Now, let's take our time. Have a cigarette. Let's talk about this week's bullfight for a few minutes." Then we can get down to talking about the problem, and the man is a little more relaxed.

C: It's important to encourage the men to come to you?

R: That's vital. The old management approach won't work any more today. We used to have the big man in the office and he had a steel fence around him, but it can't be that way any more. The idea now is that we're all playing on a team. The managers and the workers are all players. They've got one job, and that's to work for the team and to win the game for it. We have a game against costs and we have a game against quality. We've got to win them. That's the way the operation has to go. It's just like a game of baseball. Everybody's got to do his part, and everybody has got to be good. You may have lots of good fielders, but if you've got a lousy pitcher, then you're not going to win the game.

C: It's easier for some people on a team to know their job than for others, though. Take a guy who is tightening the bolts. It is a lot easier for him to know the right thing to do than the manager who has to handle the whole thing, like you do.

R: Well, I'm the pitcher and the pitcher has to decide just how to throw the ball. Now let us say that cost is up to bat. If I throw the ball hard and straight, chances are it will be knocked out of the lot and the fellow will get a home run. You've got to figure out just what sort of curve to put on each pitch to make sure that you get what you want. Now right now that's the way it is. Cost is up to bat. That is our problem. We've got a problem with costs. Our tool costs have been going up for the past three or four years. I think I know what it is, too. You see, we have a system here to make the temporary men responsible for tools. If a man can't account for a tool, then he pays for it. I think that's where our problem is. That may sound funny, but I think that the system is working just the wrong way.

C: How's that?

R: Well, if a man knows he has to pay for a tool, then I think that contributes to his making us lose the tool.

C: I don't understand.

R: Well, let us say he loses a screwdriver and then it comes toward the end of the month and he can't find it. What do you think he's going to do?

C: I don't know.

R: Well, he's going to take one from another guy. He'll go around and find some permanent worker and pull a screwdriver out of his box. Then that permanent man—he's not responsible—so he'll go to the crib and get another one out. In that way, we pile up the losses, and what is more probably everybody has got an extra screwdriver and monkey wrench stuck in some hole somewhere just in case he loses one. Now I think we ought to end that system. Then when a man loses a screwdriver, he can just go to the foreman and say, "I lost it," and get another one, and we won't have a lot of stealing going on back and forth.

C: This type of thing the men won't tell you about. You just have to make a good guess as to where the problem is, don't you?

R: It's a guess, but I think it's a pretty good guess. We get statistics on it. At the end of the month we can see how many tools are lost, and we get an idea of how they are changing hands. Now another thing, this is going to help on quality, and that reflects in costs, too. Now a fellow is on a job and he's got some big tools that he's concerned about; he's got just so much time to work on a job or watch his tool box to make sure nobody swipes his tools. What do you think he's going to do?

C: I suspect that he'll watch the box most of the time, won't he?

R: That's right. He's going to watch the box, and he won't be doing the work the way he should.

C: This seems like a pretty logical business, doesn't it? Do you think you can put the fellows on their honor not to take the tools home? How would it be if you just went to them on that basis and told them that all of this tool responsibility was costing quite a bit of money and that you wanted to cut that out and just rely on their honesty not to take tools home?

R: They'll react well if you put it that way. But they shouldn't take tools home anyway. We can't expect them to do that.

C: I didn't mean taking them home every night. I was thinking about whether they would steal them or not.

R: Oh, that's up to plant inspection. They check the workers so they can't take any tools home.

C: So you're going after this cost business now. There's always something, isn't there? First, there was quality control and now it will be the costs. I guess it should be a little easier to work on the cost control problem without the pressure from the boss you've had on this quality control business. Mr. Tarback was pressing you pretty hard on that.

R: Oh, I don't mind the pressure. That's a good thing. He's a big help. You know we've worked together for ten years, and we understand each other perfectly.

C: These problems all include the communication side you were talking about. You are always trying to get these people to do the job the way you see it.

R: Yes, it's all people. All of them with different ideas.

C: You want them all to be working for the company, but I guess they've got other things on their minds too.

R: Yes, you put it right when you were talking a while back and you said that we're all human. We sure are. Now I look at Mr. Kenyon up there in the picture sometimes. (Here he pointed out a picture on the wall of Mr. Kenyon, manager of the Racker International Division.) Sometimes I think he's smiling at me; sometimes I think he's mad at me.

C: It's a matter of how you feel that day?

R: Yes, I guess it's mostly a matter of my conscience. Sometimes I know I'm doing the right thing and sometimes I'm not sure I'm doing the right thing, even though I think I am.

C: And you have to figure out this sort of thing when you're handling people.

R: Now that's one thing that's different down here in Mexico. Up in the United States, you have a fellow working on the line and he's just in there for the money. You pay him two dollars an hour and that's all he cares about. The Latin is different. He's not satisfied just to get the money. The personal side is very important to him. The things the boss says to him are very important to him personally.

C: In the States, the worker doesn't really care about the boss?

R: No, he doesn't care what you say. Just so long as he gets his two dollars an hour. But down here, the way the boss acts is very important. Now if I go out on the line and I don't say hello to people, they're going to wonder what's happening. They expect me to say "Que Tal" and "How's your family?" and all of that. If I don't do that, they feel bad.

C: You have to keep up personal contacts with them all?

R: We do. Now that's what is so good about Mr. Tarback. He can remember names, he knows all sorts of names. He knows the people. That gives him a good contact with them.

C: He's a good man that way, isn't he?

R: Yes, he's quite a man. We've worked together for a long time, you know. I don't know what it will be like when he's replaced.

C: It will be pretty hard for a new man.

R: I suppose so.

C: Mr. Tarback knows so much about the country and about the people that a new man wouldn't know?

R: Well, he'd know a lot about the people. You know, they'll brief a man up there. They'll tell him all sorts of things about the men down in the plant. He'll know all about Alphonso Rodriguez and what he can do and what he can't do.

C: But that isn't like living with a man for ten years.

R: No, I don't suppose so. Well, we'll cross that bridge when we come to it.

C: He's an interesting fellow. Does he take you to dinner sometimes to find out what's on your mind?

R: Oh, yes, he takes me to dinner once in a while.

C: That gives him a chance to find out what you're thinking about?

R: Sometimes I take him to dinner too.

C: Oh?

R: I did that last week. We had a dinner party. It cost me a lot of money, but I planned it so I could have a chance to talk to him.

C: What did you do?

R: We gave a dinner in honor of his brother. We had to do it that way, you see. If I'd just invited him to dinner, him and his wife alone, he'd have known I was going to talk business, and that's no good. So we gave this party in honor of his brother, who was here for a visit.

C: You wanted him not to know it was going to be a business meeting so he'd be relaxed.

R: That's the way we set it up.

C: But it must be pretty hard to talk to him alone in a big group like that.

R: Oh, I figured that one all right. You see, Mr. Tarback doesn't like bourbon, he just likes Scotch. So I had it all set up before he got there. There was bourbon for everybody, and then the waiter came out with the tray of drinks and offered it to Mr. Tarback and so I said, right away, "No, that's not for you. That's bourbon. I've got a special bottle of Scotch just for you. But you'll have to come up to my study to have a drink." So then I took him off there, and there we were, all alone. So we could sit down and chat, and I told him all the things that I'd been planning for the production department.

C: What did you talk about?

R: Well, I talked to him about plans we have for quality control and the plans I have for the cost problems that I've been telling you about. I told him all about the things that I had on my mind.

C: What did he think about them?

R: Well, he thought they were fine. You know, we've been together a long time and we think the same way. Whenever I'm thinking up ideas, I get his advice on them this way.

C: So this party helped you get communication with the boss?

R: Yes. It set me back a lot of money. You know, it cost me 3,000 pesos for that party. I have no expense account for that. But it was worth it.

At this point a man appeared in the outer office. Mr. Rodriguez noticed him and wanted to talk to him, so the conversation ended.

Tice Electrical Company

ORGANIZATION AND COMPENSATION POLICIES

The Tice Electrical Company was established in 1950 to manufacture electronic tubes and related items for sale to manufacturers and wholesalers. The company grew steadily and an export department was soon set up which developed foreign markets, at first through distributors and then through sales branches in major markets. The export department was in New York City while the main company offices and plant were in Buffalo, New York. The export manager during this period was George Farley. Mr. Farley had been in the export business for 40 years prior to being hired by Tice to initiate the export operations, and the success of the foreign business was generally credited to his aggressive management.

In 1960 a Canadian factory was established. Previously, Canada had been treated as a sales territory under the domestic sales division. The director of sales for Canada was made head of the new manufacturing subsidiary, reporting directly to the president.

In 1962 the company decided to embark on further foreign manufacturing ventures commencing with Pavalia, a major Latin American country. The export department was redesignated as the international division, and under it a new department of foreign manufacturing operations was created. John Raines, who had been assistant to the director of foreign operations for a large electrical company, was engaged to manage this department. He was 58. In the next few months plans for the Pavalian operation were under constant discussion, and considerable friction developed between Mr. Farley and Mr. Raines. The approach of Mr. Raines to the manufacturing program received general support

The real company name, product line and some other facts have been disguised.

from the senior company officers and eventually Mr. Farley withdrew, accepting his privilege of retiring between 65 and 70. Mr. Raines became manager of the division. His former position was filled by Richard Birch from the domestic manufacturing organization. Some further adjustments were made, resulting in the organization shown in Exhibit 1.

As work on the Pavalian project proceeded, a number of administrative difficulties arose. The experience of John Martin indicates the general character of the problem.

THE PAVALIAN EXPERIENCE

John Martin was transferred from the domestic treasurer's office to work in the newly-formed financial department of the international division where he was under Michael Hudson, former credit manager of the export department. The task of developing financial and legal plans for the Pavalian operation was assigned to Mr. Martin, and he worked on them and other aspects of the Pavalian venture along with men in personnel, sales and manufacturing during late 1962 and early 1963. In June, 1963, plans for the new operation were completed and a staff of six men embarked for Pavalia to supervise construction of the plant and organization of the new subsidiary to replace the existing sales branch. Four of the men were production specialists who worked under the direction of Robert Loeb, an assistant to Mr. Birch, who was responsible for the construction

Exhibit 1. Organization, Early 1962

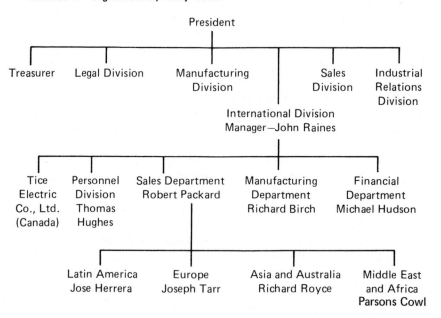

program. Mr. Martin was the sixth member of the group. The manager of the division, Mr. Raines, and Mr. Hudson told him that he was to be responsible for establishing the financial and legal aspects of the new subsidiary and that he should serve a controller's function as watchdog for the general progress of the project. He was told to stay within the framework of the plans which had been agreed upon, but beyond that he should use his best judgment in consultation with others in the group. He was to report back periodically to Mr. Hudson.

As work progressed a number of questions appeared, and they were discussed by Mr. Martin, Mr. Loeb and William Torrey, manager of the Pavalian branch. Mr. Martin found Mr. Torrey very knowledgeable about Pavalia, and he gathered from his actions that he expected to be the manager of the new subsidiary.

The most troublesome questions arose because they found that the suppliers available could not provide materials of exactly the type or quality called for by company specifications. It was necessary to decide whether to require suppliers to change their methods and help them to do so or to alter the specifications. Mr. Loeb tended to favor enforcement of the specifications whereas Mr. Torrey was prepared to make some concessions to accommodate suppliers. Mr. Martin found himself usually agreeing with Mr. Torrey both because he trusted his knowledge of the country and because helping suppliers would have added to the financial burden of the venture. Mr. Loeb felt himself to be the senior officer of the group and adhered to his position quite strongly, but in several cases accepted the conclusions of the other two men. None of the specific problems which arose was of major importance, so they were not referred back to the home office, the men feeling they could handle them adequately within their own authority.

Mr. Martin was also confronted by a number of strictly financial questions. He received several instructions from the treasurer, Mr. Hudson, which changed the original plan. While most of these were quite acceptable, a few of them seemed of doubtful value for the operation. For example, he was told that the working capital would have to be reduced and the deductions should be achieved by reducing the allotments for advances to suppliers which seemed to weaken the operation at a crucial spot. Similarly, Mr. Loeb was receiving instructions from his superior periodically, most of them involving alterations in the manufacturing plan to incorporate innovations in domestic manufacturing processes. Mr. Loeb and Mr. Martin agreed on a general policy of accepting them. Mr. Martin did write to Mr. Hudson every four or five weeks, giving a summary of the progress to date and the work still to be done.

In March, 1964, the plant was completed and the new subsidiary came into being with Mr. Torrey as president. The home office staff returned to the United States except for two of the production men who remained as advisors. On his return, Mr. Martin was disturbed to find his work in Pavalia subject to considerable criticism by Mr. Birch, head of the foreign manufacturing department, and Mr. Packard, the sales manager. They felt that he had injected himself unduly into decisions about the supply situation, and that rather than take sides in the matter, his responsibility should have been to encourage Mr. Loeb and Mr. Torrey to refer their differences back to the home office. Mr. Hudson also expressed some displeasure at the extent to which the final financial structure varied from the initial conception, though he said he thought Mr. Martin had done a generally good job in handling the many problems of starting a new venture.

Mr. Martin's problems continued after his return. From time to time he received letters from Mr. Torrey asking his advice or approval of some action. For example, three weeks after his arrival in New York, Mr. Torrey asked if he would approve an advance to a supplier whose production was essential to the operation but whose quality had on several occasions fallen a little short of company standards. In view of the criticism he had received, Mr. Martin made a practice of routing all such inquiries to Mr. Hudson, Mr. Loeb, Mr. Birch and Mr. Packard and of taking any differences of opinion through Mr. Hudson to Mr. Raines. He was distressed, however, at the time required for this process.

GENERAL REORGANIZATION

The recurrence of problems of this nature led to a major reorganization. Thomas Schilling, a consultant, was brought in as assistant to the director of the international division late in 1964. After consulting at length with members of the management he established the structure shown in Exhibit 2. The regional directors shown on the left were given full line authority for their territories while the staff men on the right were assigned advisory and supporting responsibilities. The senior men in the organization were consulted as to what positions they would like. Mr. Birch elected to become director for Latin America, and Mr. Packard chose the marketing manager post. Men were then assigned to other posts according to the management's evaluation of their capacities.

In the months which followed Mr. Schilling worked with the Tice executives to make the organization function effectively as the operations grew with new plants in three other Latin American countries and one in Europe, in addition to expanding sales organizations in about 20 countries. Particular attention was given to keeping the staff from assuming improper authority or interfering with field operations on trips overseas and to achieving sufficient collaborative action without complicating the organization with excessive procedures. The success of these efforts was tested in many cases. One such was the handling of requests from the Latinian subsidiary for adjustments in salary scales.

THE LATINIAN PAY QUESTION

The Tice salary policies for overseas personnel had been established after an extensive review of the practices of other companies. They were designed to

Exhibit 2. Organization, Late 1964

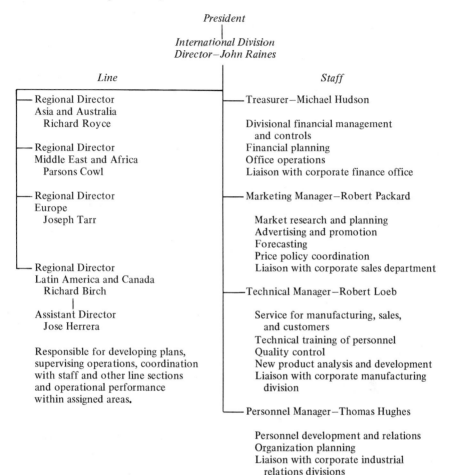

President
|
International Division
Director—John Raines

Line	*Staff*
— Regional Director Asia and Australia Richard Royce	— Treasurer—Michael Hudson Divisional financial management and controls
— Regional Director Middle East and Africa Parsons Cowl	Financial planning Office operations Liaison with corporate finance office
— Regional Director Europe Joseph Tarr	— Marketing Manager—Robert Packard Market research and planning Advertising and promotion Forecasting Price policy coordination
└ Regional Director Latin America and Canada Richard Birch	Liaison with corporate sales department — Technical Manager—Robert Loeb
| Assistant Director Jose Herrera	Service for manufacturing, sales, and customers Technical training of personnel
Responsible for developing plans, supervising operations, coordination with staff and other line sections and operational performance within assigned areas.	Quality control New product analysis and development Liaison with corporate manufacturing division └ Personnel Manager—Thomas Hughes Personnel development and relations Organization planning Liaison with corporate industrial relations divisions

assure compensation adequate to hold competent men in the organization. The company did not attempt to match the salaries of other companies exactly or to follow cost of living rises automatically. Rather it sought to maintain a pay level at which turnover was held to a reasonable rate. The main lines of the policies are given in Appendix A.

The Latinian subsidiary had initiated manufacturing operations in mid-1966. Previously the company had been organized solely for sales and service with the manager, Timothy Finch, serving essentially as the sales manager, and the treasurer, Ramon Rivera, being the only other employee of significant management status. Mr. Finch had been in Latinia for several years and was made manager of the new operations with a salary increase to cover his enlarged responsibilities. Herman Kranz, a German who had been with the Pavalian operation for two years, was brought to Latinia as assistant manager. He received a new salary in accordance with the established policies (see Appendix A), but no cost of living differential as Latinian costs were below those of Pavalia. Mr. Rivera also received a raise as his job was enlarged. One of the sales supervisors, Ricardo Jesus, was promoted to be sales manager and his pay was set by considering his former pay and that of comparable jobs in Latinia. Another Latinian, Alphonso Rojas, was hired from outside the company as production manager. He left in September 1967 to set up a company with a group of friends, and Robert Fales was sent down from the parent company to handle the job until another competent Latinian could be located. His pay in povars was set at the same level as that of Mr. Rojas, the balance due him being paid in dollars. The initial salaries of all these men are shown in Exhibit 3.

In April, 1967, the union to which the Tice workers belonged demanded a 15 percent wage increase to compensate for cost of living rises. In the face of a threatened strike, the company agreed to a 10 percent increase, and this advance was also extended to salaried local employees.

In the second week of July 1967, Mr. Birch made one of his regular visits to Latinia. On separate occasions during his visit, Mr. Finch and Mr. Kranz talked to him about their pay situation. Both expressed the opinion that the cost of living had advanced to a point where they should receive an increase. (Cost of living data are shown in Exhibit 4.) Mr. Birch returned to the home office on July 20th and the next day talked with Mr. Hughes, the personnel manager, about the men's request. Mr. Hughes pointed out that the company did not pay cost of living allowances unless costs in the foreign post were determined to be higher than those in the United States so that the situation would have to be

Exhibit 3.   Management Salaries in Latinian Subsidiary: Monthly Payments in Povars in Latinia and Dollars in United States*

	June 1966	July 1966	April 1967	September 1967	February 1968	April 1968
Mr. Finch, Manager	3240P	3700P	3700P	3700P	3700P	4030P
	$300	$340	$340	$340	$340	$340
Mr. Kranz, Asst. Mgr.	($700†)	2900P	2900P	2900P	2900P	3160P
		$265	$265	$265	$265	$265
Mr. Jesus, Sales Mgr.	1750P	2150P	2370P	2370P	2450P	2540P
Mr. Rivera, Treasurer	1850P	2150P	2370P	2370P	2370P	2370P
Mr. Rojas, Production Mgr.		2400P	2640P			
Mr. Falcs, Production Mgr.				2640P	2640P	2890P
			($700†)	$340	$340	$347

*Company exchange rate: 5 Povars = $1
†Dollar equivalent of salary in home country

Exhibit 4.   Cost of Living Indices (1963 = 100)

Year	Month	Latinia	United States
1964		107	100
1965		109	100
1966	January	109	100
	February	110	100
	March	113	100
	April	114	100
	May	114	101
	June	115	102
	July	114	102
	August	113	102
	September	114	102
	October	114	103
	November	116	103
	December	116	103
1967	January	117	103
	February	119	104
	March	122	104
	April	126	104
	May	128	105
	June	130	105
	July	133	106
	August	134	106
	September	137	106
	October	141	106
	November	142	106
	December	145	106
1968	January	145	107
	February	146	107
	March	147	108
	April	149	108
	May	152	108

studied. Because of the circumstances under which the men were assigned to their present jobs there had never been any thorough check of their salaries in relation to comparative costs of living. Therefore, Mr. Hughes engaged a consulting firm which had done such work for the company before to survey the cost of living for the men in comparison with that in Pavalia and the United States. The survey in Latinia consisted of pricing a selected sample of products covering the following elements in the cost of living: food purchases, household services, household operations, housing, transportation, medical care, personal care, recreation and tobacco and alcohol. The consultant made his survey accompanied by the two executives so that they would know the procedure for future checks. As a result of these studies, Mr. Hughes determined that the cost of living in Latinia and the United States were essentially equal. He discussed the situation with Mr. Birch and they agreed that no increase should be given and Mr. Birch wrote the men to that effect on August 25th.

On December 11, 1967, Mr. Finch wrote a letter to Mr. Herrera requesting approval for a general pay increase of 10 percent for all local employees. (Mr. Herrera had line responsibility for operational matters of this nature.) Mr. Finch included in his letter cost of living statistics since the time of the last general pay readjustment in April 1967. He pointed out that the index had risen substantially and that the personnel were entitled to higher pay.

Mr. Herrera passed the letter on to Mr. Hughes and after discussing it, Mr. Hughes wrote the letter appearing in Exhibit 5 in which he proposed that a detailed survey of comparable jobs be made before any salary adjustments were made. He had several thoughts in mind in writing the letter. First, he regarded education of the field personnel as one of his major responsibilities, and much of what he wrote was intended to convey specific information to Mr. Finch and to get him to thinking along lines of effective management, for example, in seeing the need to set salaries by competitive considerations, not just on cost of living indexes. Second, he was relating the handling of the immediate problem to basic company policies. The observations on objectives of salary administration were derived directly from the company manual. Mr. Hughes had always found reference to such policy statements both sound and safe. Third, he was using this situation as a vehicle for moving the Latinian operation toward a better personnel system. Specifically, he was pushing for better job descriptions. He had been encouraging them in this direction for some time but so far their approach had been rather haphazard. Now he had a specific situation in which job descriptions were important and he hoped to get some real progress.

Ten days later Mr. Herrera received the letter from Mr. Finch shown in Exhibit 6, suggesting that an interim raise be given immediately with the full study to be made later. Mr. Hughes and Mr. Herrera discussed this letter and in the next ten days several telegrams were exchanged with Mr. Finch on the subject. Mr. Finch held firmly to his views, and Mr. Hughes refused to recommend any increase without a survey. Finally, Mr. Hughes concluded that in view of the other pressures on the Latinia staff it was impractical to require a survey at this time so he undertook a survey in New York with the personnel managers of five companies with somewhat comparable operations in Latinia. He was not pleased with this as an approach to the problem because the records of some companies were inadequate and it was difficult to determine from their job descriptions what jobs were comparable with those in the Tice subsidiary.

Exhibit 5

Memo to Mr. Finch
From Mr. Hughes

Request for Cost of Living Increase

Mr. Herrera has passed to me your letter requesting cost of living increase for personnel in Latinia.

Your recommendations have been carefully considered in the light of the cost of living data you supplied.

We realize the urgency with which you make your request for a cost of living increase. Before being in the position to approve an increase of this nature there are certain relevant factors to be considered. It has not been a general policy of the company to give cost of living increases per se. We have considered cost of living, however, in conjunction with other conditions such as availability of labor and community rates in giving a "General Increase."

Your recommendations were explicit and conformed to the cost of living changes as indicated by government statistics. Application of the pay ranges you have proposed, however, do not show that we are in step with community rates. It is possible that in some cases we may be lower than the community rates and in other cases perhaps higher and we feel that we should determine where we stand competitively before giving increases.

It is felt that this would be an excellent time to align ourselves with community rates. We do not wish to prolong this problem but we feel that you will find this approach to be more beneficial for you in the long run.

Objective

To determine whether or not our wages and salaries are adequate to attract and hold desired employees and also to assist in maintaining a high level of morale. It is our policy to pay wages and salaries which are fair to each job and individual employee. We attempt to pay salaries which are fair and in line for comparable jobs with other companies in the community. To adjust these rates it is necessary to determine the prevailing rates for comparable jobs within the community surrounding our operations.

Step 1—Job Description

Pay rates should be based upon a clear and accurate definition of the duties and responsibility of each job. To determine just what duties are performed by each individual, a brief but clear and accurate definition of the duties which are normally performed by each employee should be set down in the form of a job description. This job description should contain as concisely as possible the general and specific duties involved. This job description can then be used by you in making your survey to make sure that you are comparing like jobs with other companies. It is not necessary to compare every job but an adequate selection of key or benchmark jobs should be used. (Key or benchmark jobs would be those that have certain basic characteristics that are easily identified in any company such as a secretary, chauffeur, accountant, etc.).

Step 2—Selection of Survey Comparison

Pay rates should reflect market conditions and represent the amount required to attract and hold desired workers. To determine whether or not we are paying adequate rates, a selected group of companies within the community should be chosen. In selecting these companies we must first decide on the geographical area we plan to use as our "community" in which we will conduct our survey. This is usually the area surrounding our plant or office from which we normally expect to hire our people. For instance, we might draw a circle with a radius of 10 to 25 miles with our plant or office as center. The community would be represented by this circle and almost all the companies selected for the community survey would fall within this circle.

First choice of companies to be selected from within our community circle would be those which are in the same or closely allied businesses. Second would be those of comparable size, reputation and working conditions. Third would be those which we might not otherwise include but with whom we are in competition for labor. Within an area such

Exhibit 5. (cont.)

as yours, your selection would include a broad category of industries of comparable size and reputation rather than just one industry.

Once such companies have been selected, they may then be contacted for salary and wage information. This may be made on a reciprocal basis.

Step 3—Comparison of Jobs

Although other companies will seldom have identical jobs, it is possible to determine which jobs are close as to level of work (education and experience required, responsibilities and judgment involved, work hazards, pace of work, etc.).

In making a survey such as this it is best to make personal visits to the companies from whom you wish to obtain the information. If this is not possible, you should clear the path for the individual who will be assigned to the task so that the information will be given to him when he calls.

Whoever gathers the information should be qualified to discuss the positions, i.e., who knows the operations, has a good idea of the jobs being compared, and is a good analyst. He should be careful not to accept a job as comparable just because job titles might be the same. The job should be examined for content.

The foregoing information is general in nature but it is essential that some method such as this be used in determining what salaries are to be paid for various jobs.

In obtaining your information the following should be noted for each job:

Job title, date rate established, minimum of rate, maximum of rate, and actual rates being paid; also the approximate number of employees at each rate.

Upon completion of your survey, the information should be forwarded to this office for review and will be discussed with Mr. Herrera for salary adjustments. Your prompt cooperation would be appreciated so that we may conclude this matter as soon as possible.

However, it did serve to give a rough measure of the competitive salary scales. The results of the survey completed on January 20th are shown in Exhibit 7. They indicated that the sales personnel were significantly underpaid, and an increase of 7 percent seemed justified. For other jobs, however, the salaries seemed generally reasonable, though some individual jobs might be out of line. On this basis, Mr. Hughes and Mr. Herrera agreed to a 7 percent increase for sales personnel with no change for others except that individual adjustments might be made if inequities were determined to exist. Mr. Finch was then advised that no further increases would be considered until a full survey had been made.

In March of 1968, Mr. Birch visited Latinia, and the two men again raised the salary question. They asserted that the cost of living had risen significantly and, if their pay had been correct in June, it certainly was not correct in the light of the rise in costs since then. Mr. Birch took the matter up with Mr. Hughes upon his return and they agreed that a new study was justified. Mr. Finch was directed to make a check of costs following the procedure the consultant had established. This study showed a 9 percent increase in costs since June 1967, and the men were given an increase in that amount on 70 percent of their total salaries. (See Appendix A, sec. A(2).)

Exhibit 6

From Mr. Finch
To Mr. Herrera

Subject: *Request for Cost of Living Increase*

The program outlined by Mr. Hughes in his memo of December 18th represents the ideal approach to the problem. We are in agreement with the various objectives set forth. In fact, we have attempted without much success to obtain this basic information from our local industry association. However, my personal opinion is that we will not obtain this information from them due to its confidential nature.

Also, we have requested to be included in a study by another United States company but have been refused because they have as many companies as they can handle. This survey for the most part includes big companies.

As you can appreciate, it requires considerable time to start and to complete our own survey. Frankly, with the number of problems we have relative to our new production plans, to our training program and to the indoctrination of Mr. Fales, there just is not enough time to do everything.

However, we do know that industry, as reported by our association, has on the average increased salaries over 30% since last April. Thus, some leading companies must have increased salaries materially more than the 30% to result in an industrial average of over 30%. Thus it is felt that the adjustment now proposed will not change our relative position in the industry, i.e., our new salary levels will not be out of line with other companies.

It is requested that you consider approving our request, and then in March when Mr. Hughes plans to come here to work with us in making a comprehensive wage survey, to help us make our personal programs more effective and to review what has been done and future plans in connection with personnel training programs, the matter can be reviewed.

You have a certain degree of security if you do favorably consider our proposal and that is with the accentuated ascending cost of living index, another adjustment will probably be needed next year just to keep even.

Before this next adjustment is made, we can complete the comprehensive survey and adjust any unusual situations that might be found.

It will be appreciated if you explain in more detail to Mr. Hughes the problems we are facing with new production, etc., and request that he reconsider his request and postpone the formal salary survey. Honestly, I feel certain we will not find at that time that we are out of line with the industry.

Exhibit 7. Latinian Salary Survey (Monthly Salaries in Povars)

| Company | Average salesmen's salary | | | Rate range |
	Base	Commission or bonus	Total	
Tice	1400	100	1500	1350-1800
A	825	825	1650	
B	1300	100	1400	1075-1750
C	1654	...	1654	1125-2100
D	650	850	1500	600-1300
E	...	...	1550 Up to 2 years	970
			Up to 4 years	1035
			Over 4 years	1130
				Commissions may vary radically from year to year

| Factory and office employees | | | | | |
Job title	Tice	B	E	A	F
Packers	175	150-200	156	150	
Watchmen	438	...	460	312	
Cleaning women	188	...	...	155	
Messengers	188	...	205	155	
Drivers	344	...	340	345	
Secretary, asst. manager	438	410	600	350	
Chief accountant	2300	...	2900	1900	
Secretary to manager	875	...	1000	935	1270
Accounting clerk	375	300	300	414	
Sec'y to chief accountant	400	250	...	391	
Stock clerk	225	...	...	...	300
Plant superintendent	2300	...	...	...	2500

Appendix A

BASIC POLICIES FOR COMPENSATION OF
OVERSEAS PERSONNEL

All Tice overseas personnel were divided into three groups:

1. Parent Company Personnel—hired in the United States and assigned to a foreign post other than their native country.

2. "Third Country" Personnel—hired in one foreign country and assigned to another.

3. Local Personnel—employed in the same country in which they were hired.

A. *Parent Company Personnel*

1. *Salary.* The basic salary was derived from the salary for a comparable position in the United States to which was added a geographic bonus ranging from 0 per cent to 35 per cent depending on the nature of the foreign post. General increases in the United States pay scales were also applied to salaries of parent company personnel overseas.

2. *Cost of Living Adjustment.* When the cost of living in the overseas post was lower than in the United States no adjustment was made. When it was higher, a differential was given on 70% of the basic salary. This was the portion of the salary assumed to be spent by the average employee for living expenses at the overseas location. The differential allowed each individual was usually determined when initially assigned to a post by a study of all available data including comparative cost of living indices from the U.S. State Department, banks and other sources. At the same time the company made a survey of costs for selected items and an analysis of the spending pattern of the particular individual.

425

Subsequently adjustments in the cost of living differential were based entirely upon changes in the local cost of living without regard to the situation in the United States. The company felt that as an individual adjusted to life in the foreign post, it was the local costs only which were significant. An objective of reviewing cost of living changes every six months was set but in practice the reviews were made at varying frequencies depending upon local conditions. Field personnel were asked to advise the home office when significant changes took place and they were never slow to do so.

3. *Specific Expenses Paid by Company.* The company paid the cost of (*a*) travel required for company business, (*b*) two months' vacation every two years in the United States including transportation for employee and family, (*c*) costs of education for children where residence abroad forced the parent to pay more for education than he would have in the United States, (*d*) membership in social or business groups essential to company standing in the community, (*e*) income tax differential where taxes were higher than in the United States. (When taxes were lower than in the United States this was considered as an offsetting factor in determining cost of living allowances.) (*f*) transportation and moving expenses between assignments.

4. *Pensions.* Employees were treated like domestic personnel in pension benefits.

5. *Method of Payment.* Basic salary and cost of living differentials were computed in dollars but the company sought to pay the maximum portion in local currency (using the exchange rate determined by the treasurer's office for all intercompany transactions). As a general guide line employees were allowed to receive 30 per cent of their pay in dollars in the United States, 70 per cent being the portion assumed to be required for living costs. In some instances, employees were allowed to receive more in dollars and in others the company set a higher portion as desirable for employee relations. Tice, like other international companies, generally had to pay expatriates more than local personnel for comparable jobs. The management explained to the latter that this difference was justified by the fact that the expatriates had to be given an incentive to work away from their native lands, but in view of the emotions involved purely logical explanations were not always fully effective. Therefore, the company tried to restrict the amounts paid to parent company personnel in local currency to the same level as those received by local personnel in comparable jobs.

B. *Third Country Personnel*

1. *Salary.* The salary was taken as the average between the salary for a comparable job in the place where the individual was hired and the salary for a parent company employee in the country of assignment.

2. *Other Provisions.* Cost of living differentials and specific expense payments were made precisely as for parent company personnel except that the place of

hire was used as the base rather than the United States. Third country employees were not eligible for the company pension plan unless they established the United States as their base. The portion of payment not received in local currency was generally paid in the currency of the country of hire but might be paid in dollars under special circumstances.

C. *Local Personnel*

Salaries of local personnel were established according to local pay scales. General increases were based on the over-all local situation considering competitive rates, productivity, the cost of living and other factors.

Rogers Company

ORGANIZATION FOR INDIAN AFFILIATE

In 1972 the Rogers Company was in the process of strengthening its operations in India. The company had recently begun the assembly of office machines in India and had made some progress in manufacturing components. Of particular interest in building up the Indian operation was the creation of an effective organization and the development of Indians for senior positions.

EARLY OPERATIONS IN INDIA

The Rogers Company had started selling in India during the 1940s. Sales had been accomplished through a distributor in Calcutta who resold to dealers in various parts of the country. In 1954 Rogers had established its own office in Calcutta with two Englishmen as manager and assistant manager and an Indian clerical staff to facilitate service and traffic work.

It was convenient to sell through the distributor because of his widespread distribution system and because he relieved Rogers of much of the accounting and traffic work. However, during the 1950s it became apparent that some further sales effort by the company might be worthwhile since the distributor was not promotion minded. Therefore, they set up the organization shown in Exhibit 1 to permit active promotion down to the dealer level. The service training supervisor was responsible for training the salesmen in service tech-

The real company name, product line and some other facts in this case have been disguised. Copyright © by the President and Fellows of Harvard College. Reproduced by permission.

Exhibit 1. Organization 1954-1966

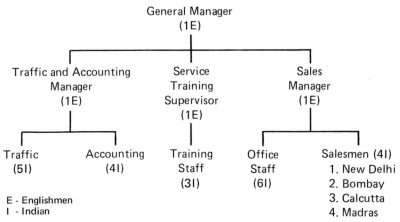

Note: The normal number of Englishmen (E) and Indians (I) are indicated in parentheses. These numbers fluctuated somewhat during the period.

niques and periodically running classes for the dealer servicemen. The distributor continued to perform the actual selling functions.

The salesmen traveled about the main cities of India, visiting dealers, encouraging them in sales promotion and training their service personnel. The market in India was not very competitive at this time, so the salesmen were not expected to be intensive in their efforts. For the most part, they were concerned with relatively simple sales methods and particularly with being sure that the service facilities of the dealers were adequate.

The salesmen were all Indians. They were chosen in various ways, but the typical man was either a former stenographer or serviceman who had shown an interest in expanded activity. For example, Mr. Swami, who handled South India, had been a stenographic clerk in the Calcutta office. In 1954, when the sales organization was set up, he had told the general manager that he would like to try sales work. At that time he was about 24. He did not have a college education but came from a high caste Indian family and was personally likable. He had proved alert in learning how to service machines and had done an effective job of getting around to see dealers in his area.

ASSEMBLY OPERATIONS

In 1966, Rogers decided it should undertake assembly, and eventually manufacture in India in response to the strong interest among Indians in development of manufacture. During negotiations with the government on this matter, officials also exerted pressure on Rogers to take Indian capital into the venture. Therefore, 51 percent interest in the subsidiary was sold to several Indian investors, thereby also providing much of the capital needed for the new operations. The Indian stockholders had no interest in management of the firm and were agreeable to continued operational control by Rogers under a 20-year management contract along with licensing and procurement arrangements which assured continuity in the operations of the firm as part of Rogers' international system.

In 1967 work was started on the assembly plant which was completed late in 1968. Operations were limited to assembly work until 1969 when a few of the simpler parts were manufactured, and, in 1972 plans were under way to manufacture other parts. As yet, no plans had been made to manufacture the parts requiring great precision which accounted for the bulk of the content of machines, but this step was expected in due course. At the same time, the company took over all distribution functions from the Calcutta firm.

ORGANIZATION IN 1968

These new activities required changing the organization from that shown in Exhibit 1 to that in Exhibit 2. In 1968 the general manager and the three second-line executives shown in Exhibit 1 were Englishmen, but the company was aware of the intense desire of the Indians to have companies in India run by their nationals, so it was intended that all jobs be turned over to Indians as rapidly as possible. It was felt that no existing Europeans would be displaced before retirement but that with the development of Indians, it would be unnecessary to recruit further Europeans for the Calcutta branch.

When the job of production manager was created, the vice-president for foreign operations in New York, Mr. Mason, wrote the general manager, Mr. Ross, telling him that he felt an Indian should be found for the job. Mr. Ross replied that he felt the desire to bring Indians into the important jobs was

Exhibit 2. Organization in 1968

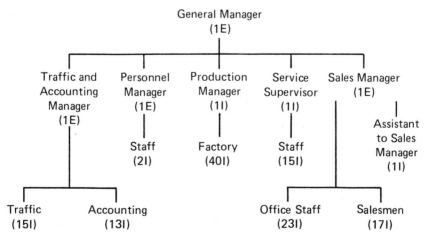

commendable as a matter of policy, but that it would be unwise to hire an Indian for such an important assignment. He said that he had looked into the matter, and the Indians available did not have sufficient sense of responsibility and technical competence, especially in light of plans for undertaking manufacture soon. Mr. Mason had learned in the meantime about two Indians who were getting advanced training in engineering in the New York area and who were about to return to India. He had met them and felt that they had real promise for production management work. He therefore wrote Mr. Ross that he knew of two men who he was sure could handle the supervision of the relatively simple assembly operations which were to be undertaken initially and could be developed for the more complex work to come. He would be glad to sign one of them up for the company if Mr. Ross could not find anybody in India. Within a few days he received a reply from Mr. Ross saying that after further investigation he had been able to find an Indian who was about 32 and had had some experience as a production supervisor. He was not outstanding but seemed competent to supervise assembly operations.

At the same time, the sales department was expanded so it could handle the full selling function. The position of assistant to the sales manager was created to handle the daily details of order processing and promotion programs. Mr. Rau, a 26-year-old Indian who had shown great ability as a salesman for two years, was given this job. Mr. Rau was the son of a farmer in northern India who was moderately prosperous, though socially of little standing. Mr. Rau had gone to college. He had a very pleasant personality and was alert and aggressive. Within a short time, the management had realized he had great promise and the job of assistant to the sales manager was created in part to give him greater responsibility and prepare him for further advancement. Subject to the appearance of a better alternative, it was believed that he would advance to assistant sales manager and eventually take over the department when Mr. Lawler, the present sales manager, retired.

The field sales force was also expanded to 17 men covering each major city. The new salesmen were all young college graduates. The company sought and was able to find intelligent men with aggressive sales ideas. They sold both to dealers and to large industrial and government buyers. Salesmen were paid salaries with no commissions. Like other workers, they paid 5 percent of their salaries to a provident fund. The company also paid 5 percent, and the total accumulation was returned to them with interest when they retired. The Indians seemed to prefer this system to a pension scheme with regular payments upon retirement. Most of them lived with their families after retiring and had no obligation to contribute to the regular support of the family. They liked getting a large lump sum with which they could splurge according to their inclinations.

The third change was the addition of the personnel department. Mr. Simpson, who had been service training supervisor, was put in charge of the department. Because of his previous work, he knew the men in the organization well, and he had an interest in training which would be useful. An Indian who had been his assistant took over the service training job.

POST-1968 EVOLUTION

In 1969 Mr. Shah, another Indian, was added to the top organization as treasurer, supervising the financial and accounting office which was created by dividing the functions of the traffic and accounting department. The manager of this department had reached the regular retirement age (58) and left. Another Indian took over the traffic department.

Mr. Shah had been chief accounting officer for a large British firm in which position he had been very well paid (3,000 rupees a month). However, Mr. Shah, who was only 42, felt that there were no further opportunities for advancement in that company so he was interested in getting in with a new, growing concern. One of Mr. Mason's friends in India had told him about Mr. Shah during a trip in 1969, so Mr. Mason had talked with him. He felt Mr. Shah would be extremely valuable in handling tax and financial negotiations with the government and was impressed with his over-all understanding of business operations.

Though he was hired only for the position of treasurer, he was, in fact, regarded as the number two man in the company and potentially the top man if the entire organization was Indian. In order to attract him to the job, he was given a salary somewhat greater than those of the sales manager and personnel manager. Ideally, Mr. Mason and Mr. Ross would have liked to make him assistant general manager. The growth of the operation and, consequently, Mr. Ross's work justified creating such a position. However, it did not seem wise to make such a move. On the basis of seniority, the sales manager, Mr. Lawler, who was 48, should have been the man to promote to this position. However, it appeared that Mr. Lawler had reached the limit of his capacity as sales manager and that he would not be effective in a position requiring responsibility for production and finance in addition to sales. Therefore, it was decided not to change the organization but simply have the treasurer relieve Mr. Ross of most governmental negotiations so that he could give full attention to the internal management of the company. Mr. Ross was 52.

In 1970 Mr. Mason had given some attention to making the organization more orderly in a procedural sense. Up to that time new jobs had been added as circumstances required and individuals taken on for whatever pay was necessary to get them to work for the company. The result was satisfactory in the short run, but as the organization grew in size, a more systematic approach seemed worthwhile, with jobs clearly defined and the pay ranges for each made explicit. Therefore, when he was in India in 1970, Mr. Mason suggested to Mr. Simpson, the personnel manager, that an organization manual be put together and efforts be made to hold the organization to it.

Mr. Simpson devoted considerable time to the manual. He interviewed most of the people in the management and clerical staff, wrote up descriptions of their work and responsibilities and established pay ranges for each position in consultation with Mr. Ross. In 1971 Mr. Simpson left the company to work for another concern, shortly after completing the manual.

While Mr. Mason was in India in that year, he discovered accidentally that the manual had had effects on the organization which were broader than had originally been anticipated. One evening he had dinner with one of the senior accountants whom he had known for some time. In the course of the conversation Mr. Mason remarked that the men would probably miss Mr. Simpson whom he knew had been personally liked. The accountant said that he was missed and that he had been well liked. He observed, however, that in the last year there had been some talk against him because of his program of freezing men in their jobs. On the whole, he felt that most people were not sorry to have him leave.

The accountant had not elaborated on this remark, but Mr. Mason felt he understood its meaning. He talked with Mr. Ross who said he had not heard such a remark before, but he concurred in Mr. Mason's analysis. Essentially, Mr. Mason felt that the Indians on the staff had considerable ambition. Their ambition might never be fulfilled, and they probably realized this to some degree. However, as long as there was no specific ceiling set on their advancement, they were content in the thought that they might achieve substantial progress. The creation of the manual with specific jobs and salary ranges probably did not reduce the actual chances of advancement for any individual, but the men evidently felt that it had.

No replacement for Mr. Simpson had been obtained at this time, and, in view of these developments, Mr. Ross and Mr. Mason discussed the idea of eliminating the job entirely. Eventually it was decided that the job would be kept with one of the older Indians filling it. The work would, however, be restricted to routine personnel processing, with any matters like the manual handled by Mr. Ross.

SALES DEPARTMENT REORGANIZATION—1971

In 1971 a further change was made in the organization. Mr. Rau had developed satisfactorily, and it was felt necessary in view of increasing competition to strengthen the sales force as much as possible. He was given the position of assistant sales manager as shown in Exhibit 3, in which job he was responsible for keeping day-to-day contact with the activities of the salesmen. He checked their daily reports of calls on dealers, their expense accounts and their use of promotion materials, and he instructed them as to suitable changes in their activities.

The management realized that this promotion for Mr. Rau would probably cause significant reactions among the sales force and some of the other office personnel. Being young, and of a relatively low social standing, he was not highly

Exhibit 3. Organization in 1972.

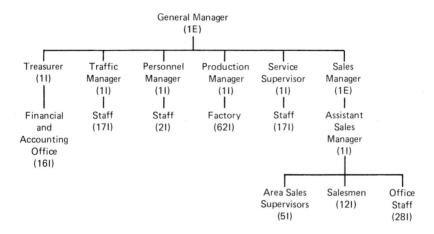

regarded by the older salesmen, even though these men did respect his actual ability. In order to ease the situation, some of the older salesmen were made area sales supervisors. The supervisors were instructed to help the younger salesmen in their districts. They continued to serve as salesmen themselves for somewhat reduced districts, and most of the decisions on sales activity were still made in the Calcutta office, to which all salesmen reported their activities directly. The area supervisors, in effect, were advisers and counsellors rather than administrators.

While this process made it somewhat easier for the older salesmen to accept Mr. Rau, it did not fully satisfy them. During a trip to India in 1972, Mr. Mason was taken aside by Mr. Swami, the salesman mentioned earlier, who had been employed in 1954. This man talked to Mr. Mason at some length about the sales program of the company and asked a number of questions about the size and type of organization which was proposed for the future. He also asked him what promotion policies were proposed in picking men for senior jobs as the company grew. At the end of the conversation, he asked whether, now that Mr. Rau had been placed above him and the other older men, it was possible for one of them to bypass him and take over Mr. Lawler's job when he left. Mr. Mason replied that it was impossible to predict the future; the company would simply have to pick the best man available for the job when that time came.

Mr. Rau was evidently concerned about the point of view of these men because he took Mr. Mason aside during the same trip and asked what Rogers did with old salesmen in the United States. Mr. Mason explained at some length that it was inevitable that most men would not go to the top and that the job of management was to make them feel satisfied with their work. In the United

States, Rogers had many salesmen in their fifties who were doing good jobs and were happy about their status.

Mr. Mason felt that he should concentrate his efforts in developing Mr. Rau along more moderate lines in management of men. There seemed no doubt of his intellectual capacities in sales planning, but his ability to handle men was not yet satisfactory. He was inclined to giving orders and curt comments rather than attempting to develop an easy relation with subordinates which would encourage cooperation in sales work. Mr. Rau was very proud of being a "modern" Indian and being independent of old habits and traditions. Occasionally it appeared that he had not made a complete break. For example, he created a minor problem in May 1971, when he suddenly asked for two weeks' vacation to get married, starting a week later. The sales manager had been planning for six months to take a vacation that month. He knew Mr. Rau was going to get married, but understood it would come later in the year. It developed, however, that Mr. Rau had been told that May would be a more appropriate time to get married according to certain signs.

On the whole, however, Mr. Rau ignored custom in his own life and was rather disdainful of the other Indians in the organization who conformed more closely to the traditional Indian social and religious practices. Mr. Mason felt that it would be essential for Mr. Rau to develop respect for the ways of others though he was uncertain as to how this could be accomplished.

While he was in India in 1972, Mr. Mason also discussed with the general manager the possibilities of applying in India a management development program recently adopted in the domestic organization. The program provided for careful evaluation and planning of the progress of all junior and senior executives. The procedure consisted of appointing a committee of three men to be responsible for each individual. The committee would review carefully the man's qualities and make recommendations for whatever action was needed to develop him for the greatest advancement he was apparently capable of achieving.

General Foods Corporation—
International Division (B)

PROFIT AND MARKETING PLANNING AND CONTROL

During Fiscal Year (FY) 1965 General Foods Corporation's net sales of convenience grocery products amounted to $1,400 million, of which $151 million was contributed by the corporation's International Division. The International Division, whose headquarters were located in Rye, New York, maintained manufacturing and marketing organizations in Great Britain, Ireland, France, Italy, West Germany, Denmark, Sweden, Brazil, Mexico, Venezuela, Australia and Japan. During FY 1964 the International Division contributed net earnings after tax of $4.7 million to General Foods' consolidated after tax earnings of $83.5 million. In FY 1965 the figures were $4.1 million and $85.0 million, respectively.

This case describes the information flow system utilized by the top management of the International Division to fulfill its responsibility for division-wide profit planning, control and marketing management support. In addition, the case examines the management of certain of the division's overseas subsidiaries and the relationship between these field systems and the International Division.

PLANNING AND CONTROL REPORTS

The thirty-odd financial reports received by the top management of the

This case was prepared by Prof. John Fayerweather, New York University, by condensing material in General Foods Corporation (A) (ICCH9-310-105), (D1) (ICCH9-313-213), and (D2) (ICCH9-313-214). The original cases were made possible by the cooperation of the General Foods Corporation, and prepared by David F. Hawkins, Assistant Professor, and Derek A. Newton, Lecturer, under the supervision of the Advanced Management Program Faculty, Harvard Graduate School of Business Administration. Copyright © by the President and Fellows of Harvard College. Reproduced by permission.

International Division from their field general managers could be classified into two groups: those related to profit planning and those showing actual financial results. All of these reports were channeled to the Division Controller, whose staff of accountants and analysts in turn translated them from local currencies into American dollars, analyzed the actual results against planned results and consolidated and summarized the reports for the consumption of both the division and corporate top management. All of the divisional and subsidiary activities concerning accounting reports were constrained by the policies and procedures established for *all* divisions by the corporate controller. General Foods' accounting reports were based on a fiscal year running from April 1 to March 31, inclusive. In addition to the financial reports, there were a number of marketing reports submitted by the overseas companies to Rye. Most of these marketing reports included sales and cost data which tied into one or more of the regular financial statements.

Planning Reports

There were six principal types of planning reports:

(1) *The Annual Profit Forecast* of the International Division was submitted each February to the Corporate Controller and reviewed by the Corporate Operating Policy Committee meeting with the International Division's top management during early March. These profit plans set forth the division's profit goal for the next fiscal year and summarized the resources management planned to use in achieving this end. The division's plan was a consolidation of the Annual Profit Forecasts of the various foreign operating subsidiaries, which were forwarded to Rye in late December and reviewed by the division president and his staff during January. As part of this divisional review of the subsidiary's plans, the general manager of each subsidiary and selected members of his staff were required to make an oral presentation of their plans to the president of the International Division. Once final approval was gained from the corporate management for the division's plans, the annual profit figure became a *fixed* objective. The Annual Profit Forecast covered two periods: the forthcoming fiscal year's profit plans and a plan for the succeeding two years. The longer-range profit plans were required primarily so that "those planning the current year would see how it fitted into some overall plan." Only the next fiscal year's plans were approved; the longer-range plans had to be resubmitted on a year-by-year basis for later approval.

The instructions covering the preparation of the FY 1965 Annual Profit Forecast were sent to the division controller on November 18, 1963. He revised them and sent them to the general managers of the foreign subsidiaries on November 20. The plans covered by these instructions were due at the International Division headquarters on or before December 23. The division's FY 1965 plans were due at the Corporate Budget and Analysis Department on February 10, 1964. Included with the instructions were the following forms to be used in submitting the forecasts to divisional headquarters: (a) Significant ($50,000 or more) adjustments to the prior year's planned profit and loss statements; (b) Return on Funds Employed; (c) Manpower Statistics; (d) Annual Profit Forecast and Long-Range Plan; (e) Annual Physical Volume and Gross Sales—All Products; (f) Quarterly Physical Volume and Gross Sales—All Products; (g) Trend of Cost of Sales; (h) Administrative Manpower—Salaries, Wages and Benefits; (i) Research Expenditures by Established Products and Development Products; (j) Quarterly Inventory Plans; and (k) Market Research Expense Analysis for Product and Process Improvement and New Products Research. In addition, each field general manager provided information about his operations in a prescribed format on charts bearing the following titles: Marketing Background; Major Problems and Opportunities; Fiscal 1965 Objectives; Plans for Accomplishing Objectives; and Marketing Prospective—New Products. According to one executive, the tentative market plans outlined in these charts were "the foundation upon which the annual profit plan was constructed." Later these details were expanded considerably in the Annual Marketing Plan submitted in early April (see below).

The principal financial statement included in the Annual Profit Forecast was "Form F" which highlighted the following items: total volume, gross sales; net sales; gross profit; total marketing expense; profit before technical service fees and interest expense; profit before taxes; and profit after taxes. A Form F was prepared by each subsidiary's management for the subsidiary as a whole and for each of its products.

The "Return on Funds Employed and Cash Flow" was another financial report which divisional management considered important. According to General Foods Accounting and Financial Manual: "Return on funds employed measures profit efficiency rather than profit dollars, which can be misleading during inflationary or deflationary periods.... This calculation also can provide a comparison of current performance against the historical and standard return. Moreover, it helps top management determine the areas in which to invest funds."

(2) *The Annual Capital Program* included all capital expenditures over $5,000, the amount above which headquarters approval was required. At the time the annual capital program was considered by the divisional and corporate top management, only tentative approval was given. These projects had to be resubmitted to headquarters management for final approval before funds were actually committed to the project.

The Annual Capital Program consisted of two parts: current and long-range programs. The current portion of the Annual Capital Program included detailed estimates for all projects for the coming fiscal year that had progressed far enough in their engineering and cost estimates to permit reasonable projections of fund requirement and benefits. Long-range projects were those for which studies had progressed far enough to identify major segments of the project or to make necessary financial evaluations.

Once the profit and capital plans were approved in March, the International Division's various subsidiaries prepared their *Annual Marketing Plan* and *Two-Year Cash Plan*, both of which were submitted to Rye during late March or early April.

(3) *The Annual Marketing Plan* described in detail the subsidiary's marketing plans by major products for each quarter of the coming fiscal year. The plan showed the expected volume in standard cases; the volume and costs related to specific promotional deals; the costs of advertising media; selling costs; burden and gross profit per case. FY 1965 was the first year all of the overseas subsidiaries were required to submit Annual Marketing Plans to Rye. In those cases where no reliable data concerning market share and competitive activity existed, the overseas managers were required to make estimates. The headquarters marketing staff spent about 40 percent of its time reviewing the annual plans and their quarterly revisions. Each plan was reviewed by at least two people. Comments were prepared for each plan received at the headquarters. These comments were abstracted by the various area directors and forwarded with suitable comments to the related subsidiary in the form of recommendations, which the subsidiary was free to follow or disregard. Appendix A summarizes the plan and headquarters comments for Kool-Aid for Mexico as one example of this process.

Once a subsidiary's Marketing Plan was settled upon, the subsidiary was expected to conform to the plan. If a product manager wanted to deviate from the plan, he had to obtain the permission of his subsidiary's marketing manager and general manager. The International Division also had to be informed ahead of time of any major changes in the marketing plans of its subsidiaries. Usually, permission to spend additional funds was granted if the additional funds generated incremental profits beyond the level established in the Annual Profit Forecast. In these situations, however, the subsidiary was held responsible for obtaining the previous profit goal plus the incremental profits. Seldom was a subsidiary given permission to spend more money on marketing if the expenditures did not generate incremental profits above the Annual Profit Forecast level. A subsidiary had considerable leeway in shifting marketing funds from one product to another, from one quarter to another and from one type of promotion to another, as long as it kept within its marketing budget set forth in the Annual Profit Forecast.

(4) *The Two-Year Cash Forecast* was prepared on a quarterly basis for the coming fiscal year and on a twelve-month basis for the second year. This required forecast was updated during October of each year.

(5) During the year *three quarterly revisions of the Annual Profit Plan* were submitted to Rye headquarters, showing the significant changes in the subsidiary's plans during the rest of the fiscal year. The main purpose of these revisions, which were known as the *First Revision, Second Revision* and *Third Revision*, was "to get the people in the field to plan ahead so that they know

what they have to do to meet their original profit goal set forth in the Annual Profit Forecast." Typically, these revisions were forwarded to Rye during the first weeks of May, August and November, respectively.

Wherever possible, the subsidiary was required to provide the reasons for the variations, including the effect of changes in (a) price and cost, (b) market size and/or market share, and (c) competitive activity.

(6) Each quarter, during the fifth and ninth weeks, the *Fifth and Ninth Week Trend Reports* were submitted to Rye. The Ninth Week Trend Reports were often included as part of the quarterly revisions to the profit plans. The trend reports indicated the subsidiary's best estimate of the actual quarterly results and contained brief descriptions of why the anticipated actual results were different from the subsidiary's earlier projections.

Historical Reports

The principal financial reports showing actual results were the monthly, quarterly and annual financial statements prepared by the foreign subsidiaries. Other principal historical reports showing actual results were the Annual Operations Review and the Weekly Activity Report.

Matters concerning financial reporting were closely controlled by the corporate controller's staff. All of the monthly, quarterly and yearly *financial statements* forwarded to Rye were prepared on forms which were standard throughout the corporation. In order to meet the corporate requirements regarding the due dates of divisional financial statements, all of the overseas subsidiaries closed their accounting records prior to the end of the month. For example, during the September quarter the foreign subsidiaries closed their books on July 25, August 22 and September 19, whereas the domestic divisions were able to meet the corporate due dates by closing their books on the last day of each month. In addition, the corporate accounting groups specified the chart of accounts and the broad accounting principles governing the preparation of financial statements. Also, from time to time, corporate internal auditors visited the foreign subsidiaries and submitted reports to headquarters management based on these visits.

Every April, following the preparation of the year-end statements, each subsidiary and division was required to prepare an *Annual Operations Review*. The review consisted of two forms: a listing of unit sales, net dollar sales and profits before taxes of every product marketed by the division; and a listing of all research expenses by projects showing total expenses to date, variations from plans, estimated future expenses and completion date. Comments explaining significant variations from earlier plans were also included.

Each week the foreign subsidiaries sent a *Weekly Activities Report* to Rye. These reports were in turn summarized and consolidated into a division weekly report which was forwarded to the chairman, General Foods Corporation. The weekly report was a two-page narrative report on such topics as competitive activity, employment situation, financial highlights, organization changes, sales results, marketing programs, and major political, social and economic events.

Also, each week a cable reporting total gross sales in units and dollars was sent to Rye, followed through the mails by a detailed report of the data contained in the cable. These weekly product transmittals reflect "a preoccupation on the part of management with sales, rather than finances," one executive said.

In addition to the above formal reports, the division top management exercised control over its subsidiary operations through personnel visits. For example, one International Division executive estimated he spent about one-half of his time overseas.

ADMINISTRATION AND USE OF PROFIT
PLANS AND CONTROL REPORTS

This section provides information on the administration and use of the division's information flow system from the headquarter's point of view and selected comments of overseas personnel.

Headquarters

By June 1964, all of the overseas subsidiaries were "more or less" on the accounting system used throughout the General Foods Corporation. In 1965, the International Division was trying to establish planning and control procedures and criteria useful to a division operating in the international environment. Management believed this review was necessary since historically the International Division's accounting and planning system had been dictated in large part by the staffs of the corporate treasurer and controller, both of whom had primarily a domestic orientation because of the relatively short time GFC had been active on the international scene. Also, the division has not been able to follow its policy of "letting the overseas people control themselves" since a number of the managers of overseas subsidiaries, who were former owners of businesses acquired by General Foods, had difficulty conforming to the General Foods report structure. Finally, three further problems encountered in administering and using the information flow system were: the great distance involved; the shortage of experienced financial analysts at headquarters; and a shortage of internal control staff trained to review the internal control systems of the foreign companies and assist them in their own programs.

Robert Howell, Vice-President, International Division believed that the division should have more direct control over its cash management, instead of leaving this area to the corporate treasurer's office. Unlike the other divisions of General Foods, the International Division's subsidiaries financed their operation with capital internally generated or borrowed locally. He also believed that not enough attention had been directed to tax management in the international area.

"Again we operate more like a company than a division. Unlike the domestic divisions, we pay taxes directly to foreign governments. Thus, while it makes sense for the domestic divisions to leave tax matters to the corporate treasurer, we are a different 'kettle of fish.' "

Mr. Howell also believed the methods and procedures related to the division's information flow system needed attention, particularly at the subsidiary level. This was true because of two factors: cost accounting as practiced in the United States "was practically unknown overseas"; and a number of the recently acquired foreign subsidiaries had primitive accounting and internal control systems which, while they satisfied the former owner-managers, did not meet General Foods' tight standards.

By August 1964 E.M. Wells, who became Manager, Finance and Administration in early 1964, had defined his function and created a small staff. He had made a number of changes in the reporting format and procedures of the division; saved the company about $30,000 through a reorganization of the banking relations of the Swedish and French companies; and had explored a number of ways to save taxes by restructuring the legal relationships of the overseas subsidiaries.

He had been unable, however, to make significant changes in the division's internal controls. According to Mr. Wells, he had defined the function of internal controls in the division, developed a program to implement the required improvements and estimated the cost of carrying out this program. The division management, he said, was reluctant to spend the estimated $95,000 a year to do this job at this time.

Every manager was measured primarily on his ability to meet the annual profit goal contained in his Annual Profit Forecast. Corporate policy indicated that managers should be held responsible for the return on funds employed in their operations. However, this standard was not generally regarded as a critical measure of performance by the various divisions. As one International Division executive said:

> In theory this measure should motivate the manager to manage his investment well. However, at the moment, return on funds employed is not particularly meaningful. There is just not enough pressure on the subsidiary managers to pay much attention to these figures. We have no standards for return on funds employed. In every area the various managers agree or do not agree to shoot for a particular return. Nobody presses them. This is due partly to the fact that we have had enough cash and very few people in the organization worried about investments. Now the management is becoming more concerned about conserving cash and looking at inventory and accounts receivable levels.

Because of the distances involved and the shortage of financial analysts at division headquarters, the International Division management found it difficult in the short-run to maintain control over their foreign operations. All of the detailed reports were air-mailed to Rye. Since the mail from Italy and Japan sometimes took as long as twelve days to reach Rye, there was a considerable lag between the date when the period covered by the report ended and the time the report arrived in Rye. Thus, because of the need to prepare a variety of reports for corporate purposes and the lack of skilled analysts, the division had "not really pushed hard for tight monthly control from Rye over subsidiary operations," according to Mr. Wynn, Controller, International Division.

Finally, during 1964 the division had embarked upon a new training program in an attempt to improve the skills of both the overseas controllers and the division's financial analysts. Under this scheme, selected controllers of the overseas operations were brought to Rye for about six months to work with the division's accounting group. While a subsidiary's controller was at Rye, his place in the field was taken by one of the financial analysts on the headquarters staff. In addition, from time to time the division's financial analysts made field trips to help subsidiaries solve particular problems, such as developing a credit policy.

Field Management

During an examination of the operations at three subsidiaries (England, Mexico and Brazil), six major conclusions regarding the administration and use of the International Division's information flow system were expressed by field management:

(1) Generally, the top management of the overseas subsidiaries recognized that close attention to the control function was critical to the success of their operations. For instance, the general manager of the Brazilian subsidiary, Kibon S.A., claimed nearly half of his time was spent in the financial control area. Close attention to cash flow, product costs and credit levels was needed, he said, if Kibon was to survive in the rapidly changing inflationary economy of Brazil. Another manager who thought that operating in an independent fashion was essential for his "style of management" said, "It is important to me that Rye has confidence in the reliability of the reports I forward to them. As long as headquarters has faith in your budgets and financial statements, they will leave you alone."

(2) The top management of the subsidiaries also agreed that the emphasis on planning and review was desirable. As one general manager said:

> An important contribution General Foods has made to the management of my company is budgetary control. The Annual Profit Forecast calls for a profit goal which I must deliver. This is a great discipline which, frankly, many overseas companies lack. As I see it, if you are tied to a fixed profit objective you have to know what's going on. . . . Also, the International Division's financial analysts located at Rye are continually asking me to explain my operations. I don't view this as an annoyance, but rather with respect since having to defend my actions keeps me on top of my operation.

The lower levels of management, however, did not always share this enthusiasm for the General Foods emphasis on budgets. As one product manager said:

> I recognize that there are very good reasons why we have to have annual and quarterly budgets in order to predict cash flows, etc., but sometimes the quarterly budget restricts us. . . . Sometimes we make decisions in marketing which are poor in order to meet a quarterly budget target. If competitive activity hits you at the beginning of the year, you have time to reallocate your expenses among quarters so as to keep profits up. However, should you get hit by competitive activity in the last quarter of the year, if you are to meet your profit goal, you can generally do nothing but cut your advertising budget. Clearly, reducing your advertising budget is not wise in terms of building a long-run market share. . . .

(3) Most of the overseas managers agreed that the Annual Profit Forecast was of limited use to them in controlling their operations, primarily because the budget was prepared in November, nearly four months before the beginning of the fiscal year. Therefore they used the First, Second and Third Revisions as control plans, rather than the Annual Profit Forecast.

(4) Several overseas managers claimed the General Foods' information flow system was not "discriminating" and was more relevant to domestic operations than foreign activities. For instance, one general manager said:

> In my opinion, in the area of financial reporting the International Division might well find it worthwhile to differentiate between the types of operations it has. Perhaps this could be on the basis of management sophistication, profits or sales. For example, we must now resubmit to Rye all of our capital budget requests over $5,000 for reapproval before we can actually spend the money. This may be essential in the case of some of the lesser developed subsidiaries, but I doubt if it is really necessary in the case of the more sophisticated companies.

Another overseas executive claimed the report structure was based on the accounting capacities of the domestic divisions. He said:

> Because most of our bookkeeping is done by hand, we have to start early next month (July) preparing our Second Revision covering the September and Final Quarters. Thus, when this report is being prepared, the actual results of the June quarter are not fully tabulated. . . . The report schedule is dictated by the Corporate Controller's office which, I believe, is tied more closely to the domestic division's needs and capabilities than to those of the International Division. For instance, I feel sure that the Corporate Controller's office assumes that the actual June quarter's results are fully known before work on the Second Revision is begun.

(5) A number of the overseas managers regarded some of the corporate internal auditors who periodically visited their subsidiaries as "inexperi-

enced." One general manager observed that this was "unfortunate" because the overseas companies needed considerable help in this area.

(6) A number of executives both in Rye and abroad pointed out that, by requiring the foreign subsidiaries to report in as much detail as the domestic divisions, their costs were increased, principally, because they have "to maintain large accounting staffs as well as pay full taxes." A number of the local businessmen against whom the foreign subsidiaries competed did not keep financial records in such detail. "This helps them," one executive said, "to keep the overheads low as well as escape many of the taxes General Foods pays!"

HEADQUARTERS MARKETING SERVICES

We think the marketing skills that have made General Foods a leader in the domestic convenience foods business can, with allowances for local variations, be successfully applied overseas to build a world-wide franchise for a whole host of present and future products. General Foods is primarily a company marketing products with relatively low technological content. We look for opportunities where our marketing skills can be usefully applied to products with high gross margins. This means, of course, that we should be in nonstaple items and possibly in countries with a relatively high standard of living. It is not clear whether we should always acquire going businesses or start new companies, but we do find it useful to maintain the brand names of acquired companies as these have an acceptance in the market.

A GFID executive gave this expression of the General Foods philosophy regarding its overseas marketing activities. This section describes the organization and activities of the GFID staff marketing department which was charged with the responsibility for assisting the managements of GFID subsidiaries in the conduct of marketing activities and the development of product lines. The sections which follow describe how GFID subsidiaries in England, Mexico and Brazil developed their marketing strategies and how these strategies were shaped both to meet local market conditions and to take account of the relationship with a large multinational organization.

Headquarters Organization

Before December 1961 the staff marketing function was performed by a small marketing services group which concerned itself primarily with the dissemination of information and product samples from headquarters to each of the overseas subsidiaries. At the end of 1961, with GFID exhibiting rapid growth, management felt the need for expanding marketing services to the subsidiaries. As of 1965, the size of the GFID marketing staff, while small relative to the financial staff, had increased and offered a range of services to the subsidiaries.

The staff marketing group was headed up by B.L. Humphrey, the staff marketing director, who had transferred to GFID in June 1964, after three years in the Maxwell House Division as Associate Product Manager, Product Manager for Instant Maxwell House, and finally Advertising and Merchandising Manager.

R. Simpson, the advertising and promotion manager, devoted a large part of his time to problems in the Far East, but was also available for assignments in other areas. In addition to advertising and promotion, Mr. Simpson was also responsible for assisting subsidiary management with trademark and copyright activities. He had one assistant to help him.

E.F. Conner, the product planning manager, had joined GFID after five years with the domestic Maxwell House Division. He was believed to be particularly well qualified to deal with coffee marketing problems. Mr. Conner had also worked many years in advertising agencies and in marketing research before joining the Maxwell House Division.

Dr. A. Ruedi, the product development manager, had spent five years with General Foods Corporation in the field of new product development, working on both corporate and domestic division projects, before joining the International Division in 1958. He had extensive experience in technical research, production and quality control and, with his assistant, served in an advisory capacity to subsidiary management and as a liaison between the area directors and the GFC product research facilities at Tarrytown, New York.

Finally, the GFID marketing department included a marketing services manager, F.L. Keller, who was responsible for circulating marketing information to the subsidiaries. Two assistants helped him in this activity. Mr. Keller's marketing background included work with an advertising agency, a GFC domestic division, and another food manufacturer. He had been with GFID for approximately five years.

Headquarters Activities

In discussing the activities of their department, GFID staff marketing personnel pointed out that their job titles did not always indicate accurately their individual activities. Thus, a problem involving advertising and promoting coffee in the United Kingdom might be forwarded to Mr. Conner instead of Mr. Simpson, because of the former's experience in the domestic Maxwell House Division. Likewise, a product planning problem presented by the Australian subsidiary might be handled by Mr. Simpson instead of Mr. Conner, because of the former's familiarity with subsidiary management in Australia.

The GFID marketing staff served as liaison with the domestic divisions, with many of the GFC staff departments and with the New York offices of the GFC domestic advertising agencies. Upon request, GFID staff people prepared special studies ranging from an analysis of a product or business category to reports on the economic conditions of countries in which GFID was investigating possible acquisitions. Working with GFC marketing research people, the GFID marketing department personnel were able to assist subsidiaries by suggesting the kind of marketing research that should be undertaken by them and later, by helping subsidiaries analyze the results of surveys. Whenever a project was judged to be of broad interest to the International Division, and adequate funds were available, there was a possibility that the GFID marketing department would undertake a research study for a particular subsidiary; for instance, as it did recently on dehydrated fruits and vegetables in England.

Marketing counsel. GFID marketing staff personnel offered overall marketing counsel to subsidiaries on many kinds of marketing problems that arose overseas, including problems on pricing, distribution and sales organization. While GFID staff executives made no claim to know all the answers, they did believe that collectively their qualifications and background, their familiarity with US marketing methods and their experience in GFC domestic divisions could be of advantage to the subsidiaries.

GFID marketing staff personnel were available for extended visits to subsidiaries as consultants on major products and for emergencies. On only two occasions had GFID marketing personnel been called upon for this purpose: Dr. Ruedi spent several weeks with the Brazilian subsidiary in 1963 assisting in setting up new product development programs; and Mr. Conner spent six months in 1963 with the Mexican subsidiary studying the soluble coffee market and advising General Foods de Mexico S.A. on pricing and on positioning its instant coffee products in the Mexican market.

According to one executive, some subsidiaries were more reluctant to seek help from staff departments than others because of the psychological differences among people, and the size and sophistication of the subsidiary. GFID marketing executives stated, for instance, that they had relatively little contact with the British subsidiary because of its large marketing organization.

Advertising counsel. GFID staff marketing executives welcomed the opportunity to study, discuss among themselves, and comment to the subsidiaries on their advertising campaigns. In addition to offering suggestions which might improve the advertising, GFID executives kept subsidiaries posted regarding advertising themes, photography, art work and commercial films that showed promise of being applicable to more than one country. For instance, the theme "America's Favorite Coffee" was first used by the British subsidiary, then followed, with variations, by the German, Australian and Japanese subsidiaries.

The GFID marketing staff also became involved in the selection of advertising agencies. Although the decision to appoint or to discontinue an advertising agency was left to subsidiary and area management, GFC required all divisions to notify corporate headquarters of agency changes, and GFID required the subsidiaries to advise its marketing department of any agency appointments before they were made.

The GFID marketing department was currently in the process of building a complete file of all TV commercials and print ads used by GFID subsidiaries. This advertising record was designed to keep GFID management posted on the subsidiaries' advertising activities and to identify themes, copy points or techniques that had application elsewhere.

Package design. The GFID marketing department was responsible for processing all subsidiaries' package designs and redesigns through the GFC carton committee. This activity involved getting the necessary clearances from the GFC legal department and technical research people. The main value of this clearance procedure, according to GFID management, was to check the many details the subsidiaries had to consider in planning packaging. In addition, GFID marketing staff personnel welcomed the opportunity to review and evaluate the package designs themselves. No attempt was made to encourage subsidiaries to have the design work performed in Rye, because the cost would probably be prohibitive and, in many countries, subsidiaries had access to designers who were as good as or better than ones in the United States.

Because packaging was considered an important element for success in the food business, GFID executives placed a lot of emphasis on upgrading the appearance and construction of the various containers. But in some countries, where GFID would have liked to see the most improvement in product packaging, the fewest package designs were submitted for approval. According to one executive: "Many of our subsidiaries operate in countries where good packaging and package designers are not available. As a result we find that 'the poor man is afraid to show up in his rags'—they are ashamed to submit new designs to us."

Dissemination of marketing information. Beginning in 1963, GFID management made efforts to advise all subsidiaries of the marketing activities in each of the overseas companies and in the United States. The vehicle for the dissemination of this marketing information was *Marketing Highlights,* a monthly news brief which presented in capsule form GFC marketing activity in both the US and overseas, and offered further details to a subsidiary upon request. Mr. Keller, who was responsible for *Marketing Highlights,* commented as follows:

> I would estimate that perhaps half of our domestic marketing ideas cannot be assimilated by any one subsidiary. Local conditions account for this and we have to depend on local management to weed out the inapplicable ideas. As we attempt to determine what information subsidiaries might be able to use or might make them feel more like a part of the General Foods family, we hope we do not throw out any babies with the bath water. Actually, the danger is that these local people tend to get overenthusiastic. For instance, our Japanese subsidiary borrowed the idea of a carafe-pack for soluble coffee from the domestic Maxwell House

Division after it had seen the success that our British subsidiary had with the same idea. Management in our Japanese subsidiary thought the empty carafe would make an ideal soy sauce jar and ordered thousands of them to tie in to a particular Christmas promotion. We cautioned them to go easy on the idea and, fortunately, they did reduce their order somewhat— but not enough. They sold about 60 percent on their original promotion and, although they will eventually get rid of them all, they were still involved with moving the carafes through the channels six months later.

Review of marketing plans.   This role was described in the previous section.

Product planning and development.   Although GFID marketing staff personnel were organized to guide the development of the subsidiaries' product lines, the final responsibility for determining the suitability of a GFC domestic product to a particular foreign market rested with the management of that subsidiary. Dr. Ruedi described the GFID policies with regard to overseas product line planning as follows:

> General Foods has not desired to become engaged in marketing staple foods overseas, and this philosophy has been injected into much of our long-range product planning. The reason for this choice is twofold: first, General Foods is in the convenience foods business in the States; second, General Foods entered the international game at a later stage when the food retailing practices of most countries had undergone forms of development which led us to believe that convenience foods held both short- and long-run profit opportunity. General Foods has undertaken a series of rapid acquisitions in the past few years. Because the corporation saw these activities as the fastest way to grow, the companies acquired were chosen more on the basis of past success than a product line similar to that of General Foods. The idea now is to build on to these operations those products that General Foods has been successful with in the United States and that we anticipate will be successful overseas.

Dr. Ruedi described his activities as falling into three categories. The first one was to offer technical assistance on product development such as, for instance, the reformulation of a gelatin dessert when a foreign subsidiary was unable to obtain the same raw materials available in the United States. Sometimes this assistance required calling upon the resources of the GFC technical facilities at Tarrytown, which might involve billing the subsidiary for technical services. Whether the subsidiary was so charged depended on whether GFID interest in the particular product was high, for instance, as in the case of bubble gum, or low as in the case of products with only national or regional sales potential. In this latter instance the subsidiary would be billed for the technical services.

Second, Dr. Ruedi attempted to keep the subsidiaries up to date on research activities undertaken by the domestic GFIC divisions. These research activities were communicated to subsidiary management either informally or by memoranda sent to the respective area directors.

Dr. Ruedi's third function was to evaluate the new-product activities and opportunities of each of the subsidiaries and recommend to them and to GFID top management the amounts of time and money that GFID should spend on the various projects open to it. This last activity, according to Dr. Ruedi, occasionally placed him in a rather uncomfortable position. Explaining this assertion, he commented:

> Generally, the smaller subsidiaries are the ones who need the most help, have the hardest fight, the smallest market, and the fewest dollars to spend. By and large, each subsidiary must generate its own funds for product line expansion and development. But if the subsidiary can justify the investment, and the International Division can recommend to the corporation that additional monies be sent to this subsidiary, then in some areas these recommendations are approved; in others they are not. I am sometimes left with the job of explaining to a subsidiary general manager that his local political and economic situation precludes long-range investment on our part. How do we do this without lowering his morale and stifling his own product development activity?

Dr. Ruedi stated that although GFID had few written policies with regard to product development, it had developed certain procedures to review and assess the new product activities of the subsidiaries. Each subsidiary was required to present its new product program at the Annual Profit Plan review held in Rye at the beginning of each calendar year. GFID management required all subsidiaries to submit complete test marketing plans before any new product was launched on a national or regional basis. Dr. Ruedi commented on these activities as follows:

> The earlier we can get into the subsidiary's new product development work, the more we can influence it. If the ideas are weak, the subsidiary can often be talked out of them and, by the same token, we can also talk them into projects—provided we present our ideas in a way that can be assessed in terms of their local situations. Of course, our product planning forms are rudimentary and we run the risks of oversimplification when we use them. Nevertheless, we feel that our requiring these forms to be filled out and requiring market tests forces a local management to think through the advantages and disadvantages of every "hot" idea it gets.
>
> General Foods acquired many one-man operations that were quite efficient in their way. These businesses didn't need targets, schedules and formal plans. These managers could intuitively develop ideas without market research and payback period considerations. These trial and error approaches were primitive but, in many instances, they were effective. If the local operator felt he could afford to, he would expand his product

line. If not, he didn't. And many of these products could be introduced by the owner appealing to his friends in the trade to plug his ideas. Our plans and figures, on the other hand, are an attempt to avoid costly mistakes or inactivity.

According to Dr. Ruedi, GFC's most vital problem, both in the United States and overseas, was the development of new products. Domestic division general managers and general managers of foreign subsidiaries were sometimes reluctant to take on new products at the risk of hurting annual profit performance. According to Dr. Ruedi:

> The issue of whether product development should be centralized or not is an interesting one, particularly when so much emphasis must be placed on local profit responsibility and these local product decisions bite into profits, and consequently, into performance evaluation and bonuses.

ALFRED BIRD & SONS, LIMITED

Alfred Bird & Sons, Ltd. (AB&S), the GFID subsidiary in England, was heavily dependent on two products; namely Maxwell House Instant Coffee and Bird's Custard products. It was becoming increasingly difficult to expand sales volume for these products. The product line had been extended since 1947 to include a wide range of GFC products including breakfast cereals; cake mixes; nuts; "Trice" and "Rice-Fit" instant rice puddings; "Garni"—a garnish; Gaines dog food; "Dream Topping," a lemon pie filling; "Instant Whip"; and ground coffee. These other products, most of which were still in the development stage, accounted, however, for a small fraction of AB&S sales volume which, as of fiscal year 1965, was approximately $41.2 million. Subsequent to their introduction, the cereals and cake mixes had been dropped because of inadequate market acceptance.

AB&S executives believed that they were relatively independent of GFID staff marketing control, primarily because the company had always made its profit commitments to GFC. Also, the uniqueness of the competitive situation in the United Kingdom made AB&S executives feel as if they had to "chart their own course." An example of this unique competitive situation was the instant coffee market. In the US, Maxwell House Instant Coffee enjoyed a 40 to 50 percent market share, with the Nestle product, "Nescafe," in second place. In the UK, the positions were reversed. Also in contrast to the US, coffee was the secondary hot beverage consumed in the UK. On a cup per capita basis, tea drinking was thought to be about six times as large. AB&S and Nestle engaged in strong competitive activities including pricing, packaging and premium efforts at various times. While AB&S essentially determined the strategy followed, GFID influenced some major decisions. For example, because of price advantages offered by Nestle, by September 1963 Bird's market share had dropped to about

30 percent. Having to hold committed volume and profits levels to GFID in the face of a sudden decline in Bird's market share, marketing executives recommended to Bird's top management in November that AB&S reduce its volume target and step up its case rate expenditure on advertising in order to "pull more coffee through the channels" and no longer attempt to be the leader. Neither Mr. Burgess, Bird's managing director, nor GFID headquarters agreed to this proposal, and AB&S was held to its original volume and profit commitment. AB&S executives believed that Maxwell House Instant Coffee merchandising practices had made the company the premium leader in Britain both with regard to containers and premiums.

According to management, considerable caution had to be exercised in introducing in the UK products that had enjoyed success in the US. An example was Bird's experience with Gaines "Gravy Train," a dog food product. There was evidence that the dog food market was large and rapidly expanding. Bird's management asked for a shipment of the Gravy Train product from the United States which was placed for market test with over 200 dog owners in 1961. A callback was made on each participant in the test one week later. The results were not conclusive. The management recognized that the product idea—one product to satisfy all the dogs' nutritional requirements—was a totally new concept to the British dog owner, and extensive education would be required before the idea was accepted. There were also price problems. They did not know what an acceptable product for dogs was, with no experience in this area and experience in the States having limited bearing. The British have a different attitude toward dogs. They are considered part of the family and, as a result, are much more pampered than they are in America. This accounts for the high incidence of table feeding in England. It might also be hard to sell large containers of dog food in England where people prefer to shop daily for "fresh tins" in the half-pound or one-pound size. In spite of these difficulties, in 1962 GFID executives decided to build a dog food plant in England. Sales results for FY 1963 and FY 1964 were $35,500 and $13,300 respectively. In terms of profit, AB&S executives estimated that the net loss over the two-year period was $223,000.

After this experience Bird's executives desired to put their new product development activities on a sounder footing. B.F. Allen, new business development manager of the domestic Post Division, was loaned to AB&S for an assignment commencing April 1964 in charge of the firm's research and development activities. Mr. Allen established a comprehensive new product system including organization, policies and procedures following much the lines of US experience.

AB&S executives noted the advantages of being a GF subsidiary. "For one thing, we are organized as a marketing company. Therefore, we don't have to fight to get a marketing idea across. This difference in attitude is a process which has been difficult for the average British company to accept. The result of this

'American' attitude is to make us more flexible." "On the whole, the trade attitude is very favorable because our sales practices depart slightly from British firms. We do not sell at different prices to competing channels, something often practiced by British firms. We have one price list, we stick to it and we are admired for it." AB&S was also well respected by the trade because of its "American" promotional know-how. Company executives believed that the trade recognized that AB&S knew how to move merchandise, and therefore it tended to get excellent cooperation on promotions and placement of point-of-sale material.

There were disadvantages in being an American company, according to one executive, who stated that the trade expected AB&S to be so much more efficient. "Some British firms can be a month late on a delivery and no one thinks anything of it. We promise goods to be delivered on a Monday, say, and if the shipment isn't there when the grocer unlocks his door that morning, all hell breaks loose."

AB&S management believed that one of the most important tangible benefits of being a GFC subsidiary was in the technical area in product and packaging improvements. "If we run into a problem, we can get professional assistance from General Foods that we could not afford to pay for ourselves. One of these areas is research. People in the States are quick to respond to our questions regarding soluble coffee processing or such things as product formulas."

Mr. Burgess mentioned that the product manager concept at Bird's and the idea that each product should make a profit were contributions from the parent company. The idea of setting quarterly profit goals was another GFC contribution, although this practice was questioned by some members of management. Mr. Burgess believed that his management team had accepted the necessity for having annual sales and profit objectives, but some of his managers thought that having quarterly profit objectives often led to poor marketing decisions. Also, he was aware that some AB&S managers believed that it was bad policy to give profit responsibilities to a product manager. In their opinion, a product manager should not be forced to build immediate sales volume but should be expected to build a product line viable over the long range.

Applying other GFC marketing concepts, AB&S had organized salesmen's calls and provided them with promotional material in order to give them something to talk about to each customer every time a call was made. Each product manager every six weeks had some selling point the Bird salesmen could discuss with the retailer. Also, GFC had introduced the concept of marketing research. Previously, AB&S management had no idea of market share, how the market had been going, in which direction it was likely to go, and how consumers felt about the product. However, internal research activities were still limited by the scarcity of people.

One area of mild annoyance to some AB&S marketing managers was the GFC requirement that all labels must be approved before they were placed on the market. According to one executive, approval could take as long as four or five weeks. When this period was added to the time needed to do the artwork, the whole process became, in his words, "rather burdensome." However, recently, one of the product managers had added a paste-on label featuring a "Pence-off" promotion. This label had partially obscured the product ingredients and, as such, had violated both the law and GFC regulations. Many thousands of the particular label had already been distributed through the trade, and the company could do little about the problem by that time. The company people involved with the illegal label had been subject to a stern lecture by members of AB&S top management concerning the need to observe requirements.

Most of the marketing ideas, according to executives, originated with AB&S product group people or Bird's advertising agencies. AB&S used two agencies to allow each agency to concentrate its energy on a single product group. This decision, according to one AB&S executive, was made in the United States. Executives admitted they would borrow any useful ideas they could from GFID staff personnel, but they had to rely primarily on their own resources because of the sheer volume of ideas they were forced to develop. According to executives, the most successful idea borrowed from the United States was the carafe pack for Maxwell House instant coffee. Subsequently, AB&S had introduced the storage jar pack—two months ahead of the Maxwell House Division in the United States—and introduced a sachet of coffee attached to a print advertisement run in a women's magazine which the Maxwell House Division had also copied for its Yuban Instant Coffee.

Product planning decisions in AB&S were strongly influenced by GFID headquarters personnel, according to AB&S executives. The chairman of the board of GFC had encouraged GFID, and AB&S in particular, to market "Dream Whip" as soon as possible. The product was being test-marketed in the North of England, and response from the trade was considered by AB&S executives to be very good. Instead of a targeted 60 percent distribution level for the test, the product had achieved a level of 80 percent distribution.

The original Dream Topping market plans submitted to GFID provided for the manufacture of the new product by AB&S commencing in March 1965, with the opening of the new manufacturing facilities. Until then, the product would be supplied by the Jell-O Division according to a decision made by the chairman. From October 1963 until March 1964, however, AB&S executives were handicapped by inadequate supplies of Dream Topping. Working through J.R. Sorenson, President of GFID, AB&S then made an arrangement whereby the Canadian subsidiary would ship over the product in bulk and AB&S would pack it and market it.

GENERAL FOODS DE MEXICO, S.A.

Prior to January 1963, the marketing department of General Foods de Mexico, S.A. was organized around one marketing manager with S.N. Taylor as sales manager and another man as advertising manager. Reporting to Mr. Taylor were four district sales managers. L.D. Walker, who joined the firm as general manager, at that time indicated this was a primitive organizational setup which neglected adequate supervision over the operations of the individual product lines. "Rosa Blanca, because it was our most important line, was getting all the attention, and the other products were neglected. It seemed to me that, if we were going to be more effective in our over-all marketing strategy, we needed to get somebody responsible for each of the particular products." Mr. Walker, recognizing that GFID could not provide the necessary talent, went out and hired managerial personnel. Mr. Taylor was the only marketing executive who was originally a GFC employee, and he had been assigned to GF de Mexico slightly less than a year and a half prior to Mr. Walker's arrival. The other marketing personnel had either "walked in off the street" or had been referred by GF's advertising agency.

Although many of the promotional and sales techniques which were effective in the US were also applicable in Mexico, GF de Mexico executives believed that certain differences in the Mexican market existed which called for different treatment and different activities from those successful in the United States. For one thing, the Mexican market was highly regionalized, making it difficult to develop copy platforms applicable on a national basis. Good trade relations were considered to be particularly important to successful marketing activity in Mexico. The typical wholesaler could not be relied upon to provide the degree of promotional support that many of them provided in the United States, so personal selling effort had to be focused on individual retailers, of whom there were more than 35,000.

It was estimated that less than 10 percent of consumer packaged goods were sold through self-service stores which catered to the middle and upper income groups. Packaged goods were sold mainly through small retail outlets catering to customers in different economic classes. In these small stores the merchandise typically was kept "under the counter" and was not well displayed. Retailers purchased in small amounts because they often did not have cash to buy in quantity, so salesmen had to call on these outlets frequently. The Mexican retailer evaluated a product by the speed at which it moved off his shelves. Since trade custom dictated that products which did not move off the shelves could be returned to the manufacturer for credit, selling to the trade was practically on a consignment basis.

These environmental differences led the management of GF de Mexico to rely heavily on its two advertising agencies, the Noble Agency and Foote, Cone & Belding, for marketing assistance over and above the preparation of design and promotional ideas, as well as generating information on the characteristics and peculiarities of the Mexican market. In general, reliable market data were scarce in Mexico.

Between FY 1962 and FY 1965, GF de Mexico increased sales from $1.9

million to $6.2 million. During FY 1965, the soup and coffee dollar sales volumes were about the same, together constituting nearly 70 percent of total sales. Candies and Jell-O desserts accounted for about 10 percent and 17 percent respectively, and Kool-Aid accounted for about 2 percent. Soups accounted for 50 percent of gross profits and coffee 25 percent of this figure. Much of the gross profit on coffee had come from sales to the domestic Maxwell House Division, but by 1965 this agreement had been terminated.

In the summer of 1963, Nestle Nescafe which had pioneered soluble coffee sales, accounted for approximately 90 percent of the market, while GF de Mexico brands Oro and Pronto held about 8 percent. To gain such a commanding position for Nescafe, the Nestle management had used a lottery-type promotion known as a "sorteo," with prizes totaling about P$2 million. Just as GF de Mexico management was getting set to combat the effect of this sorteo with two-for-one deals and apothecary jar packs, Nestle announced another lottery for late 1963 to carry forward to August 1964, which involved both Nescafe labels and Maggi soup labels with prizes worth P$3 million.

Until 1963 Nestle's Maggi soups were sold in dehydrated form and packaged in envelopes which contained four servings. The Rosa Blanca best seller was the "Triangulitos" pack, an individual serving of dehydrated consomme. Nestle introduced a similar single serving pack at the time the P$3 million lottery was announced in the fall of 1963. GF de Mexico management decided, therefore, to announce a P$5 million lottery based on Oro, Rosa Blanca and Jell-O because it believed that the Nestle lottery was a "dagger aimed at our heart," since any damage suffered to the Rosa Blanca soup franchise would place the whole company in jeopardy. Although extensive damage to the brand share of Rosa Blanca soups was averted, and a modest gain in Oro coffee brand share was achieved, the overall cost of this sorteo promotion ran in excess of P$15 million.

Mr. Walker planned to expand the company's product line, using the Rosa Blanca name which had wide recognition in Mexico. One product under development was "mole" made from the chili plant. The finished product was sold in cans or jars in a paste form and in different flavors. According to Mr. Walker, this was a "tough item to make," but he decided to add this product to the GF de Mexico product line in the near future because in Mexico no company had been successful in bringing out "mole" in sufficient quantity and adequate quality to establish a brand following. He estimated the market for mole was about P$60 million annually. Mr. Walker had hired a chemist to produce the formulae, and employees had built the necessary production equipment out of idle plant machinery and unused steel drums. The only out-of-pocket cost to GF de Mexico was a stone grinding mill for processing the chili, about $1,000.00. Other products unique to the Mexican diet were being considered for the future.

GFID management had suggested to Mr. Walker that he visit GFID's French subsidiary to investigate the possibility of adding taffy-like candies and chewing gum to his existing candy line. The GF de Mexico candy line was currently absorbing about $80,000 a month in overhead charges, and it was estimated each incremental sales dollar would contribute an additional 57¢.

Items in the GFC domestic line which Mr. Walker wanted to introduce included Dream Whip and some of the GFC cake mixes. Mr. Walker was prepared to add those GFC products to his product line which he deemed appropriate for Mexican consumption. He was deterred from taking on more products, however, because he did not think his marketing organization was large enough to assume the added burden.

According to Mr. Walker, the advantage of being a GFC subsidiary in Mexico was that he and his marketing people had access to good advice from people within the domestic divisions and GFID itself. For example, Mr. Walker mentioned Mr. James of the Maxwell House Division who had supplied him with advice and technical assistance in the promotion and packaging of coffee; and Mr. Conner, a member of the GFID marketing staff, who had spent several months in Mexico analyzing the marketing opportunities for the various products in the GF de Mexico product line.

GF de Mexico executives maintained that they were stimulated by the cross-current of ideas emanating from the monthly bulletin, *Marketing Highlights.* They believed that some of these promotional ideas gleaned from this bulletin had been applied to Mexico with considerable success. For instance, the company had packed instant coffee in apothecary jars. Nevertheless, GF de Mexico executives believed that most of their promotional ideas emanated either internally within the company or from one of their advertising agencies. One example was a single package containing three individual packages of Jell-O in the regular or double size which was mounted on a backpiece that displayed a plastic Walt Disney figure, such as Pluto or Mickey Mouse. The plastic figure had movable parts which could be disassembled. The three-pack would sell for a price equivalent to three individual packets of Jell-O, and the figurine would be free to the consumer. During a sales test over a weekend in a Mexico City supermarket, sales of Jell-O increased 1,000 percent with this premium.

Because it was the general custom in Mexico to pay supermarkets for display space, GF de Mexico personnel designed "dynamic" point-of-sale displays. One such display was a miniature coffee roaster, operating in the midst of a pile of coffee beans, that wafted the aroma of fresh coffee throughout the supermarket. Another example was a moving wooden Walt Disney figurine, designed to support the three-pack Jell-O promotion, that company executives stated could be built for about $12 each, including the electric motor. The management found that a number of display ideas transmitted through *Marketing Highlights* were too expensive to set up in Mexico. On the other hand, many of the ideas originated there could not be used in the States because they would be too expensive to install.

Mr. Walker commented on the need to resist home office ideas in some cases. "A couple of years ago the company was under some pressure from people in

Rye to promote the brand name of Maxwell House in Mexico. The company spent a lot of money in an attempt to get the name across to the Mexican consumer. In my opinion this was a mistake. The Maxwell House name is almost impossible for Mexicans to pronounce and is totally meaningless. It was my understanding that it was General Foods' intention to make the Maxwell House brand a worldwide one. In my opinion, what success we enjoy in Mexico is due to a large extent to the fact that we are using Mexican products with Mexican names."

KIBON, S.A.

Of the sales of $11.6 million by Kibon, S.A., the GFID subsidiary in Sao Paulo, Brazil, about 58 percent came from ice cream, 17 percent from candy, 11 percent from chewing gum, and the remainder from Kool-Aid, eggs and cereals. D.F. Jarvis, Kibon's President and General Manager, believed that the rate of inflation had considerable effect on marketing practices in Brazil. Yet frequent price increases made it difficult for Kibon to strengthen its market position. Mr. Jarvis commented:

> Every price rise cuts us off from a segment of the market that can no longer afford these particular impulse items. Our problem is to undertake price increases only as the need arises and to do this in a series of small steps so as to minimize the impact on the consumer. If you are able to make a small jump, say from 50 cruzeiros to 60 cruzeiros, you need to have some sort of promotion to offset the shock. For instance, one of the ways to do this is to use a marked popsicle stick. If the consumer gets the popsicle with this marked stick, he can come down to our factory and exchange it for a free bicycle. Thus far these kinds of price promotions have been effective but I feel that lately we've gone into them much more than we would really like to. To attach these gimmicks to our quality image is not, in my opinion, in the best long-run interests of the Kibon name.

It was the company's policy to indicate to the trade new prices in advance of the effective date. As the trade reacted by loading up with merchandise at the old price, Kibon was forced to correct the situation by means of additional "pull" type promotions at the consumer level. Because continual price rises had caused customers to lose any idea of values in consumer products, the usual "money-off" kind of deal that was popular with consumers everywhere was not effective in Brazil. On the other hand, deals involving "one free with two," for instance, were believed by management to be very effective.

According to Mr. Jarvis, Kibon's promotional practices were patterned after GFC's experience, although adapted to the special marketing conditions in Brazil. Also, since GFC did not sell ice cream products anywhere else in the world, Kibon executives had to rely on their own experience and imagination in marketing this line.

Kibon's promotional activities in ice cream, of which it held 80 to 85 percent of the Brazilian market, were an attempt to build a year-round product image. In the past, Kibon had curtailed ice cream advertising during the winter because Brazilians rarely eat ice cream when the temperature falls below 68°F.

Promotional activities for "Ping Pong" bubble gum (which held approximately 75 percent of the market) took two directions. First, Kibon used an in-wrapper airplane series, pictures of antique airplanes wrapped around the gum and designed for children to collect and trade. Second, was the "Bola da sorte," or "Lucky Bubble" scheme which awarded prizes to consumers using coupons enclosed within the bubble gum wrapper. These coupons could be exchanged for the prize printed on the coupon, for instance, a soccer ball or a bicycle, at any one of a number of company redemption centers.

Company executives believed that one of their most serious merchandising problems was that of gaining adequate display space for Kibon products in stores and public markets. The candy line and "Q-Suco" (Kool-Aid) were sold mainly in "mom and pop" stores and public markets whose stalls might measure perhaps 10' x 10', and whose proprietor might have a single shelf on which to display his merchandise. Most of the products were sold as a result of a customer asking the retailer for a specific item. Reaching down underneath his display counter the retailer handed the item to the customer. The retailer did not typically take on additional merchandise because either he had no place to display it or store it, or the product was not well enough known for the customers to ask him for it. Kibon managers were attempting to solve this problem by developing a display counter that could be suspended from the ceiling by wires, and they were investigating the use of self-dispensing units which could be attached by means of a nail to the wall of the store.

About 40 percent of product development work was spent on ice cream. The management felt that the constant necessity to raise prices meant they would lose market share unless it was cemented through a continuous stream of new product variations.

New products, which involved about 40 percent of development time and attention, centered on gelatin desserts, chewing gum and a soya protein as a raw material for ice cream and as a substitute for milk products. Interest in soya proteins had been sharpened at Kibon as milk became more expensive and soya prices remained low. Kibon management felt this particular area for investigation had not only a profit opportunity but might serve as a hedge against short milk supplies. The Brazilian Government had not developed soya by-products, nor had it influenced any private firms to do so. The idea had been developed by Kibon executives, and the whole idea was, of course, new to GFC in the United States.

Mr. Jarvis observed: "General Foods' experience in marketing in the United

States is frankly not too helpful. Our people here know more about marketing in an inflationary economy than do the people in Rye." Kibon marketing executives mentioned several areas in which GFID could provide marketing assistance. One executive mentioned that he would like to see GFID send him more technical material, such as *Harvard Business Review* articles and articles dealing with modern techniques in international marketing. *Marketing Highlights*, in his opinion, was very interesting but had not been of much specific help to him. He also believed that GFID should attempt to keep him up-to-date on current promotional practices in the United States and not limit these ideas to what was going on at General Foods.

Another executive mentioned that he expected to be calling upon GFID for help in the area of carton and package design. He had recently requested and received some sample Jell-O cartons which he intended to adapt to the Brazilian market. This executive believed that it would help him to have a record of General Foods' previous experience bound into a handbook so as to provide a ready reference to successful merchandising practices throughout the world. He believed this handbook should be supplemented by visitors from GFID who could show Kibon executives what GFC was doing in the marketing area. He did not believe it was necessary to send experts to work in Brazil because, in his opinion, it would take these people too long to understand the Brazilian market. He would much prefer to be able to borrow ideas from these visitors and retain the responsibility for translating these ideas into effective practices for the Brazilian market because he did not believe that US merchandising practices could be adapted to the Brazilian market without a full understanding of the Brazilian way of doing business.

Mr. Jarvis felt that the main direction of expansion would be an extension of the present business, making product refinements on current lines and moving toward other products which they could make on present equipment. He did not believe that very many GFC products marketed in the United States were yet appropriate for Brazil. For example, he mentioned "Minute Rice." Nearly everybody in Brazil ate rice but, in his opinion, Minute Rice was too expensive since many of the people who could afford a product like Minute Rice had servants to cook and wash rice and were, therefore, not likely to pay a premium for it in convenience form. Another product he cited as seemingly good for the Brazilian market was soluble coffee. But Mr. Jarvis did not believe GFC should get into this market in Brazil at this time because Nestle had been trying to sell soluble coffee in Brazil for many years with little success. It required a tremendous investment to break down cultural barriers against drinking coffee in soluble form. The convenience factor was not believed to be sufficiently important to warrant a higher price. And, finally, Brazilians traditionally preferred coffee in a strong, demi-tasse form.

✳ *Appendix A*

ANNUAL MARKETING PLAN:
GENERAL FOODS DE MEXICO—KOOL-AID

The Annual Plan for the Mexican subsidiary for FY 1965 included a thirteen-page plan for Kool-Aid, the main points of which are summarized here.

Disappointing sales in the previous three years were reported as due probably to poor distribution, inconsistent marketing strategy, inferior product quality, inferior packaging and incomplete selection of flavors. The previous product had not met solubility standards, but the formula had been changed and was now considered satisfactory. A new package following US design was to be adopted. Additional flavors were to be added.

The plan was based on three assumptions about the market: (1) Kool-Aid would appeal to economy-minded housewives because the cost per glass was thirteen centavos compared to 27 for bottled drinks; (2) the product should have great appeal to children based on US experience; and (3) the greatest potential lay in the upper-half income group where water pollution and refrigerator ownership were not problems. The strategy for FY 1965 was to be "devoted to the primary task of attempting to learn how and if Kool-Aid can be sold in Mexico. To realize this objective, total advertising and promotion funds will be invested in two test market areas. Each area has been assigned a different sales objective in accordance with population and buying power potential."

In Monterrey, advertising would be directed at children of age five to twelve using Walt Disney character premiums with Kool-Aid purchases. Advertising would be placed on the 1/2 hour Mickey Mouse Club show in July-October and in a spot saturation campaign on TV and radio in May-June. In Chihuahua and

Culiacan, high temperature areas, the tests would focus on promoting Kool-Aid to housewives as an economical substitute for bottled soft drinks. A saturation radio spot campaign for April-August was proposed with the copy emphasizing Kool-Aid as a family treat, eight glasses from a package, six natural fruit flavors, and only 14 centavos per glass.

Extracts from the response by the headquarters personnel to this plan follow:

General Statement
The plan submitted for Kool-Aid does not appear to us to reflect the positive attitude which we believe this product warrants. . . . We believe that the plan should be based on the assumption that Kool-Aid *will* sell but that the most effective and potentially profitable method of marketing need be determined. Testing of the nature contained in the recommended plan is, therefore, necessary but not to the exclusion of the remaining 85 percent of the country. Kool-Aid has a large enough contribution margin to support self-liquidating volume generating activities such as door-to-door sales, demonstrations, etc., particularly if tied in with similar activities planned for developing the Rosa Blanca business. . . . We do not believe, as stated in the plan, that refrigeration ownership should be a factor in the use of Kool-Aid. It has already been proven to be highly successful in markets with relatively less of such facilities. Further, water pollution and preparation time do not appear to have been important deterrents to the use of Kool-Aid in markets similar to Mexico. To the contrary, preparation methods might very well be a positive attribute in that Kool-Aid can always be readily available and does not involve the problems generated by the use of bottles.

Further, we do not believe it should be assumed that the marketing potential is primarily the A and B economic classes. The very factor of economy, which has been one of the primary selling points of Kool-Aid, should make it attractive to the lower income groups. Since the proposed plan is essentially a test program, we would recommend aiming more broadly and letting the product find and identify its own market.

[Comments were also made on specific elements of the plan, including the following.]

Pricing
— We would urge consideration of price increase which would provide greater funds for marketing this product. As long as the price remains below one peso, it is not believed that the product would run into any major competitive pricing problems. Even at 90 centavos it would still be a far cheaper drink than Coke. A test at a higher price is recommended.

Distribution
— Experience has shown Kool-Aid to be a high impulse item as is the case with candies. Therefore, display will be of critical importance. This could mean that secondary outlets such as candy shops, etc., can become

important to the sales of Kool-Aid. Consideration of using the proposed candy sales group for Kool-Aid to achieve this secondary distribution seems worthwhile.

Advertising
— The test plan is basically designed to measure the relative effectiveness of aiming marketing efforts toward children and toward their mothers. However, the recommended plan creates several other variables which may make it difficult to evaluate the results of the test. These additional variables are: (A) ratio of advertising to promotion; (B) different basic media, radio versus TV; and (C) different timing and duration of advertising effort. We would hope that these variables can be reduced or eliminated without reducing the effectiveness of each of the marketing plans.

About the Editors

John Fayerweather and **Ashok Kapoor** are Professors of Management and International Business and Marketing and International Business, respectively at the Graduate School of Business Administration of New York University.

Dr. Fayerweather has played a leading role in the evolution of education for international business for over 25 years. While serving on the faculties of Harvard, Columbia and NYU he authored three previous textbooks, *Management of International Operations, International Marketing* and *International Business Management.* He was the first president of the Association for Education in International Business and has worked with several national bodies for advancement of education in the field. His current research concerned with the interaction of nationalism and the strategies of international corporations has resulted in three books, *The Mercantile Bank Affair, International Business-Government Affairs* (ed.) and *Foreign Investment in Canada,* and numerous articles.

Dr. Kapoor has pioneered in developing the international business negotiation exercise for training and research purposes. He has conducted research and training programs on international business negotiations for public and private organizations in Eastern and Western Europe, the USA, Latin America, Asia and the Middle East. His recent publications include *The Multinational Enterprise in Transition, Planning for International Business Negotiations, International Business-Government Communications: U.S. Structures, Actors and Issues* and *Asian Business and Environment in Transition.* Dr. Kapoor advises private and public organizations in international business.